THE GREAT INDIAN ROPE TRICK

Roderick Matthews is a freelance writer specializing in Indian history. Born in 1956, he studied Modern History at Balliol College, Oxford, and has written articles and reviews for a number of British and Indian publications, including the *Observer*, the *Literary Review*, and the *Times of India*. His great-grandfather, George Jennings, was Principal of Muir Central College in Allahabad and tutored the young Jawaharlal Nehru through his Harrow entrance exams, while his wife, Maud, acted as governess to the Nehru family's two daughters. Another great-grandfather, Charles Roberts, was Under Secretary of State for India, and ordered M.K. Gandhi to return to India in late 1914 to safeguard his health, thus both saving the Mahatma's life and inadvertently bringing down the British Empire.

Roderick's published works include *The Flaws in the Jewel: Challenging the Myths of British India* and *Jinnah vs Gandhi*. He has his own website at historydetox.com.

Praise for *The Great Indian Rope Trick*

'Roderick Matthews takes the reader through the twists and turns of democracy in India, Pakistan, Bangladesh, Nepal, Myanmar and Sri Lanka, and comes up with valuable insights from a forest of events... The patterns and insights he draws from all of South Asia should be of interest to democrats everywhere.' – *Business Standard*

'Matthews becomes one of the few commentators on India who examine the history of India not as a standalone phenomenon but in comparison with other similarly placed societies. The most attractive feature of this book…is its ability to make bold and yet fair comparisons between ideas of democracy and their implementation in the lands of South Asia.' – *Tribune*

'This British historian's eye brings a universal perspective to the subject… a perspective that Indian historians, more influenced by the immediacy of political issues and engaged at closer range, have neglected.' – *Hindustan Times*

Also by the same author

Jinnah vs Gandhi

Praise for *Jinnah vs Gandhi*

'I recommend this book to every person who wants to gain an insight into the minds of these two men.' – Jaswant Singh, former Union minister and author of *Jinnah: India, Partition, Independence*

'Matthews' book contrasts Jinnah and Gandhi's vision for a nation…a clear tripartite exposition that puts events, people and systems of political thought beside Gandhi's stated public actions.' – *Tehelka*

'Matthews sets out to tell us the broader story of Indian politics in the first half of the twentieth century through the story of Gandhi and Jinnah's political fortunes… A solid introduction to the lives and politics of two of South Asia's most prominent leaders.' – *Mint*

'The most interesting fact about *Jinnah vs Gandhi*…is that it strips down the aura of sanctity around two of the most important personalities of the last century.' – *New Indian Express*

'As a study of two great contemporary leaders this book has few compeers.' – *Free Press journal*

The Great Indian Rope Trick

DOES THE FUTURE OF DEMOCRACY LIE WITH INDIA?

RODERICK MATTHEWS

First published in India in 2015 by Hachette India
(Registered name: Hachette Book Publishing India Pvt. Ltd)
An Hachette UK company
www.hachetteindia.com

This edition published in 2016

SRD

ISBN 978-93-5195-001-1

Hachette Book Publishing India Pvt. Ltd
4th & 5th Floors, Corporate Centre
Plot No. 94, Sector 44,
Gurgaon 122003, India

Typeset in Baskerville 11/14
by Saanvi Graphics, Noida

Printed and bound in India
by Manipal Technologies Limited, Manipal

Contents

PART 3: DEMOCRACY IN SOUTH ASIA

PART 4: PROSPECTS

Timeline

1931

Sri Lanka: Donoughmore Constitution introduces universal adult suffrage; replaces special electorates for minorities with system of committees.

1939

India: Viceroy declares India a combatant nation in the Second World War; Indians deployed in the battle against the Axis powers.

1940

India: Muslim League proposes the formation of a separate nation for Muslims living in India.

1942

India: Congress launches Quit India movement, under the leadership of Mahatma Gandhi, adopting the path of Satyagraha (non violence).

Burma: Japan invades Burma aided by Japanese-trained Burma Independence Army; it later transforms into the Anti-Fascist People's Freedom League (AFPFL) and resists Japanese rule.

1945

Burma: Britain liberates Burma from Japanese occupation with help from the AFPFL, led by Aung San.

1947

India & Pakistan: British Raj comes to an end followed by partition of the subcontinent into India and Pakistan – a state divided into East and West wings separated from each other by more than 1,500 km of Indian territory. The partition is marked by large scale bloodshed and violence on both sides of the border.

Burma: Aung San and six members of his interim government are assassinated by political opponents led by U Saw.

1948

India: Hindu extremist Nathuram Godse assassinates Mahatma Gandhi on 30th January. Sheikh Abdullah becomes the prime minister of Jammu and Kashmir as India enters into war with Pakistan over disputed territory of Kashmir. India recaptures Dras, Kargil and Poonch.

Burma: Attains independence with U Nu as prime minister.

Sri Lanka: Gains full independence.

Pakistan: Founding leader of the country, Muhammad Ali Jinnah, passes away.

1949

Bangladesh: Bengali nationalists establish the Awami League to campaign for East Pakistan's autonomy from West Pakistan.

1950

India: Becomes a republic on 26 January under a new constitution; elects Rajendra Prasad as the first President.

Burma: U Nu, along with Indian Prime Minister Nehru, Indonesian President Sukarno, Yugoslav President Tito and Egyptian President Nasser co-found the Movement of Non-Aligned States.

Nepal: Alliance of India-based anti-Rana forces and the monarch brings an end of 'Rana rule' in Nepal. Sovereignty of the crown restored and anti-Rana rebels in Nepali Congress join the government.

1951–52

India: First general election of independent India. Universal adult franchise adopted by the then Chief Election Commissioner Sukumar Sen. Congress wins the first election under leadership of Jawaharlal Nehru.

1953

Nepal: Edmund Hillary from New Zealand and Sherpa Tenzing Norgay from Nepal become the first to climb Mount Everest.

1955

Nepal: King Tribhuvan dies, King Mahendra ascends the throne. Nepal joins the United Nations.

1956

Sri Lanka: Solomon Bandaranaike, as a result of the rise of Sinhalese nationalism, makes Sinhala the sole official language of the country and adopts other measures to bolster Sinhalese and Buddhist feelings. More than 100 Tamils die in widespread violence after Tamil parliamentarians protest these new laws.

Pakistan: The new constitution declares Pakistan an Islamic republic.

1958

Pakistan: General Ayub Khan takes over following the declaration of martial law.

1959

Nepal: Adopts a multiparty constitution.

Sri Lanka: A Buddhist monk assassinates Bandaranaike. He is succeeded by his widow, Sirimavo, who continues nationalization programme.

1960

Nepal: King Mahendra seizes control and suspends parliament, constitution and party politics after Nepali Congress wins the elections.

Pakistan: General Ayub Khan becomes President.

1962

India: Loses war with China over disputed territory in regions of the north-east and Ladakh.

Burma: Military coup led by General Ne Win ousts U Nu's faction. General Ne Win abolishes the federal system and inaugurates the 'Burmese Way to Socialism' – nationalizing the economy, forming a single-party state with the Socialist Programme Party as the sole political party and banning independent newspapers. It paves way for a military rule which will last till 2011.

1964

India: Prime Minister Jawaharlal Nehru dies.

1965

India & Pakistan: Second war over the disputed territory of Kashmir.

1966

India: Nehru's daughter Indira Gandhi becomes Prime Minister.

1969

Pakistan: General Ayub Khan resigns and General Yahya Khan takes over.

1970

Bangladesh: The Awami League under Sheikh Mujibur Rahman wins election by majority votes in East Pakistan. The government in West Pakistan refuses to recognize the results, leading to rioting.

Sri Lanka: Sirimavo Bandaranaike returns to power and extends nationalization programme.

1971

India, Pakistan & Bangladesh: India enters into third war with Pakistan over the influx of immigrants from East Pakistan into Indian territory to take refuge from the ongoing civil war between East and West Pakistan. Leads to the formation of Bangladesh, formerly known as East Pakistan.

1972

Nepal: King Mahendra dies, Crown Prince Birendra ascends the throne.

Bangladesh: Sheikh Mujib returns, becomes Prime Minister. He begins a programme of nationalizing key industries in an attempt to improve living standards, but with little success.

Sri Lanka: Buddhism is given primary place as country's religion, further antagonizing Tamil minority.

Pakistan: Signs the Shimla Peace Agreement with India to tackle the Kashmir issue.

1973

Pakistan: Zulfiqar Ali Bhutto rewrites the constitution and is re-elected Prime Minister.

1974

Burma: New constitution transfers power from the armed forces to a People's Assembly headed by Ne Win and other former military leaders.

1975

India: Prime Minister Indira Gandhi declares a state of emergency after being found guilty of electoral malpractice. Riots and violence spread throughout the country.

Bangladesh: Sheikh Mujib becomes President of Bangladesh. The political situation worsens. He is assassinated in a military coup in August. Martial law is imposed.

1975–1977

India: Government imprisons nearly 1,000 political opponents and implements compulsory birth control policy in the aftermath of emergency. Violence grips the country and riots spread.

Bangladesh: General Ziaur Rahman assumes the Presidency. The constitution adopts Islam.

Sri Lanka: Separatist Tamil United Liberation Front (TULF) party wins all seats in Tamil areas. Anti-Tamil riots leave more than 100 Tamils dead.

Pakistan: Reels under riots erupt over allegations of Zulfiqar Ali Bhutto's Pakistan People's Party (PPP) rigging the votes. General Zia-ul-Haq launches military coup.

1976

Sri Lanka: Liberation Tigers of Tamil Eelam (LTTE) is formed as tensions increase in Tamil-dominated areas of north and east.

1979

Pakistan: Military leadership hangs Zulfiqar Ali Bhutto.

1981

Bangladesh: Abdus Sattar succeeds Ziaur Rehman following his assassination during military coup.

1983

Sri Lanka: The first Eelam war begins with the death of 13 soldiers in an LTTE ambush and the subsequent Black July anti-Tamil riots.

1984

India: Operation Blue Star carried out. Troops storm Golden Temple to flush out Sikh militants pressing for self-rule. Blue Star is completed successfully, but the bloodshed inside the temple causes widespread uproar amongst Sikhs. Indira Gandhi assassinated soon after by Sikh bodyguards, following which her son, Rajiv Gandhi, wins a general election and becomes prime minister.

1985

Pakistan: Martial law ends and the ban on political parties is lifted.

1986

Bangladesh: Ershad assumes the presidency following the parliamentary and presidential elections; lifts martial law and reinstates the constitution.

Pakistan: Zulfiqar Ali Bhutto's daughter Benazir returns from exile. Heads PPP in campaign for fresh elections.

1987

India & Sri Lanka: India deploys troops for a peacekeeping operation in Sri Lanka's ethnic conflict between the Tamils and the majority Sinhala community after signing an agreement with the Sri Lankan government.

Burma: Currency devaluation leads to massive anti-government riots.

1988

Burma: Thousands of people die in anti-government riots; the State Law and Order Restoration Council (SLORC) is formed.

Bangladesh: Islam becomes state religion. Floods cover three-quarters of the country. Tens of millions made homeless.

Sri Lanka: Left-wing nationalist party Janatha Vimukthi Peramuna (JVP) begins campaign against the Indo–Sri Lankan agreement.

Pakistan: General Zia, the US ambassador and many Pakistani army officials die in mysterious air crash. Benazir Bhutto's PPP wins the general elections.

1989

Burma: SLORC declares martial law, arrests thousands of people, including advocates of democracy and human rights and renames Burma as Myanmar. The capital, Rangoon, becomes Yangon. NLD leader Aung San Suu Kyi, daughter of Aung San, is put under house arrest.

1990

India & Sri Lanka: India withdraws troops from Sri Lanka. Second Eelam War begins as violence between Sri Lankan army and separatists escalates. LTTE expels thousands of Muslims from the north.

Nepal: King Birendra agrees to new democratic constitution as a result of Jana Andolan I – a pro-democracy agitation coordinated by Nepali Congress and leftist groups.

Pakistan: Benazir Bhutto is dismissed as prime minister following charges of incompetence and corruption.

1991

India: Suicide bomber sympathetic to LTTE assassinates Rajiv Gandhi.

Burma: The Norwegian Nobel Committee confers Nobel Peace Prize on Aung San Suu Kyi.

Nepal: Nepali Congress wins first democratic elections. G.P. Koirala becomes prime minister.

Bangladesh: Begum Khaleda Zia, widow of President Ziaur Rahman, becomes prime minister; changes constitution to render the position of President ceremonial and gives primary executive power to the prime minister.

1992

India: Hindu extremists demolish Babri mosque in Ayodhya, triggering widespread Hindu–Muslim violence; thousands killed.

1993

Sri Lanka: President Premadasa dies in LTTE bomb attack.

Pakistan: Benazir Bhutto returns to power.

1994

Nepal: Koirala's government loses no-confidence motion. Manmohan Adhikari forms country's first communist government following fresh elections.

Sri Lanka: President Chandrika Kumaratunga comes to power pledging to end war; opens peace talks with LTTE.

1995

Burma: Aung San Suu Kyi is released from house arrest after six years.

Nepal: Communist government is dissolved. Start of Maoist revolt which continues for more than a decade and kills thousands. The rebels want the monarchy to be abolished.

Sri Lanka: Third Eelam War begins when rebels sink naval craft. The war will last till 2001 with the Tigers bombing Sri Lanka's holiest Buddhist site and carrying out a suicide attack on the international airport which destroys half the Sri Lankan Airlines fleet. President Kumaratunga is also wounded in a bomb attack.

1996

Burma: Aung San Suu Kyi attends first NLD congress since her release; SLORC arrests more than 200 delegates on their way to the meeting.

Bangladesh: The Awami League comes to power after winning a re-run election. Sheikh Hasina Wajed, the daughter of Sheikh Mujibur Rahman, becomes prime minister.

1997

Burma: Becomes a member of the Association of South East Asian Nations (ASEAN); SLORC renamed State Peace and Development Council (SPDC).

Nepal: Prime Minister Sher Bahadur Deuba loses no-confidence vote. Period of increased political instability ushers in.

Pakistan: Nawaz Sharif becomes prime minister for the second time.

1998

India: BJP forms coalition government under Prime Minister Atal Bihari Vajpayee.

1999

India: Vajpayee makes historic bus trip to Pakistan to meet Premier Nawaz Sharif and to sign bilateral Lahore Peace Declaration. However, the conflict over the disputed territory of Kashmir eventually leads to the Kargil war. India successfully drives out Pakistani forces from Kashmir.

Pakistan: Benazir Bhutto leaves the country following corruption charges and jail sentences served on her and her husband, Asif Ali Zardari. In October, General Pervez Musharraf comes to power after a coup.

2000

India: Marks the birth of its billionth citizen. US President Bill Clinton makes a visit to improve ties with India.

Nepal: G.P. Koirala returns as prime minister, heading the ninth government in ten years.

Pakistan: Nawaz Sharif is sentenced to life imprisonment on hijacking and terrorism charges. Goes into exile in Saudi Arabia after being pardoned by military authorities.

2001

Nepal: Crown Prince Dipendra shoots King Birendra, Queen Aishwarya and other close relatives and then himself at the Royal Palace. Prince

Gyanendra, Birendra's brother, ascends the throne. Maoist rebels step up violence. Prime Minister G.P. Koirala quits and is succeeded by Sher Bahadur Deuba. King Gyanendra declares state of emergency after more than 100 people are killed in four days of violence; orders army to crush the Maoist rebels. Hundreds die in rebel and government operations in the following months.

Bangladesh: High Court confirms death sentences on 12 ex-army officers for killing Mujib. Sheikh Hasina steps down, hands power to caretaker authority, becoming first prime minister in the country's history to complete a five-year term. Law guaranteeing lifelong security to former Prime Minister Sheikh Hasina and her sister Sheikh Rehana is repealed.

Pakistan: General Pervez Musharraf declares himself President while remaining head of the army.

2002

India: The death of 59 Hindu pilgrims returning from Ayodhya in a train fire in Godhra leads to communal riots in Gujarat, resulting in the death of thousands. Retired scientist and architect of India's missile programme A.P.J. Abdul Kalam is elected President. Pakistani President Musharraf visits; expresses regret over excesses carried out by Pakistan during 1971 war.

Burma: Aung San Suu Kyi's 20-month house arrest ends and clashes between her supporters and those of government ensue; she is taken into 'protective custody'.

Bangladesh: Lajuddin Ahmed becomes President.

Sri Lanka: Government and LTTE sign a Norwegian-mediated ceasefire. De-commissioning of weapons begins; the road linking Jaffna with rest of Sri Lanka reopens after 12 years; passenger flights to Jaffna resume. Government lifts ban on LTTE. Rebels drop demand for separate state.

Pakistan: President Musharraf takes steps to curb religious extremism by banning two militant groups – Lashkar-e-Toiba and Jaish-e-Mohammad. President Musharraf wins another five years in office in a referendum criticized as unconstitutional and flawed.

2003

Burma: Khin Nyunt becomes prime minister; proposes to hold convention in 2004 on drafting a new constitution as a part of 'road map' to democracy.

Sri Lanka: LTTE pulls out of talks. Ceasefire holds.

Pakistan: Declares Kashmir ceasefire; India follows suit.

2004

India: UPA, a Congress-led coalition, wins the general elections. Manmohan Singh becomes prime minister. India, along with Brazil, Germany and Japan, files an application for a permanent seat on the UN Security Council.

Nepal: Joins the World Trade Organization (WTO).

Bangladesh: Parliament amends constitution to reserve 45 seats for female MPs.

Pakistan: Commonwealth readmits Pakistan.

2005

India & Pakistan: For the first time in 60 years, bus service start between Srinagar in Indian-administered Kashmir and Muzaffarabad in Pakistani-administered Kashmir.

Nepal: King Gyanendra assumes direct control and dismisses the government. He declares a state of emergency, citing the need to defeat Maoist rebels. However, in April, he lifts the state of emergency amid international pressure.

Sri Lanka: Sinhalas, Tamils and Muslims agree to share nearly $3 billion in tsunami aid. State of emergency is initiated after foreign minister is killed in August by a suspected Tiger assassin. Prime Minister Mahinda Rajapaksa wins presidential elections.

2006

India: US and India sign a nuclear agreement during a visit by US President George W. Bush. US gives India access to civilian nuclear technology while India agrees to greater scrutiny of its civilian nuclear programme. Hu Jintao visits India in the first visit by a Chinese president in a decade.

Nepal: Jana Andolan-II begins, with political parties seeking reinstatement of Parliament; after 19 days of massive countrywide protests, Gyanendra reinstates Parliament under G.P. Koirala. Maoists declare unilateral ceasefire, and once the Parliament agrees to strip the king of his powers and declare the country a republic, the government and the rebels sign a peace accord – the Comprehensive Peace Accord – declaring a formal end to the 10-year-long civil war.

Bangladesh: Opposition Awami League ends year-long parliamentary boycott.

Sri Lanka: Peace talks fail in Geneva.

2007

India: Signs an agreement with Pakistan aimed at reducing the risk of accidental nuclear war. Government announces its strongest economic growth figure of 9.4 per cent in 20 years. Elects Pratibha Patil as the first woman President of India.

Burma: China and Russia veto a draft to UN Security Council urging Burma to stop persecuting minority and opposition groups. Burma and North Korea restore diplomatic ties after 24 years following the debacle of a deadly attack on the visiting North Korean president.

Nepal: Parliament approves abolition of monarchy as part of the peace deal with Maoists, who agree to join the interim government, a move that brings them into the political mainstream.

Bangladesh: A state of emergency is declared amid violence in the election run-up. President Ahmed postpones the poll. Fakhruddin Ahmed heads a caretaker administration. Sheikh Hasina is charged with murder. Begum Khaleda Zia comes under virtual house arrest. Arrests of several other politicians are made in an anti-corruption drive.

Pakistan: Wave of protests grips the country due to the suspension of Chief Justice Iftikhar Mohammed Chaudhry by President Musharraf. Ex-Prime Minister Benazir Bhutto returns from exile. Suicide bomb blasts targeting her homecoming parade in Karachi kill dozens of people. Supreme Court challenges Musharraf's victory at presidential election. Musharraf declares emergency rule, dismisses Chief Justice Chaudhry and appoints new Supreme Court bench, which confirms his re-election. Former PM Nawaz Sharif returns from exile. Benazir Bhutto assassinated at election campaign rally in Rawalpindi.

2008

India: Series of coordinated attacks by gunmen on the main tourist and business area of Mumbai between 26–29 November kill nearly 200 people and injure hundreds more. India blames Pakistani militants and demands that Pakistan take responsibility and act against the militants.

Burma: Government publishes proposed new constitution, which allocates a quarter of seats in parliament to the military. The new constitution also bans Myanmar nationals married to foreigners from holding the presidency – a move interpreted as blocking the candidacy of opposition leader Aung San Suu Kyi.

Nepal: Former Maoist rebels win the largest bloc of seats in elections to the new Constituent Assembly, but fail to achieve an outright majority. Nepal becomes a republic. Ram Baran Yadav becomes Nepal's first President. Work begins on writing a new federal, secular and republican constitution.

Bangladesh: Local elections take place paving a way to restore democracy. Awami League wins by capturing more than 250 of 300 seats. Sheikh Hasina made prime minister.

Sri Lanka: Military claims to have captured the important Tamil Tiger naval base of Vidattaltivu in the north.

Pakistan: Pakistan People's Party (PPP) nominee Yusuf Raza Gilani becomes prime minister at head of a coalition with Nawaz Sharif's Muslim League party. President Musharraf resigns after the two main governing parties launch impeachment proceedings against him. MPs elect PPP's Asif Ali Zardari, the widower of assassinated former PM Benazir Bhutto, as President.

2009

India: A Delhi court decriminalizes homosexuality, overturning a 148-year-old colonial law. In latter part of the year, the government gives consent for the formation of Telangana, by carving out a part of the southern state of Andhra Pradesh, leading to violent protests.

Nepal: Prime Minister Prachanda resigns in a row with President Yadav. Maoists leave government after other parties oppose integration of former rebels into national army. Communist leader Madhav Kumar Nepal becomes new prime minister.

Bangladesh: In a ruling on the decades-old dispute between the two main political parties, the High Court decides that it was the father of Sheikh Hasina and not the late husband of her arch-rival Khaleda Zia who proclaimed independence from Pakistan in 1971.

Sri Lanka: The LTTE is defeated after government troops capture the northern town of Kilinochchi, their administrative headquarters, and overrun last patch of rebel-held territory in the northeast. Military says LTTE leader Velupillai Prabhakaran was killed in the fighting. Tamil Tigers surrender. First post-war local elections held in northern region. Governing coalition wins in Jaffna.

Pakistan: President Asif Ali Zardari hands control of Pakistan's nuclear arsenal to PM Yousuf Raza Gilani.

2010

Burma: Government announces new election laws, with provisions for an electoral commission decided upon by the citizens of the country. Government changes country's flag and national anthem.

Nepal: PM Madhav Kumar Nepal quits under Maoist pressure.

Bangladesh: Five former army officers executed for the 1975 murder of founding PM Sheikh Mujibur Rahman.

Sri Lanka: Mahinda Rajapaksa wins presidential election by a big margin. The outcome is rejected by his rival General Sarath Fonseka, who is then arrested on corruption charges and jailed for 30 months by a military court. He is convicted of further charges in November and sentenced to another three years in jail. President Rajapaksa dissolves parliament, clearing way for elections in April. European Union suspends Sri Lanka's preferential trade status because of concerns over its human rights record.

2011

Burma: Thein Sein swears in as President of a new, nominally civilian government. In latter half of August, President Thein Sein meets Aung San Suu Kyi in the capital, Nay Pyi Taw. In November, pro-democracy leader Aung San Suu Kyi announces plan to stand for elections. In December, US Secretary of State Hillary Clinton visits, meets Aung San Suu Kyi and holds talks with President Thein Sein. US offers to improve relations if democratic reforms continue.

Nepal: Jhalanath Khanal is elected premier in February, ending a seven-month stalemate during which Nepal had no effective government. He resigns in August after the government fails to reach a compromise with the Opposition on a new constitution and fate of former Maoist fighters. CA elects Maoist party's Baburam Bhattarai as prime minister. He vows to forge a cross-party consensus over the new constitution and the Maoist fighters issue.

Pakistan: In April, American Special Forces kill the founder of al-Qaeda, Osama bin Laden, in Abbottabad. In November, Pakistan shuts down NATO supply routes after a NATO attack on military outposts kills 25 Pakistani soldiers.

2012

India: Pranab Mukherjee of the Congress is elected President, beating his rival P.A. Sangma. In November, Mohammad Ajmal Amir Qasab, the sole surviving gunman of the 2008 Mumbai attacks, is executed.

Burma: NLD candidates, including Aung Saan Suu Kyi, attain a massive victory in by-elections. The European Union suspends all non-military sanctions against Burma for a year. In May, Indian Prime Minister Manmohan Singh pays first official visit. US President Barack Obama visits to offer 'the hand of friendship' in return for more reforms. He urges reconciliation with the Rohingya minority.

Nepal: Prime Minister Bhattarai dissolves CA before it can agree on a new constitution.

Sri Lanka: UN Human Rights Council adopts a resolution urging Sri Lanka to investigate war crimes allegedly committed during the final phase of the conflict with LTTE. Sri Lanka says the move usurps its sovereignty. In May, former army chief Sarath Fonseka is freed after two and a half years in jail. His terms of release prevent him from running for public office for seven years.

Pakistan: Supreme Court disqualifies Prime Minister Gilani from holding office after he declines to appeal against a token sentence in President Zardari corruption row. Parliament approves Water and Power Minister Raja Pervez Ashraf as his successor. In July, Pakistan agrees to reopen NATO supply routes to Afghanistan after the US apologizes for the accidental killing of 24 Pakistani soldiers. In October Taliban gunmen seriously injure 15-year-old campaigner for girls' rights Malala Yousafzai, whom they accuse of 'promoting secularism'.

2013

India: The Supreme Court reverses the 2009 Delhi High Court order decriminalizing homosexual acts, saying Parliament, not the courts, must resolve the issue.

Burma: President Thein Sein visits Washington. President Obama praises Myanmar's political and economic progress, but criticizes violence against Rohingya Muslims.

Nepal: Chief Justice Khil Raj Regmi forms an interim unity government. Elections are held in November for a new assembly (CA-II) which will write a new constitution. Political deadlock as no party wins a majority.

Bangladesh: War crimes tribunal sentences prominent Muslim cleric Abul Kalam Azad to death for crimes against humanity during the 1971 independence war. He is tried in absentia, as he has fled abroad. In April, Prime Minister Sheikh Hasina vetoes Islamist bill to outlaw criticism of Islam. President Zillur Rahman dies in March; Abdul Hamid elected as new President.

Sri Lanka: Parliament passes impeachment motion against Chief Justice Shirani Bandaranayake, following 14 charges of financial and official misconduct. The government's senior legal adviser, Mohan Peiris, replaces her. In March, UN Human Rights Council, and in April, Amnesty International attack the country's violation of human rights during the civil war. Despite the criticism Sri Lanka prepares to host the Commonwealth Heads of Government Meeting (CHOGM).

Pakistan: President Zardari and Afghanistan's President Hamid Karzai agree to work for an Afghan peace deal. Musharraf returns from exile in Britain to contest parliamentary elections. In April, court orders the arrest of Musharraf over his attempt to impose house arrest on judges during military rule in March 2007. Parliament approves Nawaz Sharif as prime minister after his PML-N wins elections. In July, Parliament elects Mamnoon Hussain as President. Lt Gen Raheel Sharif takes over as head of the army on the retirement of General Ashfaq Pervez Kayani.

2014

India: The Hindu nationalist Bharatiya Janata Party leads the NDA coalition to victory in general elections. Narendra Modi becomes prime minister.

Burma: Relations with US sour as the latter extends some sanctions for another year, but stresses that despite recent reforms, there have been rights abuses and army influence on politics and the economy.

Nepal: Nepali Congress leader Sushil Koirala secures parliamentary support and assumes the office of prime minister. CA misses deadline for agreeing a new constitution in September, and extends it till January 2015.

Bangladesh: Opposition BNP boycotts parliamentary elections. Prime Minister Sheikh Hasina returns for third term in office with a massive majority.

Sri Lanka: President Mahinda Rajapaksa declares that a UN team investigating allegations of war crimes will not be allowed to enter Sri Lanka. He announces an early presidential election to be held in January 2015.

Pakistan: Musharraf goes on trial on treason charges. Nawaz Sharif government and Taliban meet in North Waziristan for peace talks, with a ceasefire at the top of the agenda. Attack on Karachi airport in April. Supporters of Imran Khan and Tahirul Qadri occupy the Red Zone in downtown Islamabad in August–September, demanding the resignation of Sharif for corruption and electoral fraud. Parliament rallies behind Sharif. The army requests that the PM 'shares space' with the army.

Prologue

2014: The Triumph of Indian Democracy?

Democracy and India – do they really go together? Wise heads used to think of one as modern and egalitarian, and the other as ancient and hierarchical. But such assumptions always underestimated the adaptability of both. Today it would be hard to deny that democracy is currently very much alive in India, has been a boon to her people, and looks set to continue to work well.

Compared to her society, India's democracy has a short history, but it is a complex tale. And it is far from over, for the arrival in 2014 of a majority Bharatiya Janata Party (BJP) government – the moment when the Indian nation first turned to the right by clear popular demand – has not put an end to questions about how the state will treat its citizens, or how it will cohabit with its regional neighbours. The most we can say for now is that India has made a choice for strong national leadership.

Large popular mandates – sometimes called elective dictatorships – are both a blessing and a curse. They are reassuring for a nation and empowering for politicians, but they are not determinative; they can assure us that most of us have agreed, but they do not actually dictate what will happen. And democratic electorates can change their minds in the light of experience. Permanency, we must remind ourselves, is not a democratic norm, and it is too much to expect that turmoil and conflict will be stilled forever by the decisive parliamentary verdict delivered in favour of Narendra Modi.

What, then, can we expect from Prime Minister Modi? He had campaigned on broad themes of good governance and development, so on Day One he had little to restrict him. Early indications saw him slim down government at the top, reach out to regional leaders, and declare a commitment to China-style growth via four coloured revolutions – saffron for power, green for improved agricultural practice, white for a dairy renaissance, and blue for better management of fisheries.[1] But will India grow? And if not, will his own party be able to make the self-made hard man step down? Will we see a split, a BJP (M), and a swing to authoritarianism? Will the Indian electorate get a chance to remove him if he fails to deliver?

It is too early to say if or how the Modi victory might permanently change Indian politics. India has ingrained patterns to her political life that have developed over decades, and one election will not necessarily disrupt them greatly. But 2014 certainly marks an important historical moment for India, and it should be placed in context, along with three other pivotal points since Independence:

- 1946–50: The writing of the independent constitution. Modern India was laid out on paper, guided by concerns for social justice, inclusion and restitution.
- 1975–77: The Emergency, which marked the limits of how far India could be shoehorned into the image of one party or one leader.
- 1989–92: A confused period which saw four significant developments that transformed the party system, the economy and the national debate:
    1. The beginning of an extended period of coalition government.
    2. The introduction of the Mandal reservations, which marked the high point of the state's old welfare policies.
    3. The economic liberalization of July 1991, which marked a revision of the role of central government.
    4. The destruction of the Babri Masjid, which marked the assertive re-emergence of traditional social identities.

India lost a clear national voice during this short period, and only recovered it in May 2014, after 25 years of social and political fragmentation.

It is not hard to see why Modi won in 2014, but one of the most extraordinary aspects of his victory is that it was based squarely on promises of development and good governance. This is the Indian equivalent of an American presidential candidate running on a platform of 'motherhood and apple pie'. How did something so apparently banal prove so successful and persuasive? Surely no aspiring candidate anywhere has ever campaigned in favour of poor governance, and development was indelibly printed into India's political psyche many decades ago. Does this not pose deep questions about India's democracy? Has it failed so badly? Or is it that, although the Congress – the dominant party in Indian politics for six decades – can justifiably take credit for lifting India to the highest heights of national idealism, must it not also take the blame for dragging her down into the lowest depths of party expediency, as exemplified by the last years of UPA-II? For, as surely as the 2014 election marked the rise of Modi and the BJP, the scale of the victory also marked a catastrophic fall for the Congress.

Some remarkable things can be said about the 2014 results. A record national turnout installed the first non-coalition government since 1984 and the BJP became the first non-Congress party ever to earn a majority. The BJP famously won more seats in Uttar Pradesh (71) than the Congress did across the whole country (44). But the BJP won 52 per cent of the seats (282) on only a 31 per cent vote share. In 1967 Congress got 283 seats on a 41 per cent share. How could this happen and what does it mean for the future? Has a pro-BJP bias developed within the system, or is the party now just better at contesting elections?

One all-embracing explanation is that the Congress was going through a gradual decline across the years 1967 to 2014, which was masked by other factors and thus appeared misleadingly precipitous at the end. After 1980, there was certainly a reshuffling of right-wing forces, which eventually produced a coherent popular opposition that was able to install a government on less than a third of the popular vote. This was a remarkable development in a country that had adopted socialism so wholeheartedly. Why the change?

From the outset India's politicians always used socialism to garner support among the poorer classes, who constituted the vast bulk of the population. The demands of democracy started India on a left-wing footing, but several long-term factors – the growth of a middle class, a desire for strong leadership and disillusionment with the cynical use of the idea of secularism – pulled the political centre of gravity of the country gradually rightwards. Despite the continued presence of a great deal of poverty in the country, India's electors voted in 2014 to step away from many of the shibboleths of Indian politics. More remarkably, many of them ignored their own short-term interests, in terms of welfare, in favour of a faith in better long-term prospects for themselves – and the nation. Here is the triumph of Indian democracy, whose demise has been predicted many times.

In a sense, Narendra Modi has reinvented national politics in India – as the first person to present a clear national agenda on the right, to personify it and to make it credible by his own example in both his life story and his record in office. Reassuringly, on the morning of his victory, he told the adoring public in Vadodara that in democratic politics 'there are no enemies, but only competitors'.[2] Politics was instantly recast as business, not war – an attitude he had previously evinced about foreign policy.

Such instinctive understanding of the central essence of democracy indicated that an emphatic mandate might not turn his head, and India would be safe in his hands. But can we be sure? If such an ambitious and driven man is given so much power and adulation, who or what might be safe?

The Modi coronation was important because it was the moment at which India spoke with one voice again – a voice, however, that was no longer that of Nehruvian socialism. But it might still be the voice of an ancient tradition of accommodation, albeit with a less nervous concern for some of the weaker members of society. How much polarization will follow? No one knows for sure yet. Some are fearful, others confident or simply indifferent.

More pertinently, we can also ask: how much more polarization does Modi need to win again in 2019? The answer might be 'no more', if he merely wishes to hold onto what he has; he could even get by with less. But the logic of party politics usually rewards attack more than defence, and Modi has frequently expressed a wish to rid India of the Congress entirely. The Narendra Modi–Amit Shah leadership team has demonstrated its determination to expand the BJP's presence in state assemblies, and there are signs that the strategy of local polarization, which proved so successful in UP and Bihar, may be an integral part of this drive. But this is a high-risk strategy that may alienate some of the voters who came over to the BJP in 2014, lured by promises of clean government and development. What Modi needs most is not religious friction but economic success; electoral success will then surely follow.

And what of good governance? Can Modi reboot the Indian political and governmental machine? Does he really need to, in order to remain in power, if remaining in power is his and his colleagues' sole objective? Or will we see radical changes in governmental style and policy? With a traditional Congress approach to government, all he would need would be an obedient party, an absence of rivals, and a large war chest – of at least 56 inches.

Opponents can take some comfort from the fact that the massive victory of May 2014 was not sustained through three rounds of by-elections held in the ensuing months. The BJP came up short in several states, losing out to the Samajwadi Party (SP) in UP, and to the Congress in Rajasthan and, surprisingly, Gujarat – all states where it had won decisively in May. Was this an instant backlash delivered by voters who had not seen the '*achhe din*' they had been promised in Modi's record-breaking tweet on victory morning?[3] Or was it simply the ancient localism of India resurfacing as voters refocused on their nearer concerns? Either way, the trend was not continued through the following months. In Assembly elections in October 2014 Haryana went saffron, while in Maharashtra the BJP trounced not only its opponents to the left but also its erstwhile allies, the Shiv Sena, to its right. Then in December 2014, the BJP was able to form the first-ever majority government in Jharkhand, while in Jammu and

Kashmir, though it fell well short of a majority, the party enjoyed its best ever showing.

With local and national trends still seemingly at odds, what, indeed, is the nature of the political culture that confronts Narendra Modi?

India can be a law unto herself, or sometimes an anarchy, but several interacting factors can be identified as major influences on the unique flavour of Indian democracy:

- The modern Indian state did not emerge from indigenous society; it grew out of colonial rule, and politics then grew around the state. This left India with a big society and a small government, a mismatch that has profoundly affected the way ordinary citizens interact with the state, encouraging a proliferation of mediators and dealers in influence and access.
- Central government in India has maintained very similar policies under different administrations. Priorities in the fields of welfare and development have remained fairly constant, within parameters determined by available revenues and global conditions. Voters have therefore had a restricted set of options, and this has lent a generally pragmatic and personal character to India's national politics.
- Large political parties have proved unwieldy, vulnerable to internal rivalries and expensive to run. India therefore has a large number of small political parties. Some stay small because of their roots in particular social groupings; some are too ideological to grow into mass movements; and a great many are the products of splits based on ideologies, personal rivalries or thwarted ambitions.
- Building national political organizations is formidably difficult in such a large, diverse country. India therefore has a great many regional parties, with politicians keen to find support in local, sectional groupings. This means that successful politicians often have a regional as opposed to a national base.

- In India, being in opposition – exclusion from power – withers parties very quickly. They cannot survive without the nourishment of power, meaning the discretion to dispose of state funding. Parties are therefore highly amenable to inclusion in coalition governments at all levels, and this further reinforces political pragmatism.

India's political, geographical and cultural nature requires top-down leadership to create a national pattern; movements emerging from below are likely to stay local, bounded by India's well-rehearsed diversities of language, religion, caste and regional identity. India's size makes it hard for local movements to coalesce. This creates an important role – perhaps a need – for figurehead leaders, even if they are largely symbolic. In fact, it helps if they are symbolic, because it widens their potential appeal. India's diversity means that large socio-political alliances are almost always oppositional; it is easier to assemble large followings by being against things than being for things. Large followings are more likely to form in times of stress or moral clarity, when there is something obvious to oppose.

Truly national leaders are therefore rare in India. In the twentieth century there were perhaps only two: M.K. Gandhi and J.P. Narayan. The Mahatma had the satanic British to oppose, and JP the autocratic Indira. The present century has just found its first such leader in Narendra Modi, who could set himself against the UPA-II government that had been overtaken by inflation, mired in scandal and clinging to blatant minoritism. It is too early to admit him to such august company, but the national forces and moral factors that created Gandhi and JP have had a hand in creating Modi too.

There are, however, significant differences that may permanently deny Modi a similar standing. He is in office, whereas the others never endured the sullying effects of true political responsibility. There is a danger that he might simply join the list of those, like Sheikh Mujib or Barack Obama, who looked much more impressive as rebel outsiders. He has also achieved his eminence on only one poll, in which he was awarded 31 per cent of the vote on a 66 per cent turnout, i.e. around one in five voting Indians. He will need to improve on that if he is to attain an equivalent exalted status. In his favour, meanwhile, is his very evident ability in matters of organization. This may put substance to his vision and allow him a more worldly kind of success, and may yet make him a great leader.

No one should doubt the formidable difficulties that political organization in India presents. It was largely a result of a long process of trial and error and a series of historical accidents that the pre-independence Congress found solutions to the kind of problems that India imposes, and it took about seven decades for a second national party to emerge with a coherent popular programme and a charismatic leader. Those decades saw India's founding political institution decline from idealism into cynicism, and Modi's election, on at least the economic level, augurs a return to centre-ground pragmatism.

Does the Modi victory change anything? Yes, very much so, and in two important areas. In the short term it represents a break with the policies and politics of the last 30 years. But it also opens up some new potential avenues in the future of Indian democracy, and allows a new retrospective analysis of the recent past. Till 2014, the main view was that India was a fractured polity, coping with its own disparities in a hand-to-mouth manner, condemned to limp from coalition to coalition, a nation without a clear mind of its own. Now clarity has been restored in a way that has not been in evidence for decades; some say since 1984, some 1977. The telling difference now is that those two moments of apparent unity, one anti-Indira and one pro-Rajiv, is that they were both moments of crisis. The 2014 verdict has been calmer and much more reflective. No deaths, no disasters, no dictatorship, but perhaps a moment of realization – that the debate over social equity had moved from static redistribution to dynamic empowerment. From handing out fish to handing out fishing rods.

How permanent this change, in both outlook and alignment, might prove to be remains unknown, but assuming for a moment that it is at least durable for a decade or so, we can discern a new shape to the political history of independent India.

We can see a dominant Congress system being dismantled between 1969 and 1989, a period of maximum instability between 1989 and 1998, and a degree of solidity recovered between 1998 and 2014. Then comes a change, an end to the makeshift political decentralization of the decades since the Emergency. Now we have a party newly arrived at true national status, a traditionalist party that has finally made its accommodation with modernity and the global economy, a party of the high castes that has framed an appeal to the lower, as proof of which it has taken a leader from their ranks. This fits neatly with a parallel narrative of decline in the Congress, which collapsed from a national party to a dynastic sideshow.

In 1947, the one fact of Indian political life was the existence of the Congress as a national institution. The party had built itself up over decades, unified in its opposition to the British, but diverse in its internal character. If India was going to be a successful democracy, the question became whether she could somehow accommodate and accept her own diversity. Was India to be one thing, or many? And would democratic politics help this process, or simply prove to be a way of dismantling herself? Now we have answers.

Like many aspects of the country, India's democracy often seems chaotic, but it has survived despite the original pessimism of many observers about its prospects after independence. It had always been the British Raj's prime self-justification that Indians had demonstrated an inability to govern themselves, and should not be allowed to try again. This line of thinking was topped off with the Partition of India in 1947, possibly the greatest undemocratic act of the twentieth century. Four hundred million Indians were left unconsulted, while the decision was made by a very small group of key players at the centre. Had the question been put to the whole nation, the vote would have been against it, by a margin of perhaps three to one.

The special conditions of the time ruled out any such consultation, and as a last act of imperial power, two new countries were born. These were not nation-states that had discovered themselves; they were entities drawn on maps, left to constitute themselves as best as they could.

It is perhaps worth noting that the prospects for democracy in Germany at this time were also considered very bleak by some observers. Germany had just undergone defeat, occupation and partition, disasters that came on top of a history of autocratic rule and strong regional identities. There was talk that Germans were unable, by their very nature, to live under democratic rule – that they were prone to fanaticism, too easily led, too politically naive. Yet despite initial problems of hunger and disruption, Germany went on to become the most democratic and stable state in Europe, generating huge prosperity in a country now noted for its scrupulous attention to civic rights. Rather than a belligerent Fourth Reich, Germany gave Europe the Green Movement. Rather than falling apart, divided Germany went on to reunify and build a smooth-running federal system. We can now see that there was perhaps more hope for a democratic India hidden in the ruins of Germany than anyone in 1947 realized.

And even, perhaps, some hope for other South Asian countries – a reassurance that military defeat, dismemberment and alleged cultural unsuitability for democracy could be overcome. The missing factor was surely prosperity; Germany recovered hers very quickly. But here we come to the first of many chicken-and-egg questions about democracy: does democratic freedom stimulate people to become prosperous, or does prosperity persuade people that they can live amicably among neighbours who are their equals, no matter what their economic standing? Do democracies create prosperity, or are they simply a better way of sharing it?

Most democracies are more prosperous than most authoritarian states, but this is not an invariable rule. Over time, many in Pakistan came to associate better economic times with military government, not rule by elected politicians, and undemocratic regimes all across eastern Asia have – sometimes – proved to be compatible with high growth rates.

Wealth takes some of the edge off political tensions, just as hunger and fear tend to sharpen them, but how early and how strongly does the prospect of wealth bind people to democratic institutions? So far it seems to have done so in India, but there are problems and dangers.

India has always had an unusual social profile for a democratic state, with a very high proportion of the population officially living in poverty – over two-thirds in 1950 and about a quarter at present. How has deprivation on such a scale affected Indian politics? The large numbers involved have allowed the lower orders to elect their own representatives without having to appeal to anyone else, and this has been the genesis of caste parties, which are usually local parties. One effect of mass poverty has thus been to make it more difficult for national parties to exist or organize. But more remarkably, the very large reservoir of potential resentment within the system has never turned to sustained militancy. Instead, India's political elite has effectively bought off a revolution by poor-friendly welfare policies, which have in turn acted as a kind of modern divide-and-rule policy, with the lower economic classes competing amongst themselves for advantages. Policies of reservation have always been popular in principle, but in practice they incite intense economic rivalry, which has expressed itself in competitive political organizations.

Older capitalist societies like Britain or France were relatively richer when they adopted mass democracy, but they still courted the risk that the poor would organize and vote themselves into a socialist utopia. India faced a more acute version of this possibility, especially under leaders who professed to be socialists. But the left never managed to convince the peasantry en masse that it had the answers, and it was instead the caste-based parties, who stood on narrow, localized platforms, that since the 1980s have mopped up a significant portion of the lower class vote. But will this continue to be the case? Have the demographic effects of poverty permanently resolved themselves in India? The 2014 election suggests that they have, at least in part, if not in full measure.

This is just one of the unknowables about India's future. Democracy in India certainly faces major challenges.

Democracy comes up from the people via elections and parties, and it goes down again via government services. India has struggled with both directions of this flow. There are fiscal problems, with a tiny tax base, and over 80 per cent of the workforce in the informal sector. There are problems of law and order, with up to twenty per cent of rural districts affected by armed Maoist insurgency. There is a backlog of legal business which, at present rates, may take 200 years to clear, while corruption touches as much as two-thirds of the population in dealings with officials. But every democracy in the world is afflicted by problems of all kinds – social, political, monetary, and ecological. Every generation thinks it faces serious problems, which is true. Over time, the difference lies in which problems are resolved by agreement or design, and which are rendered irrelevant by unforeseen, sometimes catastrophic, change.

So, how well is India doing? And how can we tell? How, indeed, should we judge the success of any democracy?

Holding frequent and fair elections is a basic requirement in a democracy, and India has certainly managed to do this. Even better, in terms of percentage turnout, India can claim a good record, which also contains an unusual and encouraging feature. In the long-established democracies of the West there is a clear trend that turnout is proportionally lower at the lower end of the income scale; the poorest in society are the least engaged with elections there. In India, however, the reverse has proved to be true. The poorest, least literate classes have taken to participatory democracy in an enthusiastic and, thus far, consistent manner.

One reason for this is that, especially in recent times, the system has worked sufficiently well for the lower divisions in society, both by enriching them directly via handouts of various kinds, and in the perceived beneficial effects that electing some of their own people, through caste-based parties, has had. There is nothing quite comparable to this in the mature democracies of the West, where the poor often shun the whole political process. This disengagement has some technical and administrative aspects; electoral enrolment is often connected to systems of local taxation which many seek to avoid, and the poorest in society are the least likely to have a permanent place of residence, which is usually a basic qualification to vote. But most of all, there is the simple curse of apathy – that having voted for generations, the poor are still poor and see no way in which distant, upper-class politicians are going to help them. Parties of the left in Britain have always had a high proportion of leaders from privileged backgrounds, and this is roughly paralleled by the profile of Congress leaders in India. India's caste-based parties, though, are axiomatically led by members of the caste concerned. In this sense, democracy in India really has put new hats into the ring, and in a way that convinces spectators that the game is real.

Because the less well-off make up such a large proportion of the Indian electorate, political parties are keen to chase their votes, whereas in richer societies they are not. Parties in the US are known to court women, blacks or Hispanics, but they do not chase 'the poor vote'. In this sense democracy has been a huge success in India, and schemes of agricultural subsidies, food provision and guaranteed employment have made significant social and economic differences to the country.

The relationship between poorer people, who are always in a majority, and democracy will therefore remain a crucial factor in India's development. But this connection contains a danger that governments will try to win elections simply by bribing, directly or indirectly, the less well-off at the expense of the public treasury. The recent collapse of the public finances in Greece provides a salutary lesson in how state credit can be deployed to satisfy an electorate, but only at the risk of longer-term disaster. Democratic politicians must live with the constant temptation to overspend, and thus mortgage the state's future for their own immediate advantage. This is potentially a greater temptation for India's politicians than it has proved to be for Greece's, because of the size of the numbers involved, and because, historically, the centre has struggled to restrain public spending by the states. India's political relationship with poverty has played, and will continue to play, a crucial role in her democratic development, unless and until the proportion of officially described poor people diminishes to electoral insignificance.

In terms of regular elections and political inclusion, India has certainly done well. But most people who live in democracies like to think that there is more to the freedoms they hold than casting a vote every four or five years. Between elections, voters are still citizens, with many pressing concerns other than occasionally approving political leaders. Democracy as a daily experience includes a range of entitlements, contained in an interconnected set of rights; elections are simply an expression of one of these rights – the right to vote. For above all, democracy carries assumptions about equality and about the delivery of real freedoms.

A successful democracy should therefore be able to boast a track record of wealth creation, a good level of literacy, an independent and efficient judiciary, a diversity of national print and broadcast media and some indication of business vitality, such as a stock market. India is doing reasonably well in most of the areas connected with the encouragement of creativity and self-expression, though the benefits conferred are almost all enjoyed by the wealthier in society. And while India certainly has a democracy that discovers and truly expresses the will of the people, the day-to-day running of the country has yet to attain the quality citizens might expect under truly effective popular sovereignty. The lives of the masses would benefit from a clear improvement in the standard of basic governance, meaning the supply of reliable services including public health and education, utilities such as water and electricity, speedy justice and a reliable police service. Simply electing leaders, no matter how freely, guarantees none of these things.

If we look at democracy like this we can see that it is closely linked with expectations. Especially in newer democracies like India, it is intimately bound to the idea of change – social change and cultural modernization; traditional societies have never been very concerned to alter their internal balances. Democratic development, therefore, can produce not only new winners but also new losers, and this has been very evident in the history of democracy all across South Asia. Anti-democratic forces – principally military cliques and religious movements – frequently represent social elements that perceive themselves as losing out in altered circumstances.

Democracy is a great accelerator of social and economic change because it relies on an ideal of equal access to political power, based on the concept of equal rights. Traditional societies do not encourage such notions. Mass democracy is essentially a modern and a modernizing idea; it sits uncomfortably with much that traditional communities venerate and admire. The notion of rights, especially new rights, can be highly disturbing to patriarchal families and traditionally religious societies. Undemocratic forces therefore attract support from those who value order, repelled by the risky and unstable prospects that democracy opens up. Appeals to the authority of history can carry great weight in traditional societies, especially where respect for ancestors is mandatory. But democracy is a licence to rewrite tradition; it puts the current generation – or at least a majority of it – in charge.

This new mental world has produced all sorts of reactions across South Asia, and has been central to the birth of identity politics, a process in which communities suddenly find that they have 'rights', and then must define and discipline themselves as a group to defend interests that previously they had been only vaguely aware they possessed. This realization has had a significant impact on both majority and minority groupings.

Here we come to another chicken sitting on another egg: do traditional societies touched by modernity reach a pitch of social instability that can then only be resolved by democratic processes? Or do such societies become more economically flexible and equal within themselves, so that a demand for democracy is simply the most convenient way to satisfy new aspirations? Is the transition to democracy a form of crisis management, or a natural evolution?

This leads us to yet more questions: Are all societies suited to democracy? Can it be introduced everywhere with good effects? Currently, the answer to this hangs in the balance all around the world. Democracy is still problematic in large parts of Africa, prompting sharp debates about whether it is the legacy of colonialism or of traditional social structures that causes greater difficulties. While South America has now generally come to terms with democratic government, several major countries in the Middle East, including Iraq, Syria and Egypt, are struggling with the transitions from dictatorship, casting doubts in some quarters as to whether Islam, or Islamic culture, is compatible with democracy. Radicals and conservatives say 'no', but there is a liberal wing of Muslim opinion which believes that it is. And religion is a relevant factor in South Asia too. Conservative Hindu forces helped sustain a monarchy in Nepal until 2006, and Buddhist monks have sometimes supported an authoritarian government, as in Sri Lanka, and sometimes opposed one, as in Burma.

Is India a society that can thrive on democracy? Most observers would consider India to be safe – under normal circumstances – from an undemocratic lapse, because Indians broadly accept that the only way they can get along within such a diverse society is through democracy. The enormous size of the country has also forced a pragmatic acceptance of a degree of federal localism that does not compromise the central tenet of national sovereignty. Indians have learned to live with the idea that political authority can be pooled in a central government so that no group feels excluded or dominated by other groups. This recognition is of fundamental significance; as long as it persists, there is hope for refinements in democracy and improvements in governance.

The acceptance of a shared future is also an area in which Indians have arguably surpassed Europeans. Though India has had a long history of internal wars, these were largely in the pre-modern era and, apart from invasions, they were less devastating, less professional, and less ideological than those in Europe. Most of them were arguments about dynastic succession, or the payment of back rent.

Peace in Europe was eventually born of exhaustion. A generation of far-sighted politicians then used the resulting truce to build the modern European Union (EU), a body committed to democracy based on pooled sovereignty. Exactly the problems that Indians used to have – and to which the original Indian National Congress was the answer – were thus solved by loose political alignment. But many in Europe have been intensely suspicious of the whole supra-national European project, and there are substantial political segments in all EU member countries that are dedicated to spreading suspicion of foreigners and what they regard as the dictatorial rule of faceless bureaucrats in Brussels. Mrs Thatcher's own political demise in 1990 was directly precipitated by her suspicion of Germans and her unshakeable conviction – not that any of her convictions were very shakeable – that the European 'community' was a clandestine German scheme to secure domination of the continent. Indians can afford to look on all this with a wry smile.

At the end of the Second World War, India was facing a broadly similar range of problems as Europe – a jumbled legacy of ancestral culture and historical identities, but Indians found a way to reconcile them in an astonishingly short time. India is now perhaps the most successful recent example of the voluntary adoption of pooled sovereignty. The US took it on as a necessary founding principle over 200 years ago, and then built its politics around the idea; Europeans are still wrestling with it. India's way of preserving and developing her various distinct legacies has been to think of them not as merging but as running in parallel, and dealing with the most important points of friction as they arise.

For some in Europe, though, the sour legacy of overweening nationalism means that all the points are frictional. Getting 'out' of Europe is the battle cry, in defiance of geography, common culture and a plethora of shared interests.

There are, though, very few Indian voices striving to get out of India, a drastic course that has only ever appealed to India's geographic and cultural fringes, where the historical background provides strong alternative identities, as in the north-east, or Kashmir, or in the more extreme forms of Sikh or Dravidian nationalism. On the whole, the argument remains not about if, but how India should be. In this sense India has a culture of unity anterior and superior to that of Europe. But it is not necessary to argue about its merits. We can simply note its existence in passing as a corrective to so much propaganda from previous eras in which Indians were roundly told that in running their own affairs they should act more like Europeans. Europeans effectively smashed up their own house before learning to share it peacefully (for now). Indians had their house possessed by others, yet it remained for most of them still a home. On repossession they have argued more about who sleeps where, or who has the TV remote, rather than whether the family should stay together.

All this should remind us that democracy is never a way out of tensions; it is a way of controlling and resolving them. Violence, the most anti-democratic force on earth, can only resolve tensions through complete extermination – the silence of the graveyard. Otherwise violence offers only a way into further tensions. A well-run democracy should, and will, greatly reduce tensions, if not entirely eliminate them.

One of these tensions lies in trying to define the exact relationship between what we now call nations and states. Do nations create states or vice versa? Who can have a state and who cannot? How can different ethnic or religious groups combine to create a shared communal project? Is patriotism a learned affair, or is it somehow naturally acquired? A century ago a Polish nationalist leader, Józef Piłsudski, felt able to assert: 'It is the state which makes the nation, not the nation the state.'[4] Was he right?

South Asia now provides several illustrations of how he has been proved mostly right, but occasionally wrong. East Bengal's Muslims decided they would not be Indians in 1947. Then in 1971, despite still being Muslims, they decided that they would not be Pakistanis either. On neither occasion had their state made a nation of them, and indeed had denied them that status. Nor did this happen on a sufficient scale in Sri Lanka, despite the island's distinct geography and long history. Yet in independent India – a far more complex case than either East Bengal or Sri Lanka – the new state has managed to nurture sufficient support within its borders to avert large-scale social conflicts. This achievement is more in line with recent history, which shows that states, including fairly artificial, postcolonial examples like Pakistan and Nigeria, can in fact generate intense loyalties over relatively short periods among the mass of their populations. Indians might by now think of themselves as Midnight's Children, but they are also Piłsudski's children on the quiet.

Europeans learned their lessons through the damaging effects of warfare, whereas Indians picked up most of theirs from the negative experience of colonialism, while taking advantage of its main benefits – internal disarmament and the establishment of the institutional framework of national unity. The process of anti-colonial mobilization was essentially democratic after 1857, and the way that differences were buried brought forward several generations of gifted leaders, all of whom chose, but were in equal measure obliged, to speak the language of national unity. This allowed the formation of a body of central allegiance, which managed not just to include but to surpass provincial and religious partisanship. The original Congress ideology was always an all-India ideology.

This did not, though, simplify the problems of decolonization beyond a certain point – the point of bringing pressure to bear on the colonialists to leave. What was to follow was not entirely clear, apart from the commitment of the senior Congress leadership to principles of justice and democracy.

History can show that democracy did not create India or the Indian state, but by now democracy has done a great deal to change Indian society. This is as the generation of 1947 had originally intended. They wrote the constitution as they did because they did not believe that Indian society possessed the power or willingness to change itself.

Some intricacies of the Indian constitution are still being worked out, but the original principles, especially the culture of dispersal of power, the prospectus of positive social change and the flexibility of 'the idea of India' have produced enormous benefits and a vital sense of civic cohesion. While Britain, in the years of her greatest dominance, had a strong sense of national identity but an unwritten constitution, India has benefited from the reverse – a loose sense of national identity and a deliberately explicit constitution. Of these two elements, the constitution has been more influential in the legal and political functioning of the country, despite the numerous ambiguities and contradictions that it harbours.

India's founding fathers, though, made themselves quite clear in the constitution's preamble. This declares the intention to set up a republic, to establish justice and to promote classic democratic ideals of liberty, equality and fraternity, first linked in France in 1789.

It is worth remembering what these three words mean, why they are important, and why, in combination, they are such indispensable parts of democracy:

- Liberty, because people are free under self-government
- Equality, because all votes count the same, and people have equal rights
- Fraternity, because the system will not work unless we trust our neighbours and feel connected to them.

In more recent times, the concept of fraternity – brotherhood, *bhaichara* – has been re-identified under a variety of names, including fellow feeling, community spirit, tolerance and human solidarity.

Fraternity has always tended to go missing in political writing, losing out to its two glitzier partners. Fraternity, by comparison, is slightly vague and tends to excite our animal passions rather less. But something important underlies this persistent neglect of fraternity. Liberty and equality are demands we can deliver to our rulers, whereas fraternity is something we require of ourselves. Fraternity is the one element of the French revolutionary trinity that is something we *give*. It is hard to enforce it or to demand it from others, especially if we do not embrace it ourselves.

We must not underestimate the actual everyday power of fraternity, despite its imperviousness to legislation and its resistance to measurement. Fraternity is the presiding spirit of democracy, the most difficult of its preconditions to generate and the first to evaporate in times of trouble. It is what makes social living real, and it is far more enjoyable than either liberty or equality. Liberty is easily assumed and soon becomes invisible; it is a potentiality that gives us nothing that we do not give ourselves. Equality is actively distressing to many people in a great many aspects of their lives; equality is a political, not a social, comfort.

Fraternity, however, is actively enjoyable, endlessly varied and pleasantly unpredictable. No one can build a social life exclusively on the principles of liberty or equality, and no society that loses the spirit of fraternity can long endure in any form, democratic or otherwise. The first thing that dictatorships attack and pervert is fraternity – the willingness to work together for collective ends, the ability to trust other people and the capacity to accept others as connected with ourselves, regardless of socially specific characteristics.

Fraternity is how and why democracy works. It is democracy's life force. Understanding it also gives an insight into democracy's greatest weakness, because fraternity has a dark side. It is also the presiding genius of identity politics, for it is the essence of community feeling, and the perceptions of self that it generates can often unleash violent and destructive forces.

This is closely connected to a fourth political desideratum – security, which never appeared on the banners of the French revolutionaries, and did not feature in the great face-off between liberty and equality that the ideological left–right battles of the twentieth century were supposed to be about. Nor was it included in the Indian constitution of 1950.

In trying to understand democracy and the limitations of its appeal, it is important to appreciate how a combination of fraternity and security can have real mass appeal. People will happily settle for this combination in troubled times. Liberty is often belittled as an illusion, and some religious people actively despise it. Equality can be deeply unpopular in any form that carries compulsion.

Fraternity and security are what populations in South Asia have often settled for, and this – despite the incredulity of some American political scientists – is the daily reality of mass politics around the world. Compromised liberty can be acceptable, as long as fraternity and security are attended to – not perhaps security against the state, or to enjoy unlimited rights of expression, but security to lead one's daily life, including the chance to get rich. This makes life unsafe for democracies, especially if they cannot promote, protect or generate a suitable mixture of fraternity and security along with their other objectives.

So when are democracies in trouble? They may be struggling when we hear the sound of complaints. But it is important to listen to the actual content of those complaints and map them onto a wider scheme of society, to see how many people it is that are complaining, and exactly what their grievances are. Loudness and apparent quantity, or even vehemence, may not be reliable indicators of the malaises of a democracy. They may, rather confusingly, be symptoms of its health. This is the most magical quality of democracy, its ability to deliver stable instability, or more accurately, instability within limits. India provides the prime example of how this works.

India's problems, however, are real enough, and are rehearsed daily in the national press. Poverty exists, though it is reducing, and it still exerts effects on elections. Equally pressing are problems of judicial delay, bureaucratic obstructionism, corruption that ranges from petty larceny to outrageous embezzlement and grievous underperformance in health care and education. And while national democracy persists and even thrives, internal democracy in India's political parties struggles to asset itself. We must remember that effectiveness of the right to vote depends crucially on who is put up for election. India's voters may feel they have the right to pick the political players, but the secretive, often autocratic temper of party leaders means that they have often not possessed the direct ability to select the eventual teams.

Under such conditions, politicians inevitably shrink in stature, and this, combined with the difficulty of effecting change in Indian society through governmental action, means that any hope of using individual votes to promote some conception of the public good becomes a distant prospect. Some notion of the common good is required in democracies to guide public policy if it is not to drift, or to be bent towards selfish outcomes for sectional interests. Public policy must encompass more than the maintenance of the ruling elite to be truly public. Democracy, above all, is a collective project, and it must reinforce and emphasize its commonality if it is to function well or survive for long.

India has hit democracy on many of its weakest spots. Poverty, illiteracy, scale and checkerboard identities all supposedly work against managing to run fair elections while delivering social cohesion and viable governance. How India fares is central to future global development. The world need not look to China for leadership in this, for China is dealing with the problems of dismantling authoritarianism. The US is experiencing a long crisis of government paralysis, beset with debt, welfare demands and visceral political animosity at its heart, torn between reactionary constitutional fundamentalists and liberal progressives. The EU, which is the nearest analogue to the multi-ethnic, multi-linguistic, multi-faith state that India represents, has done well in a limited sense of peacemaking, but has fallen short in creating any kind of separate identity or widely accepted legitimacy in the minds of its citizens.

In the mythical Indian rope trick, the rope stands straight up, apparently without support. Onlookers know, however, that the rope is staying up because the fakir wills it to stay up. India's democracy is much the same. Some observers have found it hard to see how it could support itself, and many have expected it to fall. But it will stand if Indians want it to, and use their collective will to give it strength.

And we must all hope that the rope stays up, not just for the sake of India, but for the rest of the world too, because India currently needs to solve the same range of economic, political, social and environmental problems that confront all modern societies. If democracy cannot provide suitable answers for India, then modernity may be doomed. And if so, are we bound for dictatorship or archaism? We need to know, and India may be able to tell us.

Part 1

Democracy

Democracy is a principle of government, not a fixed system. It is a practical approach to conflict resolution, and it has no single, ideal form. It can come in different varieties – direct, indirect, formal, representative, parliamentary and presidential – to suit different local conditions.

Common elements of democratic systems include elections, representative institutions, orderly transitions between governments, the rule of law and mutual recognition of rights, including freedom of expression, association and movement. Democracy relies on the principle of popular sovereignty, the idea that the power of government comes from the people who live under it, not from God or the right of conquest or the sacredness of the land. Popular sovereignty justifies two principal pillars of democracy: reciprocal recognition of equal rights, and accountability, meaning that those delegated to wield power must answer to the community from which that power has been derived. In a democracy the collective will of the community is monitored and respected in a continuous process of consensual change, meaning that any leader, or any law, can be replaced by another.

Democracies are not all the same because humanity varies all over the world in detailed matters of tradition, and in the size and uniformity of community groups. If democracies express the nature of their constituent human parts, which is something they aspire to do, it follows that democracies will vary as much as human societies do.

1.

Past, Present and Future

In 1941 there were fewer than a dozen democracies in the world. Monarchy was still common, dictators ruled several major states, and the European empires had not yet fallen. But at the end of the Second World War, a war which Western powers allegedly fought for democracy, the democratic count did not go up; rather, it went down. Communism took hold of Eastern Europe, and the Cold War then promoted and protected various kinds of autocracy and dictatorship all over the globe. Today, around 120 of the world's 195 states are democracies. So, why did over a hundred countries become democratic between 1941 and now? And if democracy is so desirable, why are all countries not democracies? Above all, where did such a powerful idea come from?

There are conflicting claims about who invented democracy, when and where. Perhaps democracy, in some form, did originate in ancient India or Africa, as some nationalist partisans claim, in defiance of the Eurocentric tradition that awards the crown to classical Greece. But is it really necessary to be definitive on this subject? Such claims are difficult to substantiate, and they might all be valid. It is therefore as chauvinistic to claim an exclusive right to the invention of ancient democracy as it is to deny it to others.

Archaeology has revealed the kind of small social groupings that early humans lived in all over the world, and anthropology has given us clues as to how they operated. They seem to have been fairly egalitarian by the standards of much of what followed, and this should not surprise us unduly. In societies where respect was paid to wisdom and where the division of food and goods was not systematically unequal, it would have been quite logical to ask group members what they thought about important matters, and then decide collectively who had the best ideas. This would be likely to keep a small, self-sufficient group together. It would also be the best way to maximize its collective brainpower, and to give it the most extensive access to its own experience. We can recognize this way of taking decisions as a form of 'democratic' self-government, and a range of early societies could all have arrived at their own versions of such a system by trial and error – and without reference to each other.

When it comes to the 'invention' of democracy, priority in time is not provable, exclusivity is not likely – and both are irrelevant, because these systems did not turn into modern democracy by any connected chain of developments. Indeed, democracy of this type disappeared to be overtaken by systems of government more suitable for larger groupings and designed to cope with more sophisticated objectives.

The significant factor here is the massive complications involved with the move towards large-scale agriculture and urban dwelling. Somewhere in this process, collective decision-making profoundly changed. It is apparent that the Axial Age (c.800–200 BCE) was an era of bloody clashes between large militaristic empires. In such a world, any democracy, which would necessarily have to be small, would have found it difficult to flourish. The miracle is that such a thing did appear and survive, for a while, most notably in Athens but also in other prominent Greek cities, such as Thebes and Argos, and across the broader Hellenistic world, in Sicily and southern Italy, North Africa and Asia Minor.

But it must be emphasized that democracy as practised in ancient Greece was a distant cousin to what we now recognize by that name. It grew to its fullest expression in Athens because of the local occurrence of three propitious conditions – security, education and community feeling. All three of these were highly restricted by modern standards, but they all played a part.

Athenian democracy was a system for free male citizens. It did not include women, slaves or anyone outside the propertied classes. It was a direct democracy that required constant assemblies and relied on citizen juries, magistrates and officers elected by lot as well as by open vote. Athens was also an incomplete democracy in that it had democratic ideals at home but behaved as an empire abroad. Certain Athenians may have been equal to each other in a political sense, but as a body they were definitely superior to inhabitants of other lands and cities that they conquered, from which they levied tribute.

Democracy in the Athenian sense was not a matter of comfortable, bourgeois serenity. In Athenian minds, it was recognized as a system of modified conflict, a way of avoiding mob rule – ochlocracy – while maintaining orderly relations between rich and poor in the close confines of a city-state. Though it was recognized as a form of popular as opposed to autocratic government – the word meant literally 'rule of the people' – it was not favoured by the intellectuals of the era, who considered it an extreme form, to be avoided in favour of more mixed systems that included elements of monarchy and aristocracy as well. Plato thought it was essentially a false and degrading system, founded on untruths with which demagogues would flatter and mislead the people, appealing to their worst instincts. Aristotle considered democracy to be a deviant form of constitution, because it was likely to be dominated by the poor. He preferred the rule of the many via what he called 'polity', in which middle-income people had a dominant say.

While allowing a certain precedence to the Greeks based on the written records we have and on the way they intellectualized what they were doing, it is unwise to trumpet western exclusivity in the invention of democracy, meaning deciding matters of public interest by debate and majority opinion and/or governance by elected representatives. The need to make decisions well, and to have them widely accepted, will always pull societies back to forms of collective discussion.

One crucial factor here is the problem of the losers. The defeated party may not accept or abide by the loss, except under coercion. Therefore, those in possession of military technology, skill or organization would rarely, if ever, be on the losing side for long, because if they were, they could reverse the decision by other means. Medieval history is largely the story of how this pattern played out all over the world – how trained fighters came to monopolize political power within societies in which the rest of the members were generally priests, merchants or peasants. Feudal societies were dominated by a knightly (i.e. violent) landowning class and were not democratic at all, though they acknowledged the desirability of consensus within the ruling elite – what might be termed 'sectional democracy'.

Feudalism revolved not around general consensus or consultation, but around strictly controlled relationships of protection and loyalty, connected to land and food. In societies which moved beyond subsistence, two skills emerged as central to life – growing food and handling weapons, and two specialist classes evolved from this distinction. With a clear division of labour set between these two groups, democratic ideas became redundant. Something like this seems to have happened all over the world in more complex societies, though not in societies of nomads or hunter-gatherers.

Democratic forms, however, appeared and persisted in many religious traditions. This may have been because the religious mindset often recognizes that wisdom can be shared, or revealed to many people. Buddhism had a strong collective, discursive tradition within its monasteries, albeit under the authority of abbots. But abbatial power cannot have been all that strong, because Buddhism spilt into 20 or more schools within a very short period of running its sangha system.

The medieval Catholic Church also practised a form of majoritarianism in the Conciliar Movement (1409–1517 CE). This movement relied on the high-minded idea that in a gathering of holy men, God was more likely to speak truly through majorities than minorities on non-scriptural issues, such as Church reform. This, however, is only an analogue of what we might think of as democratic procedure. The franchise was exclusive – holy orders – and the guiding principle was spiritual insight, not interest in the public good. But the idea was powerful. It has come down to modern times, and still provides the rationale for the elaborate election of popes.

Islam can also boast a tradition of consultation, or 'shura', relying on much the same idea – that rightly guided men can ascertain God's will, even in large numbers. This is, however, an unwieldy idea at the best of times, and although Muhammad Ali Jinnah was proud to declare that Muslims had been practising democracy for 1,300 years, he was telling the truth rather than the whole truth. The process of shura is not binding on an Islamic ruler, and the system of 'election' of a Muslim leader – *bay'ah* – is not temporary or revocable; it is for life and includes an absolute obligation of obedience upon those who swear allegiance.[5] The followers of the Prophet could not agree collectively on a clear line of succession after his death, and the historic Sunni–Shi'a split was the result. Ever since, the orthodox practice of Islam has been guided by scholars and jurists, not by majority votes in majlis or jirga.

Pre-modern, religious 'democracy' was never properly political. In another important difference, minorities in religious debates were, and still are, heavily at risk whenever the principle of right-mindedness is in play. Religious minorities are often called heretics, whereas it is a basic principle of modern democracy that a divergence of opinion cannot be taken as proof of moral wickedness.

Democracy in its modern form was practised nowhere until the Middle Ages were long over. Italian city-states did have forms of republicanism, but these were like the Athenian model, with limited franchises among very small, privileged citizen bodies. And one crucial element of modern democracy – lawmaking by popular consent – was never present anywhere. Divinely appointed rulers generally made laws on advice from select groups of courtiers, scholars and priests, either in accordance with what was perceived to be God's will, or with what was manifestly in the interests of important sections of society. The idea of putting up laws for general approval would have seemed both absurd and unwise.

What can count as modern democracy was not apparent in the constitutional history of England either, especially in anything like the degree asserted by British historians who began to study medieval documents in a new spirit of critical enquiry through the nineteenth century. The once popular idea that 'the barons' who extracted the list of promises known as Magna Carta (the Great Charter) from King John in 1215 CE were somehow tribunes of the people was quite misplaced. The barons spoke for no one but themselves, and though they touched on good governance, the promises they extracted were not about any kind of agreement with the wider realm. They wished to establish binding rules on King John, who was especially prone to making things up as he went along. Nor was Simon de Montfort, slain as a rebel in 1265 CE, the true father of the English Parliament as it became familiar to great Victorian politicians such as Gladstone or Disraeli. Like the barons 50 years before, de Montfort was trying to set up standard procedures of consultation, and to limit the influence of unsuitable courtiers, especially foreigners.

The idea that medieval barons were defining modern political liberties was a staple of British school history for about a hundred years before 1970, and was part of a chain of connected, cumulative developments referred to as 'Our Island Story', meaning 'How we became best at everything'. This teleological approach has long been discredited, as has the much-vaunted idea that ancient Anglo-Saxon 'freedoms' were snatched away by the evil, invading Normans after 1066 CE.

'Liberties' were mentioned frequently in medieval documents, but the word should not be understood in its modern sense. It was equivalent to what we would call privileges – a word that literally means 'private laws'. Medieval lawyers understood these to mean local capabilities outside royal supervision; rights, certainly, but rather the opposite of universal rights. Slightly more democratic was the clerical tradition of majority rule that spread out through municipalities and guild bodies and found a congenial home in universities, but in terms of recognizable modern democratic elements – regular elections, wide franchise, secret ballots, free speech, transparency in appointments and so forth – English/British democracy is a very young creature. On the road to democracy, just as important as charters, were: a costly and very bloody civil war in the seventeenth century that asserted the power of Parliament, the increasing independence of the judiciary, the secularization and depersonalization of government and a massive decline in social and judicial violence, all of which allowed a culture of civility to grow up within and between classes. These processes created a notional national 'centre', around which the culture and institutions of the country could arrange themselves without anyone ever having to locate or define that centre precisely.

Historians are rarely satisfied with such vague and scarcely visible processes, and are keen to discover significant milestones. The patrician liberals of late Victorian England preferred to see the barons as constitutional exemplars, and it was the Marxists of the 1940s who rediscovered the proto-democratic demands of the various radical sects during the English Civil War, such as the Levellers and the Diggers. Commentators with less revolutionary tastes now like to declare the dawning of democracy to be in 1832, the year of the Great Reform Act, but democratic principles were only truly established after the Second Reform Act of 1867, which laid down a new set of recognizably modern assumptions and entitlements. The evolution of British democracy was further aided by yet more electoral inclusion in 1884, and in terms of franchise the current British system only came into force in 1974, when 18-year-olds could vote for the first time.

Democracy has enjoyed a slow growth, and has not always been greatly helped by revolutions. Despite much of the rhetorical output of modern Americans, the revolt of the 13 colonies in the 1770s did not mark a truly democratic dawn. Most of the leaders of the American Revolution did not subscribe to egalitarian ideas, and political rights in the original United States were very restricted by modern standards. The new American Union was a republic based on individual property rights, not a democracy based on universal political rights – hence its apparent comfort with the institution of slavery. The US was not properly a democracy until the enactment of the 14th and 15th Amendments in 1868 and 1870. Even then, female suffrage was not fully in place until 1920, much as it had to wait for full implementation in other countries, with New Zealand leading the field in 1893.

So where can modern democracy first be seen to appear? Most credibly it can first be said to have taken shape in France after 1789. This is not because the French set up a fully functioning democratic system, because they didn't; the 'Revolutionary' constitutions of 1791, 1793 and 1795 all fell short of the modern model in various respects. But after 1789 the principles of universality and equality that underpin democracy were fully stated and widely supported across French society. The contents of the Declaration of the Rights of Man (1789) were genuinely groundbreaking. This is not an anachronistic or sentimental view; contemporaries who supported the old order – from diehard Catholic absolutists in France to rational Whigs in England – were equally appalled by its implications for monarchy and the 'natural' order with which they were familiar.

Democratic impulses, of more and less radical nature, emerged within French society over the revolutionary period 1789–1815. Ideas such as popular sovereignty, universal suffrage (for males over 25) and equality of civil rights became markers, then permanent gains of the Revolution. But the promise of a new beginning soon fell away. War, instability, faction and repression undid the infant democracy, and the nation passed through Jacobin terror and Napoleonic absolutism, only to return to conservative, hereditary monarchy with the restoration of the Bourbons. It is an abiding irony that the less democratic American Revolution easily outlasted the more radical French variant.

The new democratic principles of 1789 were soon declared in India too. Public debate in the French enclaves of Pondicherry and Chandernagore was passionate, as the expatriate French tried to decide whether the new principles of equality and fraternity applied to Indians too. The answer, though, was generally 'no'. Undaunted by this reluctance, Tipu Sultan of Mysore took up Jacobin principles of popular sovereignty in 1798, and just as the colonial French were prepared to make an exception for Indians, Tipu was prepared to make an exception for himself. In allying with republican France he required his followers and subjects to declare implacable hostility to all kings, except himself. But this was a dead end. India did not get democracy or revolutionary principles. Instead she finally got a very watered-down version of British liberalism in the early twentieth century, having endured a long intermediate period after 1784, under a sort of Whig aristocratic government that neither consulted its subjects directly nor provided anything but the most basic protection for ordinary Indians from the force of unaccountable government.

This extended political hijacking meant that Indians were given scant opportunity to take a role in the development of modern democratic institutions. However, there are two fields in which Indian contributions must be acknowledged. The first is in the perfection of civic nationalism. The Indian National Congress rejected ethnic nationalism of the European type and demonstrated how an ethnically and culturally diverse state could be created and maintained. The second is in the construction and management of federalism. Unlike the US, which aligned pre-existing discrete units, or Australia and Canada, which received their federal architecture from above/abroad, India's federal structure, uniquely, was created from within by consensus. Under imperial rule, agreement could not be reached; after Independence, the matter was settled quickly and without rancour.

In two vital areas – how to create a democratic community and how to scale it up to continental size – India greatly expanded the reach and range of modern democratic systems.

India, though, was sidelined during the period 1789–1945, when the crucial elements that enabled mass democracy to find its feet were falling into place. Chief among these was the creation of the modern bureaucratic state, without which mass elective democracy could not come into being. It was not the other way around. Democracy needs rational administration, and modern systems permit this. Modern states also recognize popular sovereignty as their foundation, and this idea most easily grew up within nation states, because nation states have fixed borders that act to distil and concentrate 'national' identity, thus creating a common power that is not just technological or bureaucratic but socially collective. Mass democracy developed as a way to harness and direct this enormous, potentially unlimited power.

Jean Jacques Rousseau, the eighteenth century *philosophe*, was dead before this process had fully developed, but his ideas played a part in it, principally in helping to secure nationalism as part of the European political imagination. He developed a new idea of the nation, as the embodiment of a collective spirit he called the 'General Will', which transcended the sum of all individual interests. He believed that this Will would emerge on important occasions to express the deepest wishes of the nation. This idea acted as a comfort to nations embarking on their journey as states, but it has occasionally had a sinister side, when the personification of the nation has been taken too literally. Any such unanimous expression of common social objectives has never appeared anywhere, and Rousseau's belief in it reflects some kind of mystical yearning on his part for a more natural, less constrained society. He was wrong in believing that national will is comparable to the will of an idealized, virtuous individual – unchangeable, consistent and discoverable by simple introspection, and his conception of General Will is based on a simplistic and deeply flawed theoretical parallel between the nation and a human being. If forced parallels have to be made, national will is actually much more like that of a real person under real world pressures, i.e. conflicted, inconsistent, venal, easily swayed, selfish and prone to bouts of temporary enthusiasm.

A nation does not 'naturally' know its own will, no matter how ethnically pure or culturally conformist. Nations have a much simpler role: they create and guard borders. Once those borders are set, the collective will of the nation can be discovered, but only by the totally non-mystical process of day-to-day political consultation and collaboration. Attempts to short-circuit this tedious process by emotional appeals to higher, romantic conceptions of social nationhood risk unleashing undesirable forms of majoritarian empowerment.

States, borders and democracy are inseparable, because democracy has no strong internal force that sets the boundaries within which it can operate, i.e. be accepted as legitimate. Unlike military conquest it has no natural edges to its own hegemony, no defined outer limits to its reach. Lucky states have clear geography. Those denied this boon often struggle; islands are most favoured. Democracy is a net that can collect only the willing. Any self-defined group can opt into a democracy, but the rules for opting out are much less clear. Nation states thus make natural containers for democracy, but only when they already exist.

All too often democracy is imprisoned by historical circumstances, condemned to cope with unresolved issues that have been suppressed by conquest or have been artificially solved with too much high-handedness. This has been a curse all across the postcolonial world, where the collapse of undemocratic military empires left borders that were often democratically illogical.

Simplicity and practicality have condemned us to live with nation states for now, because democracy needs a defined container; it has no power without one. It requires certain technical definitions in order to work – borders, voting rights, and rules of inclusion and exclusion. The nation state is the most coherent and visible container yet invented, because the people are the nation. This is not true in other forms of political organization. Athens was a container and could tolerate and sustain democratic government under certain conditions, but the Delian League, its imperial offshoot, could not. Nationality within borders both creates and enforces democracy, but also ensures that it remains human. Nation states and democracy thus go together, not just because of rights, but also because of people.

Democracy makes the state the servant of the people. Not God or king or race, but the people as they are here and now. Modern states without democracy are terrifying, cruel, impersonal creations, too easily tempted to sustain themselves at the cost of those they rule. Put at the disposal of a Stalin or a Pol Pot they can become irrationally voracious. If we wish to live in states and to enjoy the advantages they bring, we have no option but to use democratic institutions to run them. If we do not, then there is little to stop a state becoming a self-serving entity like North Korea.

Self-government by consent, with an appropriate degree of public invigilation, is the only way to run a successful modern state, to compel it to take on the extra responsibilities and functions that come with welfare systems, public health, mass education and so forth. Defence and law enforcement can be sustained without close democratic supervision, because they involve the use of force, but the soft functions of modern government cannot. They need humanity as much as they need efficiency. Nor can economic growth which, in harness with political liberty, is the main boon of modern democracy. In the absence of these things, no state, regardless of what it calls itself, can be considered democratic.

Democracy, if it has ever meant anything, has always meant self-government. Details, such as who exactly can vote and how often, pale into insignificance before the importance of attaining self-government. Monarchs rule by hereditary right or by right of conquest; their subjects have no say in the matter. Using the benchmark of popular self-government is a much clearer way to assess democratic status than narrow constitutional details. Late-colonial India had representative institutions that mimicked some aspects of democracy, but the fundamental element of self-government was not present.

After the 1945–65 period of decolonization, self-government was (re)implemented all over the world in areas where it had often not been formalized beyond systems of custom and tradition. But the postcolonial world was vulnerable to many stresses and strains that had not accompanied the often slow emergence of democratic systems elsewhere. Democracy found it difficult to sustain itself wherever economic underdevelopment, recent conflict, personal ambition or continuing proxy wars prevailed. Some of India's near neighbours succumbed to these problems, as did many states in Asia, Africa and Latin America.

Persistent failures of democracy in the developing world and the continued existence of the Soviet bloc led some observers into deep pessimism about the long-term prospects for democracy. The economic chaos and under-achievement of the 1970s further clouded the outlook, and democracy's apparent inability to control inflation or suppress terrorism gave rise to serious doubts that it could survive, let alone win the Cold War somehow.

But the 1980s were to bring a dramatic reversal of fortunes, when the collapse of communism at the end of the decade reintroduced democracy to Eastern Europe. This took much of the tension out of global politics, which further aided the spread or revival of democracy. One significant and immediate benefit of the détente was the dismantling of apartheid in South Africa, where official policies of white supremacy, racial segregation and 'separate development' had made the country not only an egregious example of undemocratic minority rule, but also an international pariah. With the collapse of global communism, the regime's credibility as a bulwark against the Red threat evaporated. The subsequent establishment of majority rule in 1993 was the single greatest global advance for democracy since the Indian elections of 1951–52.

This so-called 'third wave' of democratization seemed about to carry all before it, as it toppled tyrants from the Philippines to Romania, and then unravelled the Soviet Union. But protests in Rangoon and Beijing failed to institute democracy, and the Arab world remained under the rule of monarchs, generals and dictators.

Prospects for democracy darkened again in the new millennium. The 'War on Terror' that followed the 9/11 attacks on the US was often an anti-democratic force, as American strategists sought 'strong' allies where they could be found, and the invasions of Iraq and Afghanistan both turned into bloody civil conflicts. Though the Arab Spring of 2011 may have discredited dictatorships across the centre of the Muslim political world, it has yet to install democracy as the only choice for the Arab peoples. So far, only Tunisia and Egypt have managed to write new constitutions and hold national elections, but in Egypt this process has been deeply flawed. Elsewhere the wave of popular discontent unintentionally reduced large parts of the former Ottoman Empire to political chaos. Lebanon had already gone through a drawn-out and destructive civil war from 1975–90 as it threw off its double imperial-colonial past. Now a number of regional states, including Libya, Iraq and Syria are undergoing a similarly traumatic process as they finally confront their own long suppressed social complexities. Democratization can be a two-edged sword, unleashing majority power in states where majority demographics did not determine their political complexion. Just as the British Empire played havoc with some aspects of India's demography, so the Ottoman Empire did likewise across much of its extent, from Bosnia to Basra.

The recent Islamic State (ISIS/ISIL) advance into Iraq is clearly related to the advent of democracy in states where it had no deep roots. Tribal societies, like Iraq, could get by when authoritarian rule, by either Ottomans or Baathists, meant that none of the tribes had direct access to power over each other. Democracy changed this.

It is worth stressing that 'religious' conflicts of the type recently seen in the Middle East are not about religious detail – theology – but about raw power – securing domination over others. The rise of the Islamic State reflects an attempt to create new politics by recourse to old religion. It is not a popular movement but an elite military affair, obsessed with violent dominion. But the weak political structures of Syria and Iraq have proved completely incapable of mounting effective resistance.

Politics only manages communities, whereas religion creates them. Armed militant religion can also destroy them. On a day-to-day basis, politics is a better way of doing civil business, because it sets boundaries on our ability to interfere in our neighbour's affairs. Religion, when given anything like temporal power, tends not recognize those same boundaries, and can then set individuals, and eventually whole communities, against each other. This is the tragic result of the extreme naivety about power that religious extremists exhibit, which generates their equally naïve faith in high moral justifications for violence. Many ancient faith communities spread across Syria and Iraq are now suffering under the burden of Sunni militancy that appears to have no concept of how endless their struggle to impose their will promises to be. Where next? Shi'a Iran with its 60 million heretics? When will these people ever live in peace with their neighbours? Do they want to?

All of this forces us to ask again whether democracy can flourish everywhere and anywhere. Only thinkers who can broadly be described as liberals have felt the need to talk up democracy's prospects, while the main players in the world who are not advocates of some kind of liberal democracy are either under the black flag of Islamism or the red banner of communism. The communists had their day, in that there were extended experiments through the twentieth century in running mass societies on the version of democracy that communists preferred, which was non-consultative. The Islamists are currently having their turn, but they show no more inclination to implement any version of democratic popular sovereignty.

The failure of communism may not haunt Islamists, but it should. Both projects believe in an all-powerful state and the enforcement of puritanical personal codes. The difference is that one is modernist and in thrall to science, while the other is archaist and bound by scripture. But both have a horror of diversity, and both have had regular recourse to extreme violence, which has not remedied the unpopularity that absolute principles always bring with them. And both degenerate swiftly into the rule of small cliques, determined to freeze the social activity of those they rule. One has already collapsed as a global project. The other will never manage to escape the ungoverned spaces of the modern world.

Liberals generally like to believe that democracy has the virtues and energy to hold the ring for an indefinite period, but they remain nervous, because liberalism must allow for dissent. In the liberal mindset, anti-democratic forces have ultimately to be defeated and disarmed by force of argument, which can sometimes seem insufficient in the face of fanaticism.

Immediately after the end of the Cold War, the cheerleader in chief was Francis Fukuyama, whose *The End of History and the Last Man* appeared in 1993. Optimistic, even triumphal, it is squarely based on nineteenth-century ideas from Hegel and Nietzsche, but it reads like a summation of the 'last' war, the cold one, against communism. It explains that liberal democracy works because it provides universal mutual 'recognition' for citizens.

Fukuyama was attempting to resurrect 'Universal History', meaning a grand, all-embracing account of where humanity is heading, based on a directional, Hegelian idea of progress, in this case with liberal democracy as a final destination, or 'end'. History as a series of 'events' had not ended, said Fukuyama, but history as an ideological struggle had now been decided, with liberal democracy the winner.

This thesis has since been attacked, defended, refined and restated till it is almost meaningless. By now we understand Fukuyama to have said that democracy is popular, and nothing else is as popular or as compatible with human aspirations. Meanwhile, the darker side of his message – the Nietzschean fear that human beings risk becoming vapid, hopeless creatures without the nobility of ideological struggle to invigorate and ennoble them – has become increasingly lost.

Where Fukuyama was mostly hopeful, his former teacher Samuel P. Huntington was decidedly pessimistic, as he explained in his *Clash of Civilizations* (1996), which was a thinly disguised lament for the decline of Western supremacy. This unjustly famous book takes on a range of global enemies, lumped crudely together by its author as anyone not American or not a democrat. Adopting a tone of high authority, Huntington manages to be both irritatingly vague and confusingly self-contradictory. He never properly defines the two terms in the book's title, remaining content merely to list what other people have meant by 'civilization'. He himself goes as far as to say that it refers to an 'overall way of life', and is 'culture writ large'.[6] But he also admits that 'cultures can change'.[7] So where are the hard edges that will 'clash'? He refuses to admit that cultures trade far more often than they clash. Clashes, however, are anticipated, for no better reason than he says they will. The 'African' and 'Sinic' (i.e. Chinese) cultures are currently very busy trading rather than clashing, and look set to continue to do so. How they could ever clash at such a distance is baffling. His confusion and imprecision even extends to an inability to count how many civilizations there are in the world. He settles for 'seven or eight',[8] but his map shows nine.[9]

Not content with confusion, Huntington also sallies into offensiveness, by finding a 'paradox' within democracy, namely that it is a Western institution, but non-Westerners use it to elect governments that are not pro-Western! How anyone ever took such a book seriously defies belief. It is a screed of fearfulness about Muslims and the Chinese, and further details of its multiple failings need not detain us here. Its one instructive element is its emphasis on the potentially contrary stances of religion and politics on a regional basis, though it takes no trouble to explain this systematically.

Religion does not necessarily challenge civilization, let alone confront it, though it can easily present a direct challenge to democracy, which is a rather different matter. Religion and democracy derive their authority from entirely different and incompatible sources; one from the celestial, the other from here below; one is rooted in permanence and eternity, the other in the ever-changing present. Religion also gives desperate people some hope of salvation, or eternal life, and such things are not in the gift of governments. In the minds of some, pleasing God will always seem a higher goal than pleasing man, and will always appear so to those prepared to accept certain premises about the existence of God, about our ability to know His will, and about who is allowed to supervise the enforcement of His will here on earth. Taking a view on these things is easier than understanding the justifications of democracy mounted by the likes of Fukuyama, with all their codices about market economics. Religious fanaticism also has a more personal, more practical aspect; it tells you what to do in a way that free market economics do not.

Yet it has always been, and will continue to be, easier to be specific about the will of the people than the will of God. The anti-democratic religious forces that still exist in the world today subsist on violence and have an agenda of resisting modernity and the culture of equal human value. The most prominent among these groups are currently Muslim, though this may not continue to be the case. If there is a problem with Islam in the modern world it is not primarily to do with violence, though certain interpretations of the faith concentrate on justifications for violent struggle. It lies in the way that even traditional interpretations of Islam concentrate on the international extent of the umma, and the universal scope of sharia law. These two aspects ensure that Islam can all too easily challenge the sovereignty of states and the validity of statute law – two main pillars of democracy.

Above all, the conception of Islam as a connected community diverts its most fanatical adherents from feeling social solidarity with anyone other than Muslims, and the special feelings of injustice that this can evoke in young men has had terrible effects. No one can be safe when jihadi logic dictates that any Muslim can visit divinely approved retribution on anyone anywhere as punishment for any offence committed against Muslims.

Jihadi groups, among whom the ISIS or Daulat-e-Islami (DeI) is currently the most successful, recognize no borders, administer summary justice and inflict collective punishments. All this is entirely contrary to democratic practice, and stems from the idea that all of the earth is God's, and that Muslims have divine authority to do whatever they wish to non-believers.

Radical Islamism thus does not co-exist comfortably with the modern global state system, and its adherents are heading for certain failure trying to set up a state without acknowledging how states actually work. This is why jihadis have failed to take lasting control of any substantial area, ever. Currently there are only people who want to *run* such states, and unless large numbers of people actually wish to live under such intensely strict Islamic government, such states are not likely to emerge. It is quite possible to live the life of a devout Muslim in any liberal democracy. Success will continue to elude radical Islamists unless they can all agree among themselves on what exactly their priorities are, who will be their leader (and how they will choose the one after that), how to split the loot and how they will deal with the billions of people who do not share their views.

Despite the turbulence that accompanies Islamist control of several underdeveloped parts of the globe – Somalia, northern Iraq, the Sinai desert, parts of Afghanistan – serious threats to the world will not come from some enormous theoretical division of the planet based on 'civilizational' disputes. Political–cultural problems will arise within states as much as between them; 'civilizations' are simply not centred enough, or even different enough, to create real tensions or to wage real war. To imagine, as Huntington seems to, that anyone who does not speak your language, or spend their weekends in the same way as you do, or does not share your exact vision of the afterlife, is somehow on the warpath is no kind of sustainable intellectual case. Ignorance can be bliss, but it cannot claim to be wisdom.

Indeed it is ignorance that may be a more serious threat to democracies than fanaticism. Another defender and questioner of democracy recently appeared in the shape of David Runciman, whose *The Confidence Trap* (2013) is a thoughtful and humane look at the defects of democracy in the light of another specific context – the global banking crisis of 2008.

Runciman believes that democracy 'is trapped by the nature of its own success'.[10] It tends to generate overconfidence in its ability to solve problems, because it is good at riding out moments of crisis. 'Democracies survive their mistakes. So the mistakes keep coming.'[11] He believes democracies currently face four existential threats: debt, terrorism, climate change and the Chinese (again). In this context the threat from China is not invasion, but as a competitor model. He worries because 'democracy has triumphed but it has not grown up',[12] meaning that it displays a frivolous concern with superficialities, which tends to exaggerate both good and bad times, and repeatedly fails to distinguish between trivial and serious issues. His criticisms constantly hit home, and his lack of bombast allows us to recognize ourselves and our collective failings. Like Rousseau, he sees society as a very human construction, and as long as we maintain some faith in humanity, his message would seem to be that we can probably get by.

Most elements, or certainly more elements, of the good life are to be found in communal living, where we all service each other's various needs in different ways, while enjoying a range of common cultural entertainments. Democracies are best at this, and the history of the world's cultures confirms this repeatedly.

The idea of democracy has survived, developed and continues to attract support because it plugs into a whole network of philosophical gold standards – rationality, equality, consistency and reciprocity. And it will probably continue to do so. Its self-consistency is its great strength, and at its best it has produced all the good things human beings have ever wanted, including the freedom to obey God in the way one wishes to. Where it has been less popular is when its sole objective has been the imposition of equality across too wide a spectrum.

But while it is true that democracy is popular (in all senses of the word), what looms in the future is not a 'clash' but an important choice, a potential divide in the road forward that confronts humanity. This choice is not between democracy and theocracy; democracies will always win that fight, because they have more manoeuvrability and a store of material rewards to dispense that will always ultimately buy off all but the most psychotic opponents. Nor will scripture ever be an adequate basis for running a state; it wasn't then and it isn't now. It is only suitable to the task of dictating certain kinds of social conformity. Nor is religiously authorized violence the way ahead to anywhere worth going. The world will not become a caliphate or any such unified religious parish, under caliph, Christ, or Krishna.

The great question that confronts us is: can we live together in large multi-ethnic political units or not? This is an unavoidable choice. Political units have been getting larger for centuries, and the future of the world now lies in the hands of a few very big states, all of which, with the possible exception of China, are internally diverse. We must therefore confront the issue of diversity, because the alternative is that we retreat from it. Such a retreat would imply a progressively greater subdivision of the human family – the creation of smaller, allegedly homogenous units, internally unified by some dominant characteristic of choice. How this could be achieved without enormous bloodshed and disruption – and for whose real benefit – is not clear. Large units are a guarantee of greater peace, as long as we can develop and live by suitable socio-political structures and public attitudes.

Trying to achieve anything like 'pure' nations would also jeopardize two of the freedoms for which the world has fought over the centuries – the freedom to travel, and the freedom to marry whom one wishes. On several levels, India is working out an acceptable local form of this new world, as long as the more supremacist members of Team Modi do not insist on turning India into a monoculture.

And the West may be about to catch up in its own way. The London Borough of Newham is the most diverse borough in the UK, and its

(Labour) leaders recently made a momentous decision to divert funds away from translation services for the benefit of ethnic minorities, and towards education in English.[13] The limits of multi-ethnicity in the West may be about to reveal themselves, and this may eventually stabilize the subdivision, and therefore the potential fractiousness, of multi-ethnic states.

Diversity can, and surely will, grow within a successful democratic state, not least because outsiders will want to live there. So, democracy can promote, but struggles to emerge from, diversity.

Where any society sits on the graph of diversity is a key factor in determining whether it can accommodate or develop stable democratic mutuality. Too much diversity makes democratic power-sharing seem too risky. Voices on the right in economically advanced countries tend to say 'no' to complex forms of cohabitation, and often insist that multiculturalism – in whatever form they choose to see (and dislike) it – has 'failed'. The implied premise is that human beings all have to be alike to live together in peace. But, very clearly, we *are* all alike. We are all human. All the external variation, to which right-wing eyes and minds are so sensitive, is irrelevant as long as the meaning of the variation is trivial, or descriptive of small differences. In a world where religion is a private matter of conscience, and where public education teaches tolerance, religious differences need not enter the contested areas of public space.

The choice ahead is not religious, or even ethnic. The decision before us all is whether in the future the world is going to consist of large organizations like the US, which were originally founded on a narrow, historically determined basis and have cultural characteristics that are deemed immutable; or of large states like India, which are inventions set around an existing range of diversities. The US has never fully accepted its own diversity; India has.

Much has been written by historians and political scientists about 'state formation', the conditions under which it occurs and the processes it involves. But the main and obvious difference between democracy as found in the US and India is that the US grew up in territory that looked unclaimed to Europeans brought up on Roman ideas of possessory dominion. North America was a large, politically disconnected landmass with no modern institutions prior to its existence as a unitary state. It had no defined political character of its own, and took what it now has from recent intruders. Densely populated India, however, had long experience of both local self-government and imperial rule that gave her people a set of comparatively advanced models of political management, all of which had developed strategies to cope with diversity. No new state, large or small, will now be built on the American model. The only possibilities might be in Antarctica or on the Moon. Multi-ethnic states are here to stay.

Anyone who insists on pure nationalities and homogenized states is flying in the face of history – there has never been a good match of nations, states and ethnicities, all terms which are in various degrees invented, arbitrary, and flexible. Must we live in thrall to these categories? Are we helpless before history? If so, why? Must it determine our future in a rigid way? If we think so, if we *agree* so, then we need to think through the implications of this stance. Or, if democracy means anything, can we not choose our future?

Every unified state that ever existed has also been diverse, if we take the trouble to detect and distinguish enough categories, and stop trying to assume, or insist, that everyone must have identical qualities to agree about important matters. Democratic societies should be easy and familiar with their own diversity, but there are limits; they cannot be too diverse. There is a comfort zone of diversity, which is not measurable, but is perceptible to those living within the society concerned. If the population is too diverse, cultural coherence – fraternity – will struggle to thrive. Diversity will not bring down democracy by itself; all societies contain many degrees of diversity, and it stimulates and leavens their collective communal life. But too much diversity can. In that case, either authoritarianism will re-emerge as one group takes charge, or smaller states will be formed.

But democracy, in its nature and by its very existence, diminishes differences between individuals *in areas where they conflict*, i.e. in the public sphere. In areas where they do not, in matters of conscience and culture, democracy permits, nourishes, validates, rewards and promotes diversity. In areas of the public sphere that are potentially contentious, law, debate and rationality contrive ways to render them as non-antagonistic as possible.

How will this project fare? Will it be supported by enough powerful players? Britain and the US both have public cultures of tolerance that are unlikely to fade away anytime soon. Of the BRICS countries, India, Brazil and South Africa are democracies, but China is not, and Putin's Russia currently has distinctly undemocratic traits. And what of the next wave, the MINT countries – Mexico, Indonesia, Nigeria and Turkey? All are currently democratic, but the latter three have a history of military rule. Nigeria has some of the ethnic and religious diversity found in Brazil and India, but is coping with them less well, and President Erdogan in Turkey seems to be leaning towards a homogenous, conservative Turkish identity in defiance of both the recent secularist tradition of the country and of its internal diversities.

With seven of these vital nine countries in the democratic camp, perhaps the world will feel like a safer place for democracy over the next 20 years. But can any state, large or small, ever be entirely safe from internal undemocratic forces that promise either to enhance the prosperity of the already powerful, or to deliver discipline and orderliness to protect their citizens from chaos unleashed by development? And can small democratic states with powerful neighbours ever be entirely free from external threats? Many of Russia's neighbours are keen to pursue independent destinies as democratic states, but Russia may not be sympathetic to these aspirations.

The future presents a paradox. We need large democratic political units to guarantee peace, but we also need small democratic units to ensure that self-government seems real.

Much work still needs to be done, but the future of democracy is safe if the Indian model can be appreciated for what it can teach. We certainly cannot expect to live comfortably in a world where fake clashes are seen to be real, where the only road to unity is mapped out in conflict, and where nations can only come of age by paying a sanctified price in blood.

2.

Working Parts

All democracies share certain features that can be thought of as functional parts of the democratic mechanism. Chief among these are politicians, political parties, the majority–minority concept, and rights. These components have to work more or less well, both individually and in concert, for any democracy to exhibit the characteristics of representation and responsiveness that a democratic system is supposed to possess.

These components all have their own histories and dynamics, and all are, to some extent, necessary evils, for they all bring with them a range of problems.

POLITICIANS

Enoch Powell, who pursued a maverick career in British Conservative politics through the 1950s and 60s, once said that all political careers end in failure. His certainly did. But in the Indian context, a career in politics is much more likely to end in enrichment. Politicians make decisions, and those decisions affect people who are often willing to pay a little along the way to secure valuable objectives. Public office also opens up opportunities to gain direct access to public money in various forms.

It is certainly hard for honest individuals to thrive amid dishonesty, and a great many commentators have drawn attention to the criminality and corruption of some within India's political classes, for whom the phrase 'conviction politician' has taken on a new and deeper meaning. Large numbers of local and national politicians have criminal records or outstanding criminal cases against them. Around 30 per cent of those who sat in the 2009 Lok Sabha did, a total that has now risen to 34 per cent – 184 members – after the 2014 election. This prompts the question whether this is a case of criminals entering politics, or of the demands of Indian politics driving people towards criminality.

Regardless of how or why such people get into politics, the more important question is: how to get them out? This is not a simple matter in a free society. One strategy is shaming them. Since 2003, candidates have had to submit a comprehensive affidavit listing, inter alia, all criminal cases pending against them. This might seem to be a step forward, but as an anti-criminal measure it heavily relies on two assumptions.

The first is that a stack of outstanding cases against an individual is some measure of their character. It may be, but it is also quite common for politicians in India to be accused of all sorts of things by opponents for tactical reasons. This is all too easy to organize when local officials and policemen are not impartial, which is not unknown. Hence accusations alone have never been taken as a bar to candidacy. If they were, it would be all too simple to knock a rival out of the running. Furthermore, a long string of pending cases can easily accumulate as a side effect of India's tardy justice system, and need not be, per se, an indication of a criminal spree. Kameshwar Baitha from Jharkhand was elected to the Lok Sabha in 2009 despite 17 charges of murder against him, a legacy of his years as a Maoist insurgent.[14]

The second assumption is that the public will express a distaste for those with criminal connections, and will not elect them. This, unfortunately, is not true. The aura of toughness that accompanies a criminal reputation can actually enhance a candidate's appeal, as someone who can fight effectively to gets things done for their supporters. Figures bear this out. In the general elections of 2004 and 2009, candidates with criminal records had a 22 per cent success rate

– around three times of those without.[15] Matters do, however, seem to be improving in this area. Only 13.9 per cent of candidates with criminal records were elected in 2014, down from 14.2 per cent in 2009, and this figure was around half of that for 2004.[16] Nevertheless, the number of candidates with criminal cases pending against them went up from 1,110 in 2009 to 1,398 in 2014, nearly three times the level in 2004. People with shady backgrounds are still strongly attracted to politics, but the Indian public may now be just a little less willing to elect them.

This clearly is a complicated phenomenon, and may take a long time to solidify into fixed political norms. Political parties are reckoned, at a guess, to have spent over ₹300 billion during the 2014 campaign;[17] where did that colossal sum come from? With each candidate officially allowed to spend only ₹70 lakh, things become even murkier; where did it all go? Money is a perennially important factor in elections, and criminal connections can provide it. Or consume it.

The decriminalization of politics in India needs to be approached simultaneously from several angles, including reducing corruption and misuse of public office. But India's voters could make a strong start if they stopped supporting criminal candidates. If a candidate's 'winnability' was seen to be directly affected by criminal taint, which local electors would be in a good position to judge, then parties would stop selecting them. This is somewhat analogous to the ruling recently handed down by the Supreme Court, that though it is unconstitutional to disqualify someone with a criminal record from ministerial office, the onus is on the prime minister not to appoint unsuitable people.[18] It is not a question of legality, but of prudence, or constitutional morality. Certainly, matters will not improve at either the bottom or the top of the ladder if everyone simply looks the other way.

Let us be realistic. Politicians in India are usually not so much men and women of principle as representatives of communities and groups. This means that party loyalty is often weak, whereas loyalty to community is strong. Switching party affiliation therefore is not necessarily a matter of inconsistency or cause for shame, it can be a matter of doing the best for one's followers. It is perfectly acceptable, even obligatory, for a politician to change political horses if their current party is no longer offering the best prospects for the local people. The direction of travel before the 2014 election was mainly from the Congress to the BJP, but there were other movements. In Bihar, Ramkripal Yadav crossed from the Rashtriya Janata Dal (RJD) to the BJP, and Udit Raj, a Dalit leader from UP, also joined the BJP after years of opposing them.[19] Some went the other way: Santosh Kumar quit the BJP and joined the Janata Dal (United), winning from Purnia in Bihar.[20] Multiple switching is not unknown; Inder Singh Namdhari from Jharkhand has been a member of four different parties.[21]

How does this happen? Such people are not discredited because it is understood that although they may be promoting their own interests, they can be equally seen as promoting the welfare of others. As long as that equation stays in balance, they can be admired, respected and supported. Of course, once cast adrift from principle in this way, it is all too easy for this kind of advocacy to end up flirting with criminality, if clashes on the ground are involved, and pressure is brought to bear by the security units of rival organizations. Throw in a little biased law enforcement and the whole brew becomes a cynical and potentially violent struggle over the spoils of the state for everyone concerned. With strong obligations on local leaders to deliver benefits to their supporters, it is easy to see how the distinctive flavour of Indian politics, with its elastic alliances and unstable parties, can emerge from a few basic grass-roots pressures.

Some perspective is appropriate here. Politics is about power, and people are drawn towards politics either to gain power or to protect what power they already have. Therefore all sorts of people, in all countries and all systems, are drawn into the struggles that politics represents and perpetuates. Curbing the tendency of devolved systems to accommodate local empires is no easier than curbing the tendency of central governments to become over-mighty in strongly centralized systems. If we make government strong we are effectively making politicians strong, and this is a danger that can only be consistently contained by a two-ended process requiring both integrity from politicians and sustained public scrutiny.

Stricter accountability may just be more feasible in an age of internet connectivity, though people did have similarly optimistic expectations about the growth of national media and the introduction of telephones. But politicians can now certainly expect to be more closely supervised by more people than ever before. Popular movements against politicians have appeared in various forms all over the world, and in countries where perceptions of corruption are widespread, like Spain or Italy, such movements can gain considerable popular traction. Veteran Italian satirist Beppe Grillo decided in 2010 to form his own political party, the Five Star Movement, to fight corruption and promote direct democracy. At the general election of 2013 it became the largest single party in the Italian Parliament with a quarter of the seats. The advent of the Aam Aadmi Party (AAP) in India is a parallel development, though it is a street-level movement rather than an internet phenomenon like Grillo's campaign. It also has yet to match his electoral success, though it is three years younger.

A more typically Indian reflection of political exasperation was the campaign headed by Anna Hazare, who looked and sounded more Gandhian than mainstream politicians would ever care to. His main demand, the Lokpal, has now been conceded, and how effective this will be in regulating India's politicians out of their worst habits may shortly be revealed. Narendra Modi spoke out strongly against corruption on the stump, which may have been one factor in his victory, and he achieved the supreme office less apparently beholden to powerful interests than almost any politician in India for three generations. However, corporate interests helped to bankroll his expensive campaign, and a degree of scepticism remains as to how far will he be able to clean up the system, even if he makes life difficult for corrupt individuals.

Politicians want to get things done, or sometimes undone, for a variety of personal and abstract reasons. They can be ambitious for themselves, for the ideals they espouse, or for the people they represent. Successful politicians conflate these motivations with such skill that sometimes they themselves cannot distinguish them. It is therefore not safe to generalize about politicians as a subset of humanity, but it is an unpromising sign if the voting public considers their politicians, as a class, to be cynical and self-interested.

So, can anything be said about India's politicians as a class? It is both difficult and unwise to generalize about their character – there are rogues, idealists and saints to be found. But two things can be discerned about their general behaviour.

The first is the distance they habitually maintain from policymaking. As English politicians of another era would have put it, Indian politics is primarily about 'men not measures'. And such measures as there are, are called for in the name of 'justice', though they are often closely related to electoral arithmetic. Attitudes to national policy are very similar across the political spectrum, and they reflect fairly accurately what is deemed possible. Policy formation is dictated by circumstances, and particular measures thus attract support or opposition not in relation to any fundamental issue of principle, but as dictated by the in-out duality of executive office. Thus incoming governments in India have almost never reversed the decisions of their predecessors, despite having fought them tooth and nail from the opposition benches.

Some of this easiness with principle is connected to the inconsistent vertical separation between provincial and national politics in India. In the UK and US, a distinct thermocline divides the two political habitats; success at local level may lead to a national role, but the two systems are distinct, in terms of both personnel and powers. This is less true in India. Winning state power can promote individuals to national status, but only if policy does not stand too firmly in the way.

Another strand of distinctive behaviour concerns the constant search among the political class for ways of escaping strict accountability. This extends to matters of policy, with manifestos habitually kept short and vague, and to the area of party funding, where full transparency might prove embarrassing. When the Right to Information Act (2005) was debated, there was broad agreement among the parties that their own affairs should be exempted from the legislation.

The main objective is always to preserve executive flexibility. One exception to this is in the matter of seat-sharing agreements before elections, which by their nature must be made public. But once the votes are counted, politicians assess the verdict and can then cobble together an executive programme. This effectively breaks the link between promises and delivery, which constitutes the voters' greatest power over their representatives. India suffered from this uncoupling through the 1990s, trapped in a cycle of indecisiveness. Fewer parties or decisive verdicts are the ways out; India took the latter route in 2014.

From around the mid-1960s, when party proliferation really took off, politicians have run politics in India as a closed game, fluid, unaccountable and, above all, lucrative. The high number of parties has tended to blunt the Indian public's ability to break up the cartel character of the proceedings, by diminishing the power of collective voting. The Modi era may usher in a reduction in the profusion of parties, which might reverse this circular process. But that will only happen if he manages to deliver prosperity and stability, and maintains a strong national character to political debate. If he stumbles, he may have to revert in due course to the same tactics of coalition-making and horse-trading that have so richly fertilized the soil in which India's political parties have multiplied.

Politics is an attractive profession in India – the declared assets of most MPs show unmistakeable growth.[22] One beneficial aspect of this is that, even as the options in policymaking have remained fairly stable, the pool of leadership has widened enormously since independence. The lawyers and landowners of the original Congress high command have been joined on the *pandals* of the nation by characters from all sections and levels of Indian society, including the least privileged. The poster girl of this expanded inclusion has been Kumari Mayawati, whose elevated status as a provincial chief minister and party leader has smashed a number of barriers erected against both Dalits and women. She is only one of a whole generation of lower status politicians who have flourished, particularly across north India. These include Jagjivan Ram, who became a senior Congressman and eventually leader of his own party, and his daughter, Meira Kumar, who was Speaker of Parliament from 2009 to 2014. The leader of the Congress in the sixteenth Lok Sabha is a Dalit, Mallikarjun Kharge, and a host of other well known national figures have now emerged from lower strata, including chief ministers such as Nitish Kumar, Lalu Prasad Yadav and Jitan Ram Manjhi.

Despite this undoubted social broadening of access to political power, there are concerns that on the national stage the current political elite is entrenching itself far too comfortably. Patrick French observed in 2011 that all members of the fifteenth Lok Sabha under the age of 30 came from established political families.[23] About half of all MPs did *not* have family connections in politics, but the fear here is for the future. The list of close family relationships in Indian politics is now very long. In July 2013, *India Today* calculated that the country was essentially in the hands of 24 'clans';[24] this compares closely to the oft-levelled charge against Pakistan that it is dominated by two dozen or so families.

This familial status boost is not confined to the males of the line; there is a strong and visible presence of women in national politics all across South Asia, though they tend to be wives, widows and daughters rather than truly independent figures. Chief ministers such as Mayawati in UP or Mamata Banerjee in West Bengal are exceptions, as is Jayalalitha in Tamil Nadu, though she acquired the original basis of her fame as a film star rather than as a politician.

This again demonstrates that although there are certain privileged roads into public affairs, Indian politics is very open to anyone with a recognizable profile. Famously, two film stars from the south created their own parties and became highly influential in provincial and national politics. M.G. Ramachandran, or MGR, left the Dravida Munnetra Kazhagam (DMK) to form his own All-India Anna Dravida Munnetra Kazhagam (AIADMK) in 1972, then ruled Tamil Nadu for a decade after 1977. N.T. Rama Rao, or NTR, founded the Telugu Desam Party (TDP) in 1982, and then went on to serve three terms as chief minister of Andhra Pradesh between 1983 and 1999.

All this tends to emphasize that within India's political world, status and renown are of equal if not greater importance than principle or ideology. Indian politics remains a highly practical concern for almost everyone involved at a high level. The principal matter at issue has generally been an administrative detail – who administers.

All across the globe, the political classes are now a little more open and flexible than they were 50 years ago. This means that people from less wealthy backgrounds are involved, and this in turn, for better or worse, has brought into being the formal profession of 'politician'. This development is not always welcomed; it seems to run counter to the idea of public service. But the alternative is either that we retain a hereditary class of rulers, or that only rich people can afford to enter politics. India runs a slight danger that either or both of these things may be happening.

It is difficult to engage seriously in politics while doing other work, so we now expect politicians to specialize. We accept this, yet ironically, we also feel uncomfortable if they make an effort to train for the profession, because we are suspicious if politicians have never done anything else. Some real experience of the lives of ordinary people – an apprenticeship in humility perhaps – is often thought to be necessary to deliver rounded politicians. Otherwise we risk being ruled by a privileged class of isolated, over-theoretical, or even arrogant technocrats. This is a serious criticism of the current political caste in Britain and the US – that they move from studying politics at university to become 'special advisers' to senior figures, then, once safely under the wing of a powerful patron, they get themselves adopted for safe seats in the party of their choice. Indians might ask themselves if they would prefer this arrangement to the current conveyor belt of family members arriving in government.

In India, the generation that led the independence movement was an unusually saintly and ascetic group. Why exactly this was so is not easily explained. One reason may have been that the attractions of official political life under the Raj were not financial. Official positions therefore appealed primarily to those with a private income and a measure of comfort with colonial government. Such people were generally already in positions of high status and did not need more wealth, but quite fancied a knighthood. Official Raj politics was an amateur sport, not too heavily loaded with expectations of political change, and thus, unsurprisingly, quite like contemporary politics in Victorian and Edwardian Britain. In other words, the idealists within Indian society were likely to remain outside government, not in it.

Opposing the British regime was going to be an unrewarding life-choice, and the men and women who took it on therefore did so with their eyes open. If they were independently wealthy, like the Nehrus, they were able to live through the austerity in a little style. If they were professional people, and most of the Congress leaders had independent incomes as landowners, lawyers or journalists, they could sustain their living as it was. The moral is perhaps, that when politics is not financially rewarding, a different set of people roll up to join it.

Certainly the generation of Tilak, Gokhale, and Lala Lajpat Rai were more idealistic than most of its successors, but that generation managed to mix its idealism with social activism and an earthy sense of pragmatism. The subsequent perceived fall in the quality of India's leaders is something of an illusion. It is perhaps worth pointing out that the original founding fathers of many countries, including the US, Ghana, Tanzania and post-apartheid South Africa, also included remarkable thinkers and leaders, who were followed by lesser characters who seemed in contrast to be small-minded or corrupt. Great causes sometimes do bring out the best in people. The question might be, then, whether the rest of us have the courage to go through bad times in order to get a generation of worthy leaders.

Material rewards aside, politicians have an unenviable job. Apart from making decisions, sitting in meetings or running organizations, they are also engaged in a continuous programme of presentation. They first have to convince people inside their party of their worth. If they succeed in this and manage to attain elected office, they can then spend public money to convince people outside their party of their worth too. Indians have not been easy prey in this game, though. As an electorate, Indians are very hard on their politicians, and tend to throw them out of office very readily. This may be fickleness, or impatience, or it may be that Indians are canny consumers of political services and expect their politicians to pay a price if they over-promise and under-deliver. Anti-incumbency is frequently cited as a contributing factor in electoral verdicts, particularly at state level. Between 1989 and 2007 around 70 per cent of governments in 'sizeable' states were thrown out.[25] It can also be very apparent at national level, where six of the last eight general elections have brought defeat for the incumbent regime.

How to get better politicians must always be the question. This is not easy because public office brings such manifest rewards, and there will always be a long queue for it, containing a range of individuals attracted by high personal status, the possibility of getting things done or the very real influence that patronage over appointments and control over public procurement can give. Politics makes individuals rich, famous and powerful, and in a rather more satisfactory way than a career in popular entertainment or sport can do. Successful political careers last longer, go further and frequently pay more.

It is not possible to take the power out of politics – what use is a political system that exerts no power over its people? Politicians must be given authority, and the question then is how to get them not to abuse it. One approach is to try to dull the edge of greed, by ensuring that politicians are well-paid, though this is never a very popular strategy with taxpayers.

But it is not a practical option to take money entirely out of politics, because so much of the executive role of government is effected through expenditure. Instead money should be tagged, followed and counted regularly and well. This applies to individuals, who must not put their hands in the till, but it also applies to party funding. This is a separate and complicated issue, and an area in which individuals can collect a great deal of money without pangs of conscience about personal gain, while nevertheless engaging in dubious practices – usually trading political favours for contributions. The potential for 'sleaze' is enormous in any area of government spending, and the best countermeasure is the enforcement of proper transparency concerning where party money comes from, and what it can and cannot buy.

Some parties, though, will always end up richer than others. Incumbency attracts attention, and pro-business parties are more likely to attract rich sponsors than those representing workers or peasants. Central funding and a range of caps on contributions and spending can help to even the scores, but all democracies have been dogged by the details of such regulation for years. India, where so much business is done off the books, is doomed to struggle with this problem even more so.

So, we should pay our leaders well, but not too well, and we should respect them, but not too much. And if we are to carry on with our daily lives, we must also trust them, but not too much. Electors in the West complain about the quality of their politicians, but they have become marooned between deference and cynicism, and so can think of little to do about it. Such passive-aggressive political behaviour is not to be copied by people who want their political system to work better. Trust and transparency go together, but transparency can never wholly take the place of trust. Public culture, eventually, has to police itself.

We need some base scales against which to judge our leaders and representatives, such as ways to distinguish between pragmatism and opportunism. Pragmatism relates to fixed aims, and how to achieve them. It involves assessing all the relevant circumstances and deciding how to get the best outcome. Opportunism has no fixed goals and is simply the pursuit of advantage in the broadest sense. In politics, India needs more of the former and less of the latter.

To gain our trust, politicians must display an understanding of what was formerly called responsibility, but is now known as accountability. The classic eighteenth century understanding of responsibility was to be rewarded for doing your task well and punished (by dismissal) for doing it badly. Modern egalitarianism has kept the second element – censure and removal, but has largely rejected the idea of reward. We now like to think that the exercise of power – the essential freedom that it represents – should be enough for our leaders.

Power is now viewed as its own perquisite, and the idea of glory has not survived the arrival of mass democracy and the intrusive

24-hour news cycle. In modern times we like our leaders to be principled and modest in lifestyle. The most iconic among them are identified with some greater cause, usually connected with national aspirations – like Nehru or General de Gaulle – or sometimes with greater social inclusion – like Dr. Ambedkar or Martin Luther King. There has been a discernible transition in the public's assessment of their leaders' behaviour, with less admiration of personal qualities and more concern for representative accuracy. We now like our leaders to do our bidding and to fulfil our personal list of requirements in a much more ledger-book manner than older, grander leaders did. In this sense, Clement Attlee did much more for his people in peace time than Winston Churchill ever did while at war. Most politicians would probably prefer to emulate Churchill's grand, classless national achievements than Attlee's more prosaic, social reforms, but modern electorates actually prefer Attlee types to Churchills.

Early signs show that Narendra Modi is attempting to straddle both roles, but the demands of the modern world, and the condition of contemporary India, almost inevitably mean that his great work will not be to rescue his country from mortal danger, but to readjust its social and economic composition. Were he to succeed in this, he will surely become as revered a figure for the Indian right as Attlee is for the British left.

One last and somewhat sobering thought: In a democracy we are likely to get the politicians we deserve, because we choose them, and encourage or revile them as we please. Who else is there to blame?

POLITICAL PARTIES

Forming large groups enhances the power that individuals can exercise. Here lies the genesis of armies and mobs – and political parties, the means by which power is contested in mass democracies.

Parties are designed to act as a stabilizing influence within political systems. This has been true ever since the acceptance, in nineteenth century England, of the concept of 'His Majesty's Opposition', the idea that an anti-government grouping could also be 'loyal'. This was a breakthrough in two respects. It allowed critics of the government to be freed from accusations of opportunism, or even treason; from then on, political opponents had to be regarded as something better than scoundrels. Those not in government could also then collaborate, and political life could be balanced, with collective groups both in and out of power.

Parties are now indispensable to the running of democracy. They play a vital part in condensing social interest groups into coherent bodies that can engage in orderly debates and contests. They also act as nursery leagues for potential national leaders, training them in political manners and testing them in the public arena. In a democracy, a national leader without a strong standing in a major political party is unthinkable.

But parties have their drawbacks, be they large, small, few or many, broad or narrow. There can be too many parties for orderly governance, or too few for the representation of a full spectrum of opinions and interests. If parties are too sectional or cynical, the channelling of public interest and the emergence of leaders can be disrupted; if they are insufficiently democratic within themselves, talents are overlooked and individual voices are lost. And then there is the vital question; who funds parties, and what influence do they acquire in return?

India has encountered all these problems, and has coped with them in a variety of distinctive ways.

The first and most obvious is that India supports very few big parties but an enormous number of small ones, a remarkable thing in a country that uses the 'first-past-the-post' voting system, which tends to reward big parties at the expense of the smaller.

One explanation for the high party count is that small parties engage better with the diversity of India by appealing to particular sections of the electorate in specific regions. This is broadly true, but it is hardly sufficient to explain the persistent multiplication of parties. A more telling insight is that big parties have proportionately small leadership cliques, which dam up the channels of personal advancement, meaning that political aspirants have a strong incentive to strike out on their own. With lots of regional and national offices to fill in India, individuals can put themselves in line for them by forming their own parties, often on the slimmest of ideological grounds.

Yet a third explanation is that parties based on caste find it hard to broaden their bases and tend to fragment if they try. The original Janata Dal of the 1980s split on both ideological and regional lines. More recently, the Bahujan Samaj Party (BSP) and the SP have made attempts to expand outside their local strongholds, but without great success.

A fourth factor is in play too. Small parties formed around an individual often stay small by choice because the surest way for the leader to lose control is to expand the party's membership, thus recruiting and empowering potential rivals. The traditional antidote to the dangers of expansion is family loyalty. This keeps the issue of party leadership within narrow bounds, while the distinction between patrons and clients remains clear and is less likely to cause friction. But if India's party system can only stabilize at the level of family interests, then the future of multiparty democracy in any real sense is not bright. National parties need to have programmes and coherent outlooks, both for election campaigns and for government; coalitions of small family firms will be unlikely to provide this. There is also the risk that sections of the electorate will identify only with individual ministers, and for ministers to respond to this in inappropriate and damaging ways.

Personal ambition is a well-attested force in India's party system. The list of splits is very long, and of the national parties the BJP has been less prone to fragmentation than the Congress, which has a history of personal factionalism that has created a plethora of parties with the word 'Congress' in their names. The BJP is not, however, immune. Kalyan Singh, Uma Bharti, and Keshubhai Patel have all formed breakaways, though none proved long-lived.

Why has the Congress proved less able to reabsorb its splinters, whereas the BJP has managed to remain an attractive home for repentant members? It is partly because of the contrasting cultures of the two parties, with the Congress's more rigid tradition of dynastic succession as opposed to the BJP's more flexible internal dynamic, which is neither democratic nor dynastic, which means that room can usually be found for wayward saffron stars. There is also a more ideological aspect. A Congress split makes a certain sense within Indian national politics, as the party has always been an aggregation of sectional and regional interests. Within the BJP, however, which is committed to an organic national view of Indian society, a split is essentially contradictory, and the smaller units will always lose out to the national party if they try espousing the same line. In other words, ideological discipline and personal opportunities tend to work towards unity within the BJP, whereas the same factors tend to invite splits within the Congress.

The intense individualism that generates party instability in India has a deep historical irony about it. British colonial officials insisted on seeing India as a land of massive collective blocks, particularly religious blocks, but they were only seeing the most surface level of the fabric around them. Much self-confident prose was written about how India was a land frozen in an early phase of social organization, in which personal perceptions and individual thinking were deficient. Europeans were supposed to have transcended this group mentality, and to have moved on to the creation of Protestantism, capitalism, personal diaries, ham sandwiches and much else. The whole institution of 'oriental despotism' was read as a deficiency in the host society, not as a quality of individual rulers and their ambition to dominate.

Looking back from modern conditions, with the elements of colonialism and despotism removed, we might notice something else about India as a society. It is quite clear that Indians are as insistently ambitious and individualistic as any people on earth, and this is one reason why democracy has taken root amongst them. Is the unsplittable BJP, then, the last bastion of collectivism in India? Hardly. The irony redoubles if we consider that a great many of the BJP's supporters are the individualist entrepreneurs that have driven India's recent rapid growth.

However, political bodies in India are not fluid or fragile because Indians are peculiarly ambitious; rather, the basic nature of India's political system is favourable to the growth and sustenance of a large number of parties. In some ways this is a side effect of diversity, but there is a conceptual point too, which is that India still does not have a unified national economy or a truly homogenous political culture. Under such conditions, parties cannot latch onto the national interest or psyche very easily. Only the Congress was able to do this for a few years after independence, and that too mostly by happenstance. The unity of the freedom struggle spilled over into more peaceful times largely intact, but soon fell apart under the more normal conditions of social competition and international economic pressures.

Collective interests did not then disappear; they became less national and more sectional. This heralded another profound change – the rise of regional and caste parties. But the strand of individualism lived on to mark India's politics very strongly. In India the individual element goes right to the heart of the party unit and has helped to multiply them for two major reasons.

One concerns the remunerative possibilities of elected office, which generates a self-sustaining drive; it is worth trying very hard to get into government because once in, there are opportunities to ensure one stays in, and everybody knows it. This feeds the intensity of the competition between individual politicians, so that in the event of disputes, new parties are more likely to be formed than old ones rebuilt.

Then there is the usefulness of personal eminence; individuals who are already famous can find it easier and more rewarding to form a party than to join one. Fame itself is an enormous electoral asset. Famous people form parties; successful parties generate fame. Indian politics has always been an argument about a fairly limited range of options and outcomes, and whenever politics is relatively value-neutral, personal recognition is a huge advantage.

But fame is not always enough, and 2014 saw a number of high profile sports stars, actors and singers trying their hand at politics, only to fail. Cricketer Mohammad Kaif stood for the Congress and lost, footballer Bhaichung Bhutia was defeated on a Trinamool

Congress (TMC) ticket, while actors Mahesh Manjrekar and Raj Babbar both flopped, for the Maharashtra Navnirman Sena (MNS) and the Congress respectively. Celebrity winners included screen stars Vinod Khanna, Manoj Tiwari and singer Babul Supriyo for the BJP, who were perhaps shrewder in their choices and were drawn along by the wider successes of Banerjee of Modi. The lesson for ambitious celebrities is that in politics you have to pick a party or a seat every bit as carefully as you make any other move within your career; even enormous personal popularity may not be enough to allow you to swim against a national or local political tide.

The existence of a reasonable number of parties is a sign of political health in a society; to posit the opposite, an absence of parties would mean politics could not function on a collective basis. But the existence of too many parties ensures that none of them can deliver anything to anybody. India has a rather large number at the moment. Before the 2014 poll, the Election Commission listed six national parties (represented in four or more states), 54 state parties and nearly 1,600 unregistered parties. There are no signs that these numbers are set to fall anytime soon. This growing profusion has its own fascinating history.

Once the era of minority government began in 1989, national coalitions had to recruit smaller parties. This meant that even smaller local outfits, if successful, were able to reap a high degree of return from inclusion at the central level. It also helped if that party was non-ideological, i.e. compatible with any potential national patron, and this encouraged the formation of local, pragmatic parties that were essentially plying for hire. And even without inclusion in central government, regional parties also had much to play for locally because, after the liberalization of 1991, state governments were directly bidding for international investment.

The rise of provincial power diffused influence across the system and tended to encourage political fragmentation. This trend has now been checked, at least for the moment, by the Modi wave, which has re-established a genuine national element within Indian politics, though the dual level of electoral representation will continue to allow regional parties to exercise a powerful hold on the loyalties of individuals. It is still the states that deliver most governance to ordinary Indians on a daily basis, and power will still be contested at that level under all the conditions that have tended to multiply political entities. Hopes that greater stability might emerge if the National Democratic Alliance (NDA) and the United Progressive Alliance (UPA) could develop into more coherent, more permanent party machines have currently evaporated. The need for the NDA has disappeared with the BJP holding a majority by itself, and the UPA, as it was, cannot be reconstituted without a strong Congress, which seems an unlikely development in either short or medium terms.

Further consolidation is also unlikely because political parties in India, especially those with national ambitions, have always been subject to two critical limitations – of policy and of organization.

Indian party politics has not greatly diversified at the level of distinct policy; the restrictions on government are established, and the general thrust of state policy – development – has not varied much in 60 years, apart from a general movement, matched all over the world, from state regulation towards liberalization. This draws out an interesting contrast. Western countries tend to live with fairly stable political alliances, with a slow oscillation of government outlook and a degree of volatility within parties. India, by contrast, has instability in party alignments and internal allegiances, but has had a remarkably consistent general political tenor to national government. One great exception is the Mandal Commission's recommendations on reservations which, at the time of their delivery in 1980, represented a radical breach with the past. Though controversial when partially implemented over a decade later, they have been retained by all subsequent governments of all compositions, which means that every large political party in India has tacitly accepted them.

What has made a distinct difference in India is not policy, but the matter of organization. Originally, there was only one party with any real national structure in place – the Congress – which had built up a national framework over decades. This structure gradually fell apart through the 1950s and 1960s as local and factional disputes arose.

Indira Gandhi lost control of much of this faltering machine when she spilt from the old guard in 1969, and she then adopted direct, simple appeals to the public as a substitute. Populism circumvents the need to build an organization or to have a coherent policy programme; it promotes one leader as *the* solution. Mrs Gandhi cleverly used slogans and emotive issues to create a personal following from thin air. The drawbacks of such an approach soon became apparent, and she had to take recourse to using the state's apparatus as her personal secretariat and whips' office.

The coalition that toppled her in 1977 used a similarly informal approach, by making her the central electoral issue – a trick she had used to good effect in better times. But the successful Janata alliance that replaced her had no national independent structure of its own, and had little to hold it together as a 'party'.

There have been two other parties with national organizing capabilities. One was the Communist party, which had policy and structure, but insufficient appeal. Such as it had, it squandered in arcane debates and repeated splits. The other was the Bharatiya Jana Sangh, ancestor of the BJP, which was built parallel to the national structure of the Rashtriya Swayamsevak Sangh (RSS), with its various sub-groups, including a very extensive and disciplined women's section. But again, the limits of the Jana Sangh's core appeal denied it the national dominance enjoyed by the early Congress. It found it impossible to break through nationally to a similar level of support – i.e. well above the mid-20 per cent mark – until it had undergone a number of constructive adjustments, or modernizations. The first was the adoption of a new name, the Bharatiya Janata Party, in 1980. Next was the mellowing experience of coalition politics between 1996–2004, during which it dropped the most exclusivist features of its programme. Finally it found a leader of sufficient energy, clarity of purpose and proven executive ability to appeal to a broader constituency, especially the aspiring younger voters who had not been enthused by the party's elderly leadership. Narendra Modi also came with what political analysts call 'narrative' – he actually embodied the values he claimed to espouse. In doing all this, the

BJP eventually made national politics a bipolar affair, in which clear choices were on offer.

Below the national level there has been, and still is, a great deal of room for fragmentation, which has tended to produce a party for every cause. But when there is a party for every grievance, nothing is likely to change. The politics of grievance is only effective when grievances are widely felt. The more specific they are, the less likely the parties voicing them are to deliver results, and the less inclined people are to support any of those parties.

Sometimes the whole party system can become the grievance, and this is exactly what happened in India with the rise of AAP, which in early 2014 held power for a brief 49 days in Delhi. At first sight AAP did look very much like a roots-up party, reflecting real concerns of ordinary people, and it may yet have, if not a bright, then at least a viable future. Were it to succeed in siphoning off any significant degree of support from the major parties, it too might end up as part of a future national coalition.

But this will not be an easy trick to pull off. Protest parties like the AAP thrive on the apparent tainted nature of their rivals, but they tend not to last. Such a party often struggles to maintain its initial purity of principle once it becomes engaged with events, real responsibility and the messy business of political implementation. Anti-corruption campaigns can gradually lose support among electors, as the novel, rather austere promise of probity in government begins to seem less attractive, while the familiar promises of jobs, tax breaks, handouts and subsidies come to seem more enticing and perhaps worth risking a little graft behind closed doors to get. Parties of high principle can also prove vulnerable to internal factional disputes, and this is exactly what befell the AAP shortly after the 2014 poll, with complaints from within about cliques, personality cults and bullying.

If 'third way' parties ever come to power, they find it just as difficult as their predecessors to wrestle with the delivery of political objectives, because they have to confront exactly the same structural obstacles, especially the resistance of entrenched vested interests. Protest is easier than government, and the magic wand of principle is not always enough to deliver real change to ordinary voters. If this does not happen, the old parties begin to look better as the new begin to look ineffective. The central fallacy here is that established parties are simply unwilling to act, from lethargy or disinterest, and that the only thing required is better intentions.

Disillusionment is a constant threat within all democracies. Long experience of parties tends to foster scepticism among voters, even contempt. Western voters are prone to express dissatisfaction with political parties – they are all the same, they don't deliver, their leaders are all selfish careerists, and so forth. The paradox here is that if, despite all the wrangling and name-calling, a party system does manage to deliver long-term stability and prosperity, the difference between parties diminishes, outcomes under governments of different hues are less distinct, and politics becomes more about personalities, personal appeals and careerism. Successful national management through party politics therefore undermines the necessity for the existence of parties. The pettier the squabbles, the more the party system degrades itself.

But in the longer historical perspective, bland politics is actually much better for societies than polarization. In times of deeply polarized politics there will either be fewer parties, because the issues are so clear, or very many more, because any real concept of 'the general interest' – of coherent social outcomes – has disappeared.

Could India do without parties? No. Another clear side effect of representative democracy is that unless we all want to involve ourselves closely with detailed decision-making and administration, we need political parties to organize and stabilize the job of government on our behalf. The rewards that accrue to individual politicians – wealth and status – are a small price to pay for this.

Again, to posit the opposite: if there were no parties, elections would be about competition between individuals, and no one would know what kind of governance they could expect, or from whom. After elections, like-minded individuals would somehow have to find each other and determine how they could work together. Without party discipline before and after elections, the electoral process would be a confusing mass of detail which would have no precise meaning till after the polls had closed. Parties supply the vital link between votes and outcomes. They allow voters to make generalized and rational decisions about the future, with a reasonable expectation that their choices will carry force and meaning. At least in theory.

With fewer, larger parties, voters can choose particular outcomes and take a view later as to whether they have been well served. Large, disciplined parties are therefore good for stability and general accountability, but to be big they must also accommodate a wide range of opinions. And the larger the party, the more anaemic its general stance on almost anything. This encourages moderate political debate, but it leaves the periphery of politics exposed to inroads by enthusiasts. India, as a polity, is therefore prone to throw up single-issue campaigns, like the Chipko Movement, or Anna Hazare's anti-corruption drive. Charities and NGOs can also take up some of the slack left by the indifference of party organizations to specific grievances. But the relative blandness of party politics can sometimes leave sections of the community feeling that their specific needs are not being addressed. In Europe this has led to the rise of a slew of anti-immigration parties. In India it has left space for Naxalites and religious extremists to appear on the neglected fringes.

Large parties carry their own disadvantages, but they do allow voters to punish politicians effectively. If the government fails us, we know who is responsible and we can vote them out. In the absence of large parties we get coalition governments. Responsibility is then less clearly allocated; we can be sure that politicians will blame their erstwhile partners if they feel they need to. Similarly, when parties split, the pressure that an electorate can exercise diminishes.

Democracy is not well served in elections where voters vote for specific parties and policies, and politicians then cobble together a coalition programme afterwards, thus installing a government that no one has expressly voted for. Chaos in party politics unpicks the loop of accountability. India has accommodated this problem by the formation of pre-election coalitions with published programmes, but this practice, first used by the Janata Party in 1977, has somewhat fallen out of fashion. It worked well for the National Front in 1989, and again for the newly formed NDA in 1999, but has not been used since by either major national grouping. The change of government in 2004 was followed by the negotiation of a Common Minimum Programme, as had been the case with the installation of the United Front in 1996.

Is the large number of parties therefore a weakness in the Indian system? And if it is a weakness, how could it be addressed?

Parties almost everywhere, except in the US, do have a tendency to multiply. As collective bodies made up of individuals, they are never safe from factionalism. What else might we expect when ambitious people collect in one group? As politicians soon learn, their most dangerous enemies are not outside their party, but inside.

One measure already in place to enforce party discipline in India is the Anti-Defection Law, added to the constitution in 1985 as the Tenth Schedule. This requires elected representatives who change party allegiance to stand for re-election, unless a minimum of one-third of the party in question also defects. This is a deterrent to individual acts of desertion, but it does not prohibit the defection of parties en bloc, and this has been a common feature of Indian politics. And so it should be, some might say, because collective action is what parties are designed to facilitate. Such action should therefore never be completely outlawed, though if it takes place between elections it reflects the will of party members, not of the electorate.

The anti-defection rules operate against individuals, and are designed to prevent chaos overtaking representative bodies, but they have also had the slightly paradoxical effect of making it more likely that dissidents within a party will not join another party but will form a new one of their own. This tends to work against internal party democracy, which is already in scant supply within Indian politics.

Here is a further pressure towards political subdivision, created in the name of electoral accountability. But the worry is that the new parties that emerge will not be genuinely needed or representative, nor any more accountable than their parent bodies.

Where substantial minorities exist, especially ones that are concentrated in specific regions, small parties can thrive and can play an effective and necessary role within a diverse society. The objective must be to encourage parties with genuine grass-roots support, and discourage careerism and factionalism. Ultimately this is a matter that Indian voters can resolve for themselves, by not voting for small parties that have a track record of unprincipled behaviour. Any potential censoriousness, though, could always be counteracted if the party in question is very good at handing out rewards and benefits to its supporters. Regional parties are prone to doing just this, and a great many targeted schemes have been implemented over the years, including free electricity for farmers in Punjab and Andhra Pradesh, laptops given out in UP, and bicycles for students in Tamil Nadu.

The connection between a party and its supporters hides other contentious areas too, because some supporters not only give votes but also money. Funding parties wholly by donation keeps public money out of the equation, which is popular with taxpayers, but it does leave the parties directly beholden to their paymasters. This is not such a problem with small opposition parties, where donors are unlikely to find their contributions repaid in kind, but it is a problem with major national parties. At that level, the pressures actually begin to flow in both directions. The issue is not always that big corporate donors get their way, but that parties of government extract money from corporations.

Every major democracy has struggled with these issues, and India is no exception. Indira Gandhi politicized the issue when she made corporate donations illegal in 1968. This was interpreted as a move to cut off the supply of big business money to her non-socialist opponents. It may have done this, but it also opened up a vast field of untraced business funding to politicians, who still needed money to run their organizations and were left to find it from individuals or under the counter. An era of so-called 'suitcase politics' followed, when senior politicians were forced to carry around sums of cash too large to fit into a briefcase. This situation was so unhealthy and untenable that corporate donations were legalized again in 1985.

Additional monitoring and restriction have been put in place since then, and the current position is that all donations are fully tax deductible, and donations above ₹20,000 must be declared. Despite this, the great majority of the income of major parties, around 75–80 per cent, consists of small, anonymous donations – at least that is what the books say. The relationship of the main parties with corporate donors tells a different story. Major industrial groups tend to support both main parties in roughly similar amounts. But suspicion persists that a great deal of money stays off the books, and that parties spend much more on election expenses than statutory limits – which are fairly low – permit. Parties are understandably reluctant to commit to greater transparency in this area.

It is certainly undesirable to have parties buying elections, but the whole relationship of money to elections is very complicated, with a vast grey area surrounding how legitimate expenses should be defined and how they should be split between candidates and parties. The AAP tried to run a clean house in this regard, and did relatively well. But they did not have to sustain a national organization, and they did not field candidates in as many constituencies as the two main parties. Other smaller parties have made rather less creditable efforts; smaller sums do not naturally encourage more openness.

Thus, India has not been fertile ground for the development of the 'few large parties' model of democracy, but this does not seem to have been a serious handicap in the operation of democratic processes. Though a limited range of party options does tend to confer a degree of stability in larger countries, India already has a relatively stable history of government policy. It is debatable, therefore, whether fewer parties would bring any appreciable benefit.

If India were to have fewer parties, then more people must vote for some of those that already exist. Could this come about purely as the result of a switch in voter preference, or would it have to be driven by major changes in party policy? This comes down to the old question of whether popular political figures are leading or following their supporters. In India, the dilemma for party leaders is how to swell their electoral base while not expanding their party organizations unduly, with the attendant increased expense and risk of faction. Much of the complex political manoeuvring in UP and Bihar over the last two decades has been a matter of rival parties, particularly the BSP and the SP, trying to poach each other's support with various patterns of appeal, through handouts, the selection of candidates and targeted rhetoric. With Dalits comprising about 20 per cent of the electorate and other backward classes (OBCs) roughly another 30 per cent, the ability of leaders to tailor appeals to selected groups becomes crucial, along with making alliances with larger parties. In UP it has been the BJP that has allied and re-allied with local power brokers, and it did so successfully and very decisively in 2014. In the 1970s the Congress similarly managed to assemble various jigsaw demographic alliances, especially the notorious KHAM alliance in Maharashtra, of appealing to Kshatriyas, Harijans, Adivasis and Muslims.

Can any of India's main power blocs expand? It may not be possible to appeal to all the people all the time, yet a party that wishes to broaden its base must try to appeal to more of the people for more of the time. The BJP made a spectacular success in this respect in UP and Bihar during the 2014 campaign, with a more modest impact in West Bengal; more Dalits voted for the BJP than ever before. The party's outreach in Kerala, however, was less successful. But to attract new voters by changing policy or direction also potentially risks alienating existing supporters. The BJP was not immune to this problem in its campaign in UP, and there was a degree of friction in the local party membership about fielding several of the lower-caste candidates that the party's strategy required. How well an expansion strategy can be executed in any individual case is highly problematic. The history of political parties everywhere tends to show that they are much better at keeping the support they already have through a 'core vote strategy' – appealing to existing supporters, with attempts to convince them that everything they know is somehow in danger – than reaching out to previously hostile sections of society.

If Indian politics is permanently polarized by region, caste and religion, then the political map will surely stay as it is. The results of the 2014 poll are not entirely clear in this regard. The BJP enjoyed unprecedented success, both as a national force and in local appeals to sections of Dalit and OBC communities. Perhaps there is more flexibility in the system than many have assumed, and a degree of democratic maturity – call it shrewdness – may be developing. Or perhaps this was simply a side effect of greater prosperity allowing more people to make more reasoned decisions away from ancestral identities.

Till now parties in India have generally found it hard to grow, and the Congress remained the leading all-India party for long, mainly because its traditional electoral strategy was to reach out to the masses. The BJP has made a play for the middle ranks of society, but this will only attract a minority of the population in a country still so full of poor people. The appeal to religion has masked this tendency, and accusations of 'pseudo-secularism' aimed at the Congress can hit home, but the BJP's breakthrough to a national majority came when it stood on its least overtly religious, most emphatically materialistic platform ever. Economics must represent the way forward for a national party in India, especially as the absolute number of poor people diminishes, and the remainder of the population becomes more interested in real opportunities and wealth and less interested in subsidies and welfare schemes.

No matter how true all this might be in theory, India may well be condemned to personalization of parties for some time yet because of the regional nature of the country's culture(s), the significance of state assemblies and because the bonds of ideological purpose are weak. India has a practical political culture that is not noticeably ideological on any large scale. There are idealists within it, but they find it as hard to combine in India as they do anywhere else, leaving the fringes of politics speckled with shades of mutually loathing extremists. Indian conditions are not conducive to the incubation of abstract political programmes. The country faces enough real problems to ensure that practicalities dominate.

If the relative shallowness of party politics is set to remain, Indians should perhaps be grateful on one level. Who, after all, wants to live in politically 'interesting' times? But if that shallowness is really the result of incompetence, disinterest or even corruption, Indians would do well to make themselves aware of what they can do as individuals, and in wider groupings, to drive up standards.

MAJORITIES AND MINORITIES

Democracy is sometimes simplistically summed up as 'majority rule'. While this is certainly an important part of democratic practice, democracy also carries ideas about justice, rights and equality that promote consideration for the interests of minorities. In a democracy, the majority has obligations towards the minority – to be moderate in victory, and to remain sensitive to the way it uses its delegated power, which the participation of the minority has enhanced. This is especially true of the permanent majorities found in modern multi-ethnic multicultural states.

Lord Salisbury, the great Victorian Conservative leader, was happy to deride the idea of majority rule, declaring in 1883 that no country could be considered free in which six men could tell five men exactly what to do.[26] Salisbury was taking a very narrow example of abuse of majority, and he would probably have been horrified at political normality in America – an indubitably free country in which 50 people have often told 49 who should be President. But the abuse of majorities can take many shapes and is not directly related to the scale of the majority. Having been given only the thinnest of majorities, George W. Bush embarked on a highly partisan programme after winning the presidential election of 2000. His opponents cried foul; he simply took the view that he had won. If nine sailors in a boat cast votes to decide which one of them should be eaten to keep the others alive, whoever loses is entitled to feel somewhat hard done by, no matter if the poll is split eight–one or five–four.

Majority rule is mostly a practical matter. If more people are content than not with a decision, then it is more likely to stick and to be accompanied by civic peace. Consider the opposite: minority rule has to rely on some form of compulsion. Majority rule helps a society to cohere, but only if the majority is clear-cut, and the decision is also felt to be somehow right. This is where morality makes an entrance. It is the moral force of the decision that draws compliance from the minority. Societies that keep their minorities onside can take pride in their sense of justice, and this makes them better to live in for everyone.

Universal suffrage, the bedrock of democracy, assures citizens that they have collective power over themselves, but if they are in a majority they inevitably hold authority over others too. Majoritarian power is checked in India by a series of devices; structurally by federalism, constitutionally by a range of guaranteed rights, legally by the Supreme Court, and culturally by education and a tradition of tolerance. All this is not enough to avoid all cases of discrimination or the abuse of majorities, but it is sufficient, thus far, to prevent such abuses rising to a national level.

We as a species are becoming increasingly confident about our ability to make good collective decisions, and this bodes well for democracy. In the past, majorities were often felt to be threatening, and were sometimes regarded as axiomatically ignorant or irrational. But recent experience has tempered prejudices about the madness or depravity of crowds, and has revealed majorities as potentially benign. Now we are just as likely to hear about the wisdom of crowds, a phenomenon that is probably a by-product of mass education. Wikipedia relies on the idea that the public can assemble knowledge that is not tainted by partisanship, if collected on a wide enough basis. But it soon re-discovered the old truth that although everyone is entitled to their opinion, not all opinions are equally well-founded, and what began as an exercise in radical democratic cognition soon reverted to hierarchy and the maintenance of order via an inner circle of initiates. Wikipedia, it turned out, still needed government by the few.

And so it is within any democracy. Government involves making decisions, and democracy is a system in which some, but not all, decisions are determined by majority. Lord Salisbury may have appeared to resent the principle, but as a wealthy aristocrat he was only inconvenienced by majority rule in his role as a party leader.

Like democratic leaders everywhere today, his main problem was to refine the knack of managing the electorate – that is, asking the right questions at the right time. Democratic politicians know that it is only by putting the right questions to voters that they can engineer divisions in their opponents' parties while avoiding them in their own. Like the rules of any game, the rules of majority voting can be bent and manipulated in all sorts of ways that stop short of actual fraud. One classic stratagem is to time an election at a supposedly favourable moment, as Indira Gandhi did in 1971 and 1977, resulting in one win and one defeat. Another is to redraw electoral boundaries, around either supporters or opponents, to one's best advantage. The creation of three new states by the NDA government in 2003 can be viewed as an example of this; the BJP have certainly been rewarded with support from local populations in these states ever since.

The majority-minority concept is far from absolute. It is an inconvenient and rarely discussed truth that majorities and minorities – the fundamental units of democratic decision-making – are transitory, abstract entities. They are not hard realities, but matters of flexible definition. They are products of occasions; they assemble and dissolve, depending on what question is put and under what circumstances. The 1947 Partition illustrates all of these variable elements. If the voting pool had been the whole of British India, and if full adult franchise had been in place, there would have been a majority against dismemberment. But the June 1947 plan provided that certain individual provinces – as drawn by the British – would determine their own fate on questions of internal partition and accession to which successor state.

The minorities that suffered most in this process were those that were widely dispersed, and this is a recurrent theme in the narrative of all minority communities everywhere. The Sikhs were fairly evenly spread across the Punjab, but were not in a strong majority anywhere. Three subdivisions of the original Punjab province were subsequently created, with a major international bifurcation based on religion in 1947, and the splitting of the Indian half, based on language, in 1966. The resulting concentration of Sikhs then produced a secession movement. It is an unavoidable circumstance that a concentrated minority is also a local majority. If that group feels itself to be sufficiently large and sufficiently distinct, it may demand not only greater autonomy but also full sovereignty. In the case of the Sikhs, the 1966 reorganization encouraged a more forceful expression of Sikh religious identity, leading to demands for greater autonomy, formalized in 1973 by the Anandpur Sahib Resolution. This in turn led militants to revive the pre-independence demand for a sovereign Khalistan, and a major armed insurgency broke out in the 1980s.

South Asia has a large number of minority groupings caught up in this process. There are several small sub-nationalities in India's north-east, like the Nagas and Mizos, who now have their own separate states. Balochis, similarly, have a strong sense of identity. They have their own province, but many resent inclusion within Pakistan. Pathans, meanwhile, straddle two nation states, as do Bengalis, and neither can therefore express themselves collectively within an existing democratic hierarchy.

Wherever the geography of political states makes a sufficiently untidy match with linguistic and ethnic history, resentment and oppression can easily arise. Kurds form minorities in Turkey, Syria and Iraq, but would be a majority in an independent Kurdistan. Migration similarly creates situations where democracy throws up odd results. The character of Sikkim was permanently changed by migration, leading to a situation in which its king felt unable to seek democratic approval from 'his' people for reforms. In neighbouring Bhutan, the scale of the influx of Nepalis led to strenuous attempts by its government to expel them. This was not just paranoia. Minorities can occasionally become majorities purely by immigration, as happened in Fiji in the late 1970s, when newcomers from the subcontinent briefly outnumbered native Fijians.

Minorities and borders are inextricably linked. Some Scots want independence from the UK not from any feeling of ancestral and special nationhood, but on a purely majority–minority basis. They maintain that Scottish people, as a body, tend to vote centre-left, yet they regularly get centre-right Conservative governments based on majorities delivered by voters in the heavily populated, wealthy south-east of England. By redrawing the borders of the democratic game, Scots could assure themselves that in future they would not vote Labour and get Tories. Meanwhile, the Labour party has always fiercely opposed Scottish independence for the same reason; they fear that without the reservoir of centre-left votes in Scotland, the UK would be less likely to get a Labour government.

This kind of regional anomaly is usually mitigated by local assemblies and forms of devolved decision-making. Modern India was designed to run on this principle, but tensions have often resulted when regional governments have been of a different persuasion from that in New Delhi. This is a central weakness in all large democratic polities that can only be eased by a general commitment to moderation.

Elections, the most distinctive element of democracy, can thus only act as a partial system of control. Voting is a passive response to questions set by ruling elites, within artificial boundaries framed by history. Voting is also a one-off answer to a single question, but this is not how governance works.

Decisions constantly need to be made in societies that, even when only the size of Malta, are too big to be referred singly to the wider public. Political decisions are either simplified and pre-digested into party manifestos, or taken on the hoof as and when they arise, by experts with an appropriate degree of technical knowledge. Voters are left to cast one single vote with which they make bundled decisions about numerous issues, both foreseen and unforeseen, via their representatives.

Furthermore, elections only determine who will govern, not what they will do. In India, the repeated formation of coalition governments has further enhanced this distancing effect, both in terms of direct selection of personnel, and in the eventual policy of governments that emerge from political deals. Some European countries – such as Belgium and Italy – have endured this for decades.

But for all the various weaknesses and limitations of the voting process, the most important point about an election is that the result is binding. It is therefore serious – it affects people in their wider lives. Voting forces voters to make considered decisions, which are supposedly better than rushed, frivolous or entirely self-interested decisions. This makes democracy a serious business, and saves it from the kind of frivolity its opponents, from Plato onwards, have feared it might encourage. Unfortunately it also opens the door to the kind of collective fearfulness that underlies communal tensions within complex polities. Minority social groups can become acutely aware that they are essentially at the mercy of majority groups at every election.

This is why it is so important not to moralize the result of an election or referendum in terms of right and wrong. It is also essential not to transform greater and lesser numbers into hard categories of winners and losers. For elections to be binding, the losing side must not suffer unduly. This is where the spirit of fraternity has to take a central role. The boundaries of political action have to be limited. Defeated politicians must not fear for their safety. Once this barrier was crossed in England in the early eighteenth century when politicians stopped impeaching each other, public policy became a real thing, above and away from personal fortunes and interests. Unless they are corrupt or criminal, ejection from office should entail merely that. Where politicians still fear for their lives and liberty, as many still do across South Asia, the whole tenor of politics is different. It is more dynastic, less candid and tends to swing between periods of artificial stability and exaggerated tumult. Democratic norms are designed to reduce this range of responses.

Democratic states recognize that the constant interplay of majorities and minorities is an inevitable and inescapable part of all societies. They intersect, overlap and coexist all the time. Some, however, are more significant that others. There is a rough equivalence of males and females within society, but this is almost never a significant factor in any political arrangement. More significantly, there are, by definition, smaller numbers of highly intelligent people than of average intelligence, and fewer rich people than poor.

While taking on board the essential artificiality of much majority-minority rhetoric, we should also note that not all minorities are oppressed. Some can be powerful, in which case they are known as elites. The principle of majority rule is, by necessity, always implemented by means of an elite corps; in a well run democracy its members occupy a privileged, though temporary position. And some large groups that cannot be considered as minorities can suffer too, if they have no source of power independent of electoral processes. A very large group of this type is poor women, who always make up roughly half of the lower orders in any developing country, but who rarely if ever exercise an independent voice or are able to apply distinct pressure as a group. Amartya Sen and Jean Drèze attribute the impressive improvement achieved by Bangladesh in its human development indices to the enhanced role of its poorer women. The irony is that this has not been achieved in Bangladesh by direct electoral pressure. The lesson may be that enhanced inclusivity is good for any society, no matter how poor.

Democracy is historically unusual in that it works against the pyramidal structure of privilege, and the scarcity of natural talent – eminence. It is a denial of greatness, and a restriction upon it in some ways. Right-wing thinkers have always viewed it thus, and have hated precisely this about it. Left-wing thinkers, on the other hand, have always overvalued the commonplace, and have remained suspicious of the material and political acquisitiveness of exceptional people. Dragging down and lifting up are the metaphors in play. The liberation of genius or the moderation of exploitation are the principles.

Democracy unleashes the power of majorities, but it also serves to fetter and moderate that power. In other systems a smaller, superior group wields power without reference to others. In a democracy, a small elite group wields power but its members remain accountable.

The early advocates of democratic extension in the nineteenth century, such as Alexis de Tocqueville and John Stuart Mill, saw one great disadvantage with a wider franchise, which was that it opened the possibility that the poor and ignorant would dominate the wealthy and educated. A potential 'tyranny of the majority' was very real to these thinkers, and they were only prepared to court this danger because the principle of equality and the probable civic benefits of consultation, and of what would now be called inclusion, were so manifest. The safeguard against this possible tyranny was education, and democracy and mass education have gone together ever since.

The corollary is also true: in societies that reject democratic ideas, education is not widespread and is frequently considered dangerous. As an index of democratic intent, education is a very good guide. States that promote it are not afraid of it. In Burma it has been badly neglected. The violent Islamists in Nigeria call themselves Boko Haram, which means 'western education is sinful'.

Theocracies and oligarchies are never very concerned to educate their own people beyond the technical level required for service in the armed forces, the maintenance of basic civil amenities and the supply of vital mechanical skills. Indoctrination, or the inculcation of correct thinking, is always the real priority. One of the most shameful legacies of the British to India is in exactly this area. The Raj left primary education largely alone and committed the funds it had to higher education. Independent India picked up from a bad place in this respect, and again one of the blemishes on India's post-independence record has been the neglect of primary schools. This, though, is a lapse attributable not to the desire to exclude the masses from politics; it is more a matter of rural under-development and local corruption.

India has a special relationship to the majority–minority debate because of the exceptional variety of human conditions that the Indian state includes. Increased sensitivity to new forms of acceptable identity has only reinforced this rich crop of subdivisions and distinctions, and post-independence India has a good record of dealing with minorities. M. K. Gandhi was sympathetic towards them, but he was not willing to give any of them a separate political voice within the Congress. Unity against colonial power was the priority. But after 1947, the quest for unity gave place to a pressing, and to some critics a seemingly inexhaustible, desire to appease minority interests. This commitment to reverse injustice has had a long-lasting effect on independent India, which has been among the most sensitive of nations to minority demands, if expressed non-violently and on a secular basis.

This makes an instructive contrast with the development of Pakistan. Gandhi and all the principal Congress leaders overruled the interests of minorities in service of the wider national movement. Jinnah, by contrast, claimed special status as a minority leader, and went to great lengths in the final furlong before Partition to reassure any possible minority group within Pakistan that their rights would be fully respected. Since 1947, however, it has been Pakistan that has ignored the rights of its minorities, while India has been obsessive about observing them. This began with the extensive reservations written into the original constitution, and has continued ever since via the implementation of Mandal in the early 1990s, the formation of the Minorities Commission in 1992, and the creation of the Ministry of Minority Affairs in 2006.

Nothing in this outlook owes much to the British tradition, in which it is considered discriminatory to treat people differently. In independent India it has been considered discriminatory to treat them all the same. At its best, this attitude produces sensitivity in government, but there are limits to how much special treatment can be handed out. Some Hindus feel they were singled out unfairly with the passage of the Hindu Code in the mid-1950s, because a similar code was not drawn up modernizing Muslim personal law. This feeling was compounded in the 1980s when the Rajiv Gandhi government actually confirmed the traditional interpretation of Islamic divorce law after the Shah Bano case.

Unlike the Congress, the BJP has not been keen to recognize minority rights, preferring to promote an ideal of Indian society as undifferentiated and organic, while viewing the protection of minority rights as divisive. 'Justice to all, appeasement to none' has been the cry, emergent consensus the ideal. This stance has sometimes given the BJP an undemocratic air, especially before the late-1990s, when the Westminster-style adversarial model was often decried as fundamentally un-Indian. At other times the Hindu predominance in the country has been seen as an unassailable strength, allowing BJP leaders to embrace majority rule without fear. Narendra Modi appears to come from this school, and has played the game more successfully than any of his predecessors.

Modi's rhetoric at the national level has been inclusive; '*sabka saath, sabka vikas*' could hardly sound more generous, and he has championed the rights of women more forcefully and more publicly than any previous protégé of the Sangh Parivar. But suspicions persist that hidden within the BJP's national electoral strategy lies a complex set of attempts to polarize communities across north India, where the party feels it needs to consolidate the 'Hindu' vote while fragmenting potential opposition. These divisive tactics have included exploiting, or even allegedly fomenting Hindu–Muslim riots on a variety of pretexts, and by issuing warnings against 'love jihad', meaning mixed Hindu–Muslim marriages in which a Hindu bride is required to convert.

Why this strategy should be necessary when Hindus are in a majority almost everywhere in India might seem baffling, but the vagaries of electoral boundaries play a role in potentially over-representing minority communities, especially when the 'Hindu' vote is as fragmented as it has been over recent decades in the wake of Mandalization and the proliferation of caste parties.

The other unspoken agenda is that some Hindu nationalists fear that Muslims, even as a minority of around 13 per cent, will eventually dominate Hindus, by outbreeding them. This has created a variety of hysterical estimates about when a Muslim majority will appear in India. The year 2035 is the official RSS guess.[27] While Narendra Modi may not personally believe this, the BJP could find it useful to have the idea taken seriously as a way of garnering the naturally diverse vote bank that 'Hindus' represent. This has been easier to do in UP and Bihar, where the population divides fairly neatly into two camps, but less so where the mix is more complex, and the BJP has historically done much less well in Kerala, though steps are currently being taken to address this failing.[28]

It is worth pointing out that communal tensions are not really about religious beliefs, though they are marked by religious differences. They are connected to dominance, fear and the artificial construction of categories of 'us and them'. It can be difficult to combat this tendency when hard times make people too willing to believe they are in danger, and when advantages can be gained by the careful cultivation of exploitable human frailties. A minority has no effective defence against the power that fear can lead majorities to award themselves, if skilfully organized. Democracy is supposed to guarantee individuals power over themselves, to assure them self-government; minority status removes that guarantee.

Finally, majorities throw up one significant quirk. The majority of people in any society are poor, and the rich are always a minority. If minorities are always poorer than majorities, then why do they not simply dispossess the rich? This has never actually happened in any democracy. If it was going to happen anywhere it should have happened in India, but it has not. Why? It is a well-known argument that if all the wealth of the super-rich were to be divided among the wider population, no one's life would be appreciably or permanently improved. The most effective protection of the rich, even in India, has perhaps been that the poor want to be rich themselves, and were the concept of wealth to be removed, or the wealth pyramid destroyed, much of their hope for a better future would go with it.

Freedom, fairness, trust and hope are all vital component parts of a democracy. They are not details; they are centrally concerned with making democracies better to live in than other types of system. They are also intimately connected with the status of minorities, and with the concept of rights.

RIGHTS

Democracy and rights go together. The possession of rights – *equal* rights – is the absolute bedrock of all democratic processes.

Rights, however, are not simple. They bring questions with them, such as what they are, who decides who has them and how they can be enforced. And beyond these primary questions there lurks the inconvenient reality that rights are frequently in conflict with. This is very apparent in the area of public health, where medical care opens an enormous range of possibilities, such as where legal abortion directly poses a woman's 'right to choose' against the unborn child's 'right to life'. Conflict can also arise all across the cultural sphere, where rights of free expression run up against rights protected by laws of libel, obscenity or blasphemy. India's rich religious mix has produced a long stream of rights-based clashes, from the rights of Muslims to use amplifiers to aid the call to prayer, to the rights of Hindus to have academic works on Hinduism banned, to the rights of Dalits to enter temples, and the general question as to how far the right to hold one's faith, under Article 25 of the constitution, extends to the right to proselytize.

There are also a number of potential conflicts between the state and its citizens concerning the individual's right to privacy, the public's right to information, and the state's rights to pre-empt hostile actions against itself. States generally consider that their own rights to secrecy outrank the civil rights possessed by citizens. Like other major democracies, the Indian state has equipped itself with a formidable range of powers to combat subversion, insurgency and terrorism, leading to repeated protests and accusations of oppressive governmental overreach, under the Prevention of Terrorism Act (POTA), passed in 2002 but repealed two years later; the Armed Forces (Special Powers) Act, passed in 1958 and still very much in force; and the overarching Unlawful Activities (Prevention) Act, originally passed in 1963, but heavily amended in recent years to incorporate powers lost with the repeal of POTA.

States also believe that their right to purchase land for infrastructural projects overrides an individual's right to refuse to sell. This has played out several times in recent Indian history, with the drawn-out protests in Nandigram and Singur, and the disruption caused by the construction of major dams, which has rendered up to 40 million Indians homeless.[29] Not just individual farmers, but large sections of society have also been overridden by state priorities. India's princes were deprived of their privy purses in 1971, and the dispossession of tribal communities in favour of mining and mineral interests continues to this day.

As societies become more tolerant, economically interconnected and technologically advanced, the number of rights they enforce and supervise increases. The game becomes more complicated, so it requires more rules to keep it running smoothly. Thus the number of rights that any society recognizes can be taken as an index of its sophistication, and the amount of new rights that it generates can stand as a measure of its democratic health. Citizens, however, do not always view things this way, and it is a classic complaint of political conservatives that there are too many rights in modern society and not enough obligations; that too many people are getting without giving.

It is certainly true that the quest for rights has been largely a left-wing project, and the establishment of new rights has almost always been a matter of protecting the weaker members of society, or of addressing the inability of individuals to get something valuable by their own efforts. India's history provides many examples of efforts to equalize rights, starting with rights to vote and to government jobs in the 1940s, and running through to more recent rights, such as to information (2005) and the National Food Security Bill (2013), which gave legal force to Article 47 of the constitution, elevating the 'duty' of the state to raise the level of nutrition into a 'right to food' for all Indians.

In general terms, humanity is moving on from defining and establishing absolute rights – such as the right to a fair trial – into the difficult area of managing relative rights, such as of free speech or the protection of intellectual property. By the end of the Second World War, a full list of rights had been established, and seven of these, under broad headings, were written into Part III of the Indian constitution as 'Fundamental Rights'. These were rights to equality, freedom, protection from exploitation, freedom of religion, constitutional remedies, cultural and educational rights, and the right to hold property. This last was somewhat downgraded, in a more overtly socialist period, by the 44th Amendment (1978), which redefined the entitlement negatively, as a right not to be deprived of property unlawfully.

It is all very well to declare lists of rights, but they cannot be said to exist unless some form of enforcement accompanies them. In legal terms, rights and remedies must go together, and in India this has led, somewhat circuitously, to a uniquely Indian tradition of judicial activism, spearheaded by the Supreme Court, which has had a distinctly political tinge. The apex court became involved in political matters via its largely passive role in clarifying the original constitution through the 1950s and 1960s, but it became more active after the Emergency of 1975–77, and its ambitions expanded into the central vacuum created by the prolonged governmental instability of the 1990s.

Tensions arise within any constitution, no matter how well-written. Legislatures make laws but do not interpret them; judges do not legislate. In India, however, judicial activism adapted the common law tradition of judge-made case law – building up binding interpretations via an accumulation of rulings – and moved into the grey area within the constitution between Fundamental Rights and Directive Principles. Judges felt compelled to step into the political arena to compensate for the inability of governments to frame policy, or to drive through reform. This raised some constitutional questions concerning the separation of powers; what if politicians decided to intervene in judicial decisions? The courts have tended to see their role as limiting executive power, and this has led to sharp conflict on several occasions, such as in 2002, when the Supreme Court ruled that candidates for election were required to disclose their assets, or in 2013, when it decided that politicians should immediately be disqualified as MPs or MLAs on conviction, not after appeals were exhausted.

The wider concept that the law and the courts exist to guard and promote public welfare has now created a subsidiary tradition of Public Interest Litigation (PIL), which relies on the principle that anyone can bring a case to court, in person or by letter, regardless of whether they themselves are personally involved in the issue, or would be directly affected by the outcome. Such an approach has proved very valuable in environmental affairs, where poorer sections of society often suffer most. It has a long tradition in India by now, and can show some substantial gains, such as the ruling in 1998 that compelled buses and auto-rickshaws in Delhi to use compressed natural gas (CNG) in order to reduce atmospheric pollution. The culture of rights and PIL are now fused, and much more may yet be expected from it.

None of this, though, tells us what rights *are.* A great deal of abstract reasoning has gone into this question, and two solutions regularly emerge. One is that rights are somehow 'natural', i.e. they are granted by God or are an integral part of the natural order in some way, or originate in our humanity itself. These arguments are all extensions of a chain of thought that starts with the idea that rights should exist, and that the source of them must therefore be somehow self-evident. This is not actually true, though, in the sense of being provable by science, logic or direct demonstration. If the great Utilitarian philosopher Jeremy Bentham is remembered for anything, it is that he declared the idea of natural rights to be 'nonsense on stilts'.

Why should this be so? Bentham, who died in 1832, had his own agenda and a list of particular enemies to discredit, both radical and conservative. But serious problems confront arguments that rely either on concepts of God, as put forward by medieval scholastics such as Thomas Aquinas, or on ideas of Nature, as per more modern radicals such as Thomas Paine. Neither type of argument defines the explicit content of rights, nor how they can be enforced, even if they do manage to trace the putative source of such rights to their proponent's own satisfaction. For it is not at all clear which rights God intends us to have, or whose God we are talking about. Choose your God, choose your enforcers. And which nature are we dealing with – the vegetarian-motherly version, or the carnivorous-competitive one? Do little fishes have a right to life? And does a bigger fish have the same right to life and also therefore a right to eat the little fishes that make up its 'natural' diet? And what use are natural rights when no natural systems exist to enforce them? What status do such rights occupy in a world in which they are flouted consistently and with impunity?

There is another approach available that dissolves these abstract problems. Briefly put, rights can be defined as entitlements that others will concede to you without a fight. If you have to fight to establish your right, then it is clearly not a right in the minds of your opponents. If you fight and win, the right then 'exists' and others may claim it without the necessity of fighting. This is actually how rights have been established and accepted in the real world – specific rights to go somewhere, or do something, like to settle, cultivate land or have access to water or fish. In more recent times, the right to form trade unions or for women to vote are rights of this sort.

Rights, therefore, should not be thought of as an end to disputes, but rather as a lattice of formal entry points into them. Rights represent a provisional map of what kinds of disputes are recognized within a wider system of enforcement – in other words, the kinds of arguments that states can resolve internally. New rights, therefore, are now regularly appearing. A significant right that has recently been won is the right of disabled people to enjoy access to public buildings. In modern Britain, every public building now has wheelchair access, often via specially constructed facilities at the front. The long-dead architects of Britain's historic public buildings were completely unaware of this right, and might well consider the additions to be unsightly. Nevertheless ramps have now appeared, because the principle of disabled access seems inherently fair – even natural. This right also appeared when its host society was rich enough to afford it, and wealth is a hidden metric that is still very active in determining which rights are recognized and where. Greater prosperity will undoubtedly extend the range of rights available to ordinary Indians.

Rights involve capabilities and entitlements, some of them exclusive, some not. But they all have to be enforced to be real. How is this to be done? The answer is hidden in the word: by force. The best way we have of generating force is through political legitimacy, and the best way we have of establishing political legitimacy is democracy. Rights and democracy are inseparable. Where there are no rights, might rules; those who can dispose of force have more rights than others who cannot. In the real world, more force generally equals a louder voice and the enjoyment of 'better' rights. In a society without adequate respect for rights, social status is determined by little more than the crude ability to dominate others, and to take and keep whatever one wants by the (temporary and reversible) right of *force majeure.* No one would call a society like that a democracy.

Force without the concept of rights is just that – the threat of violence. Rights and civilization belong comfortably together, although rights and civility sometimes struggle to do so. The public debates that surround rights tend to be heated, as new rights will almost inevitably conflict with some hallowed tradition, established practice or vested interest. Sexual and gender rights are particularly susceptible to forms of incivility, and a massive amount of public debate in the West has recently revolved around the rights of women to hold religious office, and the rights of homosexuals to have relationships sanctioned by the state.

The future of gay rights looks very bleak in many parts of Africa, such as in Gambia, where President Yahya Jammeh has declared homosexuality to be one of the three greatest dangers to the planet. A struggle may ensue there, but if the cultural sensibilities of the majority of the population are sufficiently offended by gay relationships, then that struggle may be a long uphill affair, as it seems likely in Uganda. In India too the issue of gay rights has been reactivated by the Supreme Court's ruling of December 2013, which re-criminalized gay sex by overturning the effective repeal of Section 377 of the Criminal Code by the Delhi High Court in 2009. Attempts to obtain a formal repeal in Parliament may well succeed; a less sympathetic atmosphere is likely to accompany any such attempt in Kampala.

Rights and Western law traditions have a strong connection, through Roman law. The Romans did not have a concept of equal rights, but they had a keen sense of what rights were and who possessed them – citizens. Two of the most significant have entered the modern world through Western law: the right to a fair trial by a competent authority, and the right to exclusive (and freely transferable) possession of property – sometimes called dominion. This extended to land, but was more recognizable in the area of personal possessions, which included slaves – people with no rights, and animals – creatures that had no rights.

These Roman legacies illustrate the essentially local and constructed nature of rights. All through history, some cultures have not recognized the right to own land at all, and, by extension, have not recognized the right to transfer its possession to someone else. This power of alienation has struck some societies as absurd. Land just is. Ancient Indian law recognized the right to cultivate land, but not the right to sell or transfer the ownership of the physical earth. The British changed this for their own purposes, one of which was to try to wean Indians off 'usury', as Governor-General Lord Cornwallis put it, and to create a market in land that would reward farmers or landlords for investing in their property.[30]

This idea in its turn was based in the very strong conviction of eighteenth century philosophers that 'property' – the right to own things – was the absolute bedrock of civilization, meaning liberty under laws. In some of the 'primitive' societies that these philosophers were examining with interest at the time, in America, Africa and across the Pacific, the concept of ownership was rather reversed. In pre-modern societies, the dominant, 'natural' idea was often that the land owned the people who took their living from it, who were obliged to look after it as its servants. In such a society the idea of selling land could never occur to anyone, because a transfer of ownership would imply changing the occupancy of the space, that is, moving the people who lived on the land. Fighting over the occupation of land, or imposing obligations of serfdom on the existing inhabitants might make sense, but selling land – i.e. exchanging it for something that was not land – would not.

The concept of ownership – of anything – is itself a right, but one that can only be enforced by permanent, mutual recognition. The rights that come with democracy, and that create it, are not dissimilar.

This leads us to the central truth that not all rights are equally universal. An individual's right to own something, such as land, is a right that can be sanctioned – or not, as in communist societies. But when it does exist, the right to own property is not co-equal. The *general* right to own land is equal, but the *specific* right to own any particular piece of land is exclusive. Otherwise the concept of owning it, meaning that it can be disposed of or put to use in any way considered reasonable by the owner, cannot exist.

The right to graze cattle on common land illustrates how this does and does not work. Such common rights can be found all over the world, but they are very difficult to enforce or manage, and must be mediated by some spirit of community and/or published rules. If everyone grazes all their cattle on the common all the time, then soon there is nothing left for anyone's beasts to eat. Tribal people in modern India often suffer from a particularly vicious version of this problem, because their traditional way of life – to which they have protected rights – cannot coexist with the disruption that accompanies modern mining, logging or dam construction. They cannot 'share' their resources; they simply lose them.

This dilemma, often called 'the tragedy of the commons', is with us today in many areas that are not related to the raising of cattle, including the fishing of the world's oceans, the use of public roads, the extraction of water from rivers and pollution of the planet's atmosphere. All these can pit individuals or groups against each other in ways that make it difficult to see how everyone can equitably enforce their supposed rights against everyone else's.

These problems often arise in areas where no single competent authority is in charge; they are essentially interstitial and can only be resolved by either extending an existing authority, or by agreement between interested parties above the level of individuals. Recently, such areas of conflict have been addressed via multilateral international agreements, but it remains to be seen how effective these can be. The US generally opposes agreements that restrict its right to maintain its current wealth, while developing countries oppose them as restrictive of their rights to develop their potential wealth. The sense of community that is so central to the workings of democracy is still lacking in the international arena, and this is likely to remain the case while parties view themselves as potential losers. Rights are most easily established and accepted when two things are in play: an evident disparity of power, and an available remedy that conforms to an agreed standard of justice. This is still some way off in planetary terms.

Rights in different cultures vary, but the idea that individuals have certain entitlements is universal. In India, the caste system had a clear conception of rights, restricting them on one level, but protecting them at the same time, in laying out who did what within society. Whatever it was that one's caste determined one should do, no one else could do it. The balance in this system is still admired by Y.S. Rao, Prime Minister Modi's own choice as chairman of the Indian Council of Historical Research (ICHR),[31] though in *The Annihilation of Caste* (1936) Dr Ambedkar was absolutely clear that it was not merely a division of labour but a division of labourers, and was thus not equitable.[32] In Europe, feudal societies were also highly controlled, but the existence of specific rights was absolutely central to their functioning, such as the right of landowners to demand labour from serfs, the right of kings to demand military service from vassals, or the right to collect firewood, cut turf or hunt animals. The question came down to which persons were qualified to have rights (not women, children, slaves, prisoners or aliens) and in what specific areas – to own land or carry arms, to strike coins or to charge transit duties. The medium of enforcement was always a duly sanctioned court, whether based in custom or positive law. Rights simply descended from the highest authority – gods and kings – down chains of delegation to local bodies. Anarchy and feudalism were never equivalent; they were opposites.

Rights and enforcement go together, which means, in practice, the modern state and rights also go together. They are mutually supportive. The state is more powerful than any individual, and must therefore be curbed. But the power that a state wields is not imported from somewhere outside society; it emerges from within it, and is made up of individual acts of accession – at least in theory.

The contract theory of society as set out by Locke and Rousseau is full of intellectual fictions, and making a real constitution is a mysterious act of plucking something forceful out of thin air. Any such process must start with the very tricky question of who has the right to make a constitution. And if they hold the right to make it, do they then have the right to alter or abrogate it? Logically, the agreement to be bound by it must predate its creation. But what real power can a constitution ever have if it can be unmade at will? Do constitution makers have the power, but only once, at a special, unique moment?

This is the precise point that was addressed in the famous ruling in the *Kesavananda Bharati vs. State of Kerala* case of 1973, by which the Supreme Court established that the power to make a constitution must always override the power to amend it, and that the Parliament had the right to amend the constitution, but not to interfere with its 'basic structure'. This remains the single greatest judicial protection that Indian democracy enjoys, because it defends the constitution from subsequent majoritarian interference that runs counter to the intentions of its original creators. Better defined and more powerful than the notion of 'popular will', the Basic Structure doctrine is the principal force that maintains the democratic rope trick, and it represents India's greatest contribution to democratic theory.

In establishing that the Indian state has a right to exist unmolested, it helps to amplify the point that national states also possess rights. The most basic is what might be called the right to life – the right to *be* a state. Revealingly, this right is not an absolute right at all and subsists solely in the willingness of other states to accept it. Thus East Timor became a state to general acclaim, whereas Taliban Afghanistan did not, picking up nods of approval from only Saudi Arabia, Pakistan and the UAE. How any new state arrives at this critical moment of acceptance is open to chance; it might be a secessionist war, as was successfully achieved by South Sudan but not Biafra, or via a plebiscite as in the Czech Republic, or by any other way in which separate territoriality can be established, as was Pakistan by colonial British fiat.

States are containers of rights, have rights themselves and act as guarantors of the rights of individuals and groups within their populations. What precisely those rights might be is another matter. Rights of individuals within states are determined by the context of the social environment within the state, and the ability of the government to defend or concede rights on any single topic. Thus in the modern world we have new rights which would have meant nothing to Harrapans or Incans. One such would be the right to information, a modern right that bureaucratic states have been reluctant to concede, but which citizens were bound to demand eventually as a form of accountability and as a check on the misuse of data. Other modern rights might include a right to housing, to privacy, or to adopt or even conceive children. These are all very dependent on particular social and political contexts. A right to a house cannot realistically predate the provision of public housing; a right to privacy cannot run ahead of the existence of an intrusive press; a right to parenthood cannot be enforceable without in-vitro fertilization and an advanced health care system.

It is not very helpful to think of rights as universal or permanent. They are not, unless we say they are. Democracy is the way to do this. The burden is heavy and constantly shifting, but is worth carrying, because democratic rights defend us, against our governments and against each other. Those who decry rights as somehow obstructive of or injurious to the normal conduct of human society are denying the civilizing power of law. Obviously it can be annoying to be told one cannot build whatever structure one wants to on one's own property. But we can be told we cannot pick the flowers in the public park, therefore denying the rights of others to enjoy the sight of them.

Rights make democracy; rights define civilization; rights ultimately nurture and defend civilized people. To do without rights would return society to the rule of the strong. For all their occasional absurdities and contradictions, we all have rights we like to exercise, which we hope will be respected. And by their very nature it will always be the weakest who need rights and who will eventually mobilize to get them.

But we need not be too alarmed. Rights are not actualities; they only establish potentialities. The fact that everybody has a right to be

President, under the prescribed circumstances, does not mean that everybody can be President, especially not at the same time.

The debate over rights occasionally now becomes entangled not so much with the idea of democracy, but with Western double standards. Many politicians in developing countries consider that the 'human rights' agenda of the Western powers is a surrogate form of imperialism, under which rulers of smaller states can be prosecuted for infringements, while leaders of major powers can lay waste to foreign countries and slaughter their populations with impunity. They have a point. But this does not invalidate the idea of rights, or diminish their central importance to civilized behaviour. Barack Obama has not attacked his own people, whereas Bashar al-Assad repeatedly has. Killing other states' citizens has always been presented as an act of war; killing one's own is an act of betrayal. It was precisely this cardinal sin that unseated ex-President Yanukovych of Ukraine in 2013.

Rights are a work in progress, and we can expect them to continue to ramify and develop as society becomes more prosperous, more complex and less afraid to be self-critical. The extent of the culture of rights will always be a good litmus test of how determined a society is to balance itself by consent, and through published (variable) rules.

3.

Conclusion

It may seem unnecessary, even a little old-fashioned, to sing the praises of democracy, but the case has to be made and remade constantly. Why? Because historically speaking, democracy is rare. Over the last 5,000 years it has been the exception, not the rule, and it is still an immature thing. Those who wish to see it more securely established should make efforts to extol and defend it, for its future is not assured.

Democracy runs counter to many established patterns of thought and behaviour, and is alien to the instincts of many of those who covet governmental power. It is neither self-creating nor self-maintaining, and is more likely to dissolve into chaos than to emerge from it.

Above all, democracy cannot easily claim to be 'natural'. The natural world holds little that can be taken as an example of or inspiration for democratic ideas. Rather the contrary, as democracy's opponents are all too keen to point out. Raw domination, direct confrontation, the survival of the fittest and so forth are all familiar animal tropes, and democracy denies, undermines or avoids all of them. The ideal of collective welfare that is beneficial to *all* individuals is diametrically opposed to the process of Darwinian natural selection, which is not concerned with the preservation of communities but with the survival and dispersal of favourably adapted genetic material within individuals. Natural selection is elitist; it is hard-hearted towards the less well-adapted.

'Natural' institutions that are not democratic include any hierarchical social order in which rank is determined by physical strength or aggression, which covers most of the rest of the mammals. Insects are the least democratic, most hierarchical creatures on earth – and also the most successful. The price they pay is in a complete lack of individuality, and in rigidly fixed functional roles determined by gender and fertility, or the lack of it. There may be a lesson there.

Democracy can only be considered 'natural' by some discreet massaging of the meaning of the word – by saying, perhaps, that human beings flourish best under it, and achieve their highest potential for thought and deed within the freedoms and opportunities that it brings. The most 'natural' of all human institutions is the family group, which protects young and old, passes on its skills and sustains itself by various forms of work. The democratic state has taken on some of these roles, principally defence and education, but democracy liberates individuals socially and culturally in ways that families do not. It is dictatorships that seek to evoke images of and associations with the family – with a tender-hearted father-figure at the head of the family/state and the people as his children.

Democracy is not just an artificial contrivance; it can feel like a burden too. It is sometimes harder work to live in a democracy than under less consultative kinds of system, because of the high degree of participation that democratic institutions can demand. For those who would prefer to be left alone, or who would rather live in a world of constancy and certainty, democracy may seem too intrusive or impermanent, and high principles such as equality and freedom may seem too vague or even vulgar for those with a taste for glory. The soft virtues of democracy can be seen as timid when set against stirring dreams of national pride or ideals of social purity.

Democratic states also judge their leaders on their performance, and this can effectively dishonour them by turning them into mere managers. The banality of public service linked to the 'delivery' of specific social ends is another way in which democracy can seem less romantic than empire.

All of this makes mass democracy a fragile thing.

But despite the many complications that the process generates, democracy has been found to be popular and beneficial wherever it has successfully been instituted, with enough good luck to sustain the social trust that is its lifeblood. The problem with democracy is not popularity; it is sustainability.

No system is perfect, but democracy has more ways of coming to terms with its flaws than any other system. Its details can all be changed, whereas rival systems enshrine their specifics and hold fiercely to them. Such worship of permanence is intended to deny citizens the right to criticize, and non-democratic systems habitually defend laws, institutions, religious beliefs, specific persons or entire families. Monarchy relies on permanent appointments; democracy insists they must be provisional. Theocracy requires that law and scripture are coextensive and eternal; democracy insists on legislative flexibility.

Democracy has less structural rigidity than all its rivals, except anarchy, and its opponents still regularly hold up a list of its alleged failings, most of which are caricatures of its adaptability. But it can stand acquitted on its strengths. Democracies make fewer disastrous errors than dictatorships; they mobilize human resources and unleash human aspirations more effectively and at higher qualities; they please more of the people more of the time than any other system. Democracy acts as a social truce, which allows more people to share in the benefits of peaceful cooperation than any other arrangement. It accepts people as they are and permits their desires to be legitimate.

These are virtues of democracy in its broadest sense, meaning liberal democracy based on universal rights. There are other systems that have described themselves as democratic, but simply adding the word to the official name of a country does not go very far towards instituting real democracy. North Korea, officially the Democratic People's Republic of Korea, can stand as an obvious example. Highly socialistic systems grant themselves the virtue of being in tune with the needs of the people, so things like elections and judicial independence are not necessary. Theocracies are similarly convinced of their own perfection, but substitute harmony with God for harmony with the people. Such systems do not tolerate dissent, despite the fact that human nature includes argumentative, creative and inquisitive elements, which will then go unrecognized. Systems that deny the existence of fundamental human characteristics are set up to fail.

Failing systems can be sustained from outside. The major global powers did this repeatedly in the twentieth century – Vietnam, Cuba, Afghanistan – and it can work, but not indefinitely. Inherently rigid or narrow political systems are always likely to collapse and cannot be sustained by external force alone. Democracy absolutely has to be sustained from within. Fear can maintain a dictatorship, but fear will destroy any democracy, as citizens take up arms against each other or give up their liberties in exchange for security under 'strong leadership'.

Living in a democracy can be a more disturbing experience than living under an unaccountable government, because democracy involves two key elements – choice and change. The price of freedom is not so much eternal vigilance as eternal competitive sloganeering. Democratic citizens have to learn to live with contradictory messages, and a range of civic demands. Democracy promises peace and freedom, not peace and tranquillity.

Democracy is about the management of conflict, and that includes all forms of dissent, not just class economic interests or personal ambitions. As a system its genius is that it can do this and be seen to do it fairly without imposing permanent or sacred outcomes.

Significantly, democratic states have learned to lay democracy aside when at war. In times of crisis a soft heart, or ponderous, consultative decision-making – sensitivities which may be accounted virtues in other circumstances – are abandoned when leadership and central control need to be strengthened and internal criticisms and opposition muted. This was the experience of the major democracies in the last century, and critics are still wary lest these expedients are abused during times that do not justify drastic curtailment of liberties. The problem is not usually in imposing emergency powers; the difficulty is in judging when they can be safely abandoned. Politicians are always keener to take them up than to put them down. But the ability to extend or curb central authority as necessary – and with due accountability – must surely be seen as a strength.

Democracy is a multi-speed engine of government that can be revved up in times of civil or military emergency. All democratic nations reserve emergency powers to the executive. The arguments are about the deployment of these powers, not the necessity for their existence. This makes democracies different from dictatorships on a very fundamental level.

What merits can other systems boast? Can they be so bold as to stand in the dock?

Orderliness is usually at the core of anti-democratic systems, and people can develop a taste for it, especially after traumatic experiences of disorder. Thomas Hobbes, writing in the early 1650s just after the English Civil War, was one such, and to this day his arguments for unlimited state power can find echoes in Stalinism and fascism in all its local versions. Other supports for non-democratic systems are all essentially circular arguments about authority. They run roughly: 'God/the people/the workers/our race is the ultimate authority, and I represent it. And as the representative of that authority, I can assure you that it is legitimate, and that it is in your ultimate interests to obey me.' This may lead to orderliness, but not usually to inclusive and sustainable social justice, or good, disinterested governance.

Democracies are actually better upholders of law than even the most orderly dictatorships, because the source of the law is different. The former are based on popular legitimacy, the latter on brute force. Popular legitimacy provides a superior grounding because it involves the whole of society in establishing the moral force that validates the power of governments to enforce the law. Popular legitimacy rests on the principle that laws commonly made must be commonly obeyed.

The central principle of law is that it should always apply everywhere in the same way in the same circumstances, and democratic systems are more consistent with this principle than any other. Democracies are securely founded on the principle of equality – equality before the law, equality of rights – and from that basis they can proceed to create conditions for the protection and expression of liberty within the law. Citizens are defended from each other and from their government, which fulfils a delegated function and does not enjoy a superior status – since it exists only through the common popular consent that also supports the law.

Democratic systems rely heavily on two universal ideas – equality and reciprocity – that sit easily with a range of traditional philosophical 'goods', such as justice, liberty and proportionality. It would be a mistake, however, to imagine that any democratic system actually dispenses these things by itself. Again, another great merit of democracy is that it allots human beings a set of responsible roles, unlike ideological systems which reduce human agency in favour of superhuman standards.

Freedom of conscience and freedom of speech are vital parts of enabling such roles to be played, as are free exchange of goods and a degree of property rights. This last is more controversial than the rest. Eighteenth century proto-liberal thinkers believed that the protection of private property was the bedrock of political liberty. They were primarily thinking of real property – land – but there is still a massive presumption in liberal thinking in favour of the existence and protection of the institution of private property, and for a while this became the touchstone issue between liberal and socialist thinking. From the liberal angle, if an individual can be dispossessed by either the state or brigandage, civil society cannot grow or prosper. From the socialist viewpoint, private property enshrines inequality, and the desire to protect and increase it corrupts society. In India, the retreat from the right to hold property to the right not to be unlawfully dispossessed of it was prompted by unease on this account, related to the historic hostility to the 'zamindari' system.

In Europe during the eighteenth century, private property was seen as a guarantee of freedom against state power. In the modern world, property is seen not as the guarantor of liberty but as the reward of personal ambition. Thus we have returned to an ancient idea – the acceptance of inequality. Inequality is not as unpopular as it used to be, now that general levels of wealth are higher, and equality before the law is an absolute staple in all civilized societies.

Eighteenth century writers who promoted the sacredness of property, such as Adam Smith and David Hume, were perfectly willing to accept that the principle of property went hand in hand with the principle of inequality. They did not see this as a good thing, but simply as necessary or unavoidable. Their descendants in centre-left parties now frequently toe the same line, and do not talk of more equality but of less inequality. The principal component of the argument has changed its polarity under the pressure of experience.

The best examples of democratic practice are now all coupled with the word liberal, for liberal democracy is more honest to itself than most forms of socialist democracy, which tend to excuse their failures by blaming adverse circumstances rather than admitting defects in basic principles. It is not a strong argument to keep insisting that the system you advocate is ideal and would work to everyone's satisfaction if it wasn't for all the stubborn and unreformed people who stop it from succeeding.

But democracy has a persistent weakness in this area – its relative aversion to boastfulness – compared to its rivals. Democracy's virtues can only be showcased in a very diffuse way. Democracies are less keen on monuments and parades; their achievements are generally quieter and more gradual. Nor do they go in for enormous, orchestrated public displays of loyalty. Loyalty is a provisional matter in a healthy democracy. Citizens can change their minds; they do not over-invest in leaders or regard them as somehow gifted with a special, instinctive understanding of the people's best interests. Strong leaders with genuine social empathy are rare; they tend to rely on a highly developed sense of their own interests and a good understanding of how to promote them within their local conditions.

In a democracy, a citizen's loyalty is always divided between visions of a collective future and specific things in the immediate here and now. Skilful politicians give us a little of both – the hope for jam tomorrow and at least a little jam today. As a public process this is not unhealthy. Hope is a binding thing, and insecurity is no kind of basis for community feeling. Dictators offer only a parody of hope by comparison. Voters in a democracy make rational assessments about how their own interests and the wider interests of the community will interact. This is not an easy habit to acquire, and its outcomes are not certain, but once acquired it is the best guarantor of continued civic intelligence that there is.

Democracy is, as Abraham Lincoln deftly summed it up, 'government of the people, by the people, for the people'. What he missed out was how squarely this arrangement rests on agreement *between* the people – mutual trust, reciprocal recognition, shared prosperity. Confidence is the essential element of the rope trick. In a democracy, the texture of day-to-day affairs can be rough, but it tends to be kinder to citizens in isolation. Non-democratic systems have supposedly smoother running, but their impact on individual citizens can be far more severe.

Privileged with a little more experience than Lincoln, we can attempt another formulation: Democracy is self-government, but it only works well when it *feels* like self-government.

Part 2

Democracy in India

Historians of the left, especially in India, have been puzzled for years by the essentially conservative nature of India's national liberation struggle. Why, they ask, if it was a popular mass movement, did it not usher in radical social change?

One answer to this question has been supplied by 'subaltern' writers such as Ranajit Guha and Partha Chatterjee, who see the nationalist leaders as 'bourgeois' and accuse them of betraying the aspirations of the masses. But this is simply another way of saying that India should have had a 'proper' revolution to coincide with independence, and it is not so much a historical insight as an indiscriminate stricture on a large number of people.

So why was India's struggle for liberation so markedly un-ideological, especially by the standards of other regional anti-colonial movements such as in Indo-China? Why was the end of imperialism not accompanied by a social revolution? We can answer this without condemning the freedom movement as somehow inauthentic by picking out the strong strand of pragmatism that guided its leaders. This was not some kind of aberration. Mainstream Indian politics remains generally pragmatic to this day, yielding little space to truly ideological parties.

If we view the pre-independence Congress as the product of an under-politicized nation, then its general pragmatism makes good sense. Here was an ad-hoc body striving for practical ends through practical means, while challenging an enemy that raised no insuperable ideological barriers to Indian self-government. The British argument was that Indians were not yet ready to rule themselves;

the Indian riposte was to behave responsibly. The ultimate Congress objective was always to take possession of the governmental machine without damaging it, and this acted as a running restraint on the range of actions and attitudes that the movement chose to adopt. The political leadership was also of an elite nature, with little taste for massive social change. Finally, the only way that the Congress could straddle all India was from above, which imbued the party with an aversion to extreme lines of policy.

Here, then, are three reasons why the Congress never became a revolutionary body. But there is another, which carries across 1947 and beyond, and it concerns the political application of the ancient Indian concept of dharma.

While the adoption of nationalism acted as a galvanizing force in the struggle against colonial subjection, its arrival was followed by something rather more important – a revolution in the understanding of social injustice. Within the 'orthodox' tradition', the internal connectedness of Indian society had always been understood in terms of hierarchy, but the arrival of liberal values, with their assumptions about equality, inspired a new sense of general social obligation. Coupled with an emerging consciousness of nationhood, this created a new national political body – the Congress, while giving it a programme that looked beyond simple liberation.

But what kind of political discussions would arise in a country full of poor people who were about to exercise collective political power for the first time? This was a challenge that had never been faced elsewhere. Here lies the unique experience of Indian democracy – that it has been conducted in the presence of so much poverty.

What resulted was the paradox that the political classes in India took on the burden of addressing poverty, but ended up depending on it for sustenance.

DHARMA, INJUSTICE AND PRAGMATISM

Standard accounts tell us that the Indian National Congress grew up around imported ideas of liberalism and nationalism. This is true up to a point, but it does little to explain the subsequent development of Indian politics, or the twists and turns in the internal affairs of the Congress, either before or after independence.

A deeper and more complete way to understand the Congress revolves around the position that dharma holds in the fabric of Indian life, and the way that dharma and pragmatism are very closely linked. Dharma is an understanding of the world 'as it is', not as it 'should' be. Dharma in its purest form dictates that it is not in the power of human beings to make the world better by changing anything in it, or making people behave in new ways. Dharma is an explanation of what is established, not a critique of it. Indeed, it stands as a warning *not* to change it.

Dharma is simply the doctrine that individuals should conform to their allotted 'role' – the assignment they must fulfil. It is not concerned with moral 'improvement'. Dharma is the law of right action, and it is so for pragmatic reasons; dharma is supposed to have benign consequences – to pay dividends within society now, and to better the condition of individuals in future incarnations.

Christianity had a much more critical view of human nature and of society. It taught that the standard range of human behaviour, with all its social, sexual and economic vices, is offensive to God, for He made us perfect, and we 'fell'. The influence this had on Western political philosophy has been traced and is clear; modern politics of the liberal tradition grew out of a discontent with the world, which generated a determination to change it, for moral reasons.

In the dharmic view, however, human behaviour is only judged in context – as whether it is the correct thing to do in specific circumstances. Why we should do these things is a matter of practicality and self-interest, and related to outcomes; a matter of pragmatism, not of universal morality. The one great book of Hindu political philosophy is the *Arthashastra*, and a more pragmatic book has never been written.

Pre-colonial India did not have politics in the modern sense; it had social arrangements. The dominant ideas in Indian intellectual life were about accepting the social and political order, not changing it.

In such an intellectual context liberty meant little, and equality was an empty idea, clearly not in concordance with life as it is experienced. Fraternity was localized and specific. How, then, could liberalism have taken root in this soil?

The experience of colonial rule fundamentally changed the Indian notion of justice; it became the prime national demand, eventually to enjoy an honoured place atop the new constitution. The imported version of justice that arrived with British courts, and the positive law they enforced, was a real break with indigenous traditions because it ran so clearly against acceptance of the world as it is, and this duly had an influence on the political demands of Indians, though much less on internal social relations within Indian society.

Europeans gladly accepted that the world was not perfect; religiously speaking, that was the central point of their beliefs. At the heart of European religion and law was consciousness of the guilt of our imperfection. This always created conceptual problems, about how an omnipotent God could have made a world that is imperfect, filled with people who are imperfect. Much convoluted theology resulted. But the central dissatisfaction with things-as-they-are was very clear, and was repeatedly expressed in attempts to ameliorate this world through religious social teaching, teleological and eschatological theology, and even statute law. Indians though, rather than indulging in moral self-criticism, simply observed correct ritual and displayed piety. All was as it was, they thought, because it was meant to be like that.

These two attitudes were bound to play out differently in politics, and before 1885, the year the Congress was founded, they did. Even the 1857 Uprising was an attempt at restoration, at putting things back to how they were, not making them better according to some new standard.

A dharmic society is one in which people live seemly lives in their own specific ways. Good is not a fixed value, and bad is something that the cosmos takes care of in a teaching process of its own. British norms of justice introduced an idea of equality in law, which was alien to Hindu tradition, and was not entirely compatible with sharia law either. Indeed, equality in the courts was a grievance of traditionalists within Indian society, who could not see the justice of taking a poor man's word against a raja's. After that time, many progressive Indians began to view the whole British notion of justice as hypocritical, because judges were mostly, and juries were always, white, and Indians had no say in the creation of the laws that were being enforced.

All this meant that the development of modern politics in India grew up with a strong sense of collective injustice; it fitted well with what the British were doing to India as a whole. For religious conservatives, the offence was not only that kshatriyas could not rule, but also that shudras were learning to read and write. For liberal nationalists the political, economic and legal inequalities of colonial rule were clearly inconsistent and unjust.

The offence given was inclusive. For the first time Indians had one thing in common, which was not to be involved in their own government, and this alienated all Indians, no matter whether they were collaborating with the Raj or not; there were always fixed limits to what any Indian could do, or become. Here was a new unity in Indian experience, expressed in a variety of regional and national movements that ran in parallel with the Congress. The commonality of experience – of types and degrees of injustice – inevitably drew the nationalist movement into mass politics, as a way to bring pressure on the Raj. This process was further enhanced by M.K. Gandhi, who added spiritual awakening to the mix – again, a uniquely Indian refinement within a popular political mobilization.

There were, of course, multiple distinct fragments and plenty of contradictions within the broad movement that resulted, but the Congress managed to contain them all while maintaining its nationalist coherence. Pragmatism was a vital ingredient in this, and became perhaps the most important element in the Congress project, because it acted in several ways on the leadership and was a distinct influence on both Gandhi and Jawaharlal Nehru.

Gandhi rode the wave of popular discontent while preaching a kind of revolutionary universalism that was disturbing to many senior

Congressmen. But they let him proceed, content in the pragmatic realization that he was discomforting the British. And Gandhi himself was consistently pragmatic in the way he led the movement. Sometimes those around him felt that his decisions were inconsistent and betrayed a lack of determination. In reality he was very accepting of circumstances, and remained realistic about what he thought he could achieve at any point.

One crucial thing that enabled him to energize and lead such a broad movement was the way he indigenized a central aspect of democratic theory; he rebranded self-government as 'swaraj' and reoriented it not so much as a matter of democratic inclusion but as a vital part of spiritual enlightenment, as a fulfilment of dharma – taking responsibility for one's actions and conduct. This was a message that could appeal to both the masses and to individuals, and its implications obviated the need for social revolution. Gandhi was a popular leader preaching personal revolution.

Within the limits of his two unshakeable ideas, non-violence and swaraj, Gandhi's leadership and his philosophy in action still remained essentially pragmatic, a trait that has since opened his conduct to all sorts of unkind interpretations – that he lacked principles, that he was a deceiver, that he was incoherent, dishonest, and so forth. Politically, he remained the perfect outsider, and his general approach, since labelled Gandhism, was never consistent or clear enough to be converted easily into a programme of government. But dharma and pragmatism eventually triumphed through the Congress, and in the end its golden child was not Gandhi, but Nehru.

Jawaharlal Nehru was the most 'socialist' of all the major Indian leaders, with the possible exception of Subhas Chandra Bose. But when he finally had access to executive authority, his 'socialism' was distinctly limited. The programme he pieced together was not only coloured by a host of practical considerations, but it was also neither doctrinaire nor inflexible in comparison to any of the models he could have taken from the twentieth century's socialist states. He was, in fact, rather humbly accepting of the limitations that his times, his country and his party laid upon him. When confronted with the problems of ruling postcolonial India, he quailed at the idea of making a perfect world out of imperfect humans. The choices he made – in welfare provision, import substitution, industrialization and broad civic freedoms – were all compromises in the gallery of socialist options. He was a man of principle who repeatedly made pragmatic choices.

The true legacy of the pre-independence Congress was thus neither Gandhism nor socialism; it was pragmatism – the willingness to identify and solve problems in the here-and-now. This dictated everything from all-India nationalism to the acceptance of Partition. After independence the Congress found it difficult to relinquish its central role in national life, and too easily believed for too long that it represented India by its very existence, and that the fate of the nation was intimately bound to the fate of the party. Its pragmatism converted itself into a compulsion to win elections, which over the succeeding decades led the party to portray itself variously as socialist or neo-liberal, democratic or dynastic, strictly secular or religiously sensitive, as circumstances required. Ironically, the one thing Congress never adopted was 'the Gandhian path', which was a prominent element of the Janata Party's anti-Congress platform in 1977.

Mainstream Indian politics has always retained its indigenous basis, as Gandhi and Nehru both illustrate. Few in India have taken foreign ideas off the peg, and in recent years those that have done so in extreme forms, such as the Maoist Naxalites, have only found support among those whom modern India has most obviously and systematically failed. Across history, revolution seems to appeal to only a small fringe of Indian society, and in recent times the degree of distance between major political opinions is very much in line with the parameters of debate in settled democracies all over the world. So much so that newly elected governments in India have often continued or finished off the work of their predecessors, which they obstructed while in opposition. And parties are all very flexible when it comes to thrashing out deals that allow access to power. Even the very lowest in society – the supporters of caste parties – seem to prefer knick-knacks and kickbacks to social revolution.

How did all this come about?

1857–1947: COLONIAL BEGINNINGS

The story of modern democracy in India is conventionally linked to the rise of the Indian National Congress, founded in 1885. This is broadly correct, but the formation of the Congress actually marked the adoption not of democracy as we understand it now but of liberal nationalism. The early Congress was not politically more advanced in demands for franchise extension than British liberals of the same era. It was an elite professional and intellectual grouping, demanding a range of practical governmental reforms including greater political inclusion for its members. Indeed, it was so little concerned with, and even sometimes opposed to, peasant interests that successive viceroys felt confident in presenting the British Raj as a more genuine protector of poor 'voiceless' Indians in matters such as education and land tenancy than the smartly dressed Congress-wallahs.

But the birth of the Congress did represent one unmistakeable development in Indian political thinking – the permanent and irreversible rejection of monarchy as an appropriate means to express the character and aspirations of the Indian people. The Congress asserted that India was a nation – a body of people with the right to govern itself, and that Indians collectively had the right to determine their own form of government. Although these ideas mirrored European nationalism of the same era, the Congress, unlike many European movements, never flirted with monarchical forms. The collective, consensual model of national self-determination was fixed early on and forever.

Indians swore off the institution of monarchy after 1857 and, despite a superabundance of princely houses and potential royal figureheads, the concept of personal rule was never seriously resurrected in nationalist thinking. Once Bahadur Shah Zafar had been deported in 1858, the monarchs of India would be British by blood and right, not Indian. After the imposition of a distant empress in 1877, the appearance of the Congress eight years later ensured that the only way forward for the Indian nation was under some form of inclusive, democratic system. Originally conceived as a representative national forum, the Congress was a kind of Parliament in waiting; it always proceeded by discussion and majority decisions, and it held all its meetings in public. This inclusive ethos ensured that the culture of representation and debate became a permanent part of Indian politics.

With Congress leaders focused on the rights of the nation, the process of deciding what exactly the nation was could begin. This was not without its difficulties, some of which were still unresolved in 1947, but the general approach adopted by the Congress pointed India's political development in a very definite direction towards popular, democratic sovereignty.

The main obstacle was British colonial rule, which slowly addressed the demand for representative government with reform packages in 1892, 1909, 1919 and 1935. The successive expansions of the electoral franchise that these delivered never quite caught up with conditions in Britain, but the determination to hold back from universal electoral inclusion was not coming from the Congress, which, after the agitation against the partition of Bengal in 1905, became increasingly popularist.

Reform of the Raj set up elaborate systems that managed to look more inclusive of Indian opinion while preserving government control. They featured a variety of restricted franchises based on all sorts of special qualifications, including religion, income, ethnicity/race, education and even gender. Such elaborate precautions were not considered necessary in contemporary Britain, where franchise restrictions based on anything other than age were abandoned by 1918.

India's great leap into popular democracy soon arrived, but it was not the doing of the British, though it overlapped with the implementation of the Montagu–Chelmsford Reforms of 1919, which introduced a degree of provincial autonomy. Instead it came in the shape of the Non-Cooperation Movement of 1920–22, led by M.K. Gandhi. It was Gandhi who wrought an irreversible change in Indian politics by involving the masses in a direct and non-ideological way that was easily understood and was concerned with a kind of uplift, even holiness, free from the taint of economic motives. Gandhi was concerned – even preoccupied – with remaining directly in touch with the Indian masses; he lived and walked among them. He also maintained a network of grass-roots activists, and this helped the independence movement retain its focus on practicalities.

In the wake of the general Gandhian mobilization there were other, more sectional awakenings. Through the 1920s, left-wing and communist groups appeared in India, some with democratic ambitions and some dedicated to armed, terrorist struggle. They all, however, remained small. There was also an upsurge in specifically Hindu politics, conducted within formal institutions by the Hindu Mahasabha, and outside by the RSS, a 'cultural' organization dedicated to the training and disciplining of young Hindus with the object of reconnecting them with their pre-colonial identity. Founded in 1925, the RSS had no electoral ambitions and was not run on democratic lines. Instead it mixed the ethos of the British Boy Scouts with the more militaristic national movements, then becoming popular in parts of Europe; it was disciplined, religious and supremacist.

Fresh energy also appeared on the other side of the Hindu–Muslim divide, where the counterpart of the Hindu Mahasabha was the Muslim League. Originally formed in 1906 in response to the imminent arrival of electoral politics, due in 1909, the League did not start out as a party of democratic mobilization; it was led by hereditary landowners. Muslims who were primarily nationalists could opt to join the Congress, and some did. But democratic ideals held little appeal to those Muslims who felt they needed separate representation as Indian politics became more national and democratic.

Acknowledging the permanent minority status of Muslims within India, the Muslim League at first sought ways to protect Muslim interests by devising constitutional safeguards. Through the late 1920s these were repeatedly rejected by the Congress as unnecessary or divisive. This ensured that the issue of effective representation for Muslims became a matter of converting a permanent minority within Greater India to a permanent majority within a new structure, eventually to be called Pakistan. Thus the Muslim League had a dual life as a minority/majority movement; it held ambivalent views about accepting existing political boundaries and about who should and should not be included in any headcount. Muhammad Ali Jinnah, the undisputed leader of the movement from the mid-1930s, wrestled with these issues, but always claimed to be a democrat. His most successful strategy, however, was not in touting for votes; it was in creating a new state around his supporters.

In 1928 the Nehru Report was drawn up by a cross-party committee of nationalist politicians to outline how an independent India would run its affairs. It was the first, detailed draft of a future Indian constitution, and it was guarded on the exact details of the electoral franchise; it merely expressed the wish that it should be as extensive as possible. But the main characteristic features of modern democracy were all present – popular sovereignty, representative institutions and full equality of civil rights for all. Its main points were adopted by the Congress via the Fundamental Rights Resolution at Karachi in 1931.

The freedom movement then became a mass-based democratic force, with detailed, attainable national demands. Despite some wobbles along the way – including disputes over leadership and responses to the Second World War – Gandhi shepherded the movement until around 1945, when the main leadership cadre was released from wartime detention and elections were held.

Gandhi was not a convinced democrat himself. He was uneasy about the motivations of majority groups and believed that minorities were more likely to be guided by true moral impulses. In *Hind Swaraj* he had only harsh words for parliaments and parties, recommending instead leadership by 'a few good men'. But he was happy to see India united in a morally coherent and elevating cause, and he threw the stewardship of popular sovereignty open to all as a joint enterprise. He was not concerned with arcane disputes about who was and was not part of the nation. For him, everyone who lived in India was an Indian, regardless of creed, caste or language; none were to be excluded, none left behind. This graceful latitude did not feature widely in European nationalisms, which had often thrived on sensitivity to minute differences in language, culture and ethnicity, and it can be said to represent a truly Indian turn in India's democratic journey.

Gandhi had two things that European nationalists generally did not; one was a faith in *all* humanity, not just one branch of it that was deemed to deserve special consideration. The other was a conviction that power, economic or political, was better shared and dispersed than concentrated. He wanted India to be governed by thousands of small village councils – panchayats. In such a situation, people would have little power to do each other harm, and would be more likely to be rightly guided by their inner voices.

The movement headed by the Congress was national, democratic and peaceful, and India was eventually liberated not by an army or a secretive clique of revolutionaries. The transfer of power was somewhat chaotic and contained elements that were profoundly undemocratic, but the first Congress government came in on a platform of mass participation, and with a declared intention, voiced repeatedly by its senior leadership, to reform India's social and economic fabric.

1947–1950: LAYING THE FOUNDATION

Indians finally began to take control of their own destiny through a Constituent Assembly, convened in July and August 1946 under the provisions of the British Cabinet Mission Plan. It was intended to be an all-India organ, but events overtook it, and when it finally met as a fully sovereign body in the early hours of 15 August 1947, it represented not all India but only those areas that had not opted for Pakistan.

The Assembly then worked for three years to give expression to the aspirations of new India, whose people now needed to replace the heady unity of opposition to the British with a workable consensus on practical measures. Partly because of the dominance of Congress, which had been latitudinarian and inclusive, and partly owing to the authority and brilliance of a few individual figures, the debates on the new constitution were lively but not acrimonious, and the potentially divisive major issues – such as language and caste reservations – did not prove unduly troublesome. The constructive leadership provided by B.R. Ambedkar, Vallabhbhai Patel and Jawaharlal Nehru are regularly cited as crucial. These men ensured that the new India would have a rounded and unified system of centralized, secular, mass democracy.

What emerged from the deliberations was a very long document, consisting of 395 Articles and numerous schedules. The system it defined was modern and liberal in all key respects. It adopted institutions and devices from other major democracies, as suggested by the assembly's Constitutional Advisor Sir B.N. Rau, and it drew on the accumulated experience of running the Congress as a national body. The results paid little heed to the traditional wing of Indian opinion; the new state was egalitarian, it did not privilege the majority faith community, and its legal system was based on English Common Law and Parliamentary statutes. It was not very Gandhian either; government was powerful and highly centralized, and prohibition of alcohol was no more than an aspiration.

India was declared to be a sovereign, federal republic. All three of these terms were important, and all signalled new beginnings. However, purely as a matter of convenience, India accepted Dominion Status within the British Commonwealth. This was something that the Congress had opposed since 1930, a hostility reconfirmed by Nehru himself as recently as April 1947. But as part of the Partition process, Congress accepted Commonwealth membership because of its practical advantages, and because by that date it effectively meant complete sovereign autonomy; any member state could leave if it so wished. It did, however, mean recognizing the British monarch as nominal head of state, and before the new constitution was fully adopted, India was governed in the interim by a Governor-General appointed in London. This was not acceptable as a long-term solution, and Nehru then became instrumental in establishing that the Commonwealth was a purely voluntary grouping and did not imply any permanent or necessary link to the British Crown. He managed to get the word 'British' removed from the title of the Commonwealth in 1949 and brokered an agreement that downsized the role of the British monarchy to a position as simply the 'head' of the Commonwealth.

India was then free to become a sovereign republic, independent and autonomous in all respects.

The new constitution, formally adopted on 26 January 1950, contained some potentially contradictory elements, but it was clear in its intentions and practical in its details. Its structure was complex, with a careful distribution of governmental powers that acknowledged regional diversity but was clearly biased in favour of the central authority in New Delhi. Nehru, Patel and Ambedkar all had slightly different views on the relative merits of different schemes of governance, but all were solidly behind the idea that India should opt for a unitary structure with a strong central presence to hold the country together, while acknowledging the rights of the federal units – states, as they were now called – to determine the details of their own affairs in matters including law and order, education, agriculture and local government. Politically, however, the system remained highly centralized. The central government created the states, not the other way around, and it retained the right to modify, subdivide and rename the units of the union. It awarded itself powers to appoint state governors and to dismiss elected state governments in cases of emergency.

With the centre taking the main financial role in raising taxes and allocating funds, the most contentious area of centre–state relations in the initial debates proved to be the issue of language. Some Congress leaders, and especially Nehru, were determined to rid the newly decolonized country of English and to adopt Hindi in its stead. This seemed a sound move in terms of administrative efficiency, and as an aid to nation-building. But regional sentiments were strong, and many in South India were determined to resist the imposition of Hindi, which had never been the lingua franca of the region and was unknown to a very large proportion of the population. A compromise was reached, whereby English would remain in use in inter-provincial official business for 15 years.

As a result, India ended up with 22 official languages in state business, and 14 scripts, while retaining the option to use English. This was, in some ways, very much a taste of what was to come in the Indian republic – that it would be a broad and diverse country, where the limits to uniformity were accepted, and diversity, despite all its various inconveniences, would be respected. This was yet another triumph of pragmatism.

When revision of the language issue duly came round in 1965, exactly the same arguments arose, for all the same reasons. As a compromise, any further decision was left to an indefinite future date, while a formula allowing official use of Hindi, English or the local language was put in place.

The other main bone of contention was over the need, or otherwise, to make special allowance for India's historically oppressed classes. Nehru famously announced on 13 December 1946, in the Constituent Assembly's first session, that the 'backward classes' would be given help in the new India. It was entirely typical of him to want to do this, but on that day he only announced an aspiration to do it. The details were not obvious and threatened to be highly contentious; who exactly were the backward classes, and how much help should they be given?

In addressing this issue, the Assembly outlawed the institution of untouchability – the most obviously Gandhian provision in the whole constitution. Another significant concession to the depressed classes was a range of 'reservations' – of seats in the new parliament and state assemblies, and of positions in education and government employment. This was a practice that had begun under British rule, and Dr Ambedkar eloquently urged its retention. His argument was that the introduction of full legal equality in all areas of Indian life was simply a formal declaration, and that practical means had to be found to ensure the reversal of ancestral injustices. Simply announcing that anyone could apply for places in higher education or for government jobs would not be enough; it was within the government's power to do more, and there was a moral imperative that it should. 'One man one vote' would not be enough, he insisted, to bring the necessary changes to India's social arrangements. Ambedkar's socialism eventually triumphed over the various shades of liberalism and conservatism that the Congress had always carried within it, and a 22 per cent reservation for Scheduled Tribes and Scheduled Classes was agreed, as per the British definitions of these groups in the 1935 Government of India Act.

There were three other areas where the principle of equality was sacrificed, if only temporarily. One was the prohibiting of discrimination against individuals on grounds of caste, in Article 15, which sat alongside the establishment of privileges for the depressed classes in the same article. A second was in the area of religion, where sensitivities were considered too delicate for the introduction of full legal equality in the areas of family law. So the Raj-era arrangement of leaving faith communities under their own traditional rules was continued (Article 17), with an aspiration marked for the introduction of a uniform civil code in due course (Article 44). Such a code is still awaited, and the lack of it stands as the premier indictment of modern India's commitment to universal equality. Finally the state of Jammu and Kashmir (J&K) was granted special status because of its late accession to the Union and the various complications of its demography and separate history. Article 370 reproduced the accession agreement signed in October 1947 by the state's last maharaja. J&K has enjoyed a unique, semi-autonomous position within India ever since.

The constitution that finally emerged gave India a bicameral national legislature elected on universal adult suffrage. The central government was to be headed by an executive prime minister appointed by a President, but responsible to the legislature. The President's functions were to be largely symbolic, and were roughly equivalent to those performed by the British monarch. This meant that he or she was to act on political advice while taking into account the mood of the nation as expressed through elections. The judiciary was independent, and all matters relating to the constitution were under the purview of a Supreme Court. Elections were to be supervised by an independent Election Commission.

The central government sat on top of a clutch of directly administered territories and a network of regional states, which had their own elected governments and legislatures, supervised by centrally appointed governors, who wielded powers over state governments analogous to those of the President over the national government. Local government was a state subject, so specifics were left for individual states to determine, but at district level, India was still run by magistrates and collectors, in much the same way as the British had done.

This structure took into account India's traditions and the current condition of the country. It was generally agreed that a strong centre was required for national cohesion and for the supervision of planned development. Nor did anyone seriously contest the choice of British-style 'first-past-the-post' elections. Again, strong government was the objective, and the voting system, along with the unchallenged status of the Congress as a national political organization, duly delivered strong central leadership.

The constitution was an unashamedly aspirational document. Its preamble specifically included the intention to promote the often-neglected concept of 'fraternity', in order to assure the dignity of the individual and the unity of the nation. More binding were the Fundamental Rights that it contained, seven in all, which every Indian was now entitled to demand, with legal force. These included all the civil and political rights familiar to the modern world. Less conventionally, the constitution also contained a list of Directive Principles, which did not have the force of law but were a sort of memo to future governments, indicating what the aims of the state should be. The first and most important objective, though, as set out in the preamble, was to secure justice, social, economic and political, for all citizens.

The root of the whole enterprise was the desire of Congress leaders to deliver a better, fairer life to the people across a range of legal, social and economic issues. These objectives were written into the document because many of the leaders, especially Nehru, did not believe that India's social system would readily reform itself spontaneously. India's founding fathers and mothers took their time over their work and were not cynical about the language they used, or the principles they set out. The results were not perfect, and many of their aspirations are still only partially fulfilled, perhaps because the liberal, inclusive vision of the freedom movement's leaders came to seem a little too generous in the minds of many, once the shadow of colonial rule had receded.

But the task was completed in remarkably consensual fashion, and much of what was agreed has worked much better than many expected.

1950–1964: NEHRU AND CONGRESS RAJ

The new Indian state faced formidable difficulties. It was under-resourced and its inhabitants were underfed, unhealthy and under-educated. Life expectancy was a miserable 27 years; literacy stood at a scandalous 12 per cent. There were also potential conflicts between the centre and states, and between individuals and their entitlements to various kinds of freedoms.

Among all the difficulties, India had one piece of good fortune in the sincere commitment of Jawaharlal Nehru to the democratic process. It was Nehru who first fully articulated the modern Indian truism that democracy is actually the *only* way that India can be run, and that it is therefore absolutely necessary that individual Indians continuously express their commitment to supporting the nation through the exercise of tolerance – a commitment to what he called 'unity in diversity'. This paradox – one of many in Indian politics – essentially became the founding principle of the modern Indian state.

Nehru saw off a challenge for the party presidency from a traditionalist right-winger, P.D. Tandon, in 1950, and then led the Congress into the election of 1951–52, from which it emerged as by far the largest party. He then dominated the Congress, which itself went on to dominate national politics to such a degree that India in this era is sometimes called a one-party state; it would be more accurate, however, to call it a state with only one large party. This virtual monopoly brought a degree of welcome cohesion to national affairs at a time when patterns were still to be set, but it also created a situation in which those who were politically ambitious had only one destination of choice. The party's membership, which tripled between 1945 and 1950, contained many people who were not primarily interested in ideology or public service but were drawn to the perquisites of office. Through its dominance, the Congress became a vehicle of patronage as much as of public policy.

The problems that confronted the leadership were extensive: economic development; national integration; industrial management; the creation of modern infrastructure; the improvement of health and education. Under Nehru's management, solutions to these difficulties were sought in what eventually came to be known as 'Nehruvian socialism', though several features of this strategy were not particularly socialist, at least not by the standards of the day. Nehru simply took the state as a ready tool to hand; he was not a great believer in massive exertions of central power, and although he placed much faith in planning, he was more of a gradualist than a revolutionary. But his ideals were certainly of a left-progressive sort, with a commitment to greater social justice in the broadest sense.

Though inclined to dogmatism as a younger man, by the time he came to hold executive power he had shed most of the certainties of his youth and had come to believe sincerely in the indefinable essence of India, which inspired him more than Marxist economic theory. His best, most mature writing, as in *The Discovery of India* (1946), is all about this cultural–political theme. For him, India's future was as a diverse, plural society, and whenever he encountered India's complex essence, he was prepared to rein in whatever autocratic tendencies he still had, being aware of the value of consensus and conscious of the example that his own conduct would set.

It is a well-established game to try to label Nehru's outlook in some way or another. He was an educated, rather patrician man, a professed friend of the common people who nevertheless kept his distance from popular culture. He certainly seems an anomalous figure: independent India's first leader, but still recognizably British in so many aspects of his tastes, views and character. Yet he was also a man who had been imprisoned for ten years by the British, and he remained determined to erase their alien imprint from India in every way he could.

A much more pragmatic man than many Indians today will allow, his genius found distinct expression in both economics and politics. In economics he faced an impossible dilemma. He wished to free India, a capital-starved country, from industrial backwardness, while having no money with which to do so. At the same time he had a dread of selling India back to the purveyors of international capital. Self-reliance and import substitution was the answer, an answer to which there was no obvious alternative that could have delivered real and immediate progress to India's millions.

In politics he advocated and exemplified democratic inclusion, by both word and deed. He was respectful to opponents and included a substantial number of non-Congress figures in his first cabinet. He un-banned the RSS, proscribed after the assassination of Gandhi in 1948, and he was happy to allow the Communists to run in the 1951 elections once they had renounced violence. His friends portrayed him as a prime minister who liked to lead through consensus. One long-serving minister could not recall a single vote being taken in cabinet between 1951 and 1956. This is, however, a slightly ambiguous compliment to have paid him; it can stand equally convincingly as evidence of massive personal domination as of sweet reasonableness. But in his defence, he could take defeat on the chin, like when he had to in 1958, over his wish to create farming cooperatives. Once farmers and some of his Congress colleagues had combined behind Charan Singh to oppose the measure, he laid it aside, declaring coercion to be unthinkable.

He also reversed himself on the subject of language. Despite the compromise reached by the Constituent Assembly, the issue did not die away as a matter of local controversy, because the large provinces of British India, which were provisionally retained after independence, bore no relation to the details of their populations. Demands increased for smaller states based on language, most prominently in Andhra, where Potti Sreeramulu, a prominent social activist, fasted until death in 1952. After a commission and a great deal of protest, India was divided into 14 large 'linguistic' states in 1956. Nehru was not keen on the process because it threatened to turn into a never-ending parade of new demands and sub-divisions, but he conceded the point. He also accepted defeat over the national link language, which he had always wanted to be Hindi. The original opponents of Hindi had still not mellowed by 1963, and he allowed, as one of his last acts in government, that English would provisionally remain an official medium of interstate business. It still is.

Despite the dominance of the Congress, it was clear from very early on that Indians were not of one mind on many important issues. The Congress was the largest political organ, but there were plenty of alternate visions of India that could not find, or did not want, a place within the party. As a consequence, Nehru and the Congress faced opposition from both inside and outside electoral politics.

Prominent socialists within the Congress declared that it was insufficiently radical and that they could no longer support it, leaving en masse in 1948. These included Ram Manohar Lohia and Jayaprakash Narayan, both of whom went on to have long, complicated and influential careers in left-wing, anti-Congress politics. J.B. Kripalani, a former Congress president, also left the party in 1950 to pursue more socialist objectives, disillusioned with what he perceived as Nehru's lack of engagement with the party's lower ranks and his apparent unconcern for peasants.

Further to the left, communism presented a more direct challenge, with an armed insurrection in Telangana from 1946 that managed to set up 'parallel governments' in several districts. Originally against landlords and the Nizam of Hyderabad, the struggle proceeded to set itself against the whole bourgeois Indian state. It continued till October 1951, when it was called off after consultations with Moscow by the Communist Party of India (CPI). The CPI's adoption of a milder line bore fruit when it became the largest opposition party at the 1951–52 elections, albeit with only 16 seats. It then suffered a major split in 1964, after which it never threatened to gain power at national level, though the moderate wing, the CPI-Marxist (CPI-M), did well in the provinces, principally Kerala and West Bengal.

The Congress faced competition and criticism from the right too. A private enterprise alliance opposed to central state planning became the Swatantra Party in 1959, whose luminaries included another veteran Congressman, C. Rajagopalachari. Further to the right, a range of more explicitly Hindu parties also found support, including the Jana Sangh, backed by the RSS. As the standard-bearer of ideological Hindu nationalism, the Jana Sangh had a strong core of support, but it failed to reach out far beyond it and became embroiled in internal debates about strategy and the precise relationship of the party with the RSS cadre. Syama Prasad Mookerjee, the party's first leader, was not an RSS man, but its next star, Deendayal Upadhyaya, was. The BJP was to inherit this fault line, and the party's detractors are still suspicious about the precise relationship between the 'cultural' and 'political' wings of the organization.

None of the ideological or traditionalist parties gained much national traction, and it was only as the Congress slowly disintegrated over the next 40 years that the current full range of Indian political parties could find electoral space for themselves, most dramatically at regional level.

The Congress hegemony was seriously breached for the first time in the newly formed state of Kerala in 1957, when assembly elections gave the Communists a majority. Significantly for the long-term future of the Indian state, Nehru was forced to interfere directly in 1959, when he unseated the Communist administration which had gone too far and too fast in its reform programmes, antagonizing local landlords with land redistribution proposals and whipping up a storm of resistance to changes in education. The Communists, who had risen to power largely through the mobilization of lower castes, had overstepped public tolerance to such a degree that civil order was threatened – or so it appeared. Nehru availed himself of his emergency powers to call for fresh state elections when the state governor (his own appointee) reported that government had broken down.

The Communists had pulled off a classic majoritarian coup, using an electoral victory as a general permission to ignore the wishes of the minority – in this case the upper castes and middle classes, whose children were now to be taught a Communist syllabus by Communist teachers. Nehru then executed an authoritarian countercoup, and subjected the state to President's Rule pending new elections, which the Communists lost. This established two clear principles: that politicians at the centre could snuff out regional dissent, and that the greater democracy of the nation would override the smaller democracy of the region. Indian federalism was to be a fragile and provisional ideal over the coming decades.

There was another lesson hidden in the events of 1959: electoral majorities in states were no protection from the centre if they were vigorously challenged in the streets. Much of the agitation in Kerala was organized and intensified by Congress members, and the political benefits ultimately accrued to the party. Public disorder – supplied as necessary – was established as an effective tool of party contestation. Though elections became an immovable part of India's public life, riot and mayhem were also to become familiar political devices. Political scientist Paul Brass was later to write of an 'institutionalized riot system' across north India in the 1990s.[33]

But through the 1950s India remained remarkably stable for a new state, and Congress dominance had a great deal to do with this boon. The veneer of consensus was undoubtedly good for national cohesion at such an early stage, and one of Nehru's great triumphs was that under his stewardship the sustained dominance of a successful party with an unchallenged leader did not lead to dictatorship. The passage of three orderly elections, in 1951–52, 1957 and 1962, allowed time to let the system bed in. People voted and saw their votes counted fairly. This produced a 'goldilocks' moment – with not too much stability and just enough dissent, gently leading the Indian voting public into the milder sorts of democratic uncertainties. This is best illustrated by asking a counterfactual question: what if the first elections had produced deadlock, hung parliaments, heated exchanges, paralysis? Weak government can be the death of fledgling democracies. India avoided this and saw sufficient benefit from the system to stick with it.

And, it must be said, so did the politicians. This is where the Nehruvian calm actually worked against the long-term interests of

Indian democracy. The headline requirements of the system were firmly set out, and largely respected. The Election Commission worked well, the Supreme Court began to unpick some of the divergent ambitions of the written constitution, and a free press grew up and was left alone. But at lower levels of government, away from the drive for central planning and major infrastructure projects, the localism of India remained unaffected. Nehru's project to create a more socially and economically just India was left in the hands of the traditional class that had supported most of the ancestral social and economic injustices that they were now supposed to remedy. The clear devolution of powers to the states in matters of land reform and local expenditure left little likelihood that an outburst of social conscience and liberality would spring forth. Nehru, who was always primarily interested in foreign affairs and the standing of India among the comity of nations, hardly seemed to notice, or at least did little to drive the reform process harder.

There were other obstacles to social and political progress as well. The requirements of running for office placed obligations on politicians to make promises and pay back favours, and the extensive powers that government had retained from the colonial era – which seemed ideal for rapid nation-building – also came in handy for the creation of empires on a more local and personal scale. Serious scandals began to emerge from the late 1950s. In Punjab the chief minister, P.S. Kairon, was accused of vastly enriching his family, and he was only partially exonerated by an enquiry in 1964 which decided his sons had acted with his knowledge and connivance. He resigned on its publication. There were allegations against other provincial leaders, including M.L. Sukhadia in Rajasthan and Biju Patnaik in Orissa, while in Kerala C.M.R. Shankar and C.K. Govindan Nair, both of the Congress, traded accusations between them. Nor was the central government immune. In 1958 the Mundra scandal broke, concerning a series of disastrous investments by the state-owned Life Insurance Corporation in ailing businesses owned by an entrepreneur named Haridas Mundhra. These investments could not be adequately explained by anyone involved. Finance Minister T.T. Krishanamachari was forced to resign, and Mundhra went to prison.

Nehru became aware of this tendency rather late and set up the Santhanam Commission in 1962, tasked with proposing 'measures calculated to produce a social climate both amongst public servants and in the general public in which bribery and corruption may not flourish', and finding ways to secure public support for such measures.[34] It is interesting to note that Nehru understood how corruption among officials was connected to public tolerance. The Commission's report estimated that corruption was costing the country about ₹1.2 billion per annum, and the seriousness of its findings led to the setting up in 1964 of a permanent body, the Central Vigilance Commission, to monitor the problem.

The independent Indian state proved vulnerable to abuses of power from the start. As a structure it was something of a public–private partnership, inheriting all the authority of the Raj machine it had replaced, but with less of its neutrality. The more ambitious aims of the new system, including its willingness to spend more money, were left in the hands of local politicians with intimate links to their locality. They had little incentive to implement land reforms, and much incentive to spend the money where it would do most good to themselves. The temptation to favour particular projects or contractors was strong, and corrupt relationships developed all too easily. Whenever a central government delegates authority in sufficient quantity, its local agents can always find ways to evade scrutiny from both above and below. This can be a serious problem anywhere. At exactly the moment that local government began to dispense really large sums in Britain in the 1960s, corruption burgeoned in major municipalities.

Membership of the Congress slowly changed in nature. Before independence it had been a matter of idealism and sacrifice rather than of reward, but by the late 1950s the party's membership was an inventory of raw power, a register of who was already in possession of social and economic influence in the localities. The Congress was a national party primarily because it reflected who within the nation held influence; it drew the influential to it as much as it conferred influence on those who wished to gain it. The party brought together the non-revolutionary and pragmatic elements of India's political classes and became a conservative force in many ways, acting as a barrier to social change. It had never been a revolutionary party in opposition, and did not become one in government. It was able to take power at the moment of demission because it was a coherent force with a degree of responsibility – the only national body of its type. For historians keen to understand why India did not have a revolution, the social solidity that the Congress enjoyed is the answer. What happened afterwards is that social change carried on under the surface of politics, as ambitious subaltern social groups began to organize outside the Congress. These groups first emerged in full view during the Janata government of 1977–79.

Nehru's legacy was thus rather mixed. Above suspicion himself, he left a political system that was awash with public money amid opportunities to divert it to private purposes. The constitutional part of his vision – the paperwork – was in place, as was the living example he had set. But the deeper levels of economic and social progress he wanted to introduce were still some way off. Imposing socialism through the medium of the ruling classes was never likely to be a very effective strategy. But he had no choice, just as he had no alternative to trying to build up heavy industry with state backing. It was much easier to declare a democracy and build a few huge dams than it was to make innumerable small adjustments to India's social fabric.

The one very direct attempt he made to do this was his effort across 1954–56 to reform Hindu personal law, particularly in the areas of divorce and inheritance. He ultimately succeeded, in the teeth of opposition from the Hindu Mahasabha, the Jana Sangh, assorted sadhus and even the President, Rajendra Prasad. But he left the equivalent Muslim laws in place, a decision dictated by prudence rather than principle. Even the foremost Indian politician of his generation, a secularist to the marrow, was unwilling to reopen the wounds of Partition by risking giving offence to the Muslim minority. Thus the bizarre logic of daring to offend a powerful majority for reasons of high state policy, yet not daring to offend a minority on the same basis, arrived early in the history of Congress governance, and did not leave.

The Nehru years also set up two characteristic elements of Indian politics that are closely intertwined – the technocratic bent of government and the distancing of politicians from policy formation. Nehru's fondness for planning and central control, given force in 1951 by the first five year plan, inaugurated a culture of government by experts that started with P.C. Mahalanobis and came down to Manmohan Singh. The idea of state-led development, and its links to social equity, were never questioned before 1991 by any ruling party, and have only now been seriously re-examined by the Modi leadership. The intervening stasis left India's politicians with a very narrow corridor of economic manoeuvre, and their response was to talk either of non-economic issues – meaning religion and culture – or of economic sub-issues of distributive justice – meaning reservations, subsidies and handouts.

These two factors have profoundly affected the content and conduct of Indian politics ever since.

1964–89: CRISIS, WAR, EMERGENCY, DEATH, SCANDAL

In 1960, an American scholar-journalist Selig Harrison wrote a pessimistic book called *India: The Most Dangerous Decades.* Like a number of other observers he was not convinced that India's infant democracy could survive the various stresses placed upon it. But his worst prognostications – balkanization and/or a slide into permanent authoritarianism – did not materialize. This is in some ways remarkable, because after Nehru, India spent 25 years going through the most demanding rites of passage that any state can experience, including famine, financial crisis, war, riots, political lockdown, assassination and scandal at the highest levels of government. Somehow this large, poor and unruly country, with its untested system of checks and balances, strong provincial identities and hostile neighbours, managed to hold onto the central tenets of democracy and preserve its unitary form.

India survived, and emerged even from a brief period of dictatorship in 1975–77 into an era when elections, and only elections, determined who was to conduct the governance of the country. But how good that governance was going to be remained problematic. Indian democracy initially proved to be better at changing its personnel than at enhancing its responsiveness.

After three elected terms and 17 years as national leader, Jawaharlal Nehru died in 1964, to be succeeded by Lal Bahadur Shastri, who barely managed 20 months in office before he passed away. The next leader plucked from Congress ranks had initially been reluctant to enter politics and was parachuted into the premiership in 1966 as a stopgap. A group of five senior Congress figures, dubbed 'the Syndicate', nominated Indira Gandhi, Nehru's daughter, as prime minister, hoping that she had sufficient popularity to win a looming general election. She did, but only just, and her narrow victory at the polls in 1967 presaged a number of significant changes in Congress politics.

First, she felt personally insecure and vulnerable to enemies within the party, especially Morarji Desai, the senior figure within the Syndicate. This feeling prompted her to embark on what became a lifelong search for political security. Secondly, if the Congress could barely limp home relying on the old methods and policies, changes were going to have to be made.

Two factors sharpened the party's predicament. One was the generally weak state of the country. Drought and famine, coupled with poor economic performance, lent an air of crisis. Foreign aid was a short-term fix, but the way forward seemed, at least in the mind of Indira Gandhi, to be an increase in central control and an all-out assault on rural poverty. Nationalizing private sector banks and ending the state subsidy to India's princely houses were two measures designed to ease the government's cash flow and to signal her intention to modernize India at speed.

The other factor was the chronically weak state of the Congress itself. Its regional fabric was dilapidated after years of neglect and infighting, and the party's increasingly apparent failures in government had begun to alienate many of its traditional supporters among the rural classes. Mrs Gandhi compensated for this weakness in several ways that were to transform India's polity and politics.

First, she broke free of the Syndicate's control by splitting the party in 1969, losing most of what remained of the old party structure in the process. The pretext she chose is revealing. The national Presidency was vacant after the death of Zakir Hussain and she believed that Neelam Sanjiva Reddy, the official Congress candidate to succeed him, was in league with her opponents in the party. So she backed the independent candidate, V.V. Giri, who won. She thus covered her back at the centre, but only at the expense of losing much of the support she had commanded at provincial level. This manoeuvre also demonstrates to what lengths she was prepared to go to protect herself long before she faced outright opposition on the streets.

She then abandoned internal party democracy and ran her own machine from the top to ensure cohesion and, above all, personal loyalty. To the same end she developed the party's Youth Wing as a parallel framework, from which she could exclude rival influences; it became the personal fiefdom of her son Sanjay. She then set out to appeal to the masses with more radical policies, and by promoting herself as a leader who cared and got things done. This led her to interfere in state-level politics more than her predecessors had done, or had needed to do. She also went as far as to call on bureaucrats to be 'committed' – a euphemism for politicized – and to interpret the rules of seniority within the judiciary to promote sympathizers and obtain favourable judgements in the Supreme Court, which had stood in the way of several of her more radical reform initiatives.

All this demonstrated that carefully built and expensive party structures could be dispensed with, provided the slogans were right and the target audience was successfully enthused. In a country where around 60 per cent of the people were below the official poverty line, her infamous slogan '*Garibi hatao*!' made sound political sense. Electoral arithmetic trumped policy details, and the Congress party was released from ideological consistency by Mrs Gandhi's personal eminence. She broke free from local party bosses and their traditional vote banks, but as she intensified the rhetoric of elections she also raised the expectations of what governments could do. Her success showed how effective the direct connections – big personalities and simple solutions – of populism could be, and they have remained key elements of popular 'waves' in Indian elections ever since.

After her split from the traditional Congress in 1969, Indira Gandhi won a clear victory in the general election of March 1971 and then rode to even greater popularity on the back of her overwhelming victory in the war with Pakistan in December that year. But this did not exempt her from criticism, as the masses endured economic hardships and the political classes objected to her highhandedness. She experienced problems with regional unrest in Gujarat and Bihar and a prolonged national railway strike. Finally, she was found guilty of minor electoral offences in June 1975, which threatened her by nullifying her position as an MP. At this point, with her conviction yet to be appealed, she decided to impose not just President's Rule on a state (which she did 39 times over her career), but prime minister's rule on the whole country by declaring an emergency. This included the large-scale arrest and imprisonment of her political opponents – another groundbreaking strategy in independent India. By 1975, after nine years in power, it was all too easy for her to identify her own fortunes with those of the country. Surrounded by sycophants, urged on by Sanjay, and with the slogan 'India is Indira and Indira is India' ringing in her ears, the road to hubris lay invitingly open.

But she was only to learn, yet again, one of the insidious lessons of state power – that the stronger the state becomes, the less likely justice will be done. Strong law and order measures are apt to produce a degree of order, but only at the cost of undermining the law. Programmes of mass sterilization and slum clearance were pursued by Sanjay Gandhi with an enthusiasm that took them up to and beyond the limits of legality, bringing the full, unaccountable force of executive government down on some of India's poorest inhabitants in ways that made their lives even more wretched.

The Emergency, from June 1975 to January 1977, represents a major watershed in Indian democracy for three reasons. First, it completed the transition from the high-minded politics of the

Nehru era to the simple-minded politics of populism; this included converting India officially into a socialist state by inserting the word 'socialist' into the preamble of the constitution. Secondly, it unleashed a whole new range of abuses of power, with the government left to supervise itself and its underlings, a task for which it had no taste and little institutional machinery. Sanjay Gandhi held no official position in party or government and seemed answerable only to his mother, who showed no inclination to restrain him. The extent of his activities was later exposed by the Shah Commission that looked into the Emergency's excesses; he did not emerge well from its investigations. Unaccountable power on this scale has never reappeared within the Indian state. Thirdly, the net result of the 19-month period of authoritarian government was, ironically, to reinforce the popular demand for democratic change – the very thing that had prompted its imposition.

If the events of 1857–59 can be called The Uprising, the mass protests and radical popular mobilization of 1974–77, led by Jayaprakash Narayan, might be called The Awakening. The enormous upsurge of popular resentment against Indira's Congress shook the lower ranks of Indian society in a way that nothing since the agitation of 1919–22 had done. But there was a significant difference. In 1919–22 there had been a macro-politicization, the creation of a large movement, whereas the years 1974–77 marked a micro-politicization, the creation of many small movements at different levels of social and economic status. Neither religious nationalism, as later evinced by the BJP, nor revolutionary socialism, as promoted by Naxalites, ever managed to reshuffle the political pack to any similar degree. The political mobilization of the lower half of society – the 52 per cent later counted by Mandal – was both cause and effect of much of what happened in the mid-1970s. By that time, the relationships of lower-status social groups with the state had been sufficiently defined and monetized for those groups to discover and discipline themselves as political entities.

The Emergency also marks a watershed moment in the history of the Congress itself. The selection of Indira Gandhi in 1966 did not determine the development of the party; it was not yet *her* Congress. After the split in 1969, the movement ceased to be a genuinely national organ of opinion and shrank to a personal faction. During the unrest of 1974–75 it contracted even further into a dynastic duumvirate. Across the nine years of her first premiership from 1966, Indira trusted fewer and fewer of those around her and lost control of the constructive policy agenda she had inherited. She replaced it with a stubborn determination to cling to power, driven by the increasingly untenable conviction that the smaller her inner circle became, the more it was in tune with the nation. Her willingness to trust her son, and only her son, with so much unsupervised authority – matched by his willingness to take it on – marked the intellectual and spiritual death of the national Congress of Gandhi, Patel and Nehru, and the creation of Congress-II, a narrow, family concern. Though her name and her personality served to obscure this development at the time, the change was duly reflected in the fact that when the Emergency was over, the party that challenged her stood on a Gandhian platform.

New parties and a whole new political landscape thus eventually emerged from the period of the Emergency. The JP movement, in tandem with wider, global economic changes, achieved a radicalization of the less prosperous and educated classes in India, which included the galvanization of Dalit and lower caste consciousness, leading to the creation of new political structures. The first flowering of this change was the ramshackle Janata Party coalition, but the longer-term effects were clearly the creation of a large number of small regional and caste-related parties. Stars of this new generation of lower-caste leaders included Lalu Prasad Yadav, Mulayam Singh Yadav and Nitish Kumar, all of whom were to serve as chief ministers of either UP or Bihar, all of whom led their own parties, and all of whom cut their political teeth in the JP movement.

Mrs Gandhi was unaware of these deeper developments; her thoughts were all about self-preservation in the name of national security. She managed to restore order, and the country seemed collectively to recover its senses. Then, in a quite unprecedented move in the long history of dictatorship, she decided to garland her new regime by going to the polls. Why exactly she did this, and why at that particular time – at the start of 1977 is not known for sure. She must have expected to win, and may well have had a false sense of assurance about the result; having silenced all opposition voices, she had no way of knowing how deeply unpopular her government had become.

A more detailed reason why she called a poll may be connected to what she intended to do with her expected success. She may have wanted to realign the rank and file within the Congress to assure its attachment to Sanjay. By selecting candidates for lucrative Congress 'tickets', she could effectively buy a block of new supporters for her son and uncrowned political heir. An election was the natural way to carry out this stratagem, in a way that was public and sustainable. To nominate Sanjay herself would have been a gross act of public nepotism and potentially unsustainable, so the party had to be brought into line. Had she succeeded, she would effectively have found another way to avoid building a national political structure from the roots upwards.

Another explanation has been offered by veteran journalist Inder Malhotra, who wrote a biography of Indira Gandhi. He believes that she was actually forced into the poll by the over-enthusiasm of some of her supporters who wanted her to stage a constitutional coup and make herself president for life. Sanjay Gandhi apparently approved. But Indira was uncomfortable with the idea, as she preferred to remain an elected prime minister. She then set out to calm the situation by testing the temper of the Indian public without reference to Sanjay.[35] Another seasoned observer, Kuldip Nayar, concurs that the decision was hers alone and that Sanjay was not consulted.[36]

Whatever the reasons, Indian democracy was then able to pass from its worst disaster in June 1975 to its greatest triumph in March 1977, when Mrs Gandhi was trounced at the polls and replaced by a coalition that had run on the single issue of expelling her from office.

That the Janata government could then agree on little else should have come as no surprise, for the coalition was an ideologically heterogeneous grouping of opposition forces loosely connected by a commitment to the Gandhian 'path', which was contrasted in the alliance's manifesto to the road to 'national ruin' represented by Mrs Gandhi's own brand of Gandhism.

The Janata party is hard to characterize precisely, but it was an alliance naturally inclined to the promotion of farmers' interests. Its heartlands were in north India, and its principal figures – Jagjivan Ram, Morarji Desai, Charan Singh and Ramakrishna Hegde, the only southerner – were all ex-Congress leaders. This hints at another long-term trend in Indian politics, the constant bleeding of leadership talent out of the Congress, as ambitious individuals found their paths blocked by the fierce jealousy of Indira Gandhi. There was not yet a single coherent anti-Congress platform, but the Janata experiment demonstrated that there was a great deal of political space beyond Congress politics for both leaders and followers.

The Janata party enjoyed wide popularity among the newly enriched middle-ranking farmers, a group that had done well out of the Green Revolution, in progress since the late-1960s. The prosperity brought by this Revolution tended, because of its inherently high expense, to deliver its greatest benefits to those with larger plots and more capital. The same general class of rural entrepreneurs – 'bullock capitalists' – were also good at manipulating development budgets and government aid schemes to their best advantage. But the success of these farmers tended to aggravate traditional rural rivalries between various grades of landholders, farmers and labourers. The poorer end of society took on a much more complex grain, and this produced new levels of economic and political self-awareness across the Indian countryside. From then on, simply giving handouts to 'the poor' would not greatly help economic development and was likely to generate as much political resentment as gratitude.

One of Janata's main achievements – its New Industrial Policy, announced in late 1977 – not only illustrates the complex and unsatisfactory nature of the coalition, but also serves as a signpost to some of the political confusions of the next three decades. The policy was both left- and right-friendly, an odd hybrid of a kind to be found perhaps only in India. It aimed to promote cottage industries and small-scale, labour-intensive enterprises using indigenous technology, with the goal of national self-sufficiency. It was thus pro-peasant, anti-capitalist, nationalist and protectionist. That all these things were anti-Congress policies illustrates how those on the political margins were supporting economic ideas that were essentially anti-modernist and designed to promote either peasant or traditional interests, with resistance to foreign capital always an underlying motivation. The left-wing elements in these ideas never found mass support (outside of West Bengal), but many of the right-wing elements, with all their contradictions, were passed down to the BJP.

Janata's other notable act was to commission B.P. Mandal to examine the phenomenon of modern caste and the workings of caste-based reservations in employment and education. The reservations system had generated an inevitable degree of anomaly and perceived injustice at its edges, and many supporters of the non-Congress forces had grown to resent the system for not helping them. There was therefore strong pressure not to abolish reservations but to extend them. This was Mandal's brief.

But the years 1977–79 saw mostly backbiting and drift, which served only to restore the Indian public's taste for strong leadership, and Mrs Gandhi was returned to power in 1980, evidently forgiven for her excesses and newly appreciated for her talents as a leader. She was also helped by the disunity of her opponents, and this lesson was not lost on anti-Congress groupings. It became clear that with the Congress still so large and successful a body, alliances and pacts among its opponents were essential. After 1980, future challenges to Congress dominance would be better organized, both at elections and in government.

Nine years of Congress rule followed 1980's victorious return. They saw little change on the political surface and something of a vacuum in policy initiatives, but new forces were at work. Fragmentation was the new trend, with castes, classes and regions all organizing separately. Indira Gandhi's return masked the long-term decline of the Congress as a national body, and saw her effectively accelerating its decline by her own determination to cut down potential rivals within the party.

This was poignantly illustrated by her decision, after Sanjay Gandhi was killed in an air crash in 1980, to turn for support to her elder son Rajiv. He had never wanted to be a politician, but he responded to his mother's call and left his career as an airline pilot. He was certainly the helpmeet she required and not the potential rival she feared, but her decision also underlines how narrow her leadership had become. Much of the older generation of Congress leaders had ended up heading the Janata party, and most of the rest had left her in 1978, when the Congress broke into two factions, the Congress-I behind Indira, and the Congress-U led by Devraj Urs. This schism distanced her from figures of the calibre of Y.B. Chavan, Brahmananda Reddy and Sharad Pawar.

So, after 1980, Indira Gandhi found herself the unrivalled leader of a party that carried her own name, with her son at her side. This could only set the party and the nation on one course – towards a further extension of the Nehru–Gandhi line. With the 'succession' secured, she then further buttressed her own position by using fiercely nationalist rhetoric, and she remained every bit as dictatorial and inflexible in her dealings with chief ministers who either opposed her or threatened to be insufficiently loyal. She also took a very hard line against the separatist movement that appeared in Punjab. Along with her apparent abandonment of the reforming socialist drives of the 1970s, the post-Emergency Indira seemed to move noticeably to the right to counter the extensive anti-Congress forces that had emerged since the mid-1970s and their economic and cultural agendas. All these tactical adjustments did little to advance India's national well-being, but they did sterling work in consolidating her own position.

What finally brought her down was not a collapse in popularity or economic failure, or even a coup within her own party, but the side effects of her provincial policy – specifically her decision to face down the Sikh separatist movement in Punjab. Having helped to build up the radical Sikh Sant Jarnail Singh Bhindranwale as a counterpoise to the orthodox Akali Dal – her political opponents in the state – Bhindranwale proved neither grateful nor controllable. After he moved into the Golden Temple in Amritsar in 1982 and turned it into a fortress, Mrs Gandhi decided to oust him by force. The result – Operation Blue Star of June 1984 – proved successful but at a high cost in lives, structural damage and massive outrage among the Sikh community. Four months later, on 31 October, two of her Sikh bodyguards gunned her down in her own garden.

An election held after her assassination gave Rajiv Gandhi a massive majority, but this proved to be a sentimental blip, and his unprecedented Parliamentary strength, at over 400 seats, was a last hurrah for Congress hegemony.

The forces that were to end it grew from a wide range of social, economic and political causes.

Caste came into focus in a way that had not been foreseen. Nehru, and socialists in general, were all in favour of eliminating caste distinctions and the invidious social practices that came with them. Most viewed the matter as simply one of economics, and they expected caste to wither as increasing prosperity, wider education and modern attitudes took hold. But others of a leftish hue always considered this approach to be too slow, and that it missed out the vital hereditary factors that would still operate against those of lower status. More direct measures, principally reservations in employment and education, were the preferred strategy of socialist thinkers such as Ram Manohar Lohia, leader of the Samyukta Socialist Party, which merged with Charan Singh's Bharatiya Lok Dal in 1974, which in turn merged with the Janata Party in 1977.

A cruder version of this approach was adopted by the lower castes themselves as they organized into large voting unions designed to put their leaders in positions of power where they would be able to help their fellows directly. Kanshi Ram, the godfather of Dalit politics in UP, took a very simple view: power had to be acquired in whatever way possible. Democracy was a good way to do this, because the poor were so numerous. Principles, however, would be a handicap. In this non-revolutionary view, the politics of caste was best played out in hard-headed calculations of advantage. The effects of this change were to become increasingly manifest through the 1980s, especially in Bihar and UP.

There was also a rising force on the right, soon to crystallize into a middle class electoral alliance that would be socially conservative and anti-socialist. The chaotic period running from the pre-Emergency to the riots post the Babri Masjid demolition (1974–93) witnessed the condensation of an urban, aspirational and respectable constituency that did not identify with the style of politics perfected by Indira Gandhi. These people did not consider themselves as either secular or poor, and although they were not repelled by authority per se, corruption disgusted them.

Regional activism also continued to rise, with new parties representing new interests appearing all the time. Some of this was a reaction to Indira Gandhi's heavy-handed treatment of local political rivals both inside and outside the Congress, and some was a logical continuation of the language issues of the 1950s, which had activated enormously popular regional cinema industries. The wealth and fame that these enterprises created, particularly in Tamil Nadu, generated new generations of political leaders beholden to no one.

All these changes proved irreversible, and all undermined Congress dominance.

Rajiv Gandhi could not hold back the tide in his five years in government, from 1984–89. He attempted to liberalize the economy and to pacify regional and religious interests, but he was destined to fail in assembling a new Congress clientele. Sections of Indian society that had benefited from government subsidies in the rural economy had been prominent in the Janata movement, and many of them remained active in the newly formed Janata Dal, while the emerging middle classes in the cities were attracted to much of the agenda of the new BJP, formed in 1980 from the old Jana Sangh.

All the while, both Indira and Rajiv were forced to confront persistent problems of regional unrest and economic underperformance. Separatist movements scarcely yielded to either Indira's use of force or Rajiv's willingness to accommodate. Rajiv Gandhi attempted to stimulate the economy, but with disappointing results. Communal tensions then rose across 1985–86, related to a series of actions by his government. First there was the 'Shah Bano' case, which concerned alimony payments for a divorced Muslim woman. As a Congress leader, Rajiv Gandhi would have been expected to side with the widow, whose petition was upheld by the Supreme Court, but he buckled under protests from Muslim scholars, who insisted on the protected status of Islamic family law under the constitution. Forced to take action, he chose to uphold the special status of religious personal law with the Muslim Women (Protection of Rights on Divorce) Act (1986). This overturned the Supreme Court's judgement, outraging secular liberals and Hindu militants alike.

The resulting furore was followed, perhaps not entirely coincidentally, by the granting of permission in February 1986 for Hindus to reopen the Babri mosque in Ayodhya for the worship of Rama, to the consternation of the ulema. Rajiv Gandhi's attempts at appeasement thus managed to offend all religious parties with a simultaneous loss of regard in liberal secular quarters.

Finally, the high-level corruption exposed in the Bofors defence procurement scandal siphoned off the last goodwill towards the Nehru–Gandhi brand, and the voters threw out the Congress in 1989, turning again to an opposition coalition, led by former Congressman V.P. Singh, that had plenty to point at disapprovingly.

The Congress had never won an absolute majority of the national vote, and Rajiv Gandhi's high water mark of 1984 – 49 per cent on a turnout of around 63 per cent – only represented about 32 per cent in overall terms. The first-past-the-post system, combined with a great deal of social power exercised by senior Congress figures, had delivered 35 years of Congress rule out of 37 since independence. Was this democracy at work, or in abeyance? Either way, 1989 marked the end of the era of Congress majority government.

Selig Harrison was proved wrong in the short term, but after 1989 was he yet to be proved right? Without a strong Congress, what would hold the country together? Who or what could step into that massive breach? With so much organized, and even institutionalized social division in place, how could civic society – even civility itself

– be sustained? The answers were not obvious, and an era of blurred politics began.

As the period 1964–89 closed, Harrison's worries were echoed anew by Atul Kohli, in a study of Indian politics entitled *Democracy and Discontent: India's Growing Crisis of Governability* (1990). Kohli, though, was looking at India through very different eyes. He thought India had been stable in the 1950s and 1960s but was now increasingly 'not well governed' and risked descending into chaos.

By 1989 democracy in India seemed to have scraped home to, at best, a battered sort of victory; the country had yet to find a middle way between big figure leadership and big coalition chaos. Indians had sidestepped authoritarianism and shunned violent revolution in favour of the perceived virtues of democracy, whatever its shortcomings and limitations. But the relative positions of the state and those it governed had changed. Through peasant agitation and the formation of caste-based parties, the lower orders had made a calculated grab for power and had been able to get enough of it at state level to generate a degree of stability. The ballot box delivered real power and real benefits to potential revolutionary classes, and the section of India's poor that was attracted to violent revolutionary ideas remained very small.

The state had proved its worth over a sufficient period, but acceptance of its existence did not take the shape of passive support; instead, the objective in Indian politics became to use the state actively for private and sectional purposes. The formation of smaller caste and regional parties marked a significant development in this trend. Dr Ambedkar had described caste as 'anti-national', and here he was proved right. The state was beginning to be perceived not as a mediator or a common construct; instead it was treated as a table loaded with sweetmeats. The people were not the state; the people saw themselves as separate from, even opposed to, the state, and used it as an instrument of depredation and extraction.

Rather than dismantling or rolling back the state, the next decades saw attempts to extend the state's competence and struggles over access to its bounty.

1989–2004: COALITION AND FRAGMENTATION

The decade that followed the Congress defeat of 1989 saw a marked increase in political complexity. With elections in 1989, 1991, 1996, 1998 and 1999, the former rhythm of the electoral cycle was disrupted, with an accompanying rise in the fractiousness of party politics that did double duty as both cause and effect of the change. There were also more parties, and this further complicated the political arithmetic of governing at the Centre. The Janata coalition consisted of four parties; the National Front government of 1989 contained seven, the United Front of 1996 13, and the NDA and UPA-I governments of 1999 and 2004 boasted 16 and 19 respectively. The 1989 election thus marked the opening to a quarter century of coalition politics.

Many factors helped sustain this fragmentation, including the elevation of religious and caste issues to a national level. Less directly, the assassination of Rajiv Gandhi, while fighting the 1991 election, forced the temporary withdrawal of the Nehru–Gandhi family from frontline politics. Coming after the death of Sanjay in 1980 and of Indira in 1984, it meant that two generations of the dynasty were lost in quick succession.

This was not merely a matter for society columnists. As the leading national political brand, the Nehru–Gandhi family had played a significant part in the shaping of Indian politics. Congress leaders had turned to an inexperienced and reluctant Indira in 1966, just as she had turned to an inexperienced and reluctant Rajiv in 1980. When he was assassinated by Tamil extremists in 1991 there was no available candidate to take on the dual role the family had fulfilled, both as national symbols and as the centre of gravity for the Congress party, which had become increasingly divorced from any specific ideology. The party's fortunes dipped from this point as it searched for both policy anchors and strong leadership. It was only when Sonia Gandhi, Rajiv's Italian-born widow, became Congress president in 1998 that the party began to revive, and it was not until her son Rahul Gandhi took a Lok Sabha seat in 2004 that the party returned to government, its historic identity fully restored. Coincidence or not, the Congress vote revived at the same time as the young heir appeared.

In the interim, national politics seemed to lose its bearings. The National Front government that ousted Rajiv in 1989 lasted less than two years, as did the United Front that ruled from 1996 to 1998. Both were made up of smaller parties largely from the centre and left, and neither managed to govern very effectively. The intervening five years, from 1991 to 1996, were occupied by a Congress-led coalition under P.V. Narasimha Rao that came in as a minority government, and only achieved majority status in 1993, when a no-confidence vote enabled Rao to attract new allies with new deals and, as it turned out later, straight bribery. But this was at best a weak revival of Congress power, and despite the achievements of Rao's government, which included liberalization of the economy and the introduction of panchayati raj, the national policy agenda slipped out of Congress's control.

When the National Front came to power in 1989, the new Prime Minister, V.P. Singh, was committed to implement the recommendations of the Mandal Commission. He had promised to do this 'expeditiously' in the alliance's manifesto and announced in August 1990 that he intended to honour this promise.

Here, unusually, was a social issue that had never been a Congress project. The Mandal Commission had examined the condition of the very broad classes of underprivileged persons who sat above the line of 'scheduled' status, i.e. those who were poor and historically disadvantaged but had not been helped by the original schemes of reservations set out at independence. By the time Mandal reported in 1980, Mrs Gandhi had returned to power, and she decided to ignore his proposals. This was hardly surprising, as he had defined 52 per cent of the population as 'backward' and had declared that the existing level of reservations, running at 22 per cent, was insufficient, and should be raised to as near 52 per cent as possible. The maximum legal limit was 49.5 per cent, so that was what he proposed.

When V.P. Singh chose to revive this scheme, he was therefore launching an explosive charge into the social and economic fabric of India. And a good thing too, he would have maintained. But the likely consequences immediately appeared, with massive protests among the social groups destined to lose out. So worrying and widespread was the disorder that the Supreme Court suspended the programme two months later, and it was Rao's minority Congress government that eventually oversaw its partial implementation in 1993.

Objections to Mandal's proposals were very extensive and included attacks on his definitions, methodology, arithmetic and prudence, with disputes about the exact meaning of 'backwardness', the numbers involved, the efficacy of the measure in actually helping those who were disadvantaged, the validity of using one form of discrimination to combat another, and so forth. Many critics were convinced that the problem of caste was being perpetuated rather than dissolved. And all the time, in the background, lay matters of electoral strategy. Singh had hoped to benefit from implementing the proposals, and opposition to them was shaped by attempts to balance the offence they caused with the political benefits they might bring. No party could afford to flatly reject them.

Here was confirmation that, in Indian politics, deprivation was impossible to ignore, difficult to address directly and all too possible to turn to political advantage. Unless and until the passage of time and the general effects of economic growth can somehow spread prosperity, this connection will remain part of India's distinctive political culture. Like sin to the medieval Catholic Church, poverty to Indian politicians is partly an enemy to fight, but also a mainstay of their livelihoods.

The implementation of Mandal's recommendations has had some bizarre and ironic effects. One was that the fight against caste, led by the left, ended up reinforcing the institution; in order for caste to mean less, first it had to mean more. Another was that, because entitlements belonged to the poorest, the aspiration of many sections of Indian society was suddenly to represent themselves as poorer, in order to become more prosperous. Mandal also only dealt with those citizens who were nominally Hindus, since he was undertaking a survey of the inequities of caste, not economic status. Therefore both Muslims and Christians, and even the poor among upper castes, were not directly dealt with. All these factors set up new sets of rivalries and tensions. The commonly quoted post-Mandal classification of OBCs became a cliché of Indian politics, bandied around endlessly, despite the fact that it covered 27 per cent of the population, and that, as a grouping, it was heavily stratified and divided within itself. Nor was it consistently defined across different states.

Pulling strings to activate as much of this very broad stratum as possible without alienating substantial subsets of it became the daily concern of caste-based parties, who understood and were generally better at this game than national parties. Tinkering with reservations and defining qualifications for various benefits became the stock-in trade of local politicians, and a slew of new acronyms and sub-classes appeared, with Most Backward and Extremely Backward Castes, and Below Poverty Line and Above Poverty Line groups newly identified.

A third effect was the contribution Mandal made to the rise of the BJP, which was the most prominent trend running counter to the political fragmentation of the 1990s. This was to some degree an effect of Congress decline, but the process was not one of simply winning a middle ground of floating voters. The BJP spoke to a different constituency in a number of ways and adopted a different tone, at least in opposition, and seemed to represent a genuinely different – though not a particularly modern – type of political consciousness in India.

The BJP connected easily with the aspirations of the richer sections of Indian society, and it originally had a reputation as a '*bania*' party. This, naturally, aligned the party against reservations on a socio-economic basis, but the more ideological elements within the party also objected to Mandalization on the grounds that it violated the essential organic unity of Hindu society. The social engineering (or class war) aspects of the new reservations helped to establish a distinct position for the BJP within Indian politics on an issue of direct concern to millions and propelled the party into a new position of national contention.

Yet in some ways Mandal was the icing on the cake for the BJP – a wallet issue to add to the religious and cultural prospectus the party had been pursuing all along with fairly limited success. This began to change in the mid-1980s, when the party finally found a sufficiently emotive 'Hindu' issue to galvanize a national support base. This was the dispute over the temple at Ayodhya, which served as the first genuinely polarizing, nationalist-friendly issue to emerge since independence. After the limited readmission of Hindu worshippers to the Babri Masjid in 1986, a plan emerged to build a new temple on the spot, and this opened up a string of opportunities to create moments of fervent mass participation. It was L.K. Advani who fully realized this. As BJP president, he persuaded the party to adopt a more militant stance at Palampur in June 1989, and then went on to actively produce and sustain a mood of national revival and religious devotion with his *rath yatra* of 1990, leading to a first attempt to destroy the mosque in October that year. The BJP then captured UP in the 1991 state elections, and the whole mission to create binding moments peaked in the destruction of the mosque by a vast crowd in December 1992.

Propelled by strident rhetoric, energetic leadership and a single, emotive cause – and somewhat helped by a degree of disunity and disorganization among its rivals – by 1996 the BJP had become the largest party in India, with 161 Lok Sabha seats. The Jana Sangh had made little noticeable impact for 30 years, yet after winning only two seats in 1984, the renamed BJP at last bestrode the country. This needs careful explanation.

One obvious element to consider is that the BJP has been very traditional in its outlook and its philosophy; it was the first major force to appear in Indian politics that exclusively promoted home-grown Indian ideas. So, did the rise of the BJP represent the positive assertion of a strong and stable identity based on a resurgence of traditional values, much as Ronald Reagan liked to see his own rise in America as a surge of Christian patriotism? Or did it indicate some kind of disorientation within Indian politics – a dizziness brought on by too much modernity? Did the party offer an anchor to the past, a reassuring link to older certainties in a modern world that was changing too quickly for many Indians? Or was the BJP's newfound popularity due to an excess of cynicism about shallow political figures with old ideas and tired, failed solutions? Was this a protest movement against other parties? In other words, was the rise of the BJP a triumph of Indian democracy – proof of a new responsiveness, or was it an abandonment – an indication of its sickness and unworthiness, and a sign of its long-term failure?

To answer these questions we need a good answer to another: what was the real nature of the BJP? Was it really a democratic organization, or was it a Trojan horse to a narrow brand of Hindu authoritarianism – like Mrs Gandhi's Emergency, but more saffron? Any answer to this question must remain nuanced, because the BJP has always functioned as three types of party in one; nationalist, religious and fiscally conservative.

The BJP was well-supported in cities as well as in rural areas, so its success carried no obvious link to a defence of tradition within a simplistic old–new, Bharat–India division. A more satisfactory explanation is that the centre-right in India had not been well catered for. The defunct Swatantra Party had been primarily concerned with the interests of a fairly small, wealthy section of the nation, which was never going to be enough to attract or sustain a mass following, especially in an era before the growth of a large self-identifying middle class. Thus it never managed to build a mass base or a national organization of any size. It managed to become the second-largest party in the elections of 1962 and 1967, but never passed 9 per cent support. With Rajaji's death in 1972, it fell into factionalism and was wound up in 1974. For the rest, the one major party, the Congress, had never taken a centre-right stance and had attempted a kind of high-low appeal, while smaller emerging parties were generally very narrow on a regional or caste basis.

The masses that rallied to the BJP's standard through the 1990s were not all hammer-wielding *kar sevaks*, wild-eyed swamis, or crypto-fascists. They represented the largest group of politically minded Indians that had no obvious champion. And by around 1990 the relevant agenda of wealth creation, patriotism, assertive nationalism, traditional religious piety and law and order rhetoric had been perfected by a group of politicians led by A.B. Vajpayee and

Advani, who had been trying very hard to put this package together. With the RSS giving the party a connected national presence, plus the ability to put large numbers on the streets, the BJP had a full hand of political assets.

Here we need to make a distinction between those inside the BJP and those outside. This sort of distinction must always be made with any party that hits a populist hot button, because party insiders at the top are probably not very like most of those who make up the wider constituency they suddenly bring into focus. In the case of the BJP, it managed to mobilize two constituencies. The first was urban and professional, aspirational and fiscally conservative. Ironically, these are exactly the sorts of people that supported the original Congress in the nineteenth century. The other was rural, made up of newly wealthy farmers who had lined up in various antagonistic ways against other country-dwellers – the top section of OBCs, sometimes called the 'creamy layer'.

The BJP is a complex phenomenon with multiple tendencies within the party, and this is known and understood well enough. There are hardliners and moderates, whose fortunes fluctuate; the exact relationship between cultural, social and economic issues varies in the party's public utterances. Some of the continuing uncertainty about the BJP is sustained by the reluctance of the party's leaders to air their differences in public. Their reticence stems from two very Indian traditions. One is a deep commitment to the idea of India as an organic society; internal dissent is therefore a matter of some embarrassment. The other is the Indian political tradition of holding one's cards close to one's chest, in order to retain maximum flexibility on issues of both policy and strategy. As a result, outsiders can only guess where the party's centre of power lies at any moment, and who is dictating priorities. Reading the factional ups and downs within the BJP is made more difficult because most of the party's star leaders – including Vajpayee, Advani and Modi – have served an apprenticeship in the ranks of the RSS, and it is difficult to tell to what degree they are being controlled from the Sangh's headquarters in Nagpur.

In some ways the BJP resembles the original Congress, with its ambition to speak for the whole nation (as it sees it), an agenda of positive change and a set of inclusive claims that are the party's main strengths and its major weaknesses. Broadly the BJP fulfils a common, and some might say a natural, role in party politics as an organ of the centre-right, with a feel for tradition, a taste for social conformity, and a natural antipathy to socialist economics. In other words, a conservative, patriotic, free-enterprise party like many others all over the world.

But the BJP is rather more than this, because of its roots in Hindutva as opposed to secular Indian nationalism.

To understand this clearly requires a brief review of the original debate in India about the best way out of colonialism – a protracted and complex discussion that established three main solutions: the Congress way, inclusive and secular; the Muslim League way, defined by regional and non-secular issues; and the 'Extremist', distinctly religious, traditional strand represented by a range of religious and cultural figures from Tilak to Savarkar.

This last strand never found a core constituency of sufficient strength to dominate the debate or to rival the mass mobilizations led by Gandhi and Jinnah. Congress-style nationalism and the Two-Nation Theory had more immediate relevance than the third strand of Hindutva, but Hindutva did not go away. It could not, because those it spoke for and the ideals it represented – of a strong nation based in localism – did not go away. Indeed, there was always an emotional element in the Hindutva tendency that was outraged by the Partition, which lingered on to convince many in India that a more robust attitude to the Muslim minority would have avoided the whole debacle. Hindutva, sometimes described as 'political Hinduism', is not just about feeling Hindu identity, but it is also about asserting Hindu *solidarity*. This cocktail of nostalgia and identity politics, combined with feelings of betrayal, shame and outrage, was too powerful simply to vanish from collective memory. Any political doctrine that gives people purpose, pride, positive identity and a clear set of rights and wrongs will always find adherents.

The desire to recapture past glories, the yearning for a purer, simpler society and the deep need to redress historic wrongs were all present in the original Hindutva package, and in this it resembled many European forms of irredentist nationalism, though, like all of those, it had distinctive features peculiar to its location in time and space. By the 1990s it also had an urgency about it; Hindus must stand together *now* or they will be undermined internally by insistent Muslim demands for special treatment, and swept away by international capitalism with its accompanying social degeneracy.

In sum, the BJP was not the opposite of the Congress. Rather, it filled a vacuum that the Congress had denied existed.

By 1992, the BJP was a viable national party. It had a robust skeleton – the RSS; a philosophy – Hindutva; and a range of popular issues to exploit, including Mandal, the mosque, the Uniform Civil Code, hostility to Pakistan and a strong anti-separatist agenda, including a desire to integrate Kashmir fully into the Indian federal state.

But even with all this, it could only go so far. The party's rise was meteoric, considering its gain of 159 MPs in 12 years, but it still could not win enough seats in 1996 to govern on its own. It had supported the National Front from outside after the 1989 election, and had opposed Rao's Congress-led government from 1991 to 1996. National leadership would have to wait two more years.

It was Rao's government that set the scene for the sustained boom India was to experience from the late-1990s. Faced with multiple levels of fiscal and economic crisis, Rao's finance minister, Manmohan Singh, pushed through a series of liberalizing measures in July 1991 that finally began to dismantle the licence raj, a process that Rajiv Gandhi had started but had not followed through.

Rao also supervised the final implementation of panchayati raj in 1993, via the 73rd and 74th Amendments, which introduced elections for urban councils and a three-tiered scheme of rural self-government, including a 33 per cent reservation for women. This had long been in the offing. Originally a pet project of M.K. Gandhi, Nehru had also been prepared to countenance it in the 1950s, but subsequent governments until the time of Rajiv Gandhi had not looked so kindly on it. The version introduced in 1993 was not complete, as local government remained a state subject and the powers that the panchayats could wield were determined at state level. Nevertheless it represented the greatest single expansion of Indian democracy since independence.

The electorate, however, did not reward Rao, who was increasingly besieged by accusations of corruption. In the general election of 1996, the BJP finally became the largest parliamentary party, and A.B. Vajpayee attempted to build a coalition. He was forced to admit defeat after two weeks of abortive negotiations, and the ramshackle United Front then held power till 1998.

The failure to attract partners in 1996 acted in some ways to domesticate the BJP, weaning it off some of the stronger ingredients of its political brew. The party had reached the limits of religious politics in a way analogous to that in which the Congress eventually found itself delimited by its own social nature; the Congress could not be an agent for socialist revolution when staffed and led by social conservatives. Similarly, the BJP found that it could mobilize mass support by triggering religious issues of identity and fears about minorities, but this could only lift it so far. At street level its programme gave purpose, status and satisfaction to some, but within the political charmed circle, the BJP could not find partners to take it beyond its natural base of around 25 per cent support.

The politics of community identity is a limited suit; it only appeals to those already on your side. It is largely a matter of fear; not the assumption that under such and such a leadership we will be better off, but on the supposed certainty that under another type of leadership we face the certainty of being worse off. So how can an identity-based party expand beyond that base?

What finally got the BJP into government in 1998 was not assertiveness, but the deliberate building of a coalition by compromise by the construction of a pre-election coalition with a published programme.

Despite the worst fears of its opponents, the BJP-led minority government that took office in 1998 did not prove to be a sectarian tiger. Nor did it increase its representation in the national elections of the next year, forced on the party after the AIADMK withdrew its support from the coalition. Reinstalled at the 1999 election as the NDA, the BJP-dominated administration went on to rule for a full term with a comfortable majority. During this time, apart from trying to rewrite school history books, the extremist agenda never materialized. And the history issue did not go well either. The new, more 'Hindu' textbooks were not well written, and with education being a state subject, non-BJP states were able to reject them.

The new government did, however, take one very deliberate step to advertise its core principles – the nuclear tests of May 1998. This was meant to send a clear signal to the rest of the world, but principally to Pakistan and China, that India was set on a new course and was determined to elevate her position in the world. However, the belligerence was not sustained over the next few years. Prime Minister Vajpayee made a bus trip to Lahore to meet Nawaz Sharif in February 1999, and the Kargil 'war' later that year, though pursued vigorously, was not extended beyond the narrow confines of the high Himalayas. Further summits with Pakistan followed in 2001 and 2004, but neither proved productive, leading to suspicions that the Pakistanis were not serious. The terrorist attack on the Indian Parliament of December 2001 produced a tense stand-off on the border, with further suspicions about Pakistani involvement, but Vajpayee maintained a conciliatory tone.

India's first BJP government produced relatively little change, and certainly not much of a radical kind: no Ram temple, no Uniform Civil Code, no change to the status of Kashmir. Positive measures included the introduction of mobile telephony on a large scale and further dismantling of the licence raj, but foreign investment remained a sensitive area and was still resisted. Three new states – Jharkhand, Chhattisgarh, and Uttarakhand – were created, largely at the behest of their *adivasi* populations. This ran counter to classic Hindutva, which prizes a unitary India above all, but smaller states did promise better local governance, with a possible lift in local support for the ruling party. Hard-line ambitions seemed restricted to the unveiling of a portrait of the pioneer of Hindutva philosophy, V.D. Savarkar, in the Central Hall of Parliament in 2003.

The events of truly long-term significance for the NDA happened in Gujarat, with the election of Narendra Modi as the state's chief minister in 2001, and the riots and mass killings of 2002 that followed a train fire in Godhra that killed 59 pilgrims returning from the Ayodhya site. The exact link between these two developments is disputed and unclear. Opponents charge Modi with at best indifference to the ensuing violence, and at worst being an active participant in its inception and execution. Judicial enquiries have left the matter undecided, with a balance of presumption in favour of Modi's innocence. But his subsequent presentation of himself as an administrator of excellence sits uncomfortably alongside his presiding over such a sustained and bloody period of disorder, lasting weeks and costing more than a thousand lives. As the deadliest outbreak of religious violence in India's recent history this was bad enough, but the election of 2014 was to bring it forcibly back to the national agenda and root it there as a painful and divisive issue for months.

What the NDA government of 1999–2004 did best was to produce a sense of well-being, brought on by high annual growth rates. Taking credit for this whenever it could, the alliance sought to tap the positive national mood at the 2004 elections with the slogan 'India Shining'. This, however, proved insufficient to counterbalance a wave of corruption scandals that hit senior government figures, making the new, clean BJP look rather more like the older, grubbier parties it had chided while in opposition. Enough of the electorate also felt that India was not shining sufficiently in their lives, and that they would tell their rulers so.

The NDA lost, though by a fairly small margin. It gleaned about 33 per cent of the vote, with the opposing UPA, led by the Congress, picking up around 35 per cent. The BJP, with 138 seats, amassed only seven less than the Congress. Had the BJP performed just a little better in UP, where it had previously been strong, or had the DMK, an erstwhile partner, been induced to join the alliance, the NDA might have scraped home. As it was, Advani declared that overconfidence had cost them the election, and the wider lesson drawn by the BJP leadership was that good economic numbers were not actually enough for the party to win. This resulted in a re-examination of the party's basic stance, and produced a lurch back towards core issues of Hindutva. Instead of a clearout at the top and a determination to produce even better economic numbers, party leaders, as is so often the case, took the defeat too heavily to heart, and chose to do more work in secret committees and think-tanks instead of on the ground.

By the time of the 2004 election, much less had changed than some had hoped and some had feared in 1998. Why? Because government in India blunts radicalism. Change is slow and painful; the system is not geared up for it, and there are too many vested interests at every level and within every niche of society determined to thwart it. Coalition government acted as a restraint, and the usual limitations on government applied, along with the same temptations in office. After six years in power, the BJP found itself back on around 21 per cent support – just about where it had been in 1991.

2004–2014: CONGRESS RESURGENT

The unheralded Congress/UPA victory of 2004 set off a burst of governmental vitality, with a succession of constructive measures to promote the welfare of India's poor. This was the result of an unusual conjunction in Indian affairs – a political willingness to implement such schemes, and enough money to pay for them. The UPA had a strong Left component, and there were consistently high annual growth figures through the mid-2000s.

The UPA had campaigned as a loose coalition, without a set programme like that of the NDA in 1999. This deficiency was remedied, as in 1996, by the negotiation of a Common Minimum Programme by the coalition partners after the election.

The problem of the premiership proved more contentious. Sonia Gandhi had been projected as a prime ministerial candidate, but opponents had made much of her foreign birth during the campaign. On reflection she declined the post, while remaining Congress president, and the eminent economist Manmohan Singh, who had served as finance minister in the Rao government, took office as prime minister. There was some discomfort about this manoeuvre, as the new premier was plucked from the upper house of Parliament, the Rajya Sabha, and had not been elected by anyone except his own party. Some theorized that Singh was a mere placeholder until the young scion of the Nehru–Gandhi dynasty – the 33-year-old Rahul – was of sufficient age and standing to lead the party. If this was the plan, it worked smoothly enough, and no strong challenger emerged from Congress ranks over the next decade to obstruct Rahul Gandhi's further advancement.

But there was a downside too, in that the government was then effectively split into public and private sections, with a front office in full view at 7 Race Course Road, the prime minster's official residence, and a back room team, titled the National Advisory Council, at 10 Janpath, which Sonia Gandhi occupied as Congress president. This arrangement struck some as cumbersome, while others considered it barely constitutional, or even illegal. In the end it may have hampered decision-making to some degree, but it did more damage to the long-term standing of Manmohan Singh, who was never able to convince the public that it was really his government he was leading.

The new administration set out on a programme to alleviate poverty and enhance 'rights', a complex twin-track project. It introduced a citizens' Right to Information Act (2005) – a measure that had long been in the offing – and it secured the Right to Education, first introduced as a constitutional amendment in 2002. It passed the National Rural Employment Guarantee Act (2005) to relieve distress in the agricultural sector, and in the same year the Sachar Committee was appointed to investigate the status of minorities and their disadvantages. This was in some ways a logical extension of the Mandal process, which had left several backward groups, particularly Muslims, without special provision. The Committee's report, delivered in 2006, revealed that Muslims were frequently more disadvantaged than STs and SCs; Muslims were present in government employment at only about a quarter of their proportion in the population.

BJP critics alleged that all this was 'povertarianism', and that the installation of Manmohan Singh as Sonia Gandhi's puppet had set the country adrift with weak leadership. Meanwhile, it was suffering its own crisis of leadership. The aged Vajpayee stepped down, but an old guard centred on Advani remained in charge, and the party leadership that entered the polls five years later in 2009 was almost identical to the losing team of 2004. Lack of internal party democracy has given all Indian parties repeated difficulties in these kinds of generational transitions.

Drifting or not, the years 2004–08 went smoothly in most respects. People became more prosperous on average, and the government took credit for the good times, though they were equally enjoyed by many other countries across the globe that were not under Dr Singh's kindly care.

While Singh enjoyed an unchallenged status at the centre, the long-term political effects of India's federal structure became increasingly apparent, and it was in the provinces that India's brightest and most colourful political characters were still to be found. Mayawati in UP, Lalu Prasad Yadav in Bihar, Naveen Patnaik in Odisha, Chandrababu Naidu in Andhra Pradesh and Jayalalitha in Tamil Nadu all led their own parties, forming a tier of expectant candidates for national leadership. The route to personal power in Delhi via provincial status was well-established after the two 'third front' governments of 1989 and 1996, and this helped to sustain the fragmentation of politics, with the two major parties constantly seeking to improve both local and national prospects by building alliances. Leaders like Mulayam Singh Yadav, with his OBC/Muslim-based SP, or Mayawati, with her Dalit-based BSP, could deliver lower or middle ranking sections of the electorate that now lay beyond the direct reach of the Congress or the BJP. Jigsaw patterns of electoral arithmetic dictated who was friends with whom, and who attacked whom and when.

The BJP and the Congress both managed to hold together well as parties, but both faced problems. The Congress's political problem was that the UPA's majority depended on their allies to the left. The BJP's problem was more cerebral – how to reverse the unexpected defeat of 2004? If changes were to be made, what should they be? An internal battle ensued, with the usual teams of hawks and doves demanding either more of the strict Hindutva medicine for the nation or a more economically and socially inclusive agenda. The one clear development was that the party now had its own provincial rising star – Narendra Modi in Gujarat, who romped home with an increased majority in the state at the 2007 Assembly polls.

Despite the majority that the UPA enjoyed, any impression of a return to some kind of Congress's golden age proved premature, and several heavy blows proceeded to darken India's horizons from 2008. First, the UPA began to disintegrate, as the Left deserted it over the nuclear deal with the US, concluded in 2008. Fears about supporting American imperialism distressed the leftists, while the BJP-led opposition represented the deal as a loss of Indian sovereignty, in allowing inspection of India's new nuclear facilities. With the administration in real danger, it managed to survive a trust vote in July 2008, but only after a new low in Indian democracy, as BJP MPs were shown on television holding bundles of cash, allegedly offered to them in return for their support in the vital division.

The terrorist attack on Mumbai in November 2008 was another rude shock, especially as it revealed the comparative paralysis of the authorities in dealing with all aspects of the outrage. At the same time, the global financial crisis blew up, and government complacency that India could avoid its worst effects proved ill-founded. Harder times came to India, and continued to do so for the next six years, with higher prices, a falling rupee and rising inflation.

Rather surprisingly, the poll of 2009 returned the UPA with an enhanced majority, but the administration was now of a different complexion, as the left parties fared disastrously and played no part. UPA-II was composed principally of the Congress and two regional parties, the DMK and the TMC, with their leaders, Muthuvel Karunanidhi and Mamata Banerjee respectively.

Recent history is often hard to set into clear patterns, but there is general agreement that UPA-II was very different in character from its predecessor. Though again the government was stable in its Parliamentary standing, it was repeatedly battered by scandal and political turbulences. A series of revelations about scams and high-level corruption began to appear, beginning with accusations about rigged contracting for the Commonwealth Games of 2010, continuing through the sale of telecom rights (2G scam), and ending with Coalgate, concerning the allocation of coal 'blocks' without proper competitive tendering. These revelations were damaging to individuals and to the government in general, though the prime minister managed to remain free of taint. But they fed into a much wider climate of scepticism about politicians because they went hand in hand with a number of scandals concerning provincial figures. These included Lalu Prasad Yadav in Bihar, leader of the RJD party and a former Union rail minister, who was implicated in a long-running fodder scam, and the Reddy brothers in Karnataka, who were part of the BJP state government that came to power in 2008 and were alleged to have abused access to mining rights. Senior Congress figures in Maharashtra were also investigated in 2011 by the Comptroller and Auditor General about their roles in the complex Adarsh housing scam.

The enormous scale and audacity of much of this malfeasance, and the involvement of members of all parties played into a mood of outrage, and it may be that an important Rubicon was crossed in public tolerance. An initial indication of the change of mood was the rapid rise of the protest movement started by Anna Hazare and Arvind Kejriwal in 2011, which vociferously demanded legislation to create a truly independent body to police politicians – a Lokpal – at the centre. This immediately created a heated, very detailed debate about how a non-political guardian body might be designed to wield what clearly amounted to political power, yet be trusted to remain apolitical. The original movement splintered under the strain, and the more proactive wing of the movement evolved into a political party dedicated to opposing corruption, the Aam Aadmi Party, founded in November 2012.

The public mood was receptive, and was regularly bolstered across the next two years with a succession of high-profile jailings – the first of major political figures in Indian history. Until then, senior national figures accused of serious crimes had avoided incarceration by pursuing extended appeal procedures, or had been exonerated by judicial enquiry, or had had charges against them dropped for lack of evidence and/or when witnesses refused to testify. Or they had merely resigned. From 2011, ministers of senior rank began to find themselves behind bars, including Sukh Ram for a telecom scandal dating back to the 1990s, Andimuthu Raja for his part in the 2G scam, and Lalu Prasad.

Lalu's conviction in late September 2013 led on to yet more scandal. In July 2013, in the case of *Lily Thomas vs. Union of India*, the Supreme Court had ruled that politicians who were either remanded or convicted of serious charges would be excluded from Parliamentary/Assembly proceedings immediately, thus withdrawing the immunity they had previously enjoyed while cases were appealed. This went along with the public mood, but politicians saw things differently. Because the tactical use of criminal charges is so common, they said, it was unfair to disqualify MPs or MLAs so precipitately. The cabinet then drafted an ordinance allowing accused politicians, or those pursuing appeals, to stay free and to continue to participate in debates and legislative business, but not to vote or draw their salaries. This seemed to be too obviously connected to the pending sentence on Lalu Prasad Yadav, whose RJD would be a potential ally of the Congress in the upcoming general election. Rahul Gandhi stepped in at this point to demand that the ordinance be 'thrown out', and Prime Minister Manmohan Singh obliged on 3 October.

Buoyed by all this, the AAP got off to a flying start, taking control of Delhi as a minority government after elections in December 2013. But it soon encountered serious difficulties, and its leader, Arvind Kejriwal, resigned after only 49 days in office. The established parties made life very difficult for the newcomers, who found they could not implement their legislative programme. There were also, inevitably, major problems of organization and funding for such a new party. The

AAP's street-level mobilization was derided as anarchic, and examples of AAP members' inexperience, misjudgement and indiscipline soon accrued, as was all too likely among such a collection of idealists and greenhorns catapulted so rapidly into political power.

The public got their way in the end, though, with the passage of the Lokpal and Lokayukta Act in December 2013, which created ombudsmen for the Union and states respectively. This may come to be remembered as the most constructive of UPA-II's achievements.

One of its other schemes, the drive for food security, might become similarly historic, at least in the minds of its proponents. But the enormous ambition of the scheme – to provide subsidized food grains to approximately two-thirds of the Indian population – combined with the vast expense associated with it, stirred up wide ranging opposition on grounds of its cost, its extension of state responsibilities and, above all, on suspicions that the whole affair, passed into law as the Food Security Act (2013), was a gigantic political stroke intended to buy the votes of the poor at public expense.

This last accusation could also have been levelled at a large number of other schemes, implemented by parties at both the national and local levels over the previous 40 years, during which electricity, water, food grain and loans had been distributed as more or less obvious inducements to support the donors. And like many of those sops and giveaways, it didn't actually work. All the money that the UPA contrived to pour into the countryside over a decade proved of no avail in the final reckoning at the polls of 2014.

Accusations of pre-election giveaways are a feature of electoral systems all over the democratic world, and incumbent governments can usually shake them off in good times. But the mood in India seemed to be changing from around 2011. There were several new factors. Over a hundred million new voters came onto the rolls at the same time as the scams appeared, the global recession hit and the UPA's double term left its leaders with no one else to blame, if blame was merited. And a great many in India felt that blame was very much the order of the day. It is a standard political adage that an incumbent government cannot win an election by attacking its own record. In bad times, the best option is to attack opponents as unworthy, irresponsible, incompetent, unready or to malign them. This was duly attempted by Congress leaders, but the fates were against them. When Rahul Gandhi finally stepped forward to shoulder his leadership responsibilities, albeit without the official tag of prime ministerial contender, he found himself against Narendra Modi.

The soft-handed, privileged political apprentice found himself up against the self-made hard man with three terms as chief minister behind him. In the prevailing anti-establishment mood, the clash of princeling versus worker was only ever going to end one way. Modi played on his humble roots and his status as an outsider figure. He was committed to growth and prosperity for all, as he passionately explained, day after day, to large audiences. Rahul meanwhile talked of changing the system, despite the fact that he was a product of it. This was thin gruel by comparison, and scarcely convincing. It sounded much like a recipe for more of the same. When challenged fairly mildly in the TimesNow television studio, he could barely manage to explain himself.

The BJP were well aware of Modi's powerful appeal on the campaign trail, and this may be the reason why the party did not release a formal manifesto until the campaign had been running for weeks. Parties in India are persistently wary of paperwork and commitments, and Modi, with his record of achievement and aura of strength and energy, made further elaboration unnecessary. 'NaMo' was the candidate in every constituency, 'NaMo' was the programme.

The Congress could offer little to counter the so-called Gujarat model of development, apart from derision. Rahul called it a 'toffee model'. Others doubted its validity in more detailed statistical terms, but they could not diminish its seductive, get-rich-quick allure. American political analysts have a beautiful phrase for debates like this: 'If you're explaining, you're losing.' Modi declined to explain anything very much, and simply emphasized his personal history of hard work. This was easily contrasted to Rahul Gandhi's cosseted origins, but it worked well against other members of the technocratic Congress leadership too. Comparing himself to Finance Minister P.

Chidambaram, who vaunts a degree from Harvard Business School, he asked voters in Chennai whether India would be better run by 'Harvard or hard work'.[37]

Modi laid aside the traditional BJP wish list – the Ram temple, the Uniform Civil Code, Article 370 – and left more contentious themes to others in the Sangh Parivar, while he hammered home his most optimistic, least divisive messages. He appeared to be taking up the Clinton–Blair model of politics as management rather than the standard Indian political model of calculated sectional electoral engineering. He addressed the nation and its ambitions, and he seemed to reawaken the dream, long lost in India, that there is a common, public good and that he could see it.

Again, he fell into line with current American electoral theory, as expounded by US President Barack Obama's political mastermind, David Axelrod, whose mantra is that elections are won on the future, not the past.

Modi won, and he won big.

Part 3

Democracy in South Asia

As the Second World War came to an end, there were no functioning democracies to be found in South Asia. The nearest thing was in Ceylon (now Sri Lanka), where a British reform package of 1931 had introduced a degree of responsible government, including adult suffrage. Nepal, Sikkim, Bhutan and Afghanistan continued as traditional monarchies, while Burma, which had endured three miserable years as a battlefield, simply swapped Japanese occupation for a return to British colonial rule. British India was enjoying a measure of regional self-government, but it was based on a limited franchise and remained firmly under central viceregal authority; there had only ever been one round of elections, in 1936–37.

The withdrawal of British imperial power over 1947–48 from the region allowed a democratic upsurge, as local elites took the reins of power in the former colonies. With varying quantities of optimism and generosity these elites then either wrote their own constitutions, as in India, or accepted foundational documents written for them by the British, as in Sri Lanka and Burma.

But over the ensuing decades, democracy did not fare well across the region. By 1980 Sri Lanka had firmly enshrined Sinhalese majority rule, and was about to plunge into a prolonged civil war. Pakistan, Bangladesh and Burma were under military rule, Nepal was an autocracy and Afghanistan a war zone. India had flirted with dictatorship, but had pulled back from the brink in 1977.

By 2014 the picture had changed yet again, with elections held regularly in all the major states. Even Myanmar, formerly Burma, had moved to nominally civilian rule in 2011, though the President was an ex-soldier and the army remained the premier institution in the country.

Is this, then, a story of success? After the abrupt transition from colonial rule to self-government, has South Asia learned to live with democratic norms? Optimism is not yet entirely justified. Although the results of elections are now generally respected in the region, the quality of the polls is not always beyond question. Armed groups still operate in parts of some states, and the self-serving nature of ruling elites still denies good governance to many. How robust are the democracies that have emerged, and will they put down institutional and cultural roots that can survive the buffeting of natural disasters, regional tensions, international terrorism and the personal ambitions of politicians? Bloodless coups may be a thing of the past, but how soon will South Asia enjoy bloodless elections?

Generalizations about the region are hazardous, especially if connected to any putative inability of non-Western people to manage democratic institutions. The very apparent differences between the historical arcs of North and South Korea, the capacity of several semi-authoritarian regimes to nurture prosperity, or the ease with which the Japanese took to social democracy should provide ample warning that glib statements about Asian people and democracy are inappropriate. For comparison, we should consider that judgements made in 1969 about any supposed affinity for democracy among Europeans would have had to include the fact that France had recently undergone a massive popular revolt; Spain, Portugal and Greece had regimes that could safely be described as undemocratic if not actually fascist; while Yugoslavs, Bulgarians, Albanians and Romanians were under varieties of Communist dictatorship.

The long history of colonial rule in South Asia ensured that there was no experience in the region of running a truly popular democracy, and the former British colonies – India, Pakistan, Sri Lanka and Burma – were all to fare very differently. Among these four – eventually five – states, only Sri Lanka has maintained a continuous record of democratic government, though this did not save the country from a vicious and protracted internal conflict. Of states that had never been under British rule, Nepal and Bhutan were eventually to become democracies, Sikkim was absorbed into India, and Afghanistan ran through a variety of arrangements – monarchy, anarchy, communism, theocracy and eventually, nominal democracy.

What these experiences might tell us about democracy as a system or about South Asia's political temperament have absorbed several generations of political scientists, and will continue to do so as long as speculation about the future of China and India as superpowers remains of interest and the tangled issues surrounding Afghanistan, Kashmir and Pakistan continue to ripple out into the affairs of major nations far away.

If more democracy is the answer to any of South Asia's persistent problems then we need to understand why India has managed to retain democratic institutions and avoid civil war while other states have not. It is immediately apparent that in 1947 India lacked a list of qualities considered essential to sustain a system of mass democracy. The Indian population was too large, too diverse and too poor to coalesce around ideas of democratic rule, it was felt – by almost everyone except the Indian leaders of the day.

Are there any themes to be found within the experience of neighbouring states that can help us to understand how and why India seemed to go right, where others seemed to go wrong?

1.

Pakistan

Pakistan began life in August 1947 buoyed up by enormous optimism. Independence, combined with escape from Hindu domination, meant that two long-term, negative historical factors – colonial rule and minority status for Muslims – had suddenly been left behind. But euphoria proved a flimsy tool to tackle the critical weaknesses that afflicted the new state. These problems are well understood in hindsight and endlessly rehearsed in writings on Pakistan, but they still make a daunting list – untidy geographical extent, economic underdevelopment, over-commitment to defence, social inequality and lack of clear political goals.

The new nation was a crossbreed, a complicated entity, and was not quite what its creator Muhammad Ali Jinnah had asked for. Jinnah had wanted all the provinces of British India that contained a Muslim majority to be assembled into a new state in which Muslims would be free of the threat of entrenched Hindu domination. The British listened indulgently to him all through the Second World War, but proved rather less compliant after it had ended. They resolved not to give him undivided provinces but contrived a package of areas in which Muslims were in a majority. Jinnah fought the internal partition of provinces to the end, and would not concede the logic that if Muslims were at risk in an independent Greater India, then non-Muslim 'hostages' would similarly be at risk in parts of it rearranged as a Greater Pakistan. In the end, Jinnah got a Lesser Pakistan, made out of three whole and two half provinces of British India.

The idea that Pakistan would be predisposed to political unanimity solely by virtue of its Muslim character was soon exposed as mistaken. The country faced a range of internal political disparities that were to prove troublesome, even insoluble. Chief among these was the fact that the majority of the new state's population lived in Bengal – its eastern wing – and had little cultural or historical empathy with the inhabitants of its western wing. Newly minted Pakistan had inconveniently combined the most sophisticated political region of British India with the most underdeveloped. Bengal had been longest under British rule and had developed a complex political consciousness that reflected some of the class-based subdivisions of Bengali society as well as of the religious. In effect, it was more likely to elect left-wing leaders and parties. This contrasted strongly with the political character of West Pakistan, which had been under British rule for the least time, was generally more conservative and contained a number of potentially troublesome disparities of its own. The population of the upland tribal areas, which had given the British their most persistent problems with insurgency, was poorer, more traditional and religious, and had a long history of effective autonomy now threatened by rule from Karachi. There were also longstanding tensions between smaller regional groups such as Sindhis, Balochis and Pashtuns and the politically and economically dominant Punjabis.

Further, the Punjabis were obliged to compete not only with the political elite in Bengal but were also required to accommodate another significant grouping, the *muhajirs* – high-status refugees from the Muslim minority provinces in India, many of whom had taken leading roles in the movement for Pakistan. It was going to be hard to reconcile the expectations of all these groups within one state, let alone one that had yet to define its own detailed structure. Leadership was required, but Pakistan was denied it on two counts, one tragic, one ironic.

The tragedy was the early death of Jinnah, who was universally revered, and might have, with sufficient energy and luck, navigated some of the rough waters ahead. But his life was already hanging by a thread as independence came, and he was dead 13 months later.

Jinnah was too prominent and died too soon for the political health of Pakistan.

The irony was that the Muslim League, the party that had driven the demand for Pakistan, had very little presence on the ground there, and thus could not easily act as a 'natural' party of government in the new country. This was because Pakistan was, by definition, composed of Muslim majority provinces, and the Muslim League had never been strong in such areas; it had been able to offer little in the way of deliverance from Hindu domination to any Muslim who lived in a Muslim majority province. The party had its intellectual roots in the old Muslim heartlands of UP, and had picked up most of its support in Muslim minority provinces, chiefly Bombay, where Jinnah himself was based. The League never enjoyed a strong following in any of the four provinces of West Pakistan, and had never had more than a minimal presence in Punjab.

For all these reasons, the new state lacked a 'natural' dominant centre of political gravity. Most of the senior army leadership were Punjabis, where links with the British Indian Army were of long standing, and in the end this proved more significant than any other factor in the future political course of the country; the one readymade national institution that Pakistan enjoyed was the army. A new bureaucracy and a new currency had to be set up virtually from scratch, but the rudiments of the army already existed, though not one single complete unit came from British India. Reshaping and equipping this force was a clear priority, especially once hostilities with India began in Kashmir only ten weeks after independence.

It proved a tremendous burden. Jinnah had to make do with some of the poorest parts of India – the swamps of East Bengal, the deserts of Sind and the hilly regions of the northwest, with only the port of Karachi and the rich plains of West Punjab to fill his treasury. Worse, Pakistan had extremely long land borders, all of them potentially hostile. This had been pointed out to Jinnah repeatedly, and some senior British officials considered that the burdens of defence would be so great that Pakistan should not even be admitted to the Commonwealth, as it represented a potential drain on the other members. But Jinnah pressed on. The 'moth-eaten' Pakistan he had once derided was offered, accepted and then duly admitted to the Commonwealth. As was India, which seemed the best, or at least the cheapest way of reining in the two new countries, and assuring that their strained relationship remained pegged at frosty and did not heat up into war.

War with India was to come though, in 1947, 1965 and 1971, with an extended skirmish in 1999. None of these wars profited Pakistan, and the 1971 conflict was disastrously expensive in terms of lives, treasure and the loss of the eastern wing of the country.

Why did Pakistan so frequently engage in war with its much larger neighbour? The answer lies in the decision-making process within the state, which was always heavily influenced by military concerns. In an experience repeated in many postcolonial societies, the armed forces in Pakistan became not only a major expense of the state, they became a central player in its governance and eventually an integral part of the country's economy.

The rise of the army to a central role in governance was driven by perceptions of necessity among the nation's leaders, but politicians proved repeatedly unable to ride the military tiger. The army was happy to fit in whenever necessary within the programme of nation-building, and this included taking political power for itself. The culture within the Pakistani military was very much on the British model, and not very different from that in India, but there were two crucial differences in context. One was in the quality of civilian leadership, the other in the constitutional vacuum that lay at the heart of Pakistani politics. Both of these factors are intimately connected with Jinnah, his personality and his vision, or lack of it.

As a leader, Jinnah spent most of his years effectively in opposition – to both the British and the Congress. During this 'long march' he developed a style that was enigmatic and solitary, which worked well enough to keep his opponents guessing, while his autocratic manner kept those within his own organization at a distance. But he assumed supreme national leadership just as his health and energy finally deserted him, and he left no clear blueprint for how the new country should be set up – particularly how exactly its constitution should relate to the Islamic principles he had declared made it impossible for Muslims to live alongside Hindus.

With the nation in mourning, this task was left to the Constituent Assembly, led by Prime Minister Liaquat Ali Khan. A Basic Objectives Resolution was agreed in 1949, but the general principles it set out – that Pakistan was to be an Islamic, federal, democratic state – were not fully specified, and each of these terms is still problematic today. What was 'Islamic' was not defined; by the 1990s it had been accepted that, legally, this aspiration could be limited to *forbidding* what was wrong rather than *prescribing* what was right. The federal structure that Jinnah preferred has been consistently reshaped, undermined or disregarded by strong leaders. And democracy has been only intermittently respected, with leaders often preferring to justify past actions via a retrospective referendum rather than hazard their future authority in an open national poll.

Subsequently, Pakistan has found it very difficult to live either with elections or without them. This is the result of a degree of internal diversity on both national and regional levels that has worked against the formation of stable political organizations and has instead promoted charismatic and populist leaders. Elections have produced results that have been too clear (1970) or too crooked (1977). For long periods elections have not been held at all (1956–70 and 1977–85), with military rulers content to secure approval via the courts.

Young Pakistan did not acquire the electoral habit early and found it difficult to acquire later. The Constituent Assembly – the only representative voice that the nation possessed – was elected indirectly before independence to do nothing more than write a constitution. But it was replaced in 1954 after seven years of discussion, after it threatened to limit the powers of Governor-General Ghulam Mohammad, who dismissed it using the legal justification of 'necessity' as sanctioned by the Supreme Court. This seemed convenient at the time, but the central issue that had been raised – whether executive or electoral power was to take precedence – had merely been postponed, while a definite impression had been created that the courts would be subservient to purposes of state.

A second Constituent Assembly was nominated by provincial assemblies that had been elected between 1951 and 1954. This body agreed a new constitution in 1956, by which it converted itself into a unicameral National Assembly, with equal representation from the eastern and western wings – the result of the newly adopted One Unit policy, which gave formal parity to the two wings of the country by fusing the four western provinces into one. This had the beneficial effect of preventing either wing from dominating the other, but it also undermined local autonomy in the west. More pointedly, it was yet another way of compromising the principle of majority rule for the benefit of the dominant political class.

This structure produced its own resentments, and after two more years of bickering, the army finally stepped in. General Ayub Khan seized power in October 1958 and inaugurated the first of three periods of military government in Pakistan. Ayub was a straightforward career soldier and a natural paternalist. Having seen party politics fail, he introduced a more dignified system of his own invention, called 'Basic Democracy', enshrined in a new constitution ratified in 1962. It was a layered structure of representative councils, based on a prime electorate of about 80,000 'basic' electors topped off with an executive president. The new system was not a success, nor was it entirely compliant; it barely elected him President when he formally put himself forward in 1965. After an unsuccessful war with India that year, and a change of leadership in 1969, which saw the installation of General Yahya Khan, the military conceded that national elections had to be held, and a date was set for late-1970.

The two-winged Pakistan was never going to be an easy country to rule, with or without popular electoral support, and the West Pakistani-dominated leadership ran into increasing problems with the aspirations of East Pakistani Bengalis. The first point of friction was the insistence by the West that Urdu was to be the only official national language. This had been very unpopular in the Bengali-speaking East from the moment that the plan was announced in 1948, but it was also resented in regions of the West where other local languages such as Pashto and Sindhi were dominant. Riots in Bengal through 1952 forced the leadership to back down, but not before the violence had provided Bengali nationalists with their first martyrs, who are remembered and honoured to this day.

But the drive for national unity continued. When East Pakistan elected a left-leaning provincial government in 1954, it was dismissed. Nor did the abuses of democracy end there. In the next poll the Bengalis were allowed, in 1970, they overwhelmingly elected a local party, the separatist Awami League led by Sheikh Mujibur Rahman. Yahya Khan suspended the result, primarily because his regime had revoked the One Unit policy, and because West Pakistan suddenly faced rule by Sheikh Mujib, despite the fact that it had voted overwhelmingly for the Pakistan People's Party (PPP) and its charismatic leader Zulfikar Ali Bhutto. A full-scale revolt began in the east, leading within a year to the creation of Bangladesh.

This tragic chain of events forcefully illustrates how flexible the definitions that democracy relies on can be, and how high the stakes can become when politicians, with their own advantage in mind, repeatedly redefine the rules of the game. The original Pakistan of 1947 was created by undemocratic acts trailing back decades. It was destroyed, though, by democracy too long delayed and too grudgingly granted. The obsession with unitary structure and central control eventually produced enough resentment in sufficiently concentrated local form to break apart the system that sought to contain it.

Bengalis were always a majority within Pakistan, but the Pakistani state was never able to find a way to reconcile itself to this fact. As a test of the state's resilience and sensitivity, this was ominous, for Pakistan had, and has, a number of minorities – some, like Bengalis, considered themselves as local majorities. The Basic Objectives Resolution of 1949 laid down that 'adequate provision' would be made for the rights of minorities, but this was generally interpreted as a grant of religious freedom of expression, not a charter for local political autonomy. In practice, neither religious nor political minorities have proved able to assert rights against the central government.

In the wake of the poll of 1970 and the schism of 1971, Zulfikar Ali Bhutto's clear electoral majority in the West left him as prime minister, and he set about stabilizing the new, smaller Pakistan. He rewrote the constitution in 1973 to reflect his taste for powerful central control, creating a bicameral legislature and granting extensive powers to the prime minister, an office he retained after elections that year. These changes promised to solve one of the most pressing long-term problems within Pakistani politics, i.e. defining the exact relationship of the major institutions within the system. The prime minister was now chief executive answerable to an elected assembly, while the office of President became largely ceremonial.

This balance between the three main organs of government had never been explicitly clear since independence. Jinnah had taken up the role of Governor-General, i.e head of state, and had treated it as an executive office, with Prime Minister Liaquat Ali Khan very much his number two. But this arrangement did not survive the personal relationship it embodied. The struggles of the 1950s then reflected the ambiguities bequeathed by Jinnah, which was exacerbated by the lack of a written constitution. Ayub Khan was clear enough about what he wanted to achieve, but his legitimacy was not strictly based on either precedent or consent. This, then, was Bhutto's constitutional inheritance. Unfortunately, he found it as difficult to stay within strict guidelines as any of his strong-willed predecessors.

Bhutto's energetic brand of populism – a variant of socialism, spelled out in anti-Western and Islamic rhetoric – did not assure him lasting mass support. Soon the economy was failing, and he had set up his own paramilitary force in parallel with the army. The first election under the new constitution, in 1977, delivered him a suspiciously large majority, and violent protests ensued. When faced with serious revolt in Balochistan in 1973, he had deployed the army, but the army now decided it had its own enemies to deal with, and General Zia ul Haq ousted him in July 1977.

Pakistani politics then took a turn for the worse, even by its own low standards. Despite extensive international protests, Zia had Bhutto hanged in 1979 for the murder of an opponent and went on to reform the constitution in piecemeal manner over the next nine years, using a strict interpretation of Islamic law and a narrow conception of Pakistani identity to guide him. He submitted his regime to a referendum in 1984. Having won, in 1985 he enacted the Eighth Amendment, which expanded the powers of the presidency, which he occupied, at the expense of all other branches of government. His death in a plane crash in 1988 brought back civilian rule, which then lasted for a further 11 years, marked by regular exchanges of power between Benazir Bhutto, Zulfikar's daughter, and the more conservative Nawaz Sharif, a prominent businessman. This left–right pattern continued till chronic tensions between politicians and the army were resolved with yet another coup in 1999, when General Pervez Musharraf removed Nawaz Sharif, then enjoying his second term as prime minister.

The Musharraf regime proved milder than Zia's, with a vast expansion of media freedom and a degree of economic success. Musharraf appointed himself President in mid-2001, and then tidied up his constitutional standing via the Legal Framework Order of 2002, which retrospectively justified his coup as an extra-constitutional step, taken in the interest of the state and for the welfare of the people. He proceeded to consolidate his position by holding a general election in October 2002. This returned a compliant assembly, which enabled him to enact the LFO of 2002 as the 17th Amendment. Musharraf thus showed himself willing to work with elected politicians, but he was not in a secure position. His term as President was due to expire after five years, and there was some dispute over whether he could stand for re-election while still army chief. He managed to get his term extended by the assembly in 2004, but resultant legalities were to dog the rest of his time in power.

It was Musharraf's fate to rule Pakistan in the aftermath of the 9/11 attacks, which ensured that the global agenda pressed heavily on domestic issues throughout his time in office. By 2007 he was unpopular with both Islamists and liberals, and was locked in combat with the senior judiciary. And despite his collaboration with elected politicians, there was a feeling that the big guns of multiparty politics, the figures who had dominated the 1990s, were not in play. Eventually both Benazir Bhutto and Nawaz Sharif negotiated a re-entry to national politics, with a general election set for early 2008. Bhutto was to die during the campaign, assassinated on 27 December 2007, but the tide was turning against Musharraf. He had steadied himself for the poll by engineering another term as President via indirect election in the provincial and central assemblies in October 2007, but this proved insufficient protection. His party, the Pakistan Muslim League (Q), trailed in third behind the PPP and Nawaz Sharif's PML-N. Under threat of impeachment, Musharraf resigned in August 2008, and left the country. Asif Ali Zardari, Benazir Bhutto's widower, contested the poll to succeed him as President and was elected in September.

This might have been a turning point, a moment when the people, led by the judiciary, could have united around a new vision. Most previous national moments in Pakistani history had arrived at times of real crisis, often with pressing external factors. This, by contrast, was a moment of comparative international calm, of peace with India, and with relatively experienced, relatively moderate leadership at hand. But the opportunity was not taken. Civilian rule was restored, but the transition brought only marginally better times. The government had to contend with a foreign debt crisis and was scarcely able to address the multiplicity of domestic, social and economic problems that had been accumulating for decades. The military retained its power but remained unchastened, while the new government saw only a return to accusations of corruption, a continued failure to address the country's deep-seated problems of sporadic economic growth, inadequate infrastructure and armed insurgency in the western uplands.

By 2008, civilian rule in Pakistan – totalling 27 years out of 61 – had a record as the bringer of chaos and corruption, government incompetence and economic drift. Of these 27 years, only the last 11, from 1988 to 1999, had seen anything like multiparty politics, and they had been the worst years of all. Pakistan's entrepreneurial middle classes appreciated the stability of military rule, but the heavy-handed nature of that stability tended to exacerbate the tensions generated by the inherent – some might say inconvenient – diversity of the national project.

Under the twin banners of national unity and Islamic orthodoxy, Pakistan has remained broadly in denial of her own diversity from the beginning. These ideals have been promoted by both military and civilian rulers. Religious minorities – and women – have not fared well, especially under the Islamization policies followed by General Zia in the 1980s, but a greater worry has been the refusal to accommodate provincial and regional demands. Much of the upland west of the country has long cherished ideals of autonomy, and a strong local movement also sprang up in Karachi in the early 1990s, asserting the rights of the *muhajir* community, bringing violent clashes to the city.

The adoption of various Islamic ordinances has definitely reduced the country's democratic essence, as all non-secular measures are likely to do. Once the will of God is taken as the prime meridian in any legal or political system, the rights of minorities – even the wishes of majorities – are bound to take second place either to the opinions of scholars, or worse, to the rhetoric of demagogues. Again, Jinnah's silence on these matters has left little defence for those in Pakistan willing to steer the country away from scripture and sectarian conformity. Where once it was only the Ahmadiyyas that bore the taint of heresy, now some Sunni organizations are calling, as a matter of public policy, for Shi'as to be officially denied the status of Muslims.

The issue of Islamic identity is inherently not amenable to public policy solutions, because Islamic identity is not undisputed. As the centrepiece of a modern state it has proved elusive and has never exhibited sufficient load-bearing strength. The contested meanings it can generate are all too familiar now, with the most extreme versions insistent on the enforcement of sharia law as they understand it.

Here we find another irony: that religious parties have never done well in elections in Pakistan, attracting only a very small percentage of the poll. But a wider background aura of religion persists, and leaders in power are compelled to talk the language of Islam even if they are not actively promoting its further grip upon the state. The Islamization that General Zia promoted – which was itself an echo of the populism of Zulfiqar Ali Bhutto in the 1970s – has proved very difficult to undo. This concerns not just the persistence of a broad Islamic political atmosphere within which politicians do not dare to appear too secular, but also the close connection of law and social policy, as in General Zia's Hudood Ordinance (1979), which is widely considered to be unfair to women. Yet a third strand concerns the space that a religious atmosphere, combined with the government's ineffectiveness, has left open for more militant organizations, such as the Jamat-ud-Dawa (the political wing of Lashkar-e-Taiba) to move into education and social and charitable works. Such religiosity has not served the wider population or the minorities well, and has, rather, served the interests of the elites and the militants.

Pakistan has both made and unmade itself. Constitutions have come and gone. The first took nine years to appear, mostly because politicians were the least organized sector of the Pakistani elite, lagging behind bureaucrats, army officers and the ulema, all of whom had their own purposes that were more easily served without a written constitution. By the time one was agreed, there had been four prime ministers, one of whom was assassinated. There were then three more prime ministers in two years, before the imposition of military rule in 1958. No national election had been held during this time; policy, choice of personnel and voting were scarcely connected. Pakistanis then learned that the army was more reliable and competent than politicians, and this lesson has not been entirely dispelled. The later military regimes of Zia-ul-Haq (1977–88) and Pervez Musharraf (1999–2008) reinforced some of these lessons by delivering a degree of growth in the economy, even if this was not widely shared.

Pakistan's political culture has remained enigmatic, and the doomsayers that surrounded both India and Pakistan in the late 1940s can still be found lingering over Jinnah's progeny. As a state Pakistan has not known how to cope with majorities or to deal with minorities. By now the country's original list of problems, chiefly its youth, poverty, diversity and strategic vulnerability, has been extended to produce several more potentially fatal weaknesses that only a miraculously perceptive, courageous and well-funded leadership is likely to be able to counter. These include a population that has tripled in 50 years, the dependence of the economy on foreign aid and overseas remittances, massive underinvestment in infrastructure that has produced problems in transport and crippling shortages of water and power, regional separatism, the rise of Islamic radicalism, sectarian violence between Sunnis and Shi'as and, crucially, the long-term interpenetration of the army and the national economy.

From where, then, will solutions to these problems arrive? Pakistanis have never been able to take comfort from constitution-making. Here we see the paradox of constitutions. The more one makes, the weaker they are. Pakistan has had three, in 1956, 1962 and 1973. The last of these has been heavily amended – itself not a good sign. The last major round of alterations was in 2010 when the government of President Asif Ali Zardari reduced the powers of the presidency in favour of the office of prime minister. This was a sensible move in a system based on a supreme legislature. It should, however, be noted that the apparently self-denying nature of this reform on President Zardari's part was balanced by the fact that the prime minister of the day was a member of the party he led – the PPP. Political leaders in South Asia have not been known to make reforms contrary to their own or their party's interests. Zardari was no exception.

Democratic politics did seem to be gaining some standing when an orderly election was held in May 2013, in which Zardari's PPP government was defeated by the PML (N) of Nawaz Sharif. The result was accepted as fair and was followed by a peaceful transition to the new regime, the first time that an elected government of Pakistan had served out its full term and was replaced by another elected government. This restored something of the atmosphere of the 1990s, when the PPP and the Islamic Democratic Alliance (IDA) coalition, led by Nawaz Sharif, swapped power three times. But it promised more. Governments had been thrown out in the 1990s by presidential order, and the army had been suspected of engineering the changes for its own purposes.

The events of 2013 seemed to promise that this pattern might have been broken, but initial optimism was soon dented. General

Musharraf had put Nawaz Sharif on trial for his life after ousting him in 1999, and now Nawaz Sharif returned the compliment. This alarmed the army. Internal security then deteriorated, with increased activity from the Pakistani Taliban and related militant outfits. The prime minister opened talks in April 2014, but a collapse in the dialogue was followed by an attack on Karachi airport in May. This elicited a strong military response and a step-up of the army's campaign in North Waziristan. Many suspected that these moves were all part of a deeper game involving the politicians, the militants and the army, in which a great deal of dissembling and double dealing was going on. Observers noted a series of moves marked out by subtly worded press releases and minor administrative changes, none of which were taken entirely at face value.

Suspicions remain that the army is still rather more in charge than it may appear to the casual onlooker. This impression has been reinforced by events such as the attempted assassination in April 2014 of Hamid Mir, a journalist working for Geo TV, who had been openly critical of the army.

Further suspicions were aroused by the extended stand-off on the streets of Islamabad through August and September 2014, as Imran Khan, the cricketer-turned-politician, and the radical cleric Tahir-ul Qadri led protests against government corruption and alleged vote rigging against their two parties, the Tehreek-e-Insaf (PTI) and the Pakistan Awami Tehreek (PAT) respectively. The avowed intent of the pair was to bring down Nawaz Sharif personally. On one level it seemed that the elections of 2013, widely accepted as the fairest ever, were being challenged extra-constitutionally and violently, in an essentially self-defeating attempt to enhance the nation's democracy. Whatever the rights and wrongs of individual cases of electoral fraud, this appeal to mass civil disobedience was potentially very risky both as a precedent and because it raised the spectre of military intervention. But it was also widely believed that the army had actually orchestrated the whole scenario to facilitate a 'soft coup' against the Nawaz Sharif government, not to topple it, but to send a warning that peace with India should be taken off the agenda and that capital charges against Musharraf should be dropped.

It remains very difficult to read a political situation that can be interpreted as completely chaotic, but may also be entirely structured. Publicly the generals merely demanded that the Sharif government 'share space' with the army.[38]

How long the army will stay out of politics is an unknown and unknowable question, but its continued power and presence are obstructing Pakistan's democratic progress. Attempts by the army to make itself relevant both nationally and internationally have been enormously damaging. Its leadership, sometimes in collusion with politicians, has repeatedly tried to trade up Pakistan's geopolitical location into an income, primarily from the US, but also from China, but this strategy has paid mixed dividends. The Soviet invasion of Afghanistan may have enhanced Pakistan's international importance to American strategists, but it had a very negative impact on the country's economic and political complexion. Military rule, particularly the encouragement and direction of Islamist fighters by the intelligence services of Pakistan, has warped the country's finances and its security status. The very obvious lesson is that Pakistan is unable to sustain a democratic recovery without some settlement of both the Afghan situation and the Kashmir issue with India, but the maintenance of these conflicts also remains the principal *raison d'etre* of the enlarged Pakistani military establishment.

Pakistan needs to live in a more orderly and less hostile neighbourhood to be allowed the full enjoyment of democratic stability. Pakistani society, which is a lusty and not illiberal entity, may learn to produce and elect better politicians, but the level of existential threat, either directly from jihadis and secessionists or indirectly from the perception of national insecurity among the military leadership, must diminish for the kind of optimism seen in 1947 to reappear. Without that, Pakistan will continue to struggle as the small vulnerable neighbour of two large powers, India and China, while the strategic aims of the US, Russia and Iran will bring various types of pressure to bear on Pakistani institutions, both civil and military. Pakistan's nuclear weapons are not enough to bridge the disparities of scale involved, and senior army leaders must eventually recognize this. But the army is so interwoven with Pakistan's economic life that it has become a new aristocracy living off the modern equivalent of agricultural surplus. It took long years and all kinds of revolutions to turf aristocrats out of government all over the world. Bearing in mind that they hold weapons, will Pakistan's generals go any less quietly?

Political analysts concentrate on the poor decision-making exhibited by Pakistan's small leadership clique over decades. Many believe that the very large amounts of foreign aid received by the country, especially under its military regimes, have acted as a kind of political anaesthetic, encouraging political short-sightedness, distorting the economic picture and repeatedly delaying much-needed reforms.

To what degree is the current leadership class capable of guiding the nation? Who knew Osama bin Laden was holed up in Abbotabad? And what did anyone think would be gained by hiding him? Was this strategic genius at work, or simply delusional incompetence? Pakistan's leaders seem to be culpably slow in learning the lesson that seeking to sponsor and control terrorist networks and jihadi groups in order to undermine their enemies is an extremely risky and short-sighted policy that has begun to eat their state alive. These groups promote violence and acknowledge no loyalty. Too many priorities have become inverted, too little has been gained in return.

Security is not divorced from civil policy. It has a significant bearing on all the practical considerations involved in economic development, water management, electricity generation, basic health care and mass education. This last is not just connected to economic uplift; it represents the best way to protect against future destruction of the polity by religious fanaticism, or sheer lawlessness brought on by unemployment, urban chaos and rampant criminality. Many of Pakistan's more isolated rural areas have long had an independent and lawless life of their own. Some observers now fear that the country's cities are becoming ungovernable, with Quetta and Lahore soon to match Karachi as violent and anarchic zones of contestation.

Peace with India, peace in the upland territories of Khyber Pakhtunkhwa and Balochistan, better education, enhanced prosperity, a wider tax base, less generalship and the growth of civility are needed now, as they have always been needed. Pakistan could become like Indonesia yet – an Islamic country committed to modern governance.

Or it could become like Egypt and stumble on with a fragile, nominal democracy permanently guided by the internal military state. Or might it become a huge Somalia, fought over by regional warlords?

The verdict of history is clear – it is very difficult to create the stability and trust that a successful democracy requires without first setting up democracy. Theory and practice have to come together in a parallel process. But the chickens and the eggs are very big and unwieldy. Military rule, especially of the more benign variety experienced in Pakistan under Ayub Khan or Pervez Musharraf, can bring a kind of stability, but the willingness of generals to risk that stability by unleashing all the unruliness and clamour that democratic processes bring is notoriously rare. Nor can democracy grow in times of conflict or chaos, while the population looks to protectors rather than representatives.

No one thinks Pakistan will bloom into a neat and well-ordered polity in any short-time scale. The three most intractable problems in play at Pakistan's inception are still biting: over-commitment to the military, an indistinct political relationship to Islam and regional diversity. One of the most baffling aspects of contemporary Pakistani politics is the multiplication of centres of power all across the state and the territory. Who exactly is in charge? Who is it that persists in ordering provocative actions along the Line of Control? And why?

Currently there is a nominally civilian government, but rumours persist that it only survives on military sufferance, and that the army may take over if it is displeased or feels its interests threatened. And there are believed to be competing centres of control within the army itself, with layers of command likely to adopt different views – an allegedly more radical lower echelon potentially at odds with a more conservative high command. Then there is the shadowy world of the intelligence services, the state within the state. Who funds them and what they are trying to achieve is not clear. Then there are the religious militants – the local Taliban and affiliates, as well as the internationally minded jihadi groups – all of whom can act as self-contained entities, but may also fragment or regroup.

Who, in such a chaotic and divided situation, can take control in a decisive, let alone a permanent way? And who is safe? The prime minister is not secure against his generals. Provincial governor Salmaan Taseer was gunned down in 2011 by his own bodyguard for taking a soft line on blasphemy. In 2012 15-year-old Malala Yousafzai miraculously survived being shot on a school bus for wanting to go to school.

This rising spiral of violence reached a sadly foreseeable peak on 16 December 2014, when the Pakistani Taliban killed 141 pupils and staff at the Army Public School in Peshawar, avowedly in retaliation for the army's anti-insurgency campaign, Operation Zarb-e-Azb. This was by far the worst single act of terrorism in the country's history, and it brought about temporary unity between all the major political players. A National Action Plan was quickly drawn up, including the reinstatement of the death penalty for terrorist crimes and the formation of new specialist courts. Prime Minister Sharif declared the policy of trying to distinguish between 'good' and 'bad' Taliban would be abandoned, and General Raheel Sharif, the army chief, promised action. Within days, one of the masterminds of the massacre, known as 'Saddam', had been hunted down and killed. In response to demands from the army, executions were immediately resumed, with a scheduled 500 perpetrators to be hanged.

But the wider regional conflict, with its competing militias, separatist elements and superpower interests, seems destined only to generate more confusion and fragmentation, with the military and political forces in the state ill at ease with each other and divided on whether talking or fighting is more likely to produce results, with either India or the Taliban. Meanwhile, what results would be most desirable, and to whom, remain open questions. Unless Pakistan can resolve its internal problems, especially the security situation, it cannot act effectively as an international player. The generals who insist on keeping foreign affairs as their exclusive domain seem to have missed this central point. And until Pakistan resolves its internal security status, its government can hardly expect to address the multifarious needs of its enormous and rapidly growing population, such as ridding the country of polio; 80 per cent of the world's cases of the disease are currently to be found in Pakistan.[39]

Prospects are not good. How can progress be made when the government's writ does not run over large areas of the country, when judges are not safe and witnesses are not protected, when the state's intelligence services are not politically accountable, and when politicians compete to exploit every twist and turn of events? How can the one effective institution in Pakistan – the army – promote democracy, when its prospects depend so heavily on preserving undemocratic practices? And how can peace be brokered with terrorists pursuing such radical aims? Negotiation has been tried repeatedly, but the Pakistani Taliban is a loose alliance of at least 13 splinters, any one of which can, and does, reject peace agreements when it suits them. Terrorists have no accountability except to each other, and sometimes not even then; smaller units are continually appearing from within larger.

Pakistan is the long-term victim of the collision of three main forces: local nationalism, US anti-communism, and intra-Muslim sectarianism driven by ultra-religious reformism. These three forces have had highly confused and incompatible goals, especially when overlaid on a markedly un-ideological regional political culture, where exploitation of advantage is still the clearest imperative. One small glimmer of hope is that the liberal English-language press has been courageous in not just condemning the Peshawar massacre, which is easy, but in denouncing a whole range of Pakistani individuals and institutions, for pusillanimity and short-sightedness. But will this bring reform? We might suspect that the political unity of December 2014 may not last. The concerns of an educated wealthy elite are not easily shared by the vast majority of the country's population, whose needs must be addressed by the familiar requirements of better education, gainful employment, personal security and speedy justice. The best aspiration for now will remain steady progress and the slim hope of spontaneous economic improvement. The key governing factor, however, will be the good luck of the region in avoiding further major calamities. Pakistan cannot become a better place until the region becomes a better region. This, ultimately, is not in the gift of Pakistanis alone.

2.

Nepal

Of all the countries of modern South Asia, Nepal has made perhaps the most dramatic political journey, moving from hereditary absolute monarchy to an elected communist government in 50 years. This transition was often a reluctant and traumatic process, and the country was not spared the various tensions usually experienced by traditional societies emerging suddenly into the modern world. Nor is that transition yet complete, with the country's political classes still unable to agree on a constitution even after six years of deliberation.

Nepal is often slightly overlooked in general accounts of South Asia, and to some extent this reflects the historic willingness of her rulers to be overlooked. It suited them, as it suited Sikkim, Bhutan and Tibet – other yams wedged between the massive stones of India and China. But as the twentieth century progressed, Nepal could not escape transformative influences from outside. Geographical proximity to India and the long-standing cultural ties between the two countries helped drive political change, promoting both democratic and communist ideals among the Nepalese, while a reinvigorated China lurked in the background, seeking strategic and economic advantages whenever they could be found.

As decolonization swept the region in the late 1940s, Nepal's Rana leaders maintained a wary distance from the accompanying wave of democratic enthusiasm. The sovereign state of Nepal had never been colonized and was a traditional monarchy, nominally ruled by the Shah dynasty, descendants of Prithvi Narayan Shah, who had created the modern state of Nepal by expanding his small kingdom of Gorkha through a series of successful conquests. This process ended in 1768, but after 1846, the conqueror's royal descendants became puppets in the hands of the Rana family, who made the position of prime minister hereditary in their own line.

The Ranas were fiercely anti-democratic in outlook and severely repressed popular demands for reform right through to the late 1940s. But they were not immune to pressure, especially from newly independent India, which was ideologically committed to the promotion of democracy in the region and was openly hosting a number of anti-Rana groups. In April 1948, as a concession to the increasingly organized opposition, Rana Prime Minister Padma Shumsher passed the Government of Nepal Act, which set out basic democratic and legal rights for the first time. Its provisions, however, were not popular within the wider Rana clan, and the Act was held in abeyance until an appropriately calm moment presented itself. Thus democracy in Nepal was launched just as its closest companion, delay, also made its debut.

By 1950 the Ranas were facing protests in Kathmandu, while the parties-in-exile based in India had united to form the Nepali Congress, plotting armed intervention in favour of the king against the Ranas. More significantly, King Tribhuvan (r. 1911–55) was actively planning to escape his tutelage, a feat he finally pulled off with Indian connivance in early November 1950. With the king in India, Prime Minister Mohan Shumsher replaced him with a royal grandson, Prince Gyanendra (who was later to become king himself). The resulting crisis prompted a small armed uprising, but the situation was eventually resolved through the mediation of India. The king returned; democracy was promised.

India's intervention was a matter of clear self-interest. Having a compliant regime to the north was considered necessary in New Delhi for a series of interrelated economic and strategic reasons, and this was not the last occasion on which India was to shape events in Nepal. Nor was it difficult for the Nepalese to accept a degree of partnership. As a landlocked country, the bulk of Nepal's trade went south, to mutual benefit. There were also a host of historic links between the two countries, based on a shared tradition of Hinduism, and because the border between them, created by a treaty with the East India Company in 1816, was arbitrary and ran across open, flat country. Republican India and monarchical Nepal were thus not so far apart. Good relations suited both parties, and a Treaty of Peace and Friendship was concluded with the Rana regime in mid-1950. This granted unusually liberal terms to the Nepalese, allowing them free movement across the border and freedom to work in India without restriction. In return, a secret protocol bound the Nepali government to consult India over arms purchases and defence policy.

Indian diplomats were to put much effort into sustaining Indian influence over the coming decades with whoever was in power, from monarchs to Maoists. Though the details varied, India was always looking to secure Nepal as a 'strategic partner', and Indian policy was aimed at keeping Nepal stable and compliant.

The British had pursued similar aims and had always supported the Ranas, who had been friendly in return and had sent troops to help suppress the 1857 Uprising. But with the 1949 Communist takeover in China, and the invasion of Tibet the next year, it became a matter of priority for the new Indian regime to settle its northern border. With increasing popular agitation, the prospect of stability under the Ranas diminished and a royal restoration seemed preferable. Pressure was brought to bear on all parties to achieve this. The king then returned under the terms of the so-called Delhi Compromise, and on 18 February 1951, he announced the inauguration of a new system of constitutional monarchy. A joint Rana–Nepali Congress government was formed, and elections for a constituent assembly were promised.

Though limited in scope, these arrangements, set out in April 1951 in the Interim Government of Nepal Act, allowed for the introduction of multiparty politics under the leadership of the king, who retained executive authority. The monarchy was extremely popular and enjoyed wide veneration within the country, the result of over a hundred years spent as a symbolic religious institution away from political dealings and the taint of corruption and repression that had attached itself to the Ranas. The king occupied centre-stage and duly acted as a broker between the Congress and

Rana elements within the government. But the resulting mixture of inexperience and ambition was not a recipe for stable politics, and there were ten separate governments in eight years. A formal constitution was finally framed in 1959, written at the king's behest and largely to his specifications. Elections were immediately held under its auspices; the Nepali Congress won a large majority, and B.P. Koirala was installed as prime minister. But only a year later, in 1960, King Mahendra (r. 1955–72) abrogated the new arrangements and took on the running of the government himself. He chose to dispense with direct forms of democratic accountability, and set up a system of 'guided' democracy. This non-party Panchayat System was based on over 4,000 councils that delegated members upwards to national level, and it bore a distinct resemblance to the system recently introduced in Pakistan by Ayub Khan. It allowed the rural, conservative forces in the country a voice but did not disturb the king's freedom of action. It was, in practice, a consultative veneer for a repressive and authoritarian regime that stifled free expression and monopolized public appointments. The system lasted till 1990, but it was not unopposed. A short-lived armed insurgency blew up after King Mahendra's death in 1972, and his successor, King Birendra (r. 1972–2001), was challenged by the 'boot polish' demonstrations in 1974, when Nepali intellectuals spent a week publicly polishing shoes to highlight their lack of involvement in national life.

A more threatening popular movement took hold in 1979, nicknamed the 'Street Poetry Revolution' because of the prominent role of satirical poets within it. Initially led by students, it soon grew much broader, and the vehemence of the public protests convinced the king to call a referendum on the future of the non-party system. The vote, in May 1980, returned a 55 per cent vote in favour of the Panchayat system. Though the fairness of the poll was questioned, the king took it as a vote for all time and continued his personal rule. The country, meanwhile, remained pitifully underdeveloped; absolutist Nepal was dogged by poverty, inflation, repression and corruption. The Nepali Congress carried on a non-violent *satyagraha* against the Panchayat System, but the movement was suspended after a series of unexplained bomb blasts in Kathmandu in 1985; popular suspicion fell on the monarchy.

The 1980s saw a gradual opening up of new avenues of discussion and opposition, with a five-fold growth in newspapers,[40] and the slow spread of telephones. Television brought news of world events, and the fall of a succession of dictators, from Ferdinand Marcos in 1986 to Nicolae Ceausescu in 1989, could not be hidden.

The final straw for the old regime was the outbreak of 50 days of mass popular protests in 1990, known as the first Jana Andolan (People's Movement). Royal autocracy was replaced by a fully elected national assembly and a return to party politics. Again India took a hand. Having been offended by the king's apparent willingness to court China, the Indian government closed the border, effectively strangling the country economically. The king capitulated, but was merely constrained, not replaced.

A new constitution was hastily drafted, which included provision for multiparty democracy and a range of political and personal rights, but it somewhat confusingly also declared Nepal to be both a democracy and a Hindu, monarchical state. Seen another way, the adjustment of 1990 was primarily between the king and the politicians, with the wider populace barely considered. Even within the political classes, only the Nepali Congress and the moderate communists, who combined to form the Unified Marxist Leninist party (UML) were fully accommodated. The Maoist-communist factions were left out, and no whisper was heard of federalism, which was becoming a demand among some of the country's minorities.

Though Nepal's new urban middle classes were generally pleased with the outcome, the more radical elements that were building up in the country were yet to find a voice. By 1990 there were at least 14 communist groupings in Nepal, and the retention of monarchy was unacceptable to the more revolutionary among them.

The new democratic arrangements also served to highlight social subdivisions, and the discovery, or reassertion, of suppressed community identities. One of the principal objectives of the monarchy, reliant as it was on the old landowning classes from the hill regions, had been to create a strict version of Nepali national identity and culture. In practice this involved reinforcing the caste system, favouring '*pahadi*' or hill people from the dominant Bahun (Brahmin) and Chhetri (Kshatriya) castes over other ethnic and regional groups in official positions, promoting Hinduism over other faiths and privileging the use – and teaching – of Nepali over all other regional languages.

Janjati (indigenous) groups now began to define and organize themselves, and an umbrella body, the Nepal Federation of Indigenous Nationalities (NEFIN), was founded in 1991 to speak for them. Regional groups, such as Newars, Limbus, Tamangs and Sherpas, had a variety of aspirations destined to complicate all political calculations in the coming decades. There was also the emergence of a 'Madhesi' identity across the southern plains – the Terai – where much of the population acknowledged a distinct Indian heritage, and where Nepali was not the dominant language.

This left the new regime with an intense backlog of discontents and grievances to deal with, and the temporary unity of 1990 was soon lost. Apart from the monarchy, there was still no preponderant centre of gravity in the political life of the nation except for the old elite, which encountered no barrier to its continuing social and economic domination. The new system, in its turn, then descended into fractiousness and paralysis. After 1990 there were ten governments in 12 years, cobbled together by minority parties. Communists were represented for the first time, with the UML as the leading centre-left grouping. The first freely elected communist-led national government in the region took power in November 1994. But politics remained a narrow affair, and the most pressing needs of the country were left unattended. An armed Maoist insurgency then took hold of large parts of the countryside from 1996 onwards.

The democratic dawn of 1990 thus brought neither good governance, nor peace, nor wider prosperity to the country. The infamous Palace Massacre of 2001 did not help the situation either, for the murdered King Birendra was replaced by his brother Gyanendra (r. 2001–08), who had even less commitment to democratic ideals.

Gyanendra dispensed with the whole system in February 2005, taking complete personal control. But the re-imposition of direct royal rule backfired spectacularly. It united all the other political forces in the country, prompting the mass protests that peaked in April 2006 (Jana Andolan II), which led to the end of the Maoist insurgency and the abolition of the monarchy in 2008. A Constituent Assembly was elected that year, and the poll returned the former Maoist rebels as the single largest party. But the Assembly was unable to agree on the details of a new constitution, and a second Assembly was elected in November 2013, charged with the same task. The new assembly (CA-II) has yet to discharge its duty, and has run into a familiar quagmire of deadlock and recrimination.

Nepal has thus taken a zigzag path to democratization and still lacks a formally approved constitution or a smoothly functioning multiparty system. Are there any basic reasons for this?

While not blessed with great economic strength, Nepal in 1950 had many of the characteristics that might abet the growth of democratic culture. It had a fairly high degree of religious unity, being overwhelmingly Hindu, and this spared the country the scourge of widespread faith identity problems. Hindu beliefs and culture do not present a barrier to democracy, as the case of India amply demonstrates, and though Nepal's population was largely poor and ill educated, this did not prove an insurmountable problem in India either.

Geographically, the country looked compact enough on a map for convenient government, but internal communication was not easy over such mountainous terrain, and history had reinforced three distinct cultural divisions of the region – hills, mountains and southern lowlands. National unity was therefore always rather more apparent than real. Demographically, Nepal's population was divided into over a hundred ethnic groups speaking over a hundred different languages, and though in recent history the region had only ever been divided into five kingdoms, there was a degree of diversity that the Shah monarchy and the Rana autocracy had always striven to suppress or underplay in favour of a unitary Nepali identity, which they claimed to embody; later, in 1960, the Panchayat system deliberately arranged the country in large north–south strips to elide differences between uplands and plains. The fundamental legal system of the country, set out in the Muluki Ain Code of 1854, had enshrined all the homogenizing pressures and integrative aims of the elite project, including the institution of Untouchability, but after 1990, the country's religious, ethnic, caste and linguistic diversity was fully revealed.

Nepal was thus not quite the suitable seedbed for democracy that some had hoped it would be in 1950. One important aspect of this unreadiness was the shallow development of political consciousness in Nepali society. The anti-Rana parties that formed in India in the late-1940s were not mass-based parties but expatriate committees of agitation, and even after the 1990 reforms, the social structure of the country supported only a very small political elite. Attempts to develop democracy have repeatedly turned into arguments within this elite. Until the entry of the radical left into national politics after 1990, party leaders were not especially interested in cultivating mass followings because, apart from the one occasion in 1959, there was no way to turn this support into power via the ballot box. Once armed revolutionaries were in the field, the ballot box had even less relevance because the Maoists were not interested in contesting elections.

The country was therefore never sufficiently internally aligned to produce a genuine threshold moment that could be seized and sustained. The nearest thing might have been the transition in 1951 from unconstitutional autocracy to constitutional monarchy, but it was a false dawn. Although 19 February is celebrated nationally as Democracy Day, it hardly marked a moment of democratic triumph. The Ranas were not driven out but merely reined in, and the Nepali people swapped an unelected Rana prime minister for a more active, unelected king. There was no ready-made democratic vehicle on hand to take power. The Nepali Congress was the only suitable candidate, but its inexperience and the privileged nature of its leadership restricted its democratic credentials. In truth, the national context was never very conducive to the growth of democracy.

An important difference here lies in Nepal's lack of a colonial past. Because there had been no foreign power to unify against and drive out, there was no climactic liberation moment as in colonial states, when power could be concentrated and redefined. In 1990 and 2006, popular protests brought about a broadening of political participation, but these mini-revolutions were balanced, in the first case by an anti-democratic royal counter-coup in 2005, which recalled a similar moment in 1960, and in the second by a prolonged electoral stalemate in which no single party managed to emerge as the authentic, uncontested voice of the people. This lack of consensus meant that the chance to correct the shortcomings of the 1990 movement was lost. Sufficient momentum to do this is yet to appear.

It all started rather more simply as a two-way fight between the politicians and the monarchy in the 1950s, a struggle that could be crudely characterized as a proxy war between forces of tradition and modernity. But as the internal development of the country proceeded, the nature of Nepali politics became increasingly confused. A major development in this process was the appearance of the Maoists, a force that was neither monarchical-traditional nor bourgeois-democratic, but armed and revolutionary. The formation of the Communist Party of Nepal-Maoist (CPN-M) in 1994 added a degree of complexity to the picture that formal democracy struggled to accommodate.

The CPN-M, under the leadership of Prachanda, conducted an armed insurgency from 1996 to 2006, and introduced two elements that had hitherto been underplayed in Nepali politics. One was armed struggle. The government's response was a reluctant escalation from police action to full-scale military deployment after 2001, when the incoming King Gyanendra insisted on a more vigorous campaign. This intensification served to enhance the national (royal) army's political influence, thus undermining the increasingly weakened political classes. The other element was the force of peasant radicalism. This had to some degree been held in check by the reforms of earlier monarchs, particularly of King Mahendra in the 1960s, as he introduced formal equality in law to all Nepali citizens and instituted a degree of land redistribution. But the Maoists managed to channel a wider range of historic grievances, not only on a class basis, as might be expected, but also on a series of regional and ethnic platforms. Essentially the Maoists were pressing not just for a republican democratic state, necessarily implying the end of the monarchy, but also for an end to the unitary structure of the historic Nepali state itself. A federal solution was promoted as the best way to undermine the entrenched power of the central elite.

Despite the confidence of King Birendra that the alliance of throne and politicians could defeat the rebels in the 1990s, this proved extremely difficult against agile and committed opponents in a mountainous country. And peasant insurgency is notoriously difficult to root out if the rural population is sympathetic, which the Maoist insurgency was, especially among the Dalits and among a range of disadvantaged ethnic groups including the Magars of western Nepal, Tharus, Limbus and Kiratis. Although the insurgency was eventually ended, it was not by force but by agreement, and it was the Comprehensive Peace Accord (CPA), signed on 21 November 2006, that presaged an end to both the monarchy and the unitary Nepali state by allowing the Maoists to participate in parliamentary democracy.

The final run-up to this pivotal moment can be traced back to the Palace Massacre of 1 June 2001, when King Birendra and several members of his close family were shot, allegedly by Crown Prince Dipendra, though many Nepalis refuse to accept the findings of the official enquiry that constituted the only forensic juridical investigation into the affair. The multiple deaths of that day, including the apparent suicide of Dipendra, brought King Gyanendra to the throne, and it was a combination of his decisions that eventually culminated in the full transition of Nepal from a monarchy to a secular, democratic republic as it is today.

Gyanendra first professed his exasperation with the democratic politicians in 2002 when he instituted a technocratic government. He then further increased his personal power with a full dismantling of democratic accountability in February 2005. At this point, the other elements in the political picture – the army, the party leaders and the Maoists – began to combine to bring the Shah monarchy to a close.

The major political players, including underground Maoist leaders, met in Delhi and hammered out a 12-point scheme of reform and reconciliation in late 2005. This Twelve-Point Agreement was the central element in the creation of trust between the principal political leaders, with the Maoists agreeing to lay down their arms in return for a commitment from the parliamentary parties that Nepal would become a secular, federal republic. Once it had been concluded and publicized, the second Jana Andolan began in early 2006. After 19 days of continuous, vigorous protest, the king's position became untenable. The last straw was the arrival of veteran Congressman Karan Singh as a special emissary from India, who informed Gyanendra that he no longer enjoyed Delhi's support, and with the loyalty of the army ebbing away, he decided to stand down. The removal of the king opened the way to a swift end to the civil war, which by that stage had cost about 15,000 lives.

But just as the Maoists laid down their weapons, the people of the southern plains began to take matters into their own hands, feeling that the CPA process did not adequately include them and their demands. Some had already taken up arms, as the Janatantrik Terai Mukti Morcha, which originated in 2004 as a Maoist splinter group of disaffected Madhesis, offended by the CPN-M's apparent unconcern for the region. Now consciousness of a Terai identity, and of *pahadi* discrimination against Madhesis, prompted mass protests across the southern plain in two waves, in 2007 and 2008, in an attempt to get genuine representation of Madhesi people by Madhesi politicians in the promised Constituent Assembly.

Elections were held for the Assembly in 2008, and yet another period of political manoeuvring ensued. Being the largest party, the Maoists led the first government under the veteran Prachanda, but were unable to carry their agenda of radical reform. There was general consensus about the sorts of rights that should be included in the new constitution, which was agreed to be secular, democratic, federal and republican. However, there was no agreement over exactly how a federal state should be set up, with disputes over the basis of any provincial divisions; the number of new provinces there should be; the powers they should be allowed; and what their relationship with the centre should be. Empowerment of ethnicities via ethnic provinces was not a simple matter; questions of geography and 'viability' made it difficult to draw clear lines around distinct groups, while the Dalits were not concentrated and so would hardly benefit from any scheme of regional devolution. There were also real political and technical difficulties about what to do with the Maoists' armed wing, the People's Liberation Army (PLA). It could have no place within a truly democratic system, but the Maoist leadership insisted that the new constitution should be written before it was disbanded, whereas the other parties all insisted that they could not write a constitution under the threat of armed coercion.

Coalitions came and went, with the three major parties all nominating at least one prime minister. The PLA was eventually disbanded, leading to a split within the Maoists, and a deal on federation was brokered in May 2012, only to fall apart a few days later. The Constituent Assembly reached the final extension of its term in late-May 2012, which led to a year of further stalemate, resolved in May 2013, when an interim government was set up under Chief Justice Khilraj Regmi. Elections were slated for November that year. The results, unfortunately, were even less clear than the poll of five years earlier. The Maoists lost ground to the NC and the UML, who jointly formed a new government in February 2014, under the premiership of Sushil Koirala of the NC.

Optimists hoped for a constitution within a year, and it seemed that the Koirala government might encounter fewer obstacles than its predecessors, principally because the Maoists were less strong. Their armed strength had been dissipated – there was now one national army – and their relatively short and largely ineffective time in government had done a great deal to undermine their revolutionary credentials, giving them a smaller parliamentary presence. Their leadership was split, and their preference for a strong presidential system seemed to have lost ground.

The balance of power in CA-II currently lies with the parties of the old dispensation, who see little wrong with the system of the 1990s that they dominated. A Westminster-style model of governance may become more likely, and the principal point of contention may come to be the number of federal provinces and whether they should be ethnic- or identity-based. It remains to be seen what any of this may mean for their populations, which will still contain majority and minority groupings of various kinds.

Why is all this still proving so difficult? One general point is that Nepali politicians have a habit of concluding deals between themselves behind closed doors, then presenting them to the wider public. This undermines accountability and generates a feeling that politics is an elite game. When polls are inconclusive, politicians are obliged to provide leadership in the wider interests of society, and Nepali politicians have found this very difficult. General progress has certainly been made, and a definite desire for change has been expressed by the populace over and over again. But details cannot be put to plebiscites, and if the competitiveness and personal interests of politicians endlessly multiply and diversify such details, the situation cannot easily clarify itself.

For understanding, we need to return to some more basic questions. Why did the civil war start? Because the 1990 system was very like the old system under expanded management. Why did the war go on so long? Because it was not winnable by either side. The Maoists could not overthrow a government that had so little material substance to it, especially working across such difficult terrain; there was no knock-out blow available to them with the forces they possessed. On the other side, the royal army could not stamp out determined resistance founded in such manifest social exclusion, economic deprivation and political injustice. The armed struggle was indecisive, and so by extension, the peace was hard to agree upon, precisely because neither side had secured a clear victory. The conflict then returned to the political arena, which was only mildly less unsatisfactory.

Why has the peace settlement taken so long? Because the details of the reform have been very complex, and power politics, personal security, peace-making and constitution-writing have all been mixed up within it. The general idea of a federal, democratic republic carried a lot of freight and was bound to create winners and losers anew, whatever the details. In the event, the CA did very little actual debating of constitutional details, because the calculus of power lacked clarity and there was no 'natural' mandate for any one specific kind of change. In other words, debates on the floor and votes in the chamber were less likely to produce results than deals done away from public scrutiny. Finally, the post-war climate was filled with distrust – the old school politicians distrusted the Maoists just as much as the latter distrusted their former enemies. Prachanda was not prepared to work with a man who had tried so long and hard to kill him, and his insistence on dismissing the army chief General Rukmangud Katawal in 2009 seriously imperilled the fragile consensus.

One way forward appeared in light of the election of Narendra Modi in May 2014. With the secular UPA gone, the small royalist grouping in the CA, the Rashtriya Prajatantra Party, began to hope that Delhi might support a royal restoration. But Nepali journalist Prashant Jha, author of *Battles of the New Republic* (2014), believes that by now there is 'absolutely no possibility' of a return to monarchy in Nepal. Some did harbour such hopes, he says, and had believed that the new BJP regime would signal India's support for monarchy. But during his visit to Nepal in August 2014, Modi declared that his government supported a 'federal democratic republican constitution', though he did not mention 'secular'.[41] Jha is less sure of the secular agenda in Nepal, sensing a concerted campaign by the right in both Nepal and India to push for a return to a Hindu state. He does not think it will succeed, but he suspects that 'we may see dilution of the secularism principle in some form'.[42]

Nepal has fallen victim to what has been called over-contestation, a situation in which arguments over very fine details become proxy skirmishes for larger struggles. Politicians begin to think that in conceding small things they risk losing out on their greater aims. Magnanimity is viewed as a fatal weakness; maximalist positions become the norm. When personal status and wealth are mixed into the picture, politics can degenerate into a messy war of attrition, only occasionally leavened with appeals to the wider populace, who are otherwise reduced to mute spectators.

Progress remains painfully slow. A four-point agreement was reached between the major parties in June 2014, but a deadline for agreement on a first draft of the constitution was missed in September 2014, and has now been extended to January 2015. Meanwhile various less democratic means of defining the Nepali state have been suggested. A new constitution technically requires a two-third majority in the Assembly to be binding, but some are now calling for a simple majority to suffice. Others are suggesting that direct popular consultation via referendum could bypass the politicians on broad issues such as secularism. The politicians have their own ideas too; a High-Level Political Committee has been delegated to thrash out constitutional sticking points, but predictable arguments about its precise remit, who should sit on it, and who should chair it have duly appeared.

All this underlines the weakness of the idea of democracy when confronted by multiple issues of insecurity, partisanship and lack of common purpose. Political deadlock discredits politicians in proportion to the degree of impotence it reveals in them, but violence promotes agendas of revenge and restitution, and secret deals breed suspicion. Constitution-making in such conditions cannot be anything but slow, and the eventual results may not command enough loyalty to exert sufficient binding force.

Lastly, federal systems are the hardest of all to build; people can so easily feel they are losing more than they gain. The Maoists, like the INC in 1947, wanted a strong centre because they trusted themselves with power. Minorities in Nepal now, as in India then, do not want a strong centre because they know that they will not be the ones to hold that central power, and they trust no one else to hold it either. The bigger picture – a feeling of inclusive national unity – has to regain the prominence it held during the two Jana Andolans, but it must somehow sustain itself long enough to generate an era of increased security. Perhaps now, leaders must argue less, consult more and take a broader view of the common good.

3.

Bangladesh

Bangladesh began life in 1971 as a nation starved of democracy. One hundred and ninety years of colonial government in East Bengal had ended in 1947, only to be replaced by rule from West Pakistan, which proved no more inclusive or responsive. Despite the numerical superiority of Bengalis within Pakistan, the government in Karachi was determined that the new state's eastern wing, which was much poorer economically, would not be allowed to dominate by sheer numbers. The two-wing Pakistan that survived from 1947 to 1971 thus had democracy written out of its political culture very early on, simply because of the demographic asymmetry of the state.

This discriminatory policy fostered a sense of resentment among Bengalis, who found themselves disadvantaged in multiple ways. They were told that Pakistan's official language was to be Urdu, which was not comprehensible to them. They missed out on senior employment opportunities within the bureaucracy and the military, and the economic priorities of the state focused on the welfare of its four western provinces. These long-held grievances came to a head when Pakistan's first-ever general election was held in 1970, and the Bengal-based Awami League won an absolute majority in the new assembly. General Yahya Khan, Pakistan's military leader, had no option but to annul the poll, setting off a chain of events that led, in March 1971, to the military suppression of protests in Dhaka.

After six months of bloodshed the Indian army finally intervened to help the Bengali resistance, and a swift and decisive victory followed.

The new state of Bangladesh, established on 16 December 1971, was thus born out of a second layer of bloodshed, imposed on the violence of the Partition of 1947.

Newly liberated Bangladesh started independent life facing a daunting range of problems, possibly even worse than had confronted Pakistan a quarter of a century earlier. The one advantage that Bangladesh had was a cultural unity. But this unity proved to be a shallow veneer, and despite the apparent popularity of the separation from West Pakistan, serious long-term divisions persisted, arising from the legacy of war and the strands of collaboration and opposition that had entangled East Pakistan during the struggle. There was also an unacknowledged problem of identity, similar to the Pakistani–Muslim duality that had troubled Jinnah and his successors. In Bangladesh this concerned whether the new state was primarily a Bengali or a Bangladeshi entity. If the new nation shared a Bengali character, then its non-Muslim members, mostly Hindus, would be entitled to a full voice in the new republic. But if the new state was Bangladeshi, i.e. defined by its specifically Pakistani heritage, then Muslim identity was paramount.

There was another aspect of the new unity in liberation that soon revealed itself as a weakness: the country was too united politically under the leadership of Sheikh Mujibur Rahman and the Awami League. Sheikh Mujib had been imprisoned by the Yahya regime, but he returned triumphantly to Bengal in early 1972 to take up the leadership of the new state, supported by the assembly as elected in 1970. Buoyed by massive popularity, he then managed to make a spectacular mess of the task of national reconstruction. This would have been a mammoth undertaking for anyone, but Mujib proved himself a better rebel than a ruler, and the Awami League leadership proved to be as adept at ignoring the national interest of Bangladeshis as the Punjabi feudals had been at ignoring the provincial interests of East Pakistanis. Corruption set in early and hard, but Mujib did little to prevent it. What wealth there was in the country soon fell into a few well-protected hands, and has barely shifted since.

A new parliamentary constitution was created in 1972, founded on four pillars – nationalism, socialism, democracy and secularism – but it was destined not to last. At the country's first general election, the Awami League won 73 per cent of the vote, which translated into 97 per cent of the seats, allowing Mujib to do whatever he wished. One of his projects was to create a militia loyal to himself, the Jatiyo Rakkhi Bahini, or National Security Force. This was to act as a counterweight to the army, which had become a fractious and disorganized body containing both professional veterans from the Pakistan era and various groups of ex-guerrilla fighters committed to a range of political creeds. Nor did the Awami League maintain its unity. Once the liberation struggle was won and minds turned to building the new country, evident divisions appeared between those who wanted to push hard for a socialist society and those who were more liberal. This had obvious economic implications, but it also lined up as a pro-Indian, pro-Western split. The same lines were drawn outside the party, with groups of radical students and ex-freedom fighters demanding revolutionary change. Then in late 1974, as he faced internal dissent and economic chaos, compounded by famine and floods, Mujib rewrote the constitution, making himself President and abolishing all political parties except his own, now renamed as the Bangladesh Krishak Sramik Awami League (BAKSAL).

With a debilitating combination of arrogance, corruption, inexperience and incompetence, his elective dictatorship became increasingly unpopular through 1975, until the army finally took action in August, slaughtering Mujib and about 40 of his closest relatives. Two further coups in November eventually installed General Ziaur Rahman as head of state. Fifteen years of military rule were to follow.

All this confirms lessons that can be drawn from other regional states. Firstly, the transition from violence to democracy is extremely perilous. Guns are a deeply anti-democratic force, whether in official or unofficial hands. Next, economic distress is not a good time for calm assessments of the national interest over one's own. Thirdly, the concentration of power in the hands of a small group, and especially one individual, is a very real threat to the continuation of democratic norms. Bangladesh has since overcome the first two problems to a reasonable degree, but the third is a persistent and systematic problem that shows no sign of abating.

Though the military were very definitely in charge after 1975, the new nation was not politically inert. General Zia had a national vision of a free market economy within a religiously conservative society, and he tried hard to enlist the support of the middle classes and richer farmers to realize it. He began by creating a new set of local village institutions in 1976, frequently compared to the Basic Democracy system of Ayub's Pakistan. He then held a referendum on his programme in May 1977. Encouraged by the results – a purported 99 per cent approval in an 85 per cent turnout – he offered himself for election as President the next year. To no one's surprise he won, and moved on to form his own political party. The new Bangladesh National Party (BNP) had a conservative, pro-business, anti-secular tint, and was called into being to enter parliamentary elections in 1979. The BNP took 207 of the 300 seats.

Zia was careful with civil society, and seems to have had a degree of vision beyond the preservation of his own position. But the army posed a greater threat to him than the politicians, and after a succession of attempted coups, he was shot dead in May 1981. A brief return to (nominally) civilian rule was then snuffed out by a further coup in 1982, which elevated Commander-in-Chief General Hussain Muhammad Ershad to power. Ershad was not quite such a shrewd operator, but he continued down the path laid out by Zia. He formed his own political machine, the Jatiya Party, and prepared to fight elections against the two main opposition parties – the BNP, now in the hands of Zia's widow, Khaleda Zia; and the Awami League, reformed in 1981 and now led by a daughter of Mujib, Sheikh Hasina Wajid, who had fortuitously been out of the country at the time of the 1975 massacre.

Ershad continued with the policy of rebuilding democracy from the bottom up, starting with local elections in 1984 and proceeding to elections for the presidency in 1986. Like Zia he carried the polls, but his tolerance of multiparty politics soon weakened his position. He allowed his opponents the chance to participate but he also gifted them a new power – that of refusing to participate. The parliamentary elections of 1986 were farcical. Ershad's Jatiya Party won a majority, but the BNP boycotted the polls, and the Awami League, which had participated, boycotted the parliament. Much of the future shape and style of Bangladeshi politics was now in place, including the renewed electoral presence of the Jamaat-e-Islami (JeI). Having been banned by Mujib as a collaborationist outfit after the war of 1971, the party was allowed back into the country in 1978, and it now took ten seats. The next elections in 1988 were boycotted by all the major opposition parties, and in a rare show of unity, Begums Khaleda Zia and Sheikh Hasina managed to paralyse the country with a wave of strikes.

Ershad finally bowed to the pressure and resigned in December 1990, leading to a general election in early-1991. The poll was close, but the BNP, which ran on a nationalist, economically liberal platform, narrowly defeated the Awami League, which stood on a centre-left, secularist platform. The BNP then formed a government with outside support from the JeI. This theoretically marked a full return to parliamentary politics, but many of the bad habits – essentially the most effective strategies – of the previous decades carried straight over into the new liberated era, which was to be marked by sustained over-contestation.

Khaleda Zia and Hasina Wajid, the 'battling begums', have dominated Bangladeshi politics ever since, and details of their tussles are edifying only in the sense that they show how far rules can be bent, ignored or rewritten by determined politicians within a nominally democratic system. Under their stewardship, Bangladesh has regularly been ranked among the world's most corrupt states, and was actually at the bottom of the list from 2001 to 2005. This was not entirely their doing, but neither of them has shown any great determination to undo it. It is as true in Bangladesh as anywhere else that no one has much incentive to reform rules under which they believe they can win.

The BNP won elections in 1991, and again in 2001, while the Awami League won in 1996 and 2008. This regular turnover of power would seem to indicate the smooth running of democracy, especially since it was always the incumbent party that was defeated. But the picture is rather more complex. On both occasions that the BNP lost power, the transition was accompanied by a constitutional crisis.

In 1991, the Awami League claimed that the polls were rigged, and continued to complain about government abuses, leading to a boycott of parliament in 1994. It then refused to contest the next election in February 1996, but the poll went ahead, producing an enormous BNP victory based on a turnout of less than 10 per cent. This was clearly an untenable situation, and a great deal of international pressure was brought to bear. A caretaker government was then installed to supervise new elections which were held that June and produced a narrow victory for the Awami League, which formed a government with support from General Ershad's Jatiya Party. One of the new administration's first acts was to pass the 13th Amendment to the constitution, laying down that all future elections must be held under the auspices of a neutral caretaker government, headed by the most recently retired chief justice of the Supreme Court, which was to be installed 90 days before the date of the poll. The AL did exactly this before the election of 2001, and lost.

The incoming BNP administration boxed more cleverly this time, and set about ensuring that the caretaker government due in 2006 would be as favourably disposed as possible. It therefore raised the compulsory retirement age of the chief justice to ensure that the most recently retired incumbent, K.M. Hasan, who was known to be a supporter, would be the caretaker administration's chief executive. The BNP then packed the Election Commission with supporters.

The next general election was due in January 2007, but a wave of strikes and protests broke out as it approached, culminating in a full Awami League boycott of the poll. Bangladesh's susceptibility to foreign pressure again produced results, with a cascade of resignations and, eventually, the installation of a military-backed interim government, led by a former banker. Elections were postponed indefinitely and a clean-up campaign of sorts began. Both main party leaders were arraigned on serious charges, possibly in an attempt to drive them into exile. But the charges were not pursued, and new elections were held in late December 2008, which produced an unexpectedly large win for the Awami League.

Lessons had been learned, but unfortunately rather to the detriment of good democratic practice. The Awami League abolished the requirement to install a caretaker administration by the 15th Amendment, passed in 2011, and an entirely predictable wave of strikes and protests then accompanied the run-up to the 2014 election. But the poll took place, and the Awami League won a huge victory on a 22 per cent turnout, winning 127 of its seats in uncontested constituencies. Slightly less predictably, the international community, so solicitous in 1996 and 2007, remained almost entirely silent, and the result has stood. Some informal polling suggested that the Awami League would have won anyway, even if the BNP had run a full campaign, but this is conjectural. Is it that the major powers actually prefer Awami League governments to BNP? Or that Bangladesh has simply fallen from international attention because of other regional factors?

Astonishingly, this is the first time in 23 years of multiparty democracy that an incumbent government has won an election. Does this mean that the Awami League truly speaks with the voice of the Bangladeshi people, or is it simply that after a great many false starts, some of the country's politicians have finally learned to pull all the right levers to run a successful election campaign, regardless of what the people say or do?

For all the apparent changing around in the top levels of society, government policy has hardly varied, while the intense party rivalry has not helped address the country's persistent problems with power supply, infrastructure and basic law and order. There has been steady growth, currently running at about 6 per cent, but politically motivated strikes have hampered economic activity, and foreign investors have been troubled by the prevalence of corruption and the capriciousness of the judicial system. Alternation of parties has actually aggravated all these problems.

But there were two clear differences of policy under the Awami League administration of 2008–14. One was its willingness to woo the Indian government with a series of measures and initiatives. The other was its determination to pursue the unresolved criminal issues from the war of 1971.

The 1971 'war of liberation' was a messy and complicated affair, and as civil wars usually are, it was marked by cruelty and ruthlessness on both sides. Opportunism and ideology played their parts in determining the loyalties of individuals, both during the conflict and afterwards, leaving a large measure of unsettled scores. Internal tensions then continued to fester after the war was won, with further bloodshed and polarization after the military coup of 1975. All the major political alignments had blood on their hands by the time democracy was restored in 1990; the country's two main leaders had lost a father and a husband at the hands of their opponents.

Of the two, Sheikh Hasina had always been keener to seek retribution for war crimes, and this attitude is credited as one factor in the rebellion she faced in February 2009, when the junior ranks of the paramilitary Bangladesh Rifles mutinied. There were casualities among the officer corps, and several accidental civilian deaths. Worse, the revolt seemed about to spread to other units who had grievances about conditions of service and corruption. There were suspicions that the uprising had been engineered by outside forces to destabilize the country; Pakistan was suspected of trying to bring down the Awami League government in order to reverse its rapprochement with India and to stymie any retrospective war crimes trials.

But the revolt did not spread. Sheikh Hasina managed to negotiate a peaceful end to the affair, and judicial proceeding later sentenced over 150 participants to death. She also successfully pursued the historical war crimes agenda, which led to the execution of Abdul Kader Mullah, a leading member of the Jamaat-e-Islami, in December 2013 – the only punishment meted out so far to a political leader from that era. There were fierce protests both for and against the execution, which serves to illustrate how divisive the war of 1971 still remains. It had always been Awami League policy to remember the martyrs of the war, while the BNP sought to downplay the whole episode, but the mission to settle old scores has now taken on an added political dimension. Two more JeI leaders, Motiur Rahman Nizami and Quasem Ali, were sentenced to death in late 2014, which proved widely popular, and nothing like the December 2013 protests appeared.[43] The effect has been to drive a wedge between the JeI and their nominal allies, the BNP, which has felt unable to condemn the verdicts for fear of damaging its increasingly fragile popular support base. In such a context, Sheikh Hasina will see no political reason not to pursue her current course, if only to keep the BNP on the back foot and unable to bring pressure to bear for a rerun of the January poll.

The events of 1971–75 have cast a long political shadow, and violence has remained a factor in Bangladeshi politics ever since. Intimidation, brutality and assassination have affected high-profile politicians, especially Awami League leaders under the 2001–06 BNP government. Police action has killed and injured hundreds of protestors from both main parties. Currently there is also concern over the high level of 'encounter' killings of criminals, especially at the hands of the elite Rapid Action Battalion (RAB), who even managed to maim an entirely innocent schoolboy named Limon Hossain in March 2011.[44] There have also been bombings by Islamic militants, with a particularly widespread coordinated attack in 2005, which killed miraculously few people – two – considering that over 500 devices were deployed.

All this represents a high degree of violence for a nominal democracy, and reflects the fact that marked divisions persist within Bangladeshi society despite 25 years of broadly centre-ground government. The original division between the support bases of the BNP and the Awami League remains fairly solid, with the middle classes, bigger farmers and the business community in the BNP camp and students, peasants and workers behind the latter. This means that the Awami League has a better chance of winning national elections if it can mobilize its support effectively. Recently it has done this, while also ensuring that all other political factors are optimized.

Since the restoration of democracy in 1990, politics in Bangladesh has not been a matter of competitive policy agendas but more like a game of musical chairs conducted in a fiercely competitive atmosphere, involving a great deal of sharp practice. Frontline politics features a great deal of noise and posturing, while the business of administration and policymaking continues more steadily underneath. It is essentially caretaker governance on a permanent basis, as politicians prioritize political advantage while underlying concerns about national development remain unaddressed. This is unfortunate, as Bangladesh faces so many of the modern world's most intractable and dangerous challenges, such as environmental degradation and population growth.

As a model of democratic practice, Bangladesh sends a warning of what can happen if the central civilities that democracy ideally requires are discarded in a process of alternate elective autocracy. Every aspect of Bangladeshi life has become polarized along party lines, so that now the national media, the bureaucracy, the police, the universities and even the foreign aid system of NGOs have been subsumed into the partisan struggle. The only virtue left in the system is that governments have actually changed at elections. The losing side routinely claims that the polls were rigged, but power changed hands regularly, at least up until 2008.

In some respects, the regular changes of the party in government from 1991 to 2008 represent a drawn-out national disaster in terms of opportunities lost and resources squandered. It is even more depressing when we consider that no matter how hard the incumbent party has tried to warp the contest in terms of patronage, fund-raising, public order enforcement and media coverage, the electorate was still able to exercise a dominant say in the power equation. In other words, all the wastefulness and poor governance were a price that the public paid to receive nothing in exchange except the privilege of determining which incompetent organization would have the next turn behind the desk.

In the four valid elections from 1991 to 2008 the ruling party was thrown out every time. In other words, being in government did not seem to confer decisive electoral advantage – or was outweighed by the contempt and revulsion that perceived failures attracted in the minds of voters. It remains to be seen whether the Awami League victory of 2014 will permanently alter this pattern. There seems no prospect of a re-run poll, as in 1996. We must ask, therefore, whether the BNP can now regroup and organize an anti-incumbency backlash, as in 2001. The party's prospects do not look promising, with reports of infighting and recrimination over the decision not to contest the 2014 poll. In all events the BNP will have to compete against a government that has had ten years to shore up its position, a very extended opportunity that in Bangladesh cannot be expected to go unmissed.

Political parties as personal fiefdoms are very clearly in effect here, but there is an even more obvious point to be made: that the country's future is being argued over by a narrow clique, consisting of relatives of a populist demagogue and a military dictator, and therefore the country is still in the same few hands, in or out of military rule, under one party or the other. How much more of a charade can democracy be reduced to than this – that nothing changes despite wasted resources and the distortions introduced to society, by the use of corruption in the delivery of public services, especially the police, and the employment of *mastans* – freelance gangsters – to enforce payment of 'black' money, or to ensure loyalty amongst underlings.

How can Bangladesh escape this cycle of misgovernment? The answer might simply be 'more democracy', but in such a tainted system it is difficult to know what this might mean. Honesty in government officials would be a major step forward, but politicians would have to allow decisions to be made on non-partisan lines for this to happen. Guidance from above has to be honest for honest administration to take root. The judiciary must be entirely independent of political influence, and currently it is not. Despite the separation of the lower judiciary from the executive power under the military caretaker government in 2007, senior appointments are highly influenced by party allegiance. A more prosperous and independent civil society needs to grow and flourish, but this is another of the many problems of serial and parallel change that arise in developing democracies.

Would the country be more prosperous under authoritarian rule? Perhaps, if it banished corruption and was solely dedicated to the public interest. But autocratic regimes inevitably commit inordinate amounts of time and effort to the elimination of dissent and extending their own tenures. Even the most un-ideological of dictators cannot in the end tell the difference between their own interests and those of the countries they dominate. It is very hard for a national saviour to know when to stop saving the country. The prime concern of dictators is always for their own well-being, and the most dangerous thing any undemocratic politician can do is to demit power.

But military rule seems a distant prospect, because Bangladesh may by now have acquired a slightly fortuitous, even a unique immunity from military coup. The army in Bangladesh earns much of its prestige, and a good deal of its perks, from its employment abroad as a peacekeeping force, and this makes it particularly vulnerable to international pressure. Its leaders are thus heavily dissuaded from taking up a political role, and without their help it may be that no civilian group can effectively exercise full authoritarian power. Bangladesh may thus be the only state currently forced to suffer all the evils of distorted democracy while being denied recourse to a military coup – the most familiar, though risky way out of democracy gone bad. The current government may be keeping an eye on this, as it has just increased its military budget by a very large 8.4 per cent, which will go mainly in wages.[45] This might seem a price worth paying for a degree of insurance against a malcontent military.

Corruption and self-seeking among the political classes of Bangladesh should, in the end, dissipate with more effective democratic accountability. But from where will this come, and who will enforce it? Offenders should be prosecuted and removed from office, but such a salutary development would have to rely on the efforts of a public informed enough to know that offences have been committed, and a law enforcement system and judicial process that is robust and impartial. Both the begums have been charged with a variety of serious offences, yet both still lead their parties.

It may well be that the political class in Bangladesh is rich enough and sufficiently entrenched institutionally to perpetuate its dominance for some time to come. While it does, the citizens of Bangladesh will have to endure the charade of democratic elections, while living in hope than one day something might actually change.

4.

Burma/Myanmar

Among the countries of southern Asia, Burma in 1945 had perhaps the least promising prospects for life as an independent democratic entity. Complex demography and geography obstructed the creation of a single national identity, and the country's recent history was of a British colonial regime that had tried to underplay or suppress ethnic friction while collecting as many disparate groups as it could under its sway. National unification under democratic government was guaranteed to be a very challenging undertaking, and the ravages of recent war could only make the task harder.

The British took over Burmese territory in three steps after successful wars against the Konbaung dynasty in 1824–26, 1852 and 1885. The last war extinguished the dynasty, and Burma was annexed in 1886, becoming part of British India till 1937, after which it was treated as a separate entity. British rule was imposed on a large and diverse territory that included several distinct ethnic and linguistic groups. The British recognized this situation and never governed Burma as a single political unit; the lowland centre of the country – 'ministerial' Burma – was dominated by Burmans, and was ruled directly, like the provinces of British India, while the hilly periphery enjoyed a fair degree of autonomy, including 34 distinct Shan states in the east, and the Karenni state in the south-east.

Around two-thirds of the country's population was Burman, and over 80 per cent Buddhist, but there were substantial minorities, some with cultural links to neighbouring traditions and polities – the Shan with Thailand, the Muslim Rohingyas with Bengal, ethnic Chinese on the long eastern border, a prosperous Indian middle class in Rangoon and a substantial amount of Christians among the Chin, Kachin (Kayin) and Karen ethnic groups.

This rich demographic and cultural mix led to deep divisions when the Japanese invaded in 1942, with sections of society taking opposite sides. The Burmans largely supported the Japanese. Historically they had been most opposed to British rule; the deposed Konbaung had defined Burman identity and had set out the borders of the state the British took over, leaving many Burmans with a sense of aggrieved nationalism. But many of the hill people, especially those who were Christian, resisted the invaders.

The war featured two main campaigns between 1942 and 1945, as the Japanese and the British mounted successful offensives in turn. The largest local force, the Burmese Independence Army, was initially on the side of the Japanese. It was dominated by Burmans, who till then had been under-represented in the armed forces. The Japanese granted Burma 'independence' in mid-1943, but the realities of the new arrangement were a disappointment. When Japanese tutelage proved to be at least as bad or possibly worse than British imperial rule, the Burman leadership, prominent among whom was the young Aung San, switched sides in March 1945 and drove the Japanese out, allied with General Slim's 14th Army. This left post-war Burma in economic chaos, with the country's infrastructure devastated and much of its urban fabric destroyed. There was also a fund of new resentments and rivalries created by the internal conflict, with the population split into heavily armed rival groups under a variety of leaders, owing allegiance to disparate groups and ideologies including revolutionary communism.

With the Japanese gone, the scene was set for the transition to independence. As with other colonies in the region, the British made no attempt to withhold self-government, and their priorities were to try to keep the new states within the Commonwealth and out of the hands of communists. Their preferred means of doing this was to make alliances with local liberal politicians and to advise on forms of constitutional arrangement that would be most helpful to them. Burma fitted this pattern very closely.

A British Military Administration was declared on 6 May 1945, and a white paper on Burmese independence was published in London on 17 May 1945, but there was no real sense of urgency in London about the process. The paper envisaged a long transition period, ending perhaps as late as 1953, and laid out a three-stage process of negotiation over the country's precise status, not an immediate grant of full sovereign independence. Its other main point of interest was that it preserved a separate administration for the Frontier Area, formerly known as the Scheduled Area, which contained the hill tribes.

More pressing were the political manoeuvrings on the ground. The newly installed British governor, General Sir Reginald Dorman-Smith, tried to build relationships with the principal nationalist leaders, but Aung San, the most gifted among them, would not join a provisional government. He demanded full independence. Dorman-Smith wanted him in, but London vetoed his inclusion; Dorman-Smith then resigned in August 1946. His successor, General Sir Hubert Rance, faced strikes and mass disruption and was forced to give Aung San and his party, the Anti-Fascist People's Freedom League (AFPFL), six out of nine seats on his executive council. The AFPFL, an umbrella left-wing coalition formed during the war, now began to act as the government-in-waiting.

Aung San called for faster progress and went to London in January 1947 for negotiations. The Attlee government proved amenable and an agreement was reached on 27 January, promising elections for a Constituent Assembly. The elections were held in April, and the AFPFL won a clear victory. But then, with prospects brightening, the first of many disasters struck when Aung San and six of his senior colleagues were gunned down in broad daylight on 19 July 1947. The guilty party was held to be U Saw, a long-term rival of Aung San's, though many still believe it might have been a British plot to eliminate Aung San and frame U Saw, thus decapitating the Burmese leadership.

The result was certainly not helpful to the future development of Burma, for it condemned the new state to what has been described as 'second eleven' leadership.[46] The chief beneficiary was U Nu, president of the Constituent Assembly, who went on to dominate national politics for a decade. Aung San's legacy, though, was a powerful one, and one that the Burmese respect to this day. Like many postcolonial leaders he had a centre-left outlook, and his main aim was to reduce exploitation by dismantling the capitalist classes that had been running the colonial Burmese state, many of whom had been aliens, principally Indians and Chinese. This meant democratic popular sovereignty, a planned economy and a secular political culture within a unitary state. Aung San had been in negotiations with the country's minority communities and had provisionally agreed to grant 'rights and privileges' to them. Two conferences on the issue, at Pandong, had been chaired by the British in 1946 and 1947; progress had been made, and a degree of trust in Aung San seemed to have been established. But the goodwill did not survive his death, and by the time the country became independent on 4 January 1948, there were serious Communist insurgencies in progress, soon followed in 1948 by a revolt among the Karen.

Independent Burma was nominally a parliamentary democracy, with a constitution drawn up by the Constituent Assembly of 111 members (all male) and agreed in September 1947. It adopted Westminster-style norms – a bicameral parliament, cabinet government, a prime minister as chief executive and a President as head of state. More importantly, it recognized minority states and granted them a right to secede after ten years. But the country was thrown immediately into a highly confused set of civil conflicts, some 'ethnic', others revolutionary, with large numbers of small groups resisting central authority. These groups frequently split up, allying and re-allying amongst themselves, sometimes funded by profits of smuggling and drugs, occasionally helped by foreign powers, principally China, which conducted a proxy war in eastern Burma till the early 1960s in pursuit of a section of the defeated nationalist Kuomintang forces which had taken refuge in the country after Mao's victory in 1949. These various conflicts proved literally interminable; peace deals were set up and broken repeatedly for the next 60 years.

This clearly did not help the new state either to become a coherent nation or a viable political system. Neither ideological revolution nor determined separatism can easily be dismantled by more democracy in centralized institutions. Military might or political leadership is required, and in the case of Burma, neither was available in useful ways. The nation's leaders had pressing economic problems to overcome, but they were constantly hampered by one abiding conceptual legacy of the colonial era, namely a determination – even a mania – to avoid foreign domination at all costs. And those costs have been high. The search for economic and cultural autarky led successive Burmese leaders, who since 1962 have all been soldiers, into a self-reinforcing cycle of repression and control.

The original prospectus of the country was a broad nationalist state socialism, considered perfectly compatible with Buddhism by U Nu, prime minister from 1948–56, 1957–58 and 1960–62. This went along with fierce isolationism, reflected in a refusal to join international organizations, principally the Commonwealth, or to be involved in any of the pan-national treaty groups that sprang up during the Cold War. Initially Burma was hostile on political grounds to all Western influence, and only gradually did China come to be viewed as a potential ally as opposed to a difficult neighbour.

This standoffishness played well enough internally, and U Nu, leading the AFPFL, was re-elected in 1952 and 1956. But the country's economic base was steadily being eroded, as rice production slumped, the costs of imports rose and the economy showed no signs of vitality. When a public and violent split in the AFPFL occurred in the late 1950s, the army stepped in to restore order before an impending election in 1958. The military caretaker government lasted 18 months and was headed by Ne Win, commander-in-chief of the armed forces since 1949.

Important developments followed. The economy improved a little, and law and order returned; both were popular. Unfortunately the generals also found that they rather liked governing the country, and thought they were good at it. Despite this new enthusiasm, the army handed back power in 1960, and U Nu was comfortably re-elected. But chaos soon returned, and U Nu's responses to it alarmed the army. He imposed Buddhism as the state's official religion; he downgraded the army's own business enterprises – the Defence Services' Institute – and opened talks with the rebels about a federal solution. All three moves struck directly at the core interests and beliefs of the army, and after two years of civilian rule, U Nu was ousted by Ne Win in March 1962.

This was the beginning of a very difficult period for the Burmese people. The army was not accountable to anyone but itself, and it massively overestimated its own ability to lead the country forward to prosperity. This misplaced belief had an ideological element. Where U Nu had dallied with a kind of cultural nationalism mixed with a command economy, the army imposed something altogether more doctrinaire and left-wing. Unlike the armies of Pakistan and Bangladesh, which always adopted a centre-right, business-friendly outlook, the Burmese generals followed authoritarian nationalist creeds from further east, along the lines of Mao's China or North Korea. What Ne Win recommended was a puritanical, virtuous programme of upliftment for the country, known as the Burmese Road to Socialism. It proved a very rocky ride.

Armies understand discipline and conformity; disobedience is anathema. The Burmese army, or Tatmadaw, proceeded to treat the whole country as a military unit, with savage enforcement of its commands. Confusingly for outsiders, this was called socialism, despite the army's continuing struggle against different groups of communist rebels that owed loyalty to either Moscow or Beijing. Ne Win's philosophy, in as far as it was ever set out, was a uniquely Burmese creation. Its objective was the building of a self-sufficient Burma marked by social equality. Ideologically, it was dominated by anti-capitalism, and it was designed to promote a culture of self-denial. The principal practical lesson it had to teach, however, was that the system didn't work. Nor was it popular. But Ne Win, like dictators from the dawn of government, was never prepared to concede publicly that he might be wrong.

A faction of hard-line Marxist economists within the army, headed by Tin Pe, took a highly ideological view of the nation's problems, while the army's leaders liked to believe that all the civil conflicts could be won with a little more vigour than U Nu had been prepared to show. All this proved disastrously misconceived, and the nation slowly descended into mass poverty.

Burmese socialism was notionally committed to democracy, so the army affected to withdraw from politics by creating a mass party – the Burmese Socialist People's Programme (BSPP) – through the early-1970s, and a cosmetic new constitution was drawn up in 1974. But one-party rule continued, and there was no appreciable deviation from hard-line socialism or isolationism. Repression and state control were reinforced. As inflation and unemployment rose, and agricultural output and foreign reserves fell, there was only intense reluctance to admit the failures.

Things were so bad by 1988 that mass popular protests erupted. The Tatmadaw replied with violent repression, followed by the eventual restoration of unadorned military control in 1989, with the creation of a nationwide system of army-approved councils under the leadership of a central State Law and Order Restoration Council (SLORC). Burma was renamed Myanmar as a sop to the minorities, and elections were held in May 1990.

The generals had a history of incompetence in their supervision of elections. They had backed U Nu's opponents in the 1960 poll that ended the caretaker government, but he was returned to power. This time, the results were even more off the script. The main opposition grouping, the National League for Democracy (NLD) which included Aung San's daughter Aung San Suu Kyi in its leadership won an overwhelming victory. Nevertheless, military control was re-imposed, and NLD members were not allowed to take their seats. The unrest and attendant chaos were declared to be impediments to progress, and a pledge from the junta to draw up a new constitution was substituted for any real political change. The framing of this new constitution was treated in an almost catatonically leisurely fashion, and was eventually completed and approved by referendum only in 2007–08.

The military, now under the leadership of the brutal Than Shwe, had just about run out of Burmese road, when another mass protest swept the country in 2007. This is conventionally, but somewhat misleadingly, called the Saffron Revolution, despite the fact that the protesting monks wore purple-red robes and the generals continued to rule undisturbed. But despite its apparent lack of immediate success, it marked a real watershed in the fortunes of the Tatmadaw. There had always been a close relationship between rulers and Buddhism in the country; traditionally, the legitimacy of rulers depended on their respect for and care of religious institutions. The personal piety of U Nu was genuine, and it played well with the public. The military had tried to associate itself with the protection of Buddhism by feeding monks and building pagodas; the new national capital of Nay Pyi Daw, under construction at the time, was filled with pagodas, and the choice of its name, which means 'abode of kings', was a naked attempt to weave the modern socialism of the generals into the longer tapestry of traditional Burmese piety and governance. But after 2007, there was absolutely no mistaking the opposition of the sangha to the junta, and the best defence the generals could devise against the protesting monks was to claim that they were all impostors.

Connected or not, important developments soon followed. The SLORC was abolished and replaced in November 2007 by the State Peace and Development Council (SPDC). The generals also deigned to complete the new constitution, after deliberations lasting a mere 19 years. Under the new system, the military effectively gave themselves a veto over all reform by building in a 25 per cent representative block for the Tatmadaw in both chambers of the Union Assembly, with a proviso that important measures had to carry a 75 per cent majority. As democratization this was hardly enough, especially in a country where thousands of political prisoners were being held in often brutal conditions, and where the most popular politician, Aung San Suu Kyi, was an apostle of non-violence and had been living under house arrest on and off since 1989. Over the next year, however, pressure for change became irresistible, even to generals living lives of privilege and luxury supported by a system of repression and corruption.

Internal discontent, economic collapse and US-led sanctions were topped off by a public relations disaster of international proportions. With a referendum on the new constitution due in May 2008, cyclone Nargis devastated the rich farmlands of the Irrawady delta, causing massive destruction and widespread distress that the world's media were all too willing to report. The government, however, denied that there was any serious problem and refused to accept foreign offers of aid. But the international community was now holding both stick and carrot. There was a new willingness in US circles to woo the junta for geopolitical and economic reasons, principally to counter Chinese influence in the region.

The final days of overt military government have been acted out since 2009 in a series of carefully orchestrated developments. Elections under the new constitution were scheduled for November 2010. The NLD chose to boycott the poll. Thein Sein, a general with a reputation as a moderate, who had been prime minister since 2007, renounced his military rank, and led the Union Solidarity and Development Party (USDP) – the Tatmadaw under another name – to a clear victory. Aung San Suu Kyi was released a few days later. Than Shwe then stepped down and the junta was dissolved in March 2011, to be replaced by a nominally civilian government led by Thein Sein as President.

Negotiations between the military and Aung San Suu Kyi resulted in the NLD's full participation in by-elections in 2012, in which it won 43 out of 45 seats it contested. Freedom of the media has since been restored in large part; some political prisoners have been released, though a few remain. Economic liberalization is proceeding, and Aung San Suu Kyi has been allowed to travel the world. Thein Sein continues to follow a conciliatory and reformist line, and has been rewarded by the international community with wider engagement and promises of investment, such as the deal concluded in January 2014 with the World Bank that provided $2 billion in loans and grants to fund health care and power generation.[47]

But several important questions remain, and few can be satisfactorily answered before the next elections due in 2015. What comes next will certainly not be some Westminster-style social democratic copy. Civil society is still very underdeveloped; above village level, there is very little social or institutional infill. And the army is still strong. It will be hard to unpick it from the national economy, and there is no independent civil institution of remotely comparable size. The NLD is a mass party, but it has nowhere near the organizational robustness of a parallel government-in-waiting. Aung San Suu Kyi has publicly been warm about Thein Sein, but constitutional change will be slow, especially if the military's 25 per cent block veto is maintained. There are still illiberal forces at work within the military and the USDP.

And if it all goes too fast, we might simply see an elite crony capitalist class stripping the country of its wealth in a rampant free market boom. There are other dangers too. Already the easing of repression has begun to reveal long-hidden fissures in Burmese society, with an upsurge of violence by Buddhists against the minority Muslim Rohingya community. Burmese society is not the first to experience such disturbances in the transition to democracy. Demographic balances have frequently been upset by the arrival of political freedoms, and the country may yet have to sit out a period of exacerbated community relations. Thein Sein has publicly stated that he believes the Rohingyas, who number about a million and are concentrated in the country's north-west, should be deported to Bangladesh, but it is difficult to see how such a measure, even if it were possible, would actually benefit anyone.

In some senses Myanmar/Burma is still in much the same position as in 1945 – with a weak civil society, a fragile economy and no clear constitutional path ahead. On the upside, nearly all the internal military conflicts have been resolved. Ceasefires were agreed through 2011–2012 with major Karen and Shan factions, and the level of internal militarization has been reduced, though fighting continues in several parts of the country, with the Ta'ang National Liberation Army (TNLA), the Kachin Independence Army (KIA) and Myanmar National Democratic Alliance Army (MNDAA) all still active. Nor has the exact political nature of minority participation been established. The constitution of 2008 makes reference to the idea of federalism, but the system of regional assemblies has never functioned. There are currently no official plans to review the constitution.

The West is keeping a close eye on the country, as are India and Bangladesh. Thein Sein has been careful not to weaken his own position, and international leaders may prefer to keep him as interlocutor for sometime yet. He has been reasonable, and it is certainly in the interests of foreigners to keep the country unified and peaceful. At the moment he may be the best way to assure that this continues. But the elephant in the room, or perhaps the giant panda, is China, whose strategic interests are heavily involved. Access to ports is a key Chinese objective, and Myanmar has been compliant in dealings with Beijing for decades, when China was the generals' only friend. Chinese influence is not popular, but Chinese foreign exchange is vital to the country's economy. With a very high public debt, Burma can only be weaned off Chinese money by heavy Western investment. Is this what we are currently seeing? Certainly the US has played its highest cards in the game, sending Hillary Clinton, President Obama and most recently John Kerry to Yangon.

Elections are scheduled for 2015, and the big question is; will the Lady run? There has been much speculation about her eligibility. She was married to Michael Aris, of Canadian-English parentage, for 27 years, and she has two children by him. Under the 2008 constitution anyone married to a foreigner or with children of foreign parentage is disqualified from election as President. And what changes, if any, would an Aung San Suu Kyi presidency actually bring, if she still has to work with the military? What, if anything, will remove the Tatmadaw from politics, or from central economic influence? The country may yet be in for decades of slow development, as education allows the population to become more involved in the democratic process, and rising prosperity (if it comes) enables the growth of a diverse civil society and more sophisticated expressions of political interests.

In 2013 Kala Mulqueeny of the Asian Development Bank believed that 'the current path is neither linear nor irreversible'.[48] She was right to be cautious. Currently Myanmar/Burma is passing through a confusing and potentially dangerous phase, in which capitalists are keen to get access to 50 million new customers – the country's first Kentucky Fried Chicken outlet is planned for 2015[49] – but where journalists are still being sentenced to long prison terms for spreading 'public alarm'.[50] And while Aung San Suu Kyi preaches non-violence, a Buddhist monk named U Wirathu is organizing the so-called '969 movement' against Muslims. Time Magazine has called him 'the face of Buddhist terror'[51] and he has allegedly described himself as 'the Buddhist Osama Bin Laden'.[52]

With 135 registered ethnicities, Burma has many of the problems of Nepal, but the heavy military presence combines this with severe versions of many of the ills that afflict Pakistan. Burma has experienced the horrors of dictatorship and civil war, and it is still cursed with ethnic and religious violence. In a recent poll 76 per cent of Burmese agreed that democracy is better than any other form of government.[53] For their sakes we can only hope that they get it.

5.

Ceylon/Sri Lanka

The island of Sri Lanka – Ceylon till 1972 – is currently a democracy, and has been for over six decades. It has a number of democratic firsts to its name, including the first implementation of universal adult suffrage in South Asia (1931), and the election of the first woman prime minister in the world (1960). It has a full compliment of democratic institutions, and has never lapsed into military government.

Despite these achievements, there are troubling questions about the nature and quality of democracy in Sri Lanka. Democratic practice has repeatedly been flouted. Incumbent governments have unilaterally extended their own powers and terms of office. Politicians have been disreputably flexible in their party allegiances while remaining all too determined to enrich themselves at public expense. Judicial independence has often been compromised, and the rule of law weakened; detention without trial, torture and extra-judicial killings are frequently reported. Elections have been manipulated by all parties, and the state's political culture includes regular recourse to violence, including everything from petty intimidation, through indiscriminate acts of terrorism, to full-scale armed insurgency. Targeted assassinations have included the killing of a prime minister in 1959 and a President in 1993.

This level of violence, and its hardy persistence, could scarcely have been envisaged in 1948, as a highly Anglicized Ceylonese elite eagerly received self-government from a British colonial regime that had always viewed Ceylon indulgently as a contented and orderly colony. The transfer of power was swift and confident, almost like a gentleman's agreement, and was accompanied by a minimum of institutional and legal protection for minorities. But in this atmosphere of serene tidiness far too many dangers were ignored that could have been foreseen. The result was a political system that was wide open to majoritarianism in a society that was not politically united or culturally uniform, and in which any tradition of competing for political power was short and shallow. The elite was more naïve and self-serving than it realized, and the nation was not sufficiently evolved and self-confident to find compromises and make them work.

Under these conditions, independent Sri Lanka came to be defined not by a legacy of united national attempts to shake off colonial subjection but by the majority community's determination to assert itself for the first time since the defeat and exile of the last Kandyan king in 1815. The lapse into majoritarian attitudes was swift, and once established, its logic was inescapable. As a consequence, the island's democracy has been variously described as either purely formal, or narrowly 'electoral', or as a 'control democracy'.

Since independence, Sri Lanka, like India, can boast an unbroken record of civilian rule, regular elections and orderly changes of administration. But whatever temptations there may be to make parallels with India, the contrasts between the two states are far more instructive. In India the state pre-dated politics; in Sri Lanka, politics has shaped and defined the state.

The British always treated Ceylon very differently from India. The island was never ruled by the East India Company, and was instead run by a governor-general directly responsible to London. There was never an anti-colonial movement as violent or as widespread as the Rising of 1857, and though local nationalist feelings were strong, they peaked in a series of Buddhist revivalist movements in the early twentieth century. After the First World War, the political climate of the country was relatively tranquil, certainly compared to India. The Ceylon National Congress, founded in 1919, was a moderate body and attempted to be inclusive, though over time it failed to reflect the social and demographic composition of the island's population, and became increasingly dominated by Sinhalese interests. The main reason for this was the introduction, under the Donoughmore constitution of 1931, of universal suffrage. With the whole population enfranchised, and in the absence of constitutional safeguards for minorities, the majority Sinhalese community took control of most of the devolved power there was to be had. In 1936, after the second round of elections under the new constitution, all seven elected ministers were Sinhalese. This was inevitable because the Sinhalese composed about 70 per cent of the island's population, but this domination ran counter to much of the informal colonial politics of the previous hundred years, which had tended to put a proportionately high number of Tamils in positions of trust and advantage under the British regime. The Tamil minority prospered under colonial rule in government service and tended to be better educated, more proficient in English and economically more advanced as traders and entrepreneurs. The Sinhalese, who were culturally more conservative, tended to be landowners and preferred to remain aloof from government. The colonial regime was not intrusive at a local level, and under pre-democratic conditions, the Sinhalese were neither deprived of their traditional status nor excluded from their traditional concerns.

Prior to 1931, there had been a series of advances in responsible government within the island, which had all involved systems of reservations and special electorates that recognized the disparity between the island's two major groupings, the Sinhalese and the Tamils, and even took account of the small number of Muslims, along with other small communities such as Europeans and Burghers, who were of mixed ethnic descent. The island had, and still has, a complex social composition that goes far beyond any simplistic Sinhalese–Tamil Buddhist–Hindu polarity. Both major communities contain Christians of various denominations, and other groups carry distinct subdivisions. Muslims were of mixed descent and ethnicity, and Tamils were demarcated between those of historic, immemorial island descent and the more recently arrived migrant workers, the so-called 'Estate Tamils', who came in increasing numbers from

India through the late nineteenth century, brought over by British and European managers as cheap labour to work in the tea and rubber plantations. They usually came with their family and kinship groups, which enabled them to retain their culture and language to a greater extent than migrant populations usually do. By 1911 there were around 500,000 Indian Tamils in Sri Lanka, comprising about 12 per cent of the island's population.

When independence came in 1948, the country already had considerable experience of self-government, but this had not served the political classes very well. Rather than an education in power sharing, it had instead sharpened potential ethnic conflicts, hardened attitudes and had crystallized a set of resentments about historic injustices, principally the over-representation of Tamils in public service and education and the advantages that 'Indian' businessmen and bankers were felt to have under colonial rule because of their easy access to sources of credit on the mainland. The Sinhalese felt they had got their country back, but they were now armed with a new weapon – the potential bludgeon of majority rule. Few, if any, among the Sinhala elite seem to have recognized that to use their unassailable majority for partisan purposes would be to play with political fire.

The elite that took power in 1948 was essentially amateur and confident. It had been spared a complicated or bloody struggle for independence, and it had used its political tutelage since 1931 to set up a rudimentary welfare state that took wide responsibility for health and education. Ceylon in 1948 was admired as a well-run and contented colony and was given a much better chance of future political success and stability than India. The British rather liked the Sinhalese elite; they were viewed as non-radical, respectable leaders who seemed keen to preserve the link with Britain. Many of them shared an education with the civil servants and diplomats with whom they negotiated the independence settlement.

A Westminster-style constitution was drawn up based on the recommendations of the Soulbury Commission (1944) in a largely private process of negotiation. The need for safeguards for minorities was not considered necessary by either side. The Sinhalese assured the

British that they knew how to behave, and the British were reluctant to raise the issue and risk slowing down the process of demission or widening it out to include other parties who might be less amenable.

For the same reasons - speed, simplicity and avoiding outside interference - the new constitution was delivered to the island in 1947 by an executive Order of the Privy Council in London. The Sinhalese leadership then took its first step towards shaping the new state by excluding the Estate Tamils from citizenship and from the electoral franchise. This had four significant, divisive effects. First, it established that Ceylonese nationality was culturally exclusive, not territorially inclusive; this idea was slowly to work itself out in highly damaging ways. It also crippled the Left parties, who had drawn much support from the 'Indian' Tamils who made up about 10 per cent of the population. Thirdly, it meant that Ceylon suddenly contained a million or so stateless persons, a situation that was only gradually resolved by agreements with India in 1964 and 1974. Finally, the willingness of the main Tamil party, the All Ceylon Tamil Congress (ACTC), to accept the citizenship rules split the organization, leading to the formation of a new body whose English name was the Federal Party. At the same time, the party that had represented the Estate Tamils, the Ceylon Workers' Congress (CWC), was effectively disabled. After the Citizenship Act of 1948, Tamils, who represented about 22 per cent of the population, were officially segmented and politically weakened.

But the Tamils, Muslims and Burghers were not removed or silenced, and radical leftists continued to criticize and oppose in Sri Lankan society. The subsequent history of democracy on the island involves three interwoven threads: a regular succession of orderly governmental changes via elections; a series of violent political processes including riots, insurgency and civil war; and a string of failed constitutional compromises to allow security for minorities while preserving the unitary state structure that has remained a non-negotiable Sinhalese demand.

What emerged after 1948 was an unusual political landscape not defined by the usual clear left–right split, though there were hints of this under the surface. The most significant political divisions to appear were between rival Sinhalese parties, paralleled with the gradual fragmentation of other political forces on the island.

The country's first government was formed by the United National Party (UNP), which represented a mainly wealthy, traditionalist constituency. It failed to win an outright majority, so the first prime minister, Don Stephen Senanayake, picked a fairly balanced cabinet that included representatives of a range of parties and communities. These included G.G. Ponnambalam, the leader of the ACTC, who had pleaded with the British to delay independence until minority safeguards were in place. When his plea fell on deaf ears, he demanded a fifty-fifty system of representation, but he failed to draw wide support from his fellow Tamils. Moderates feared his stance was too confrontational, sceptics reckoned him an opportunist trying to carve out a leadership position for himself, and separatists thought him too collaborationist. He had to make do with a seat in the cabinet, which pleased him, but it was a personal rather than a structural solution and it did little to resolve divisions between Tamils and Sinhalese. Nor did it promote unity within the Tamil community. His willingness to serve spurred on the formation of the Federal Party, which represented Tamils who thought that inclusion in a Sinhalese-dominated central government was not the best way forward and wanted greater devolution of power.

D.S. Senanayake was a shrewd and experienced operator with long years behind him working in the colonial committee system. He was himself a Buddhist, but many of the UNP's leaders were Christians, and despite its generally culturally conservative ethos, it had a pro-Western stance and agreed to allow British military bases on the island. More significantly, the party was very much a family affair; the next two premiers were Don Stephen's son and nephew; locals joked that the party's initials stood for 'Uncle Nephew Party'.

Opposite the UNP appeared a more populist formation led by Solomon W.R.D. Bandaranaike, another experienced politician who left the UNP in 1951 when he realized that the family clique at the top of the party would bar his way to further advancement. He formed his own party and named it the Sri Lanka Freedom Party (SLFP). This was the first mass Sinhalese party, a much more radical outfit both in economic policy, where it adopted socialism, and in its cultural outlook, where it was much more stridently Buddhist and intolerant of minority cultures, particularly minority languages.

The issue of a national or official language had been discussed for decades and had produced the Swabasha movement in the 1930s, dedicated to education in vernacular languages. The question had also been officially considered during the deliberations of the Soulbury Commission, but as in India, the question proved too intractable and the choice between Sinhala, Tamil or English was deferred for ten years. Bandaranaike then campaigned in the general election of 1956 on a platform of 'Sinhala Only'. He won a huge victory, and subsequently passed the Official Language Act of 1956 despite energetic protests by the Tamils. This action is widely considered to have set in motion the events that eventually led to the full-blown war for a separate Tamil state that ran from 1983 to 2009.

Bandaranaike was, of course, not to know this, and he seemed genuinely taken aback – almost paralysed – by the violent reaction his proposal provoked. He had spoken of a 'pyramid' of loyalties within his vision of nationalism, and his early development showed no traces of Sinhalese supremacism or cultural bigotry. He was Oxford-educated, heavily Anglicized in his tastes, and continued to read the English version of cabinet minutes after the passage of the Act. The standard explanation for his insistence on 'Sinhala Only' is that he thought he would be able to moderate the extremists within his party, but he simply did not understand the depth of the resentments he was exploiting for political advantage. He would not be the first politician to have accidentally unleashed mayhem while in thrall to a larger vision; Jinnah has been accused of the same thing. Equally plausibly, Bandaranaike may have been swayed by practicalities. There was an administrative argument for efficiency – that one language was better than two – and a political argument based on the very apparent lack of enthusiasm among the Sinhalese middle classes to learn Tamil, which they perceived to be of no practical use to them.

But the damage was done. A great many attempts were subsequently made to reconcile the two major communities, but all of them failed. Once the SLFP had demonstrated that populist appeals could win elections, a process of 'ethnic outbidding' began, as politicians found it all too easy to whip up tensions and too hard to resist cultivating popular outrage when others did the same to undermine more moderate stances. The relative innocence of the island's politics was lost at an early stage and thus far has proved impossible to recover.

Elections have been held regularly, and have produced repeated transfers of power between parties. The UNP and the SLFP alternated regularly before the 1970s, but this pattern was broken once governments found ways to sustain their power. The first interruption to the regular electoral cycle came in 1975 when the SLFP-led coalition government of Mrs Sirimavo Bandaranaike, Solomon's widow and the world's first woman head of government, used its majority in Parliament to extend its term by two years.

This was a cynical expedient in the face of the deep unpopularity her party was experiencing. Although she had won a comfortable victory at the election of 1970, she lost the political initiative as a number of long-term trends overtook her government over the succeeding five years. First, impatience for radical change among the Sinhala youth led to a revolutionary uprising in 1971 by the Janatha Vimukthi Peramuna (JVP). Sri Lankan national forces managed to defeat it, despite being taken off guard because Mrs Bandaranaike had downgraded the intelligence services, fearing they were working for her opponents.

She then attempted to shore up her personal and political position by completely rewriting the 1947 constitution. In 1972 she unveiled her new vision for the country, changing its name to Sri Lanka, ending its status as a Dominion, promoting Buddhism to the 'foremost place' in public life, and implicitly abandoning the doctrine of separation of powers in favour of a style of enhanced democracy which promoted the sovereignty of the legislature as the sole expression of the popular will. These steps lined up perfectly with her platform of socialism, nationalism and Buddhism, which played well with rural Sinhalese voters, who made up the majority of the electorate.

But the overall performance of her government was less well-received. Despite much socialist rhetoric and a series of nationalizations, the economy stagnated. Like several other nationalist-populists across the region – Z.A. Bhutto, Indira Gandhi, Sheikh Mujib – she found it difficult to sustain popular socialist policies across the years of the oil price hike, and that appeals to nationalist sentiments were not unproblematic. Tamils felt uncomfortable under the new dispensation, and the community reassembled its fractured political presence through the early 1970s. The Tamil United Front, formed in 1972, merged with the Federal Party in 1976 to become the Tamil United Liberation Front (TULF). The TULF then took a significant step towards separatism on 14 May 1976, when it approved the Vaddukoddai Resolution, which called for 'a sovereign, socialist state of Tamil Eelam' in the north and east of the island.[54]

All this contributed to the catastrophic defeat suffered by the SLFP at the hands of the UNP in the delayed 1977 election. The UNP's leader, Julius R. Jayewardene, then set out to use his powers every bit as ruthlessly as his predecessor. His first move was to amend the 1972 constitution to make the presidency an executive post, and to make the prime minister (i.e. himself) ex-officio President. He then enacted the Second Republican Constitution in 1978, which made several significant changes to the 1972 version. It ended the system of Parliamentary responsibility and cabinet government, confirming the creation of an elected President as head of state and chief executive. Again, this was intended to enhance democracy by giving the President a direct popular mandate. It was, of course, also another way of privileging the Sinhalese vote. The new system introduced proportional representation as a way of guaranteeing the presence of minority voices in the legislature, though this did not extend to placing those voices in the cabinet or anywhere else, because the President was not responsible to the legislature and enjoyed extensive powers of appointment over the administration, the judiciary and the armed forces. More ominously, while proportional representation can be seen as a guarantee of minority representation, it can also equally be seen as a guarantee of permanent majority rule.

This outburst of constitution-making might seem to be a flowering of indigenous democracy, which is how the politicians represented it. But it also betokened two less reassuring trends. First, these constitutions were designed for party advantage, and consequently the degree of respect that they might have enjoyed was damaged. If participants in any game can claim the right to change the rules to their own benefit, the idea of fundamental law, or of what in India became known as 'basic structure', is eroded. The 1978 document has survived to the present day, but it was amended 16 times in its first decade. The most recent alteration was the removal in 2010 of the two-term limit for presidential office. Jayewardene and his successors respected this limit, but after victories in 2005 and 2010, President Mahinda Rajapaksa has now abolished it. One can only assume that, after his victories in 2005 and 2010, he intends to stand for a third term in 2015. Politicians, thus, continue to shape the state as they wish.

By 1982 Jayewardene found himself armed with formidable personal powers, while still holding a huge parliamentary majority. He stood for a second term as President in 1982, and won. Taking up Mrs Bandaranaike's example, he then set about extending the life of the Parliament so as to preserve his massive majority, which he did not wish to risk at the ballot box after five years. He therefore held a referendum to authorize the extension of the sitting Parliament for a further six years. He won again, and passed the Sixth Amendment in 1983, which asserted Sri Lanka's territorial integrity and disbarred MPs who supported separatism, which excluded the main Tamil parties and effectively rendered most of the Tamil community politically mute. This gave Jayewardene a comfortable ride, but ensured that extramural action was now the only way ahead for Tamil aspirations.

It is not a coincidence that both Mrs Bandaranaike and Julius Jayewardene used their large majorities to rewrite the constitution to their own specifications. The original version had been a close copy of British parliamentary government, creating what historian Harshan

Kumarasingha has called an 'Eastminster' system, and was largely the work of Sir Ivor Jennings, the British constitutional expert, who in the 1950s was also to hire out his expertise to the governments of Nepal and Pakistan. The sort of moderated consensual government that had been envisioned by Jennings proved not to the taste of Sri Lanka's leaders, and their various strokes and stratagems illustrate the high-handedness that developed among the political class regarding the institutions of the country. And the Sinhalese leaders did not just use their power against the Tamils, they were quite happy to use it on each other. Jayewardene hounded Bandaranaike, having her disqualified from political office for six years because of her extension of parliament in 1975. Never has a national leader more vigorously kicked a lady when she was down.

With the side effects of party manoeuvrings and the personal concerns of politicians, Sri Lanka has endured a prolonged crisis of democratic legitimacy. This sprang from the persistent Achilles Heel of democracy – a lack of trust. The Tamil minority felt insufficiently protected from majoritarian domination, and there was ample evidence to produce in justification. More difficult to understand is the Sinhalese preoccupation with the slippery slope that Tamil 'rights' might represent. This nervousness had an obvious root – the looming presence of India, and a consequent fear that somehow giving Tamils any degree of autonomy was to invite some kind of wider Tamil formation spanning the Palk Strait that might permanently undermine Sri Lankan sovereignty. The obverse of this coin has also been a worry for Indian politicians, who have had to walk a thin line between supporting Tamils against oppression and encouraging Tamil separatism that might encourage secessionist feelings in southern India.

Sri Lankan leaders have always been aware of the sensitivities involved, and it is a continuing tragedy that none of the attempts to resolve the issue peacefully were successful. There is a long list of such attempts, and their failures are attended by a parallel history of violence.

The first serious proposal came after the 'Sinhala Only' affair when, in 1958, Prime Minister Solomon Bandaranaike negotiated an agreement with S.J.V. Chelvanayakam, leader of the Federal Party. This Bandaranaike–Chelvanayakam 'B–C' pact, which set up semi-autonomous regional councils and permitted 'reasonable' use of Tamil, was abrogated after riots in April 1958, and Bandaranaike then paid with his life for his flexibility when a Buddhist monk shot him in 1959 for betraying the Sinhalese people.

The next deal was between Chelvanayakam and the leader of the UNP, Dudley Senanayake, in the run-up to the 1965 general election. Again, this Senanayake–Chelvanayakam 'S–C' pact came unstuck because of popular protest.

The constitutions of the 1970s did not address the problem directly, though they caused a degree of concern by withdrawing the anti-discrimination clauses of the 1948 Soulbury–Jennings constitution. Relations between the communities steadily deteriorated, with a serious outbreak of rioting in 1977. Militant Tamil groups began to form with the Liberation Tigers of Tamil Eelam (LTTE), founded in 1976, prominent among them. Its military leader, Velupillai Prabhakaran, had already assassinated the Tamil mayor of Jaffna with his own hands in 1975, having declared him a traitor. President Jayewardene offered a new local government structure of District Development Councils in 1981, but the scheme was met with boycotts. At this point, the Tamils finally lost such little political presence as they had; they were also split internally over tactics and objectives.

Matters came to a head in 1983 with the 'Black July' riots, a massive anti-Tamil pogrom that began in Colombo and spread across the island. Some estimates put the casualties as high as 3,000. Certainly hundreds of thousands were displaced. The violence was sparked by an attack on government troops by the LTTE that killed 15. This act is conventionally taken to mark the beginning of the war between the Tamil Tigers and the Sri Lankan state that was to run from 1983 to 2009.

The war was an enormously damaging, cruel and costly affair, prolonged by familiar factors – the asymmetry of the two sides and their entirely incompatible war aims. The conflict also profoundly affected Sinhalese politics and influenced all the elections carried out under its shadow. One effect was that the UNP, who were in power when it broke out, became more conciliatory than the SLFP over time, and made the most sustained and constructive attempts to resolve the dispute.

The first was by accepting India as a mediator. The result was the Indo–Lanka Accord of 1987, under which India undertook to send an armed peacekeeping force to the island. The agreement also contained provisions that were supposed to secure the disarmament of all parties and guarantee regional autonomy to the Tamils. But the situation became complicated in several unforeseen ways, principally because neither the Sri Lankan government nor the LTTE saw it as likely to further their interests. It also set the Indian Peacekeeping Force (IPKF) against the Tamil Tigers, as the former was effectively adopting a role hitherto played by Sri Lankan security forces. The presence of the alien IPKF also sufficiently enraged the dormant JVP to launch a second armed insurgency in the south of the island, which was only suppressed two years later. The IPKF, which had risen to number about 75,000, then went home in early 1990, and the memory of it still blights Indo–Lanka relations.

The next UNP attempt involved the wider international community in the early 2000s, during Ranil Wickramasinghe's second term as prime minister from 2001–04. Wickramasinghe negotiated a ceasefire in early 2002, which was followed by six rounds of talks over the next two years. But the situation was not propitious. Wickramasinghe was in uneasy political cohabitation with President Chandrika Kumaratunga of the SLFP, the daughter of Solomon and Sirimavo Bandaranaike, who was opposed to the talks. Nor did the LTTE engage consistently with the process; the initiative first stalled, and was then permanently thwarted by Wickramasinghe's defeat at the parliamentary election of 2004 and Mahinda Rajapaksa's subsequent victory at the presidential election of 2005. These two political defeats for the UNP condemned the main LTTE proposal, first put forward in October 2003, for an interim self-governing authority to oblivion.

The SLFP was consistently more militant in its outlook, and President Chandrika Kumaratunga won her first term in 1994 on a platform of 'war for peace'. Once in power, however, she found it as difficult as her predecessors to deliver either victory or peace. More constructively, she produced a draft constitution in the late 1990s that provided for devolved authority within a concept of Sri Lanka as an 'indissoluble Union of Regions'. But this idea, too, ran into political opposition, raising concerns that devolution of power equalled abdication of power, and it was eventually laid aside in 2002. Eventually, it was the determination of Mahinda Rajapaksa of the SLFP to settle the argument by force that delivered victory over the LTTE, with an intense final campaign in 2009.

The argument may now have been demilitarized, but the basic issues remain. Tamils feel uncomfortable being ruled by a majority so apparently careless of their well-being, and Sinhalese suspect that any concession will destroy the state as they know it. President Rajapaksa sees enemies everywhere, even in faraway Europe, where on 16 October 2014 the General Court of the European Union (ECJ) removed the LTTE from its list of terrorist organizations, though the effects of the ban were temporarily maintained for six months.[55] The President roundly accused the opposition UNP of conspiring to bring this about,[56] thus jeopardizing the island's hard-won peace. Others, however, believe that the ECJ's decision 'amounts to a "reload" of the [government's] victory credit card' and may therefore actually help the President.[57]

The current government has taken as its motto 'maximum devolution within a unitary state'. This is compatible with the 13th Amendment, setting up provincial councils, which was passed in November 1987 as part of the ill-fated Indo–Lanka peace process, but the exact nature of the devolution of powers is still contentious. The main Tamil opposition grouping, the Tamil National Alliance, has abandoned demands for separate statehood, but it is still pressing for the fullest degree of self-government and recognition of Tamil rights. However, it gained only 14 seats out of 225 at the 2010 general election, so its influence is severely limited in national affairs.

It remains to be seen how conciliatory President Rajapaksa will be in the long term. The signs are not promising. Since his re-election in 2010, he has tried and imprisoned former head of the armed forces General Sarath Fonseka, who ran against him for the presidency; he has made legal room for a third term for himself; he has impeached a High Court judge who had ruled against him in several instances; journalists have been harried; and he has refused to prosecute anyone for alleged human rights abuses during the civil war. All this was enough to attract the disapproval of the international community, some of whose members, including Canada and India, refused to attend the Commonwealth Heads of Government Meeting (CHOGM) held in Colombo in November 2013.

Meanwhile, the cronyism that grew up under the presidential system from the 1970s onwards has, in the eyes of some, become rampant. Three senior offices of state are currently occupied by brothers of President Rajapaksa, who personally disposes of 40 per cent of the national budget. Critics argue that he has 'hijacked' Parliament and undermined democratic norms of accountability in multiple areas, including bringing nearly half of all MPs into the government, thus buying off criticism.[58] Nor has violence disappeared from the island. A militant Buddhist militia, the Bodu Bala Sena, has been linked to attacks on Muslims and Tamils, and the government seems reluctant to acknowledge its existence, let alone condemn its activities.

Nor is there likely to be any critical scrutiny of the island's affairs coming from India. Relations were expected to take an upturn with the election of the NDA, which did not need to court support from Tamil parties, and Narendra Modi immediately adopted a warmer tone in his dealings with the Sri Lankan leadership in contrast to the frosty relations under the UPA. This thaw brought the release of all Indian fishermen detained for alleged violations of Sri Lankan waters. Modi's vision of India's regional interests, especially in competition with China, led him to offer military support to the Rajapaksa government, including supplying offshore patrol boats,[59] but it soon became clear that Rajapaksa might be calculating that India needed him more than he needed India, as he seemed careless of provoking his powerful neighbour. Chinese naval vessels were welcomed in the island's ports,[60] and five Indian fishermen were sentenced to death on charges of drug smuggling.[61] India reacted strongly in both instances. The fishermen were eventually released, but relations are likely to remain fraught, because it is very much in Sri Lanka's interests to find ways to play China off against India in order to leverage aid and concessions from the two giants.

Rajapaksa may also believe that playing hardball on the international scene might help him with his domestic position, which is not entirely secure. His government performed poorly in a provincial election in September 2014, and with a renewed sense of unity appearing among the opposition, he moved to shore up his position by declaring a presidential poll 16 months ahead of time, in January 2015,[62] having carried through a populist budget packed with giveaways and tax breaks designed to appeal to rural voters; he described it unabashedly as 'a country bumpkin's budget'.[63] Though his popularity has slipped since the high point of 2010, he is widely expected to win.[64]

Rather than moving into the sunny uplands of an enhanced post-war democracy marked by reconciliation, Sri Lanka probably stands on the verge of a socially partisan dynastic autocracy, in which journalists live in fear, and against which no one can stand without risk to life, limb and property.

6.

Conclusion: India In Perspective

From a South Asian viewpoint, victory for the Allies in the Second World War brought two important benefits: it removed the threat of Japanese militarism, and it signalled the imminent end of the European colonial empires. This opened unprecedented opportunities for social, economic and political change, and all five major states in the region experimented with democracy after 1947. None enjoyed ideal conditions, and the results varied according to the interplay of factors including ethnic and religious diversity, the legacies of older conflicts, the position of the military and the willingness of politicians and elite groups to embrace change.

For democracy, in whatever form it came, did mean real change. The region had played host to a long list of empires – Ghaznavid, Mughal, Durrani, Sikh, Gorkha, Konbaung, Kandyan and finally British – but none had set up anything like the democratic nation-states constructed after the end of the war. The old regimes had never been keen to rebuild society; they had been happy to work with existing structures and all their inequalities. Now with an end to empires and dynasties, there would be changes to social and political arrangements, and to the nature and uses of violence.

Empires can be built on little more than superior force; setting up a modern democratic state requires rather more. Specific conditions have to be in place, first among which is that the general population must be willing to consider itself as one large, meta-community. Too much ethnic nationalism, too much xenophobia, too little tolerance or too few 'acceptable' identities can and will subvert democratic norms and work against voluntary social cohesion. The transition to democracy can thus ask as many questions as it answers, and developments across the region repeatedly demonstrated that majority rule rendered minorities highly vulnerable.

Democratic, constitutional liberalism was always designed to be an answer to these problems, and it is clear that it holds societies together much better than military-imperial domination does. The success of Asian societies in managing to erect viable democracies relates to the degree to which they have sincerely taken up the liberal social agenda. This means rights, especially the rights of minorities, and the genuine extension of citizenship to the whole population.

Democratic liberalism won the Second World War, but so did communism, a very evident circumstance that immediately rendered British liberal imperialism obsolete, and its long-term influence across the region thus turned out to be somewhat patchy. Indians took to liberal universalism and wrote a constitution in keeping with its principles; the Sri Lankan elite liked to think they had done the same, but neglected to implement the principles they had embraced; Pakistanis found it very difficult to mix democratic standards with traditional social hierarchy; the Nepalese eventually took contemporary regional models, not British; and the Burmese preferred socialism.

The most delicate factor in building a democracy was, and is, confidence: political confidence between leaders, and social confidence across communities. Confidence grows with the experience of peace and is encouraged by the spread of prosperity. This positive process can be very slow and is highly vulnerable. It can be undermined by political gridlock and disrupted, retarded or even destroyed by widespread violence.

Violence creates empires, but it stunts and destroys democracies; it works directly against democratic norms such as consensus, debate, accountability and the rule of law. Violence, or 'no law', is the prime resort of anti-democratic forces, including well-armed elites or irregularly organized minorities; if the majority were amenable, then violence would not be necessary. Here we can set out a sad, non-commutative equation: When democracy fails to build a nation, violence usually follows, but when violence fails, democracy does not regenerate; violence continues, or even escalates.

Violence has attractive qualities to certain classes. It promises to deliver its objective – pacification, secession or revolution – immediately. In post-war conditions of instability and deprivation, it can seem the best way out of desperate situations both for individuals and communities. It is violence above all that has influenced the region's ability to sustain democracy; its presence or absence is the single most important difference in the comparative histories of South Asian countries.

As states in the region began to grapple with their particular problems of legacy and change after 1947–48, their prospects were not even. Most fortunate, seemingly, was Sri Lanka, which had peace, secure borders, and a clear ethnic-cultural majority profile. How soon the island descended into civil strife serves as a warning that majority power is not the same thing as social cohesion. India had neither prosperity nor compact geography, but had a leadership determined to implement liberal principles in service of a national project. This contrast in elite attitudes accounts for a great deal of the difference in the fate of the two countries.

Three other states were blighted for a variety of political, socio-economic and ideological reasons. Pakistan was not a pre-existing entity at all, and had the triple burden of becoming a state, erecting an entire democratic edifice and fashioning a sense of nationhood from scratch. Burma had a terrible legacy of wartime division and destruction. Nepal was so politically and economically underdeveloped that nothing like a modern democratic state could be constructed without the goodwill of all parties, but in 1950 there were no parties and little goodwill. Bangladesh was yet to be born; when she was, war, floods and economic chaos meant that the auspices could hardly have been less favourable for the creation of the '*Sonar Bangla*' that Mujib envisioned.

Pakistan and India both had to cope with the chaotic legacy of Partition, and soon after found themselves at war over Kashmir. But India pulled away from these misfortunes relatively quickly and relatively well. India muddled through, progressing from a formal to a *jugaad* democracy, and can claim a certain status as a special case, having avoided three curses of the region that are often closely connected: civil war, secession and military rule. How was this?

India had a crucial piece of good luck that helped her avoid the worst pitfalls of young statehood. Her founding fathers did not promote a restrictive vision of the new nation; they made do with the one they had, having been made painfully aware of the various fault lines that ran across it. Multiple divisions had been highlighted to them again and again by the British, who had used them to disqualify Indians from self-government. Indian leaders thus had a point to prove – that none of these potential fissures was important. They were determined above all that the new nation should be a nation built on the antithesis of 'colonial' unity. Free India would be a reproach to British pessimism; it would be built on the unity of fellow feeling and fairness. This would not be an ideal nation, but it was a nation that could be given ideals. That was the task they set themselves.

What they had was a clear picture of the injustices they had suffered, and the watchwords of the new state were therefore 'justice' and 'democratic inclusion'. The Constituent Assembly created the constitution and expected the nation to grow into it. The leading members of the Assembly did not have an exact conception of the nation; the constitution was designed to reflect its multifariousness. The resulting structure was an enabling framework, not a restrictive mould. Nehru was always willing to think of India as a nation in the making. This allowed him to accept its faults and to love it for what it might become. His attitude was optimistic and open-minded. Such qualities in a nation-builder are invaluable.

In all this India went right in a way that a number of her neighbours went wrong. Dominant ideas of how postcolonial Pakistan and Sri Lanka should be were more rigid and deterministic. This soon bred notions of right and wrong and created exaggerated, often rather hysterical, forms of patriotism and nationalism. The Urdu-speaking, Punjabi-dominated Pakistan that Jinnah left behind was far too constricting for Bengalis. The pro-Sinhalese policies of Bandaranaike were similarly galling for Tamils.

And in its founding generation, India was also lucky in that the main characters, particularly Jawaharlal Nehru, lived long enough to pass on their wisdom in action and make good, far-sighted decisions. The dominance of the Congress, and Nehru's own pre-eminence within it, both abetted this. Had he been a lesser man, or had he decided, like Robert Mugabe, to prop up his own party and his own position from the earliest opportunity, India would have been a different place, and democracy might never have taken on the aura of permanence and fairness that Indians now freely allow it.

The lesson of colonial subjection taken by Congress leaders was that oppression and injustice were not to be sustained. The freedom struggle taught them that struggle itself is not the essence of civilized living. Where this struggle fragmented, as in Burma, or where it never had deep social roots, as in Nepal, the outcomes were very different.

The arrival of independence produced almost too much of a shock in some parts of the region. In India, with a long tradition of garrulous activism under the Congress banner, the nation did not just talk itself into being; it had already become fully acquainted with itself as a practical entity, in which the constituent elements had built binding connections and mutual obligations. Let us posit the opposite. Imagine if India had been liberated by an undemocratic, secretive organization; what then would have resulted? It would have been much harder to create a nation relatively at ease with itself and relatively well cross-connected for its size. The obverse of this process played out in Nepal, where the 'liberation' of 1951 was won by a very small faction that proved unable to tame the traditional power structures it nominally co-opted.

All this was a great help to India in avoiding the militarization of social conflicts. Myanmar, Sri Lanka and Nepal went down this route and faced turmoil. Pakistan at first managed to avoid internal militarization, except during the 1971 war, and in a sense it was a blessing for the rest of the country that East Bengal was so isolated. But the Afghan conflict, much nearer and more persistent, has poisoned Pakistani politics since the early 1980s. The influx of large quantities of armaments affected East Bengal first, and badly, but the weaponry that leaked out of Afghanistan has seriously destabilized Pakistan's western regions. The enormous growth in the availability of military hardware in Sri Lanka has similarly affected the conduct of politics since the 1980s. In both cases it has abetted secessionist groups.

Secession is an insidious weakness within democracy because democratic systems find it difficult to address secessionist grievances effectively. Democracy, in a sense, is already the problem. Large electoral units do not spontaneously break up into smaller units; a majority must expressly wish this to happen. States, therefore, must rely on political negotiation to accommodate secessionist demands, not elections. But any such process relies on the quality of leadership available, and especially its ideological tenor. History tells us that the speckled demography of South Asia can easily play host to democracy, but has found it hard to accommodate 'nation-states' with excessively ambitious centralizing tendencies. Too often the result has been conflict between old local cultures and new national states too prickly about sovereignty and what it means.

There were clashes from the start all over the South Asian theatre. In India, many regions at least had a history of being ruled from Delhi; in Pakistan, neither East Bengal nor NWFP nor Baluchistan had any tradition of being ruled from Karachi, let alone the new capital of Islamabad. The same applied to parts of Burma, where the hill peoples on the fringes of the country had not been ruled directly from Rangoon but had long enjoyed semi-autonomy within the colonial state. Sri Lanka failed to establish an equitable relationship with its Tamils, and Bangladesh had difficulties in accommodating the demands of the people of the Chittagong Hill Tracts; both conflicts drew India into the equation. Even a country as small as Nepal had internal subdivisions of significance, having been assembled by conquest from a number of independent kingdoms, while an active separatist movement is currently demanding autonomy for Madhesis in the south.

The federal-national problem has not faded away, and it is a live issue today all across the region. This is an extended tragedy, because for all the death and destruction wrought in the name of localism, only one secessionist movement has actually succeeded in separating from the mother country – Bangladesh in 1971. No other group has managed to separate contiguous territory from a postcolonial state.

Another golden mean comes into view here: How large does a regional minority movement have to be before it succeeds? The Kurds have yet to manage this fully, but the south Sudanese did in 2011. The Muslim minority in British India, at about 25 per cent, was large enough, as were the Bengalis within Pakistan, at about 50 per cent. But Sri Lankan Tamils at 12 per cent were not, nor have any of the many secessionist movements that emerged in India been successful, especially in the north-east, where their host communities are often very small.

But secession is such a direct challenge to democratic states that the only effective countermeasures against it are either military repression, which tends to make the problem worse – by demonstrating how ill-suited the majority community is to look after the interests of the regional minority – or federalism. It is quite remarkable how resistant so many South Asian states have been to the idea of federalism, at least when it is called that. In the end Nepal has opted for it, though the details are still undecided. Perhaps Myanmar will have no choice but to go the same way, despite the long-entrenched opposition to the idea from the military. Sri Lanka actually managed to crush it; Pakistan is still grappling with the problem, but remains intensely resistant. India adopted it from the start, and has bent before it ever since.

Here we might note the special role of mountains. Mountains as a geographical feature are not directly inimical to democracy, at least not on a local scale, but they are very obstructive in the process of nation-building. This serves to emphasize that democracy, in the sense of inclusive self-government, is a truly popular phenomenon. Hill people are usually keen on it, and have a natural sense of what it is. But democracy in the modern world goes with states, and mountains present problems for states – of access, inclusion and shared identity. Upland communities have often been left behind in projects of imperial conquest as too difficult to subdue. When modern states have since been formed, the separate economic and social histories of these communities can easily set them apart from lowland areas, which are often richer and more ethnically and socially mixed. There is nothing quite like isolated upland terrain for fostering a distinct sense of community, for preserving minority languages or for creating micro-economic interests. From a distance, Scots, Swiss and Macedonians can all attest to this truth.

Secession can very easily lead to militarization, with malign consequences. Separatist movements within the Indian state have been pacified politically and confronted militarily, but the latter course has created deep problems for the democratic health of the nation, especially with the use of the Armed Forces Special Powers Act (1958) amid widespread accusation of abuses. Punjab posed particular problems of religious militancy, and terrorist atrocities were met with a shocking level of state-sponsored brutality, but the willingness of moderate leaders on both sides managed gradually to depressurize the situation, which was undoubtedly also eased by the general prosperity of the region. Kashmir remains a problem, and the international dimension of the conflict means that it is singularly resistant to solutions of all kinds, including military 'victory', whatever that might mean in such a complex situation.

The longest-running separatist struggles in India have been in the north-east, where insurgency began among the Nagas in 1956, the Mizos in the 1960s, in Manipur from the 1970s, and Assam and Bodoland in the 1980s. These conflicts have been sustained to some degree by their proximity to non-Indian territory which enables insurgent groups to evade confrontation, but also by the complexity of some of the demographic aspects involved; different communities cannot be neatly separated into discrete units, and granting autonomy to the dominant group always risks doing injustice to local minorities. The Indian state has confronted these issues with a wide variety of strategies both political and military: negotiation, confrontation, detention and co-option.

India does have a relatively good record of solving problems without the use of military force, and whether as cause or effect of democracy, the country has avoided excessive militarization. The generals have been kept at a distance from political power, and this has been a virtuous loop. Politically ambitious people have not joined the military, and those in the military have never been able to develop realistic political ambitions. India has seen a good deal of armed conflict, but in relatively restricted and peripheral areas.

The secession–federalism–violence equation came right in India fairly quickly, and has stayed roughly in balance. This alone explains much of the disparity in India's experience with democracy compared to others. India became a federal state with comparative ease because of the sheer scale of the new republic. It was surely a wise choice, and one without which there would have been no viable way of running such a large polity.

This relates to another piece of good fortune. In the independent state of India, there has been only one big institution – the central government. There have been no obvious rivals in the sphere of power politics, which has not been true elsewhere. Sometimes it has been the army, sometimes a monarchy, sometimes a specific social class that has not made its accommodation with modernity. India had its hereditary privileged classes, but much of its feudal elements were either included in Pakistan or, in the case of most of the princes, absorbed into the new egalitarian Union to vanish without institutional trace. Princes can still aspire to high status, but as elected politicians.

This reminds us of another insidious danger that democracy faces – that it cannot thrive, or even survive for long, if enough powerful people do not want it. Elite behaviour matters, and an absence of generosity within elites towards fellow members and from the elite towards the lower orders can be crippling.

It has always been far too easy to degrade democratic processes into an extended charade, that is, to let the people have their say – as long as they are told what they should be saying or have their choices limited or misrepresented. All sorts of versions of these strategies have been implemented across the region. Referendums rely on a question being set. Selective or guided democratic systems inhibit or exclude real criticism. An elite can perpetuate its own position if politics is so expensive that it remains exclusively a game for the rich. Two-party systems can simply push the plate of goodies round the table, if the main players collude in preventing real change from appearing on the agenda. Or elections can simply be rigged.

South Asia does not have a good record in any of these areas, and the situation may change only very slowly. Not even violent revolutionary insurgency is likely to disrupt an unresponsive system if it relies on entrenched privilege. Shooting policemen is not the answer. What would be of more help would be concerted social intolerance of corruption along with a willingness to respect democratic norms, which always amount to forms of mutuality. Checks and balances can work within a constitution, but too often the checks are in brown envelopes and the balances are hidden in offshore accounts.

Across South Asia, the style has often belied the substance of democracy. Two-party rule may look responsive and fluid – even 'mature', but in Pakistan, Bangladesh and Nepal long periods of party alternation in the 1990s simply disguised highly oligarchic systems. Nor is a party duopoly any guarantee of good governance if it becomes simply a periodic rearrangement of personnel that disguises a static system of privilege. Peaceful transfer of legitimate authority is a good first step in the democratic development of any country. Pakistan finally achieved this in 2013, but Sri Lanka managed it many times and yet fell prey to civil war.

After nearly 70 years of sovereign independence across the region, we can see that the demand for democracy in South Asia is genuinely strong and that the thirst for revolution, even in unequal societies, has been remarkably limited. The most serious and sustained threat to democracy, though, was never a communist revolution; it was always a graduated form of authoritarianism rather than outright totalitarianism. Only Burma can be thought of as a truly totalitarian regime, from the mid-1960s onwards. But the story has hardly been straightforward. In 1962, just 15 years into the democratic era, only India and Sri Lanka were still in the democratic camp. Bangladesh started life as a democracy in 1971, but soon succumbed to military rule, while India had a brief flirtation with autocracy. In the 1980s, four out of these six regional states were under authoritarian rule, and a fifth was wracked by civil conflict. Currently, all six hold regular elections, though Myanmar is yet to manage an anti-incumbency verdict. Only one, Pakistan, is host to large-scale armed conflict, which has had a highly damaging effect upon the governability of the state.

This last fact reinforces the lesson that wars are toxic for democracy. Severe problems are likely to arise from either civil war or the military rule that it often leads to. Civil wars rarely produce clear results, which does not bode well for Pakistan, while a decisive battlefield result, as in Sri Lanka, can produce further problems of long-term polarization and suppressed desires for justice or restitution. In the absence of clear victory, the mess that civil conflict leaves behind is rarely a suitable nursery for democratic ideas. And at the end of wars long or short, decisive or drawn, the inclination to trust others with authority can remain minimal. Both Sri Lanka and Nepal are in this bind currently, and coincidentally or not, neither state has been willing to set up some kind of truth and reconciliation process. The aftermath of war does not resolve itself easily or quickly; even after 40 years it is still a political issue in Bangladesh.

Bearing all this in mind, the region holds one last major lesson – that the keystone to the arch of post-imperial democracy in South Asia is still Pakistan. Beset with multiple disadvantages, the Pakistani state has succumbed both to somnolence under forms of relatively mild military rule and to occasional outbursts of internal rage. But the militaristic nature of the state and its economy has remained almost insuperable. The stakes are high. Europe finally settled down to a peaceful and prosperous life when Germany was safely steered back into the path of liberal nationalism it had forsaken in the middle years of the nineteenth century. Somehow, if Pakistan were to be rendered stable and prosperous, and particularly if a lasting peace with India was somehow engineered, the benefits for the whole region would be enormous. Increased prosperity, the isolation of Islamic radicalism, an end to the mutual national undermining and the permission granted to democratic leaders to address the ecological and environmental challenges that face the whole region would all be immensely beneficial.

So, returning to the original question, where India went right lies in one detail of the national agenda – its logical sequence. What came first was very important. India wrote her own constitution, laboriously but above all promptly. Sri Lanka and Burma received theirs; Pakistanis and Nepalis both found the task extremely difficult and have had too many constitutions already. This early settlement was a huge advantage for Indians, and allowed them to embrace and enforce not only sovereign self-government, but also self-realization and self-acceptance.

India's leaders wrote the constitution while fully aware that they were creating a nation-state, and they used the appropriate vocabulary and concepts to do so. The democratic groundwork was clearly laid out, and whether we can truly speak of the triumph of democracy or not, the first triumph was in the idea of Indian sovereignty. It was understood to be – and could *only* be – a pooled affair. Once it had been created, it was easy to understand what it was for.

It is important to recognize that the constructive approach adopted by India's national leadership did not magically appear at the opportune moment. It had a long history and was integral to the national movement. Indians came to the concept of injustice via the idea of the nation, not via a concept of society, and justice and nationhood were inseparably linked. Preordained national destiny was not part of the Congress view, but national objectives were, and the principal objective was always social justice.

Indian democracy has not been perfect, and many would argue, like Drèze and Sen,[65] that it has not delivered sufficient benefits to enough Indians sufficiently regularly or surely. But the basis was laid publicly, by discussion, by Indians themselves and swiftly, on an agreed basis of delegated authority. No other regional state managed to do this. And once done, the path was set, and the purposes for which power had been created became naturally aligned with the basis that had created it. This is the very essence of democratic legitimacy, and India had it exactly right from the start. Whatever failures may have followed were not at the level of the system itself, and the proof of this, if any were needed, is that the ills of India have been economic, class-based and in matters of administration, not of principle. The principles have held, which is why the Supreme Court has been able to play such a constructive role in the nation's development.

One caveat: The Hindutva project is a siren-call leading India onto the path laid out by Pakistan and Sri Lanka. The class/caste system may be regarded as a problem in India, but it is one that democracy as a principle can work against, if only slowly. Class distinctions continue to endure in all democracies; only dictatorships claim to have solved this problem.

It was Indians who made India in every literal sense one cares to use: people outranked geography; the present took precedence over history; India was born and named as a joint social enterprise, not an exclusivist cultural one. The Nehruvian–Gandhian project worked, at least in principle, better than any of the rival approaches employed by India's neighbours. Indians should be proud of and grateful for that legacy.

Part 4

Prospects

1.

2014: The Long View

The NDA won a stunning victory in the 2014 general election, much bigger than anyone had expected. The margin of that victory may have been exaggerated somewhat by the first-past-the-post system, but this system operates in all other Indian elections, and in 2014 the result was unusually decisive. The verdict was so clear that it is impossible not to believe it marked a major historical event – that it reflected changes already at work within the polity, and that it will bring further changes in its wake.

So, where did it come from, and what will it bring?

Firstly, it was certainly the result of two significant historical processes that had been working themselves out for decades. One is the organization of the political centre-right in India, and the other is the decline of the Congress. The two are linked in various ways, but have distinct trajectories of their own.

The rise of the BJP had been in the making for a long time, propelled by demographic change in the cities, economic change in the countryside and the growth of cultural confidence in both. There were two principal milestones in the BJP's journey. The first was the taming process of 1996–99 that took the party from being unable to attract partners to being a major party of government. The second was the defeat of 2004, which taught the party to appear less arrogant, to address a wider and less elitist range of concerns, and to be tactically much smarter on the ground; the 2014 campaign delivered massively improved results in UP and Bihar – states in which it had not done well in recent times. The BJP also made better regional partnerships in 2014, especially in the north, and it avoided making alliances with the major Tamil parties; such pacts had not worked out well in either 1998, when the AIADMK brought down the first BJP-led government, or in 2004, when the DMK changed sides before the election.

All the pieces finally came together for the BJP in the second UPA term. It had an unpopular government to attack, and it had developed an alternative programme that was more focused, more practical and less ideological than in the past. With the selection of Narendra Modi as prime ministerial candidate in September 2013, the party shed much of its old image and associations. It began to look like a viable, modern alternative to the UPA team, which by then was bemired in scandal and beleaguered by unimpressive statistics. The BJP entered the campaign with sharper slogans, shrewder tactics and a stronger national candidate. The Congress had too much to explain away, and hardly tried to do so, relying instead on optimistic promises to reform 'the system' and attempts to project Rahul Gandhi as a man equipped with hi-tech management know-how and in touch with young India.

This explains one side of the story – the success of the BJP, but it scarcely explains why the margin of victory was so wide. For in 2014, the nation did not just embrace the BJP, it also rejected the Congress wherever the two parties were in direct opposition. Why this calamitous collapse? And if the BJP's success can be seen as based on long-term factors, are there similar factors that underlie the precipitous fall of the Congress from 206 seats to 44? Yes.

The anti-colonial origins of the Congress made it a broad-based, pragmatic party, but it began to fall apart after independence. It had held together till then mainly because of the influence of M.K. Gandhi, but once multipolar politics began in earnest, it was unrealistic to expect the Congress formula to continue to work. And it didn't. It remained safe for a while under Nehru, but potential weaknesses abounded. The first was the challenge from more ideological parties, but though these appeared on both the left and the right, they never found a mass following. The Congress might also have become vulnerable to parties that were better organized, but none appeared;

it was still too capacious and too centrally positioned to allow for the growth of other national institutions.

Eventually, internal problems would deal the party worse blows than its external enemies. Regional indiscipline and factionalism appeared strongly through the 1960s, with a bevy of satraps fully prepared to form their own organizations, such as Charan Singh, who created the Bharatiya Kranti Dal (BKD), or Biju Patnaik, who set up his own Utkal Congress. The only reply from the central leadership was to relapse into autocracy tinged with dynasticism. This merely served to foster the atmosphere of disconnection that led to the Emergency. The Janata counterstroke of 1977 marked the peak influence of former Congress leaders and their private formations, but this counter-reaction was too disjointed to displace the Congress.

Dynasticism and the cult of personality won out, at least in the short term, and Indira Gandhi set the tone for the Congress's future development. She anchored the party at the centre, looked for future leadership no further than home, and adopted a kind of hyper-pragmatism. Unwittingly she had also scored something of an own goal by rewriting the constitution to include socialism as state policy, which rather undermined her party's distinctive appeal; after the 42nd Amendment every government was nominally socialist, so it didn't matter who you voted for. But she kept the Congress clear in leadership and flexible in policy, which were both virtues at the time in the absence of other strong national figures and rival national political formations.

By 2014, such a figure and such a formation had appeared, and the quality of central leadership within the Congress had diminished. The dynastic principle dared not speak its name in the afterglow of victory in 2004; Manmohan Singh was allowed to take the top job. But it had fully remembered itself by 2014, when the young pretender fronted the campaign. However, many Indians asked, quite legitimately, why Rahul Gandhi should be given the responsibility of running the country, and whether there might not be someone else among his billion-odd fellow citizens who might be as, if not more, suited to the job.

The dynastic principle keeps things clear, but sometimes a little too clear, and in 2014 it showed that having a formidable mother and a smattering of management jargon is sometimes not enough in politics. Rahul Gandhi may have wanted to play Prince Siddhartha, whose copious heart was touched by suffering, but instead he came across as more like India's Mark Thatcher.

The comprehensive defeat of the Congress in 2014 is inextricably linked to this convoluted legacy. The party suffered the consequences of its centre-ground pragmatism – assailed on all sides, vulnerable to ideology and too complacent with its mediocre leadership. It had been too many things to too many people, and was no longer of use to enough people, either inside or outside the organization.

The Congress originally had a national agenda, and in times when politics *felt* national it did well. But an inexorable process was in play – the re-localization of Indian politics. The party gradually lost its local base and subsequently its local purpose. All states were Congress-run initially, but the party was increasingly superseded in local government from the 1960s onwards.

The old national agenda held limited appeal in regions with a strong identity, and apart from during the interregnum of 1991–98, the constrictions of kinship that prevailed at its summit meant that the party was of little use to regional figures with national ambitions to leadership. Local units broke away, and caste and regional parties formed around genuinely local issues. The intermediate farming strata in north India created their own parties and found their own leaders. Indian politics became multi-polar at state level, meaning that the Congress had to compete for Dalit and Muslim votes in increasingly complex local fights. The party increasingly lacked relevance, and by 2014 was either driven out of national politics altogether, as in Tamil Nadu, Rajasthan and Gujarat, or was relegated in states like Maharashtra, where it had to ally with the NCP, or was sidelined in states such as Odisha and West Bengal, where it was supplanted by the Biju Janata Dal and the Trinamool Congress respectively. Congress support collapsed completely in Andhra Pradesh after the bifurcation process, which is not what party strategists had expected.

They hoped that the creation of Telangana state might pay electoral dividends, as separatist protestors saw their demands met, but such gratitude as the locals felt was all directed towards the Telangana Rashtra Samithi (TRS) instead.

Can the Congress be reconstructed or re-energized at the national level, where it naturally belonged? The prospects are not good. Its ideology is weak and outdated. Notions of inclusive development have moved on, and the politics of simple redistribution are less intellectually respectable now, even if they seem to promise voter satisfaction. Having scattered so much money across the countryside for ten years, the UPA reaped a meagre harvest of votes. Will any party ever be willing to do the same again? And if the old strategy is discredited, can the party rebuild from the roots upwards?

The base from which to do so has shrunk drastically. After the 2014 polls, the Congress controlled just eight state assemblies, and of these only Karnataka can be considered a major state. Assembly by-elections in June 2014 showed some revival in the party's fortunes as it picked up seats in contests against the BJP in Karnataka and Uttarakhand. Some were prepared to credit the party's better showing across mid-2014 to the hard-line rhetoric of BJP activists such as Yogi Adityanath or to the self-imposed absence of Sonia and Rahul Gandhi from the campaign. A variety of local factors certainly contributed to these successes, and attempts to project larger trends from them soon proved misplaced. Further gains in September in Rajasthan and Gujarat followed, but the dire results in the Haryana and Maharashtra Assembly elections in October banished hopes of a grand revival. The party comforted itself by claiming that the two states had somehow voted 'for change' and not specifically for the BJP, but such reasoning was hardly sufficient to explain why the Congress slipped from positions of government to third place in both states. In truth, the BJP managed to sustain the mood of national optimism seen in May's general election, whereas the Congress could not mount a coherent defence of its own record or provide alternatives to the Modi vision, apart from telling voters they had been sold false promises.

The national trend was undeniable. By the end of 2014, after the Jharkhand and J&K elections, the Congress had only 949 MLAs, a record low, compared to the BJP's 1,058, a record high. The Congress has not yet died at local level, but its coverage is increasingly patchy. The year 2015 will see elections in Delhi sooner, and Bihar later. Were the Congress to do badly, or even not very well in them, it will be hard to see how momentum can be regained. If there are heavy losses, who will stay in the party? Neither idealists nor careerists will consider the prospect appealing.

The party has different problems staying relevant at national and local levels. Having a recognizable, energetic figure is a help at state level, and Sachin Pilot may well have been an asset in Rajasthan, but such personalities find it very difficult to flourish in the party as it is presently set up and led. It is commonly stated that the Congress lacks a supply of new leaders, and the main reason is that if they emerge in the provinces, they tend to form their own units. In policy terms, a less personal vision of a common interest is required at the national level, but the party's traditional pro-poor stance can be expected to diminish in appeal as the nation becomes richer and/or more aspirational. There are limits to the degree of enthusiasm or mobilization that conscience can be expected to produce.

And there is now a very clear limit to the degree of enthusiasm that can be expected to form around the Nehru–Gandhi dynasty. Can the family provide another premier? Sonia Gandhi seems reluctant to take on the top job, and Rahul seems not to be electable. And despite the plaintive cries of 'Priyanka *lao*, Congress *bachao*!' from among the party faithful, Priyanka Gandhi is not a viable alternative, and the slogan could stand equally well as a question. Could the party really introduce such an ingénue? She may be photogenic, but good looks were never Rahul's problem. We can ask: Does she outrank him in nous, experience or electoral relevance? Can the Congress really run another candidate who is so similarly vulnerable to accusations of being an amateur, a reluctant leader and a privileged silver-spoon sucker? And Priyanka comes with her controversial husband, Robert Vadra, in tow, so she does not represent an alternative clean slate for the leadership. We will have to wait another generation for new faces.

The party itself is either unaware of its weaknesses, or is simply unwilling to think through the consequences of doubting its own leaders. A committee chaired by senior Congressman A.K. Antony was delegated to look into reasons for the party's poor national showing in May 2014. The defeat, according to Antony, was down to manipulation of the media by the BJP.[66] This is a stunningly banal and disconnected analysis that touches on nothing of importance; it is a dereliction of duty dressed up in the finery of sycophancy. But those who speak out, such as Shashi Tharoor, still risk the party's wrath.[67]

For all these reasons, the BJP has effectively replaced the Congress as the dominant national party, at least for the near future. Nor is the end of the Congress unthinkable. We are halfway there as of now, and parties do die. In 1910 the Liberal Party in England was a political fixture, a party of government with new ideas and welfare schemes aplenty. But over the next decade it underwent a crisis of relevance that it could not have foreseen and which it had insufficient resources to overcome or outlive. The result was its estrangement from government for a century, only to return under a different name in a different era. Liberal England died, as G.B. Dangerfield explained in a 1935 book,[68] a victim of social, economic and global changes. Now, with a once-dominant party under a similar set of pressures, are we witnessing the strange death of Congress India?

Even if we are, this does not of course mean that support for centre-left politics has disappeared in India. What it means is that the Congress is having a hard time representing that demand effectively. Welfare issues are often very local in India, and this has not helped a national body like the Congress. On the contrary, it has helped socialist caste-based parties such as the SP in UP and the RJD in Bihar, which are led by local figures familiar with local issues and known to local voters. But none of these smaller parties have any realistic prospect of growing into a national force. Even the JD (U), which spans several states, has shown no capacity to outgrow its current constituency. The BSP has, at least in theory, a potential countrywide vote bank of Dalits, but recent attempts by Mayawati to expand across the country have not gone well. The BSP failed to win a single seat in Maharashtra in October 2014, and the party risks losing its official 'national' status. Indeed Mayawati may have to look to her home base, after her disastrous showing in UP, where the BSP did not win a single seat at the 2014 Lok Sabha election.

The dog that didn't bark in 2014 was the Aam Aadmi Party. The AAP picked up tremendous momentum after the Delhi assembly poll of December 2013 installed it in government. With such widespread disillusionment with UPA-II, an anti-corruption party seemed all set to do well in the national poll in May. But two factors worked against this outcome. The first was that its Delhi government did not fare well. Once in power, the party seemed amateurish and disorganized, an impression duly reinforced when Arvind Kejriwal handed back the seals of office after only seven weeks, having had its legislative programme baulked by the two main parties. Secondly, AAP was overtaken by the Modi wave. Modi was not only promising anti-corruption and greater accountability, he also inserted prosperity into the bargain. But time may reverse both these factors. AAP is likely to pick up experience and refine its structure, if it manages to keep going. It also fundamentally appeals to a different, more secular constituency, so a successful BJP does not axiomatically disadvantage AAP. And the Modi government may yet become bogged down in scandal itself. The NDA government of 1999–2004 came in on a clean-up mission but fell into traditional dark dealing after a few years. Unless NDA-II keeps its nose very clean, AAP may yet be able to recover some momentum.

It would be hard to deny that the national picture has changed both politically and economically. According to statistics, poverty alleviation has worked in the long term, both locally under Congress rule and nationally under the UPA. But the really significant change is that it does not necessarily bring political reward. There has been a law of diminishing returns in operation. India is not yet rich, per capita, but individual voters may be changing their behaviour permanently.

The big question is whether poverty, and with it caste and the reservations issue, is about to mean less in Indian national politics. And if caste is less of a factor, which is as we should suppose, then the BJP may hold the ring in national electoral contests for a while.

The 2014 election has its place in the parallel narratives of the two national parties, but it may also signal a new stage in the story of the mismatch between parties and the state. Caste-based reservations were an argument about the state and its possibilities, about who was entitled to special treatment by right. Modi transformed this argument by refusing to equate the economy and the state, and thus opened up a new area for political ideas beyond the aegis of government. This liberation had the effect of making the standard political arguments seem pessimistic, limited and limiting. His emphasis on growth changed all these equations and the other parties could not speak well on this change, or could not embrace it because their roots were buried in the system. They were the beasts that grazed on the grass, and could not do without it. Modi-nomics released the BJP from this dependence. This does not mean that the BJP cannot and will not use the reservation system to its own advantage; it just means that the cord is cut, and the issue is reduced in importance beside the greater goal of wealth creation.

In 2014 the BJP ran its most focused campaign ever, concentrating on economic issues as never before. Long-standing BJP cultural concerns were still present in the manifesto – the Ram temple, Article 370, the Uniform Civil Code – but the main emphasis of the campaign was on growth, development, better governance, infrastructure projects including roads and railways, fighting inflation, repatriating black money and reducing corruption. The campaign was slick, with a high-octane media team at work, directed by the London-based Manoj Ladwa. It used innovative techniques, including holograms and a heavy social media presence. But it also had a clever earthy charm, with '*chai pe charcha*'. There was better organization on the ground too, skillfully targeted by Amit Shah. His success in delivering seats all across Bihar and UP might seem to suggest that vote bank politics is not dead, even within an election dominated by national visions.

But perhaps it has just changed a little, becoming more flexible in two ways: the banks are smaller, and they are less loyal.

There are several reasons why this might be so. One is that caste reservations only operate in the public sector, and there are finite limits to how much of it can be reserved, especially as liberalization has curbed its growth. Both factors have tended to diminish the political significance of schemes of reservation. The political solution to this decline was to float the idea of extending reservations to the private sector. But corporate India has always been intensely resistant to the idea of non-merit based recruitment, especially if made a statutory requirement. The prospect that this might happen flickered temporarily at the end of UPA-II, but the chances of any such scheme being introduced under a Modi government are zero. The leverage that reservations can exercise on castes is thus limited, and is of increasingly less use to parties.

Another reason is that vote banks are sometimes more imaginary than real, such as the alleged Muslim vote bank that appears and disappears at different times and places, and is or is not compatible with other groupings. Yet another is that one long-term effect of Mandalization has been the subdivision of caste groups into smaller sections – so-called sub-castes and caste clusters – which are often mutually competitive. This makes it harder to assemble solid blocks of support on the basis of caste alone. Fielding the right sort of candidate is still a good way to maximize caste loyalty but, away from reservations and benefits based on social identity, it seems likely that it will be more difficult to figure out caste electoral equations or to mobilize distinct groups over wide areas.

The BJP judged this very well in 2014, which materially contributed to the scale of the party's success. One in four Dalits voted for the party, more than ever before.[69] The BSP, however, who should know a thing or two about caste mobilization, seems to have got it wrong. In 2009, the Congress got 21 seats in UP on an 18 per cent vote share: in 2014 the BSP got zero on 19 per cent, in a state where 21 per cent of the population are Scheduled Castes.[70] This serves to illustrate that in Indian elections, even with national issues in play, what determines the outcome is not swings of opinion so much as splits within social layers, which vary in their precise details. The overall effect is always then related to macro- and micro-economic contexts, and especially to the level of turnout. In a low turnout a social grouping of 10 per cent will have a proportionately much greater effect than in a high turnout. This does not mean that principles can never be part of the equation; it means that it is difficult to treat vote banks as solid entities, especially within the very wide backward caste layers. And it may well be the case that caste will remain an influence in local elections to a much greater degree than in national, based on a rough division in voters' perceptions between personal and national interests.

What will certainly remain is the willingness of India's party leaders to accuse others of using vote banks while trying to exploit them themselves. One man's vote bank is another man's targeted outreach project.

If vote banks took a less central role in 2014, big ideas certainly came to the fore. Inclusive growth was always a Congress mantra, and Modi managed to steal it by making it mean something a little different – by stressing on the growth rather than the inclusiveness. Individuals can help themselves once the growth has happened. This was his message, and he must now deliver on it to assure his place in history.

India has elected a self-declared strong leader for the first time in a while and has given him a big – slightly contrived – majority, but the irony is that the future of the country lies only partially in his hands. The states are becoming more important, and global economics affect everyone everywhere more than they ever did. Modi holds the cards as they were under the old system – he has patronage, and the public treasury is at his disposal. He might even get a following macro-economic wind with a global recovery on the way, and he might be the beneficiary of long-term economic and demographic changes, with the urban middle classes already his and the rural population more willing to listen to a man who promises them real wealth. He has the energy and the vision. He might just need a little luck.

No one will yet be betting against another Modi term in 2019.

2.

Threats to Indian Democracy

Pessimists about the prospects for democracy in India were not in short supply a few decades ago. Even Dr Ambedkar feared that the constitution he did so much to frame might not flourish in the 'soil' of India, which he viewed as historically alien to democratic, egalitarian ideas. But most observers currently believe that the skies, though not yet cloudless, are much brighter. Some may now say that Indian *society* is going to hell in a handcart for various reasons, but at present no one seems to actively predict the demise of India's democratic system.

So is India's democracy in danger? Yes, because all democracies always are. Democracy is permanently at risk from all sorts of directions. Over-mighty governments, elite monopoly attitudes, the civic stresses of diversity and the social problems that come with hard economic times can all erode the trust that holds a democracy together. As the old proverb goes, trust arrives on foot, but leaves on horseback.

Democratic institutions are like a finely spun web that requires a little tension running through it to maintain its shape but remains vulnerable to violent shocks. India is hardly insulated from such shocks, and the more she becomes integral to the global economy, the more vulnerable she may become. The decline in the value of the rupee through 2013 is one such example. Inflation is also a constant danger; no national economy is now immune from variations in international commodity prices. Extreme currency fluctuations can produce economic chaos and social distress, setting the scene for mass disorder and perhaps an opportunity for authoritarian rule. Democracies are at their least capable when sudden decisive action needs to be taken.

But India is probably too robust economically, and too accustomed to degrees of social hardship, to fall victim to the sort of fiscal whirlwind that unhinged Weimar Germany at the start of the 1930s. Indeed, India stands clear from many of the more familiar weaknesses that can bring a democracy to an inglorious end as a failed state.

Recent history tells us that democracies fail in stages; it is dictatorships that crash and burn. So what are the signs of democratic decline? Massive popular discontent can look like an upsurge of democracy, but it can act in a highly undemocratic way if it sunders communities or undermines federal compromises. The popular protests in Ukraine through early-2014 followed exactly this model. Once the elected President, Viktor Yanukovych, was ousted, the country was left facing a critical dilemma with a crisis of democratic legitimacy and a potential ethnic conflict between Ukrainians and Russians. This immediately played out in disputes over the semi-autonomous position of Crimea, and in Ukraine's relations with neighbouring Russia. Fears among ethnic Russians in the east of the country that the new regime would not respect their linguistic and religious identity escalated into a separatist insurgency, which drew Russia into annexing Crimea and supporting the rebels with arms and men. From street protests to an undeclared civil war in a few short months.

In other circumstances, an extended crisis of governability is as likely to lead to a military takeover as to a civil war, and the former may lead to the latter if the armed forces are also deeply polarized.

So how realistic is the prospect of a military coup in India? Not very. Neither the foreign exchange crises of 1967 or 1991, nor the Emergency, prompted the military even to consider stepping in. This is significant, because one of the greatest dangers to democracy in South Asia since 1945 has been from military intervention. The reasons why this happened in other countries are specific to their separate histories, but here it is worth examining why India, so far, has managed to avoid military rule.

One potential factor is the British legacy, and we could blithely assume that it must have inoculated India's military from inappropriate ambitions. But why, then, did this tradition not protect Pakistan, which shared it in full measure? The Pakistani army was officered by men with identical training and the same ethos of service – but the country they were defending has succumbed to military putsch on three occasions, and still lives under the shadow of a potential fourth. There must, therefore, be a little more to India's solid retention of civilian rule than a British hangover. Perhaps it would be better to say that even the British legacy, weak or strong as it might have been, was not sufficient to protect Pakistan against certain other factors; from the very beginning, it was an under-funded and over-militarized polity, which considered itself engaged in a deadly struggle with its larger neighbour.

Here we can appreciate that India has been much more fortunate in her circumstances. India's military spending has always been in a standard relationship to the size of the state budget, and is currently running at less than 3 per cent of GDP. This is hardly belligerent and is about a third of what China spends, but it will rise, as India replaces a long list of ageing hardware, including warships, fighter aircraft and helicopters. But the drive for modernization will also open India to outside influences, as the cap on foreign investment in defence industries has been raised from 29 to 49 per cent, and may yet go higher. The growth of a domestic hi-tech arms industry will help growth, and will not put extra pressure on the political system.

India's armed forces have never been able to create an economic niche for themselves within the wider economy, as has happened in Pakistan, Burma and Egypt. Furthermore, atomic weapons aside, military thinking in India has been conventional and reasonably realistic. Above all, the tail has never been able to wag the dog. Politicians have consistently set the military agenda, and the reverse has never been true.

This does not mean that relations between politicians and the military have always been good, or that they are not susceptible to tensions. Hasty and rather hysterical reports of an attempted coup on the foggy morning of 17 January 2012 were all too easily believed in New Delhi – by jittery newshounds at least. Other stories hinting at simmering tensions between politicians and military top brass emerge occasionally, citing disagreements on strategy against separatists in Kashmir or Naxalite rebels, and particularly over an apparent lack of public support from politicians for the military over alleged abuses and atrocities. One such story actually named General Joyanto Nath Chaudhuri, who is alleged to have contemplated a coup in the aftermath of the 1965 war with Pakistan.[71]

Tensions do exist, but are more closely connected to matters of appointment and seniority. General V.K. Singh, Chief of Army Staff from 2010 to 2012, was unusually political for a serving soldier. Approaching compulsory retirement at the age of 62, he sued the government over the way his age had been recorded; he lost and had to step down at the due date. He is also alleged to have tried to damage the promotion prospects of two senior soldiers, Generals Bikram Singh and Dalbir Singh Suhag, who were in line to succeed him, in hopes of enhancing the chances of a relative to succeed him in the top job.[72]

All these are real and continuing areas for possible friction, but none is remotely serious enough to produce a coup d'etat.

India has also been defended against its armed forces to a certain degree by geography; the scale of the country, which might be a military disadvantage in terms of defence against external threats, has proved a blessing in protecting political institutions. Any serious attempt at a takeover would have to be undertaken on a daunting scale. Small countries like Panama, Ghana or Haiti, or very sparsely populated states like Chad, present a much easier military objective. Once the presidential palace and radio and TV stations in the capital are taken, the job is largely done. Imagine trying to control the Indian media at one swoop, or how many key crossroads would have to be secured across the country to lock it down. It would also be necessary to take over all the state-level institutions, or at least to assure that they remained onside. Forming an entirely new pan-Indian organization like this would be to bite off an enormous amount at one go. Would the army really be unanimous enough within itself, officers and men, with all their regional identities, private political persuasions and personal faith traditions? And who would be the support group outside the army?

Military coups are generally in favour of some interest group or other, not just in the sole interest of the army. Which group in India is large and powerful enough to feel it is not getting what it wants, and thinks that only the army can deliver it? Bigger armies might be able to act more autonomously, but there is an optimum size for a state–army ratio that renders the state vulnerable. India surely sits well on the 'state too big, army too small' end of that scale.

The vulnerability of the Indian state to a small officer clique is very low. Indians live with a high degree of ambient disorder and are relatively used to it, so the notion that the army could 'restore' order in the country is faintly humorous from the start. And unless the whole country comes seriously off the rails politically and economically, the idea that the nation needs to be defended against revolutionary communism – the most popular recent pretext for coups, as in Greece, Argentina, Chile or Grenada – would be laughable.

At present, the dominant culture in India's armed forces is secular and liberal, broadly in line with the wider political culture. Unless and until that situation changes profoundly, India is probably as safe from military rule as any major European country or the US. Militarily, India's problems are more that the three wings of the services need better integration, arms procurement should be better supervised, dependence on foreign suppliers reduced and more civilian administrative specialists need to be trained to oversee military policy.

But the unknown factor here is insecurity. If credible threats can be talked up, increased central control to the point of dictatorship becomes a possibility. From where, then, might such threats come? India has only two neighbouring states powerful enough to threaten invasion on any scale, and she has already fought them both. We know what wars with China and Pakistan can bring. A collapse of democracy under pressure of external invasion is an extremely remote possibility, especially in view of the fact that all three likely combatants in South Asia are nuclear powers. This means that wars between them will either be very small or very, very big; so big that democratic niceties become irrelevant.

Indo–Chinese regional rivalry is rather more strategic than directly military, with China currently the more active, because of the desire in Beijing to intensify her relationships with India's neighbours, principally Myanmar and Sri Lanka. This has taken concrete form in the so-called 'String of Pearls' strategy – the attempt by China to establish economic hubs and to build railways, roads and port facilities all over the region, from the northern edge of Nepal to Chittagong, and from Kyaukphyu in Myanmar and Gwadar on the western edge of Pakistan to Hambantota on the southern coast of Sri Lanka. This certainly reflects China's drive to establish her influence, but it is not a direct military threat. China seems to be offering a partnership in development rather than imposing control at a distance, and these activities can be seen as a relatively mild version of the assertive policies recently followed by states as diverse as the US and Qatar.

There are, however, aspects of this rivalry that affect the prospects for democracy across the region, especially in relation to Sri Lanka. China is an undemocratic power with clear economic goals, and she has been buying friends, some of whom are similarly disinclined to promote real democracy. This places Sri Lanka in a special position, with Western powers attempting to promote human rights within the island and its President determined to do as he wishes. With the Chinese prepared to support him, just as they supported the generals in Myanmar, the Indian government has a hard choice to make – whether to side with the high-minded Westerners, or to compete for friendship in the region's capitals. The UPA sided against President Rajapaksa, not primarily from any calculus of humanitarian theory but because of regional electoral interests in Tamil Nadu. Prime Minister Modi has engaged with President Rajapaksa, while bringing up concerns over fishing rights and the disputed island of Kachchatheevu. He has also publicly praised China's model of business-friendly governance. Above all he seems willing to draw the Chinese into bilateral commercial relations, if only to reduce the trade deficit, currently running heavily in China's favour. With the two leaderships both committed to trade and development, the prospects for expensive military conflict seem as remote as at any time since 1962.

Pakistan remains a different matter. Islamabad has plenty to argue about with New Delhi, but the question here is as political as it is military. It has always been sound politics in Pakistan to talk up the rivalry with India, despite the rather obvious fact that India is larger and richer than Pakistan, and is unlikely to emerge badly from any conflict. But the supposed Indian threat supplies the best reason for Pakistan's military budget to remain high. Talking up tensions with India has therefore been a major obsession of Pakistani politicians and senior military figures, who have often been the same people.

But Pakistan has never succeeded in bringing any telling leverage on India through armed force. The one point scored was the revelation that Pakistan had full nuclear capability, as demonstrated by the series of tests undertaken in 1998. This was a far-reaching development, and much more significant than the attempt the next year to throw back Indian forces in the Kargil region. But in 1999, as in 1971, the immediate effects of Pakistani military action were felt in Pakistan, not India, when the tension between the then prime minister, Nawaz Sharif, and his chief of staff, Pervez Musharraf, was resolved a few months later in favour of the soldier.

Reconciliation is a treasured goal for many, and efforts have been and are being made on both sides of the border to address contentious issues and reduce the 'trust deficit' via Track Two back-channel diplomacy.[73] Delhi hosts the Centre for Dialogue and Reconciliation, founded in 2000, and in Islamabad there is the recently established Regional Peace Institute. Even the current Pakistani Prime Minister, Nawaz Sharif, has muted the anti-Indian rhetoric of previous years. The stars may not yet be fully aligned to permit a full bilateral accommodation, but the strength of the Modi government has left it a free hand to approach the problems without undue concern for electoral or parliamentary considerations. Nawaz Sharif, or any elected successor, needs to be similarly secure, though, for real progress to be made

Regional rivalries may threaten India to various degrees, but they do not seriously threaten India's democracy. Credible threats to political India are more insidious and less dramatic than foreign invasion or disastrous military defeat. The principal burden of defending India's democracy has never been the preserve of the armed forces, but of politicians. Now, increasingly, it is devolving onto the citizenry.

Thus far, politicians have played their role, and even Indira Gandhi, who accumulated more personal power than any leader before or since, never entirely lost her commitment to the forms of democracy. She was prepared to submit to the electoral test in 1977, and never made any serious attempt to impose a second emergency when things were not going her way between 1980 and 1984.

But could anyone else ever do so? Is there a real danger of a civilian coup, and a return to unaccountable, personal rule? This spectre has been raised in some quarters with the success of Narendra Modi, whose reputation as a relentless and unforgiving man intolerant of criticism is well-rehearsed. The BJP has a history of talking up constitutional reform, with a preference for a presidential system that it believes would be more consensual and directly democratic than the Westminster-style adversarial system currently in place. Could this materialize? Both L.K. Advani and A.B. Vajpayee pursued this theme in the 1990s.[74] But times have moved on, and more recently Modi has been talking less of concentrating authority in a single person and more of possible devolution of powers giving 'greater autonomy' to states in order to aid development.[75]

The creation of an authoritarian presidential regime is not likely. Modi has consistently talked the language of democracy, and India as a state, ancient or modern, has always been resistant to control by one individual. A massive amount of groundwork would have to be put in before a new dictatorship could become viable. Mrs Gandhi did a great deal before her coup, having purged or intimidated her own party ranks, provincial governors, the judiciary and the senior bureaucracy. Conditions have since combined to make such a concentration of power less likely with the rise of regional parties and the efflorescence of independent media. Any assumption of extraordinary powers would have to be, or at least would have to appear to be, a response to extraordinary events. In ordinary times, the idea that any one political leader or party could accumulate overwhelming dictatorial powers is highly unlikely. The whole Indian political system is almost designed to thwart this eventuality. And if anyone tried, the probable result would not be a successful dictatorship but a drastic collapse of central authority in the regions.

However, a more degenerative danger lurks within the structure of the Indian state, hidden within the notional separation of its powers. Democratic government is conventionally divided into three main branches – executive, legislative and judiciary. This is a theoretical scheme, and the three parts overlap and interact in all sorts of ways, not all of them unhealthy. The legislative is usually the most passive of the powers, but it occupies a controlling position. It resides in a representative assembly, and in a prime ministerial system it is this assembly's support that confers legitimacy on the executive. In a presidential system the chief executive is directly elected in his/her own right, which confers a more personal mandate, but risks creating a 'lame duck' president who cannot muster a majority in the legislature. Parliamentary systems such as India's do not create lame duck prime ministers; they are quickly thrown out by no confidence motions, followed by an outbreak of horse-trading, or fresh elections, so democracy is more directly served, and sooner.

The legislative and executive are in a relatively stable partnership in India, with the advantage clearly in favour of the latter. More problematic are relations between these two and the judiciary; the Supreme Court has repeatedly curbed the powers of the other branches. In 1973 it determined that Parliament's powers to amend the constitution were limited (*Kesavananda Bharati vs. State of Kerala*); in 1994 it ruled that the executive's powers to impose President's Rule on states was subject to judicial review (*Bommai vs. Union of India*). In the so called Judges Cases, of 1993 and 1998, the apex court also effectively took the power of appointing senior judges away from the President and into its own hands. These forays by the judiciary into the deepest workings of democracy are clearly of great importance, especially in the matter of appointments.

The rule of law can only be securely maintained if judges are competent and politically neutral. Judges are deemed competent based on their experience and professional qualifications, but they have to be chosen, and here lies the rub. The constitution originally laid down that the President would appoint judges on the advice of the chief justice and other senior legal figures. This arrangement has since been challenged and altered, so that judges now effectively appoint themselves. The President still acts on advice, partly from the government of the day, but mainly from a small group of senior lawyers headed by the chief justice called the collegium. The rules under which this body operates are not defined, nor are its procedures transparent. Under current practice, the President has to be consulted, but he can only request that appointments be reconsidered.

This system, developed through the 1980s and 1990s, was intended to eliminate the kind of political interference that Mrs Gandhi was wont to exert. However, the cure is in some ways worse than the ailment, because the present unaccountability of the system actually means that political influence can still be exercised while remaining entirely invisible. Biases of individuals may affect who does and does not receive a seat on the Supreme Court bench, but petty professional rivalries are not the danger here. Suspicions have been raised for some time about political pressure being used to secure appointments of corrupt judges. Who would want such characters to be thus favoured? Under the current opaque arrangements, no one outside the collegium can know anything.

Further alarm was generated in June 2014 when a senior and well-respected lawyer, Gopal Subramaniam, was proposed by the collegium, but the newly installed NDA, via the President, asked that his nomination be reconsidered. Reasons were not publicly given; it was hinted that Subramaniam was of unsuitable character, but senior Congress figures speculated that his role in cases involving members of the BJP in Gujarat had made him *persona non grata* to some powerful men, including Amit Shah, the BJP's president. The issue was resolved when Subramaniam withdrew his candidacy.

Judicial appointments are absolutely central to the correct functioning of the rule of law. Executive interference cannot be borne. So does the collegium system work for or against executive influence? Enough politicians and senior lawyers now believe that it facilitates it, and a bill to set up a Judicial Appointments Commission, bundled with a 121st Amendment, has passed through both houses of Parliament; it still awaits ratification by state assemblies. Whether the new system can be insulated from political influence any more securely than the previous arrangements remains to be seen. If politicians are really determined to appoint compliant judges, there are all sorts of ways to do it, such as by amending rules of seniority, or the compulsory age of retirement. India's Supreme Court has been described as the most powerful court in the world,[76] and it is absolutely imperative that its decisions remain untainted. The Modi government has the most unchallenged mandate since the time of Indira Gandhi. Indians must watch carefully.

And quite apart from creeping dictatorship or compromise of the senior judiciary, India faces another real threat to the democratic health of the nation, which is the mammoth backlog of court cases, by now running into the tens of millions. Some of this is due to archaic procedure, some because of delaying tactics by defendants. But right at the heart of the issue is the desperate shortage of judges. India has a tenth of the judges per head of population that America does. This surely has to be addressed as a matter of priority; fast-track courts and any other such innovations and expedients will certainly require more judges to make them work properly.

There are four other major dangers that threaten the quality of democracy in modern India. The first three are secession, rebellion, and inter-communal violence, which threaten dissolution of the state. The other is corruption, which threatens degeneration, with the drain of governmental resources (embezzlement), chronic national economic underperformance through corrupt elite relationships (cronyism and nepotism) and the wholesale collapse of governmental authority through bribery.

DISSOLUTION

Secession is a constant threat to large, complex political entities, and they don't come much larger or more complex than India.

The country contains an extraordinary mixture of ancient and modern elements, and its political structure represents an often fragile bridge between the two. As a cultural bloc, most of the Indian subcontinent has experienced a long, organic development, but modernization of some regions and sectors, sometimes at breakneck speed, has tended to undermine the potential benefits this might have conferred. We are all familiar with photographs contrasting squalor in the foreground with high-rise apartments in the background, or with bullock carts on three-lane highways. Writers of all stripes, Indian and foreign, are still trying to understand how exactly the new frontiers of privilege and deprivation are playing out within mass electoral politics, and how they affect ideas about national unity.

The founding generation of Indian politicians had a phobia about subdivision and were prone to overemphasize Indian unity as a rejoinder to British claims of a chaotic tendency within Indian affairs to which British rule was the only answer. The pressing need for political unity at all costs coloured Indian attitudes over the independence period, and for all his criticisms of Congress arrogance, B.R. Ambedkar was as keen to produce a unitary, centralized Indian polity as anyone else.

With the livid scar of Partition still stinging, the early Indian state was not kind to regional demands. But two factors gradually worked to create a more favourable attitude in central government policy. One was sensitivity to language, and the other was the arrival of a more relaxed attitude to regional diversity within India.

Something certainly had to be done to the basic structure of the country, because one obvious and unhelpful legacy of colonial rule was the massive size of India's provincial units, most of which had been defined without concern for the people they contained. These blocks had worked well enough within the British Raj, which undertook little of the detail that modern government requires. But post-1947, the 11 provinces of British India were evidently far too large for modern purposes. They now became 'states', and their relationship with the centre was set out in the constitution. But where should their borders be drawn, and on what basis?

While the determination in Delhi to impose Hindi as a national language persisted, this had not been a problem for the British, who had developed a flexible system, conducting local government in local languages while imposing English at higher levels. With independence, this became an active political problem, in view of the drive for national unity and an end to alien influence. With the agitation in 1953 for a Telugu language state of Andhra, a new chapter opened, and it became politically prudent to take language into account over and above existing administrative arrangements. The relentless drive for national integration that seemed to be the Congress way was then abandoned in 1956, when the linguistic reorganization of states was accepted.

The fears of the elite did, however, prove well-founded, in that language began to generate a constant stream of demands. What made the difference though, was the acceptance by both rulers and ruled that the recognition of local languages was not a rejection of the Indian polity, a trend that has continued to this day. Many observers now expect a further round of state creation in the next decade, partly as an ongoing commitment to recognize local identities, and partly as a rational concession to fuller democracy. Currently numbered at 29, some of India's states are enormous; if Uttar Pradesh were divided into four, as some have advocated,[77] its parts would still be bigger than most states in the EU. Some predict that as many as 60 states may one day make up the Indian Union. The recent bifurcation of Andhra Pradesh into Telangana and Seemandhra is perhaps only the first of many such subdivisions, which always leave at least some people dissatisfied, even as they appease others.

Linguistic sensitivities have subdivided the Indian state without breaking it up, but Delhi has not typically been sympathetic to demands for increased autonomy. Long-running armed struggles have resulted in Nagaland, Assam and Manipur, with intense conflicts in Punjab through the 1980s and in Kashmir from 1989 to the present. What distinguishes these last two conflicts is partly the extreme nature of the demands presented – for sovereign autonomy, but also the way these demands were couched in religious as opposed to ethnic or linguistic terms. Religion, the pretext for the Partition, has remained too sensitive an issue to be admitted as grounds for granting regional autonomy. Sikh or Muslim separatism has always been unacceptable, whereas a linguistic state of Punjab was conceded in 1966. The granting of more local responsibility within India, based in community identities that are not religious, has now been given a green(ish) light, and has been chiefly responsible for creating the patchwork of small states in the north-east.

Genuine secession movements, however, have been relatively rare, and have never been coordinated, so the state has picked them off one by one, much as the British did to the rajas. Since the Dravidian separatist movement backed down in the 1960s, they have also, apart from Punjab, generally been on behalf of smaller, usually peripheral states. Kashmir was never a part of British India and has always had a cultural sense of itself, which prolonged military occupation has done little to diminish. Article 370 of the constitution recognized this, and despite the ambition of nationalists to 'integrate' the former princely state, some kind of international agreement that includes provisions for continued political autonomy would seem to be the only way forward. Conceding the demands of Kashmiris will not destroy India's wider political unity or the rationale of her existence.

Political experience and the wisdom of moderation have shown that India stays strong by remaining fairly loose when under internal pressures that most states would recognize as normal. And so, over time, a modern version of the mythical Indian identity has been forged by incremental accumulation of shared experience. Films, sporting successes, nationally shared icons of all sorts, even terrorist attacks have created a large area of common ground that diversities of region, caste and language have insufficient power to destroy.

As a very large federal union, India will always be subject to the demand for greater local inclusion in the political process, and provincial state lines are the currency of this trade. As long as neither the Union nor its internal peace is compromised, bartering in autonomy will surely continue.

What is not, however, negotiable for any polity is a direct threat to its very existence. Under this heading must come the open insurgency that persists across an arc of central India, where Maoist rebels, dedicated to the overthrow of not just the Union but of capitalism itself, are waging war on the Indian state and its agencies. The rebels are promoting democracy, but the democracy of Mao, which is not easily compatible with the apparatus of multiparty politics and parliamentary democracy.

These Naxalites, named after Naxalbari, the village in Bengal where the first outbreak took place in 1967, may not present a mortal threat to the republic, but they are a troubling and costly irritant that remains highly resistant to conventional forms of repression. This is partly because the rebels are dispersed and mobile, and partly because the gospel they preach, mostly to India's more backward social and economic groups, is highly attractive in the light of the dismal experience many of these people have had of modern democratic governance. They are frequently the victims of corrupt deals and unjust treatment over land rights, and a toxic cocktail of neglect and abuse has left many within India's tribal belt all too ready to take to simple solutions pursued with violent intensity.

Experience suggests that this sort of dispersed, ideological movement is hard to combat militarily. It can only be defeated by a long process of reform and recognition of the grievances concerned, but in the interim the ferocity of state power deployed against it piles up bodies and accumulates human rights abuses that prolong the antagonism. The Naxalite movement represents a short-term threat to civil liberties, but in the long term it also offers a way in which democracy can be expanded. While everyone has a little less liberty during the campaign, a successful resolution might actually represent an enhancement of the wider democratic process. Whether the current Indian political system is capable of fully rising to this challenge may be doubted; it has not gone very far up till now. Politicians still prefer to treat the situation as a law and order matter.

The original outbreak of the 1960s was suppressed by ruthless state violence, abetted by the relatively concentrated nature of the rebellion. But the insurgency reappeared from the 1980s in a more widespread form. Attempts to find a negotiated settlement have been going on for more than a decade, and the centralization of the rebel leadership in 2004, under the title of the CPI (Maoist), should have enhanced the chances for peace, but the Maoists' demands – including land redistribution and the creation of a people's democracy – remain difficult to accommodate, and state authorities have continued to believe in the possibility of military victory. But recent history in the region doe not provide grounds for optimism about peace. In Nepal the Maoists enjoyed a much wider support base and were able to make peace as part of a national-political and constitutional settlement. In Sri Lanka the LTTE was defeated only by massive deployment of force, rendered effective by the geographical concentration of the rebel units.

Central government has not completely abandoned its faith in military might, but over the years it has learned to box a little more cleverly. Direct military action was combined with the formation of local militias, principally the Salwa Judum in Chhattisgarh, and armed force was supplemented by cash incentives offered to leaders for laying down their weapons. These 'surrender and rehabilitation' packages proved not only less divisive than setting local communities to hunting and killing each other, they also proved more effective, especially after the central government authorized a tenfold increase in their value in 2013. There were nearly 2,000 surrenders that year, mainly in Orissa.[78] The money on offer is attractive – being enough to set up a new life, but it may also be that the sheer duration of the struggle is beginning to tell heavily on the rebels; many have wives and children who have begun to hanker for a more stable lifestyle.

The main rebel leader, Mupalla Lakshman Rao, a.k.a. Ganapathy, is still at large, but he has registered concern at the success of the new government strategy.[79]

In spite of the recent successes, the problems that the Naxalite movement represents should not be underestimated. Traditional tribal societies in India have been the victims of many of the most extractive tendencies of modern capitalism, and this contradiction is not likely to be easily resolved. It is not in the economic interests of the state and its main supporters to concede to the rebels' demands. Social and economic reforms, plus political savvy, are the way forward; neat military solutions are not.

Terrorism presents very different problems, and India has had her share. Outrages by separatist groups became increasingly common through the 1970s, with Sikh groups most prominent. More recently the emphasis has been on jihadi groups, as part of the rise in global terror networks related to al-Qaeda. This has broadened out the problem, making it less susceptible to direct pressure from security forces and much less amenable to settlement by political negotiation. The personnel involved in recent high-profile attacks in India are not localized like the Naxalites. Nor are they fighting for a cause that can be recognized as a specifically local grievance – and the grievances they have are not entirely in the hands of the Indian government to solve.

How to end the use of disproportionate and indiscriminate violence on a religious basis is a question facing all major states today, but the notional grievances that impel modern Lashkar-e-Taiba style international terrorism are almost beyond the ability of politicians to assuage. Are we to dismantle everything 'un-Islamic' across the world? Here we are not dealing with dams and mineral rights or health care or police brutality; we are looking at a whole vista of heavily slanted, global–historical viewpoints which have generated 'wrongs' that are difficult to address in conventional political terms. Bombs go off in London, Spain, Bali or India that are to do with events at any point where Islamic sensitivities can be inflamed.

The attack on Mumbai in November 2008 was planned and executed by Pakistanis, but India's security services had been aware of home-grown jihadi terror cells for years before. Many were originally connected to the outlawed Students Islamic Movement of India (SIMI), though they are now also linked to transnational networks. This includes the Indian Mujahideen (IM), which has been the pre-eminent outfit since its debut in 2008, but it is now joined, or perhaps rivalled, by the recently announced al-Qaeda in the Indian Subcontinent (AQIS). All this sounds rather grandiose but the numbers involved in extremist violence are, according to President Pranab Mukherjee, 'extremely negligible'.[80] Precise totals are not available, but around 18 Indians are known to have joined ISIS/ISIL, and barely a hundred others have been recruited to other organizations.

There is now, however, a long list of homeland targets that have been attacked by native-born Indians including the Parliament building in 2001, for which Afzal Guru, an Indian citizen from J&K, was hanged in February 2013. Other Indian nationals – Shadab Baig, Iqbal Bhatkal, Abdul Mateen Damada, Ejaz Sheikh, Asadullah Akhtar, etc.,– have been linked to a series of fatal bomb blasts, including attacks in Varanasi and Mumbai (2006), Ahmedabad (2008), the Jama Masjid (2010) and Hyderabad (2013).

India is thus neither immune nor, unfortunately, any more capable of tackling terrorism than anyone else. Law and order is a state-level concern, and this has made coordinated action more difficult. Political jealousies have been pricked, and proposals for a National Counter Terrorism Centre (NCTC) were rebuffed by an alliance of regional leaders in 2013,[81] which included the Gujarat chief minister, one Narendra Modi. Long-term solutions must include surveillance, education, better employment opportunities and measures to deprive terrorist groups of funds. Less helpful would be ramped up religious rhetoric, calculated agitation by political parties and penny-pinching in intelligence budgets.

The Kashmir problem remains central, and it is to a large extent in the hands of elected governments to resolve, but the general issue of terrorism is much wider than that. Citizens can play an important role by ensuring that terrorists, who do not greatly care whom they kill, are recognized and rejected by the communities they claim to represent. Accurate intelligence is a key factor in helping governments to thwart terrorist operations, but this is not a simple process, and it can lead governments into some very murky areas, building networks of informers and double agents. It can also take a considerable time for communities that have felt unjustly treated to distinguish legitimate and illegitimate means of pursuing their grievances. Terrorists usually take considerable trouble to present themselves as heroic fighters striking back against oppression, especially at the start of the movement, and that image can give 'our boys' a lasting emotional appeal that continues to transcend their true political value.

But ultimately, terrorists are not accountable. No one elects or appoints them, and therefore it is difficult to eject them from 'office'. They represent a complete abuse of the nice democratic distinction between a delegate and a representative. There is no conceivable way in which secretive, self-appointed, unaccountable terrorists could ever claim to be delegates. They fall within the representative category, but without any of the elaborate protocols and processes that those wishing to call themselves representatives have to undergo. It is therefore almost inevitable that terrorist movements end up as entirely self-serving; history shows us precisely this effect in operation in almost every case where terrorism does not moderate itself voluntarily, leading eventually to a share in government.

Within democracies, terrorists never represent majorities. If they did they could stand for election and accomplish their ends more effectively through existing institutions. Terrorism purports to be a way of airing and resolving grievances in an all-in-one process. There is no negotiating phase in a terrorist incident. There is also no quality control on what those grievances are – how real, and how capable of resolution by the means employed, i.e. indiscriminate violence.

Global jihadi terrorism is a perverse side effect of long-standing political tensions, and India has a history of religious diversity that can easily generate and maintain such tensions. In milder forms they produce rioting, and India is not yet free from lethal civil disorder with an apparent religious aspect. Nationalist politicians of the freedom movement habitually blamed such outbreaks on British skulduggery, while the British blamed 'natural' primordial antagonisms. Neither analysis was very accurate nor entirely free of what would now be called 'spin'. Nothing can be done to ease such animosities in modern India unless it is accepted that the country's religious tensions are located squarely in the here and now. The anti-Sikh violence of 1984 in Delhi, the anti-Muslim pogrom of 2002 in Gujarat, and more recently the riots in Assam (2012) and Muzaffarnagar (2013) all had very tangible, proximate causes; some of the most significant are as closely related to party allegiances as to religion.

And it is not just the immediate impact of the violence and destruction that has to be dealt with. These events can become political footballs, kicked around by commissions of inquiry that take decades to reach conclusions, and are part of a wider landscape of partisanship that protects the guilty. Immediate political gains can be extracted from such events, and they cast a long shadow, with the Congress on the defensive about 1984 and the BJP similarly over 2002.

The politicization of religion is not, it seems, merely a street level matter, or simply a case of neighbourhood rivalry based on economics or fears of local discrimination and bias in official structures. High-level institutional exploitation of religious tensions can be alleged over a very long period, and the party political system would seem to have little incentive to clean itself up in this area when electoral advantage is perceived to be at stake. A recent investigation by the *Indian Express* found that police records in UP across the summer of 2014 show 'a running strand of attempts made by an aggressive BJP, a desperate SP and a flagging BSP to turn every clash involving individuals from the two largest religious communities into a communal issue.'[82]

Can India live with this legacy? Can it be overcome? Local versions of these questions now affect all complex modern societies, many of which have caught up a little with India in terms of social diversity over the last half-century, under the pressure of international migration. Here Huntington makes another entrance. He posed exactly these questions in relation to America, with his 2005 book *Who are We?* whose title possibly acted as an unknowing echo of V.D.

Savarkar's 1923 work *Hindutva: Who is a Hindu?* which addressed problems of Indian identity. Both books reflect their authors' belief that large countries must not be allowed to become diverse countries. Huntington was unashamedly keen to preserve American identity as an Anglo-Protestant culture, even if its core values were adopted by non-whites. Savarkar had a very similar message about non-Hindus – that they should conform and assimilate.

Neither author can, strictly speaking, be termed a racist, because ethnicity was not the issue; in both cases they were driven by a concern for conformity, and a sense of cultural supremacy based on a particular view of history. Savarkar felt that non-Hindus, primarily Muslims, were a problem, and Huntington was afraid of Hispanics. Both can be seen as cultural conservatives with a fear of the future based on an idealized version of history, but the message they carried – that diversity portends degeneration – is very easily understood and can draw visceral support wherever people worry for their own status as members of hitherto majority communities. Huntington was himself a WASP (white, Anglo-Saxon Protestant), and wished the values and heritage contained in his identity to remain dominant. Savarkar's message was more jumbled, and he admitted that the reasoning within the book is essentially circular. He never attempted to reduce his prescription for dominant Indian identity to such a memorable acronym, but he might have arrived on BHUM (brown, Hindu, upper-caste, male), a true son of the soil, which would have had a pleasing consonance with his advocacy of Bharat as a land both holy and ancestral.

Problems of secession, terrorism and social tension can always be seen as by-products of multiculturalism or social diversity. So, if diversity is the problem in India, what might be the answer?

The Hindutva project is one solution to diversity, but one that suffers from certain inherent flaws. It is mainly designed to stigmatize or exclude non-Hindus, principally Muslims, but also Christians. It works well to some degree in ancient Hindu heartlands such as the north Indian plains, but it has little relevance to the problems of a modern state. It is primarily a programme of social conformity and is much more about reducing diversity – by exclusion – than about solving real differences. In an area like Kashmir, it would prescribe restoring all the supposedly indigenous population – in this case the pandits – and either moving out all the Muslims, or getting them to reaccept their 'true' Hindu nature. In areas where there is no tradition of Sanskrit-based languages and not much trace of ancient Vedic culture, the project runs off the rails.

Hindutva inescapably contains what philosophers call an 'is–ought' problem. It does not accept India as she is; instead, it sees India as she ought to be. The force to support this transformation and to count its benefits as real is a sense of purity writ large. The nation is sullied, society is wrongly directed, it says. The central belief is not that we would all be better off if we all learned to get along – the original Congress message – it is that that some/too many of us are not behaving correctly, and we as a social unit would be better off if we all stuck to the same rules with as little deviation as possible and no dissent permitted.

Of course this is not a purely political message or programme, it is a great deal more. How this message has been conveyed, and who has picked up on it and why, explains a great deal of the varied electoral fortunes of the BJP. How the party has approached foreign policy, economic liberalization, welfare programmes and foreign investment can all be traced in detail against a baseline of Hindutva philosophy.

Enforced conformity is almost never popular anywhere about anything, yet it remains an ideal for many on the far right of politics. And although there is enough play in the Hindutva concept to embrace well-behaved Jains or Sikhs, there is not nearly enough to preserve a confident and voluntary union of India, except across its ancient heartlands where the idea could be embraced with little cultural friction. In other words, it is strong where it is strong already, and where it is weak it could be potentially disastrous.

The inflexible idealism of Hindutva accurately highlight the well-known defects of nationalism when pursued as a social ideal as opposed to a political project of self-government. All such versions of nationalism, from Irish to British to Serbian to Arab, require that we should see one significant (arbitrary) point in world history as a definitive moment when the clock of social legitimacy stopped, never to restart. In the case of Hindutva this was some point before about 1000 CE, or possibly much earlier, if the more extreme claims about the antiquity of Vedic civilization are taken seriously.

Hindutva is a massively ambitious and highly indiscriminate project, and was a minority interest for the first few decades of its life. In significant ways it is, by intention, the opposite of what the Indian government has been doing since independence, i.e. remaining fairly loose in its definition of Indian culture and identity. But those who promote it feel that under its influence genuine strength will accrue to the nation, as well as more orderliness and a higher sense of religious awareness and propriety. Its supporters, Dinanath Batra currently prominent among them, have racked up a number of successes in having scholarly works banned, suppressed or withdrawn, including A.K. Ramanujan's *Three Hundred Ramayanas*[83] and most recently Wendy Doniger's *The Hindus: An Alternative History*.[84] Others less committed may feel that such activities are not actually in the best interests of India in the long term, commercially, culturally or academically.

Modi was elected to bring development and prosperity for all, and these tensions present him with a very real political challenge – to retain the support of his old nationalist friends, who look backwards in time, while satisfying his new entrepreneurial friends, who want *vikas* and *poriborton*. He needs to chart a careful course between these two supportive but contradictory forces that must somehow be reconciled – the Hindutva brigade, who make up the RSS and the other major organs of the Sangh Parivar, and the business lobby. The former does much of the legwork for the BJP and yearns for a return to an idealized past. The latter, however, is not interested in scripture or conversion drives or new temples; they want business-friendly reforms and a domestic economic climate conducive to investment and growth. Crucially, this group is made up of the people who will actually deliver the prosperity Modi has promised.

If Modi goes any great distance to appease the nationalists, this could present a real threat to India's democratic ethos, because a sustained attack on the current social pattern of the country necessarily involves an attack on the plurality that democracy reflects and sustains, especially if this attack is ideological, non-consensual and undertaken for the sake of a notional improvement based on an exclusivist philosophy. If such changes are enforced using polarization, intimidation or discriminatory practices, the political and social fabric of India as we have known it will be changed, and for the worse in terms of the ability of minorities to express themselves.

And no matter what social purists may feel, modern societies are going to become more diverse, partly under the direct influence of democracy and its close association with consumerism and individual rights, and partly because of modern migration patterns and increasing intermarriage between social and ethnic groups. Homogenous societies may have existed in the very remote past, but they would have been very small. Homogenous states have never existed, and are less likely to do so now than ever. We will all have to cope with more types of diversity. Central authoritarian control will not reverse this trend, though it might deplore, delay, disguise or deny it.

DEGENERATION

Indian democracy is less in danger of ending with a bang than of expiring with a whimper, debilitated by forms of corruption – including cronyism, nepotism, embezzlement and bribery. Corruption steals ownership of the state from the public, undermines democratic accountability, privatizes political success and places special profits in particular pockets. Unfortunately neither centralization nor devolution guarantees that the state will be protected from those who wish to evade scrutiny or exercise unchecked power. Corruption can therefore appear at any level in any society unless a robust public culture of vigilance opposes it.

Ancient India had a system of dense social relationships mediated by all sorts of informal reciprocal arrangements. Influence was traded, services were rendered and favours were returned. Family and retainers were protected and accommodated. Such things were common all across the world, and sixteenth century England was not so different. Where a difference can be seen is in the way that modern India has both preserved and exacerbated certain elements of these social arrangements. Colonial influence was unhelpful, in that it disrupted autonomous social modernization, but the most fateful colonial legacy in this area was the creation of an administrative machine that was both unaccountable and intrusive. This naturally suited a colonial power in pursuit of colonial purposes, but it also attracted the admiration of nationalist leaders as a potential tool for nation-building. The Congress wished to preserve the Indian Civil Service (ICS) and use it to modernize India after 1947, and Sardar Patel took on the task of preserving it intact. But at the same time as the machine came under local control, another long-term Indian grievance, the disproportionate expense of the old ICS, was also addressed. So the new Indian Administrative Service inherited all the powers of the old system and some of its personnel, but not its privileged pay.

This, combined with high rates of corporate taxation, was a recipe for the creation of an 'extractive' state with powerful government officials and large amounts of unaccountable cash each seeking the other. Corruption and cronyism arrived in relationships between business and state, and the high value of government office – including the various legal immunities it conferred – created undue pressures within the electoral system. Government, business and black money have gone together ever since in India, and it is only in the very recent past that serious attempts, backed by wide public support, have begun to address problems of transparency, accountability and fairness in governance.

Why should the public oppose corrupt practices? Because they are exploitative, unfair and damaging. Corruption seriously affects the performance of a state, restricts its growth and induces disrespect for shared public concerns. Corruption also makes political office desirable to the wrong sorts of people. But it is far from easy to imagine how it can be eliminated or even reduced significantly. It tends to remain hidden by its very nature, which makes it difficult to address directly, and it has a habit of creeping forward to protect itself. If enough money is in play, individuals in supervisory and enforcement agencies can be bought off. Even worse, it has a kind of perverse popularity, and on a small scale, it can be viewed as a niche application of consumerism. If consumers – those who offer bribes – get what they pay for, where is the harm?

In this view, corruption is only a derivative market for services that opens when monopoly access to decision-making exists and desirable goods are at stake. Whenever time-consuming procedures are in place, bribery can speed them up; whenever scarce resources are to be distributed, black money can guide them to privileged hands. As an extension of the idea, sanctioned by capitalism, that money should be allowed to get what it wants, corruption then might not seem to be so unjust to many, while it is certainly a way that few can make official systems 'fairer' for themselves.

Those living within corrupt systems can develop a kind of resigned acceptance, but there is no doubt that corruption is terribly damaging to national economies and always works to preserve and sanction the least worthy personnel and the worst practices within government. Buildings fall down, baby milk is poisonous, weapon systems don't work, roads are not built, schools have no teachers, exam results are not reliable indicators of ability and criminals go unpunished while the innocent are arraigned.

India has fallen under the spell of corruption for a series of historical reasons: the government was both too strong and too weak; powerful people were accustomed to being recompensed in multifarious ways; public pay was too low; high rates of corporate taxation encouraged a cash economy for favours; and high-ups habitually intimidated the lower orders. All of this reflects India's undemocratic past. Nor did the present help. Vast sums were handed out by the central government in an attempt to drive development, but much of it found its way into the hands of those least in need of help – the traditional dominant classes. While visiting drought-stricken Orissa in 1985, Prime Minister Rajiv Gandhi famously claimed that only 17 paise of every rupee spent by the government ever reached the intended beneficiary.[85]

It is worth making a distinction here. Some corruption is the preserve of petty officialdom. It consists of small sums paid for small everyday items or benefits. This is highly morally degrading for all parties and an extra misery heaped on those with little money and no clout. It can be combated by better pay for officials and better awareness among the poorest of their rights, and it can be massively reduced by the development of online access to bureaucratic procedures. This market may run into hundreds of millions of rupees, but it is dwarfed by the more serious kinds of corruption that occur at ministerial level, which have caught the eye over recent years and involve billions. Rather surprisingly, this super-league of corruption generates little shame for some of the participants. One reason for this is that the money is not exclusively destined for individual pockets; much of it is recycled into high level politics and party funds. Kiran Kumar Reddy, chief minister of Andhra Pradesh, was quite open about it in 2013, saying that there was no need to worry about corruption because the money 'always comes back into the system during elections'.[86] Columnist and economist Lord Meghnad Desai also downplays corruption but stops well short of approving of it. He simply accepts it as 'systemic' but also 'functional', and believes that without recycled black money, politics in India would be 'crippled'.[87]

Where hope lies is in India's democratic status. Democracy does not eliminate the possibility of corruption, but it is more likely than other systems to expose it, and the culture of public accountability that democracy rests on provides justification for punishing it. Democracy offers a variety of ways forward into increased accountability, but only if the public, both as voters and payers of bribes, insist that corrupt practices are shameful, harmful and retrograde. The warping of decisions and public purposes by individuals for personal financial gain can be reduced with adequate information, or by the kind of outrage that the anti-corruption movement managed to channel in 2011.

Democracies are self-evidently not immune to corruption, but within a healthy democracy, the scope of the harm it can do is restricted. Compare the case of dictatorships, which are broadly speaking corrupt at heart, because the whole system is geared to serve the interests of the individuals at its summit – no matter what they say about the national interest or the public good. Classic oligarchy, similarly, is a system founded on and maintained by corruption – by the institutionalization of the idea that the interests of the few are put before those of the many to such a degree that the system perpetuates itself. This is a feasible future model for India if it cannot shake off corruption at senior levels. Bangladesh is a near and cautionary example.

Healthy democracy contains provisions that do allow for the interests of some to overrule those of others at times, but corruption is rather more than a matter of competing interests. It is more noxious. Corruption is making a business opportunity out of public trust. It may not be fatal to a democracy, but it runs entirely counter to fundamental democratic principles. If public servants or those in positions of trust are not looking out for the public good, then who is? And bad decisions come back to haunt governments and states; we all pay in the end for someone else's private gain.

Corruption offends the sacred dignity of public trust, and acts as an unauthorized tax on public finance. In both these aspects it cannot be defended or tolerated. Corruption is a zero sum game in which the corrupt receiver is the only winner. To fight it effectively, the public has to accept that, with its removal, individuals may lose but society will gain.

Unfortunately, corruption is a potentially elusive enemy even for societies determined to defeat it.

First, it is sometimes hard to define in a quid pro quo system of favours and traded concessions. If meetings are minuted, dubious deals are done on the phone; if phone calls are monitored, the deals are done in the lift before the meeting or at the country club afterwards, or by intermediaries somewhere else entirely. Connections within elite groups exist outside politics, and political office always confers valuable knowledge. Opportunities to buy land that is about to become more valuable is just one example of how politicians – and their cronies – can make big money without robbing the public directly; the location of the new capital of Seemandhra may be a potential bonanza for anyone with information about the decision and its accompanying rezoning, which could include anyone in whom Chief Minister Chandrababu Naidu may choose to confide.[88] Similar accusations about land deals have been levelled at other chief ministers, including Manohar Parrikar in Goa[89] and B.S. Yedyurappa in Karnataka.[90]

Secondly, unlike a range of other secret crimes, corruption is unlikely to be exposed because both parties to bribery are consciously acting illegally. This is its most insidious aspect, that the wider population increasingly begins to feel it cannot do without something that greases the wheels and expedites business, especially *my* business. And once established and half accepted, corruption spawns the idea that since everyone else has had a go at it, why shouldn't I? The idea that ending corruption is a form of self-sacrifice is deeply misplaced, and acts as a perfect illustration of its power to defend itself, and even to make hypocrites of us all.

'Power corrupts', wrote Lord Harold Acton, the great British historian, over a century and a half ago. Nothing has happened since to prove him wrong. Power is the stock-in-trade of public office, and is inseparable from it. No society can ever consider itself immune from the blandishments of power, and even the smuggest of Western countries has been beset with an absolutely appalling catalogue of abuses of power over recent years. In Britain there has been a series of major national scandals that has tainted at least eight previously respected sections of society. The list currently includes: MPs (fiddling expenses), bankers (rate rigging), media celebrities (sexual abuse of children), Catholic priests (ditto), media barons (phone tapping), policemen (accepting illegal payments from journalists, fabricating evidence), nursing staff (abuse of vulnerable patients) and sports stars (match-fixing). In some ways this sorry list reveals two things: one, that corrupt practices are widespread even in societies that think themselves relatively free of them; and two, that although those societies may indeed be wrong about themselves, their intolerance for abuses of power, when discovered, is very real.

Ordinary people are often better guardians of democratic norms than politicians; they have little to lose and much to gain in comparison. Politicians do not like to reform systems under which they are winning. This applies to almost any aspect of politics, no matter how small or technical, from party funding rules or the conduct of opinion polls, to the size of constituencies or the number of seats in an assembly. Better accountability has to be pressed for, and it usually comes in step changes, not by slow evolutionary processes.

In this respect the signs in India are improving, with a run of anti-corruption movements and measures recently – the grass-roots agitation led by Anna Hazare, the fitful success of the Aam Aadmi Party, the introduction of the Lokpal, the Supreme Court's removal of immunity of elected officials during appeal, and even a rash of high-profile jailings, including A. Raja, Lalu Prasad Yadav and, most spectacularly, Jayalalitha, who in September 2014 became the first sitting chief minister to be found guilty of corruption.

Does this mean that attitudes really are changing, and if so, is this a matter of high moral distaste or of resentment among ordinary Indians at having to pay extra to get ordinary things? Traditionally the payer of bribes gets something valuable or difficult to obtain. Ordinary Indians may now be realizing that mostly they are getting nothing extra at all – just access to standard services or universal entitlements, and that everyone else in the queue is paying too. Such a situation places a clear distinction between the exploiter and the exploited, whereas single furtive acts of 'non-compulsory' corruption do not. On the contrary, they bind giver and receiver together in a conspiracy of means and ends; they are both happy at the outcome. Is India approaching a tipping point when the givers simply refuse to pay up any longer? If a critical mass of refusal can be coordinated, the ordinary occurrence of corruption may change.

What trade union leaders call 'collective action' is the key here. If the public go on a bribe-giving strike, the power of the bribe-takers can be broken. This is a popularly available countermeasure, and if public solidarity is strong it might succeed. At the higher levels, and for greater detail, other remedies are required. India has the Comptroller and Auditor General (CAG), the Lokpal and the Lokayuktas for the elite, and will have to rely on journalists, whistleblowers and the police for the rest.

One corrupt practice is much easier to spot than any other –

nepotism – and for that reason it may be easer to eliminate, at least in public office. Within India's political parties it seems to be obligatory to promote family members, and this must stand as the most severe indictment of the lack of principle in Indian public life. If strangers cannot be expected to agree on political principle, or to act honourably and loyally around those who are not blood relatives, the country is condemned to perpetuate a kind of clan warfare carried on at the ballot box. It is also obvious that *vanshvaad* has its limitations, and currently a rash of family fights are disfiguring party politics in a number of regions, from the famous Thackeray 'feud' in Maharashtra to various complex webs of jealousy and mistrust in Bihar and UP. The moral is that only *some* family members can be trusted – absolute monarchs always live in fear of their children – and even then, political parties that rely on central nepotism can only grow so large before the servile client 'outsiders' rebel.

It has been noted[91] that the big winners of the 2014 election – Jayalalitha, Naveen Patnaik, Mamata Banerjee and Narendra Modi – have no close family in politics, and that the big losers – Congress, DMK, RJD, SP – were parties that have been well-known practitioners of often egregious nepotism. Whether this is truly a trend is yet to be seen, but it would surely be healthy if it were.

India needs to shift corruption into something more like its cashless Western versions – exchange of influence and quid pro quo. These forms of trading can never be stopped entirely; politicians will always find ways to collaborate to circumvent scrutiny when their interests align. But hands must be kept out of the till and, most importantly, regulatory bodies – in corporate affairs, academic and professional qualifications, and all aspects of public health and safety – must be kept scrupulously honest and above suspicion. Safety standards in construction, transport, medicine or food cannot be flouted, and financial probity must be maintained in both private and public sectors, otherwise corruption, cronyism and abuses of power will inevitably hobble public services, compromise security and endanger the public.

Corruption is an ever-present temptation in any system that delegates real power on a discretionary basis. Unfortunately, this means all of them; effective governance cannot exist without a degree of delegated discretion to combat rigidity. Transparency and accountability both work against corrupt practices, but cannot eliminate them if there is sufficient determination within the system to evade supervision. Whenever queues form or pinch points develop, fixers can appear to ease the problem. Rich ambitious states are less prone than poor states to corruption at the very apex, but are at least as prone to malfeasance lower down the ranks. There is no easy way out of this dilemma, but the answer must include enforcement, retribution, monitoring, decent terms of employment and public distaste.

The necessity of eliminating corruption is not just an abstract matter of equal outcomes but also of political cohesion. If trust in government is not secured, the state hollows itself out and loses its main function. If laws are not obeyed at the top, who has the moral authority to enforce them? And if relative economic standing is not addressed, if elites, and especially regional elites, enrich and perpetuate themselves unduly, all kinds of internal strains can appear.

There was a marked reduction in corruption in Karnataka between 1987 and 1991, when the regional Janata government introduced a two-tier decentralization in the state which effectively put development funds into the hands of local people. The increased accountability and wider dissemination of information produced a much wider awareness about embezzlement and slack enforcement of construction standards in the region, with the result that more of the funds went to the places they were meant to, to do the things they were intended to do. This experience, documented by R.C. Crook and J. Manor,[92] would seem to illustrate that transparency and accountability really are the way ahead if ordinary people are prepared to shoulder an increased burden of involvement.

As in many other fields, it is not more regulation in itself or more authoritarian government that promises the best way forward. Better democracy is the answer. And the future of democracy is probably assured in India. It is the quality of it and its relationship to governance that is in question.

3.

The Future of Indian Democracy

History now shows that India and democracy not only go together, they have also been good for each other. Together they have raised hundreds of millions out of poverty and sustained civic peace in an enormous country for nearly seven decades. No country has done more than India to demonstrate that, for all its turbulence and noise, democracy can work at extreme scales of size and diversity.

China may have a somewhat similar record recently in terms of peace and prosperity, but this has been achieved by adapting capitalism, not adopting democracy, and no one in China enjoys the civil freedoms that Indians take for granted. Not one Chinese leader has been chosen by the people he rules, and no Chinese businessman is entirely free from the attentions of the Communist Party. Some Indians may envy the growth rates and the futuristic cityscapes of China, but few would have relished having only one child or not being allowed to use the internet as they wish. China has yet to embrace democracy, and may well endure a bumpy ride if and when she does. India has already confronted – and overcome – the various shocks and tensions that democratization can bring in its wake.

Such an optimistic assessment of India's achievements might be countered with a more pessimistic view – that democracy has actually failed in India because the country is still home to all kinds of social and economic inequality. All indeed is not perfect, but the optimistic riposte might be that democracy, given time, will be keener than any authoritarian system to correct such deficiencies and will do so more surely and fairly than violent revolution would. Both voices might be able to agree that more democracy is the way forward. So what could that mean?

More democracy does not mean more frequent elections – India holds elections regularly enough. Nor does it mean a wider franchise; India has about as wide a franchise as can be imagined, and the poor actually use their votes. What it might mean is the development of a more effective feedback loop between popular demands and government responses, and it could certainly mean better public services, greater transparency in major state procurements, more diversity at the level of national leadership and more effective local government. Democracy should, over time, deliver all these things, and more, to Indians.

The greatest reason for optimism is that India's deficiencies are not of principle but of practice, and of practice only in certain specific areas. Elections are fair, though a little tainted at the edges; free speech is flourishing; and personal liberty is broadly protected. But the state can be heavy handed, justice is often far too slow and big money interests find it too easy to rig aspects of public life when they need to.

India has thus also demonstrated that democracy contains, and even relies on, a large element of positive illusion. Put more directly, democracy works when people believe that it is working, and many of the reasons to believe that it is working amount to window-dressing. Social structures – and their entrenched inequities – tend to remain relatively stable within democratic processes, which work indirectly, and often rather slowly in matters of social reform. No democracy has yet voted all its richest people into poverty, or managed to make all its poor people rich.

The wealth generated by industrialization has tended to obscure the reality that democracy has not, since 1945, been quite the revolutionary force that many on the left hoped it would be. The main benefits of democracy are not generally found in direct government action, but in the way it nurtures popular demands for change, to end traditional social structures of discrimination, both economic and cultural. India has suffered distinct material disadvantages compared to established societies that got rich in early modernity, like Britain and France, or newer societies that got rich quick, like the US. The fact that democracy has not yet made all Indians wealthy should not therefore come as a surprise. Nor should it be held against democracy as a system, or Indians as a people, too heavily.

India is a country that has lived with democracy while retaining a great many of its traditional social features, but it is a mistake to believe that a similar phenomenon has not been occurring in other democracies. Political scientists tend to look very closely at India's social complexities with a cultural relativism that often lends their work an unnecessarily exotic tone. The US, for instance, still maintains many of its ancestral inequities, partly because the tradition of American democracy draws clear limits around what kinds of social interaction the state has been allowed to address. In India the limitations have been more of resources than of political purposes, but the result has been similar – a degree of social conservatism.

Surface change in democracies can be swift, with the rise and fall of leaders, parties and governments, but deeper social processes are gradual. Most importantly, the poor as a block are not condemned to stay poor if political parties adopt aspirations to mass education, economic growth and the promotion of equal opportunities. In a functioning democracy they should do so, to secure the loyalty of electors, and in India they have.

For all its current shortcomings, the continued functioning of democracy in India is a success, even a triumph. Democracy is the vehicle that has delivered such gains in equality as there have been. Colonial modernization did little in this area, and non-democratic systems, especially those that shun capitalist practices, have never delivered much beyond stability. Democracy, uniquely, can provide *directional* stability, stability that is moving, and this is what India has enjoyed.

If failures are to be listed, though, it is not primarily the persistence of inequality that ranks first; it is violence. India is still far too violent in her internal dealings. Political violence is endemic, with riot and murder not rare and intimidation commonplace. Various forms of religious and caste-based violence flare up all too easily, and retain too close a connection to political calculations. Sexual violence remains disturbingly common, with stories of a genuinely horrific nature still appearing all too regularly. What can be done?

Political violence is not very directly amenable to forceful state action, which can be a way of compounding the problem. Sexual violence may take decades to eliminate, and is not very approachable via direct state levers either; rape is already illegal. Deep social reform is required, touching on traditional religious and caste practices. Discriminatory attitudes can be addressed via education, but this must include not just forthcoming generations but current senior and powerful figures in society, including members of the police. It may also be time to outlaw *khap* panchayats, especially after the efforts to enhance and reform local government in recent years, with such a clear emphasis on the greater empowerment of women. Confronting this relic of traditional patriarchy would undoubtedly be controversial and problematic in detail, but if things are to change politicians must refuse to remain mute. They must lead.

It is very difficult to take violence out of politics, let alone out of a whole society. Violent forces can only be permanently reduced by consensus, and the best way to reach and sustain consensus is via democracy. Democracy deliberately narrows the gap between winners and losers in all areas of social and economic life. It softens the sting of defeat, and over the long term it should mitigate the forces that drive violence and diminish the need for it at least as effectively as attempting to discipline the population by the use of more violence. The best hope for a cure lies in persisting with the current treatment.

One great merit of the Indian political system is that its weaknesses, such as they are – particularly in centre–state relations – encourage the exercise of moderation, and it has tended to work best when moderation has been exercised by all parties. The habit of moderation is always a help in allowing democratic systems to work well. The least moderate formations – Kerala in 1957, Mrs Gandhi's Congress government of 1971–77, and the abortive Vajpayee government of

1996 – encountered the most resistance and therefore did less well than moderate administrations.

The great virtues of Indian democracy have been its stability, its flexibility, and its increasingly inclusive nature. These have all contributed to an extraordinary achievement – of drawing the teeth of revolution while building a democratic tradition firmly grounded in genuine popular sovereignty. The solidness of this achievement means that India's status as the world's largest democracy will remain uncontested for some time, unless China opts to reject one-party rule for democratization, or India abandons the ballot box as a result of some unforeseen political catastrophe.

Indian democracy has undoubtedly been a success, but one that cannot be put down to any unique feature or institution, because there is hardly a unique element to be found within the country's constitutional framework. One candidate put forward for unique status has been the Financial Commission that determines the flow of revenues between the centre and the states,[93] but this is a marginal claim about the Commission's function, not its nature; it is a conventional committee. The system's success must therefore be found somewhere other that in its designed mechanics.

Where, then, should we look for relevant factors to explain that success without making tendentious remarks about the character of Indians or the nature of Indian society? Notoriously, all generalizations about India can be as true as they are false, but some comparisons can be attempted. Indians are as class-conscious and status-loving as the English, as materialistic and individualistic as Americans and as theoretical and argumentative as the French. Above all, Indians have a cultivated appreciation of the refinements involved in acquiring, managing and distributing power, which also makes them very like Italians; indeed, Italy was a major influence on several generations of Indian nationalists, many of whom took the great Italian democrat Mazzini as a model in the nineteenth century, and some of whom admired Mussolini in the twentieth. It should not therefore be a surprise if India's democracy exhibits all sorts of traits that can be found all over the democratic world. And it does, along with a good few eccentricities of its own. For instance, no other major democracy allows candidates to stand in two constituencies, as is the case in India.

Democracy has thrived among Indians both because of, and in spite of, all the multifarious virtues and vices that Indians display. There is no one magic explanation, and shelves of books on the subject can confirm that this is and has been true all along. There is no special quality hidden in the Indian constitution, or some unique character among Indians en masse. Democracy has flourished, in varying degrees, because of the willingness and invention that Indians have brought to the institutions of government, the (general) reluctance of leaders to use political power to hunt down opponents and the capacity of the wider political culture to absorb diversity and dissent.

Perhaps the key lies not in details at all but simply in the dynamic nature of India's original engagement with democracy. It started well and came right quickly. Once up and running, like riding a bicycle, it proved to be relatively easy to keep going. Indians, like the rest of humanity, are frequently fractious and undisciplined when structures are weak, but also compliant and loyal when social parameters are clear and accepted. With principled leadership and a balanced constitution openly agreed, the right sorts of boundaries were put in place early and were maintained. The more democracy is seen to work well, the better it will work.

Now aged 67, India's democracy is a grizzled character, witness to a lifetime of extraordinary events. Those years may have conferred a certain wisdom, but could enfeeblement, retirement or senility be on the horizon?

It is not that nobody believes in democracy in India – nearly everybody does. The question is, does it work well enough to carry the nation forward effectively, whole and improving? This is a subtler question than whether democracy can somehow survive in India in its standard, outward forms, and it is one that can be broken down into smaller, more pointed questions, such as: What latitude do incoming governments actually have in India? Can the recently recovered national voice be maintained? Is that India's only voice, or can it be modulated?

The history of general elections in India shows how well the nation responds to its circumstances. Despite the worst fears generated by the growth of identity politics, Indian elections have never become a predictable matter of pure numbers or self-serving identities. The 1967 election registered the collapse in public support for the 'old' Congress; 1971 heralded an era of charismatic, populist government; 1977 wrote a clear full stop to that era, and, incidentally, to the long-term claims of Congress to be an all-inclusive national party; 1989 brought the suspension of one-party government; 1998 and 1999 registered the acceptance by the wider electorate that Indian nationalism-II had become acceptable; 2004 signalled an end to the seemingly irresistible rise of the BJP and the neo-nationalist agenda; and 2014 declared a change of direction that promised a new take on modernity that was specifically Indian.

There has never been an entirely clear pattern. Over the decades academics and commentators have tried to foresee where India is heading, but their predictions have regularly been belied. And much of what has been written has now been rendered obsolete – again. Assessments written before 2014 tended to stress the diversity and contradictions within India, whereas the 2014 results displayed rather the opposite. So, is India really united post-2014? And where is the nation going?

To supply answers, we must step back a little, and ask again what India's premier political scientist Rajni Kothari asked in 1970: What capacities has the system developed, and what problems does it face?[94]

The basic framework of the Indian republican constitution has not changed, and by now it has proved its worth to a great degree. The one area that remains in constant dynamic development is that of centre–state relations, because these are highly sensitive to the political context, which itself is constantly shifting. The days are gone when one dominant party at the centre was automatically matched by state governments of the same stripe. The BJP currently rules some major states – Gujarat, Rajasthan, Madhya Pradesh, Maharashtra – but many states are permanently set out in effect as oppositional. Tamil Nadu has gone its own way for decades, and is presently under-represented at government level after the 2014 polls; only one Tamil party, the Pattali Makkal Katchi (PMK), is in the NDA, with one Lok Sabha seat. West Bengal, where no national party has run the state since the 1960s, remains in a world of its own.

Now that we have the strongest central government in a generation, can it be truly effective? How will centre–state relations develop, and can the states frustrate the central power?

Indian federalism, or quasi-federalism, has proved a flexible animal. The decentralization expressed in its structure was not designed as a system of active checks but more as a pragmatic recognition of provincial concerns and traditional regional identities. The country was simply too big to be run closely from the centre. But the placement of a powerful central appointee, the governor, in every state clearly reflected a desire to allow the centre to rule effectively if it wished to. The system thus carries a heavy susceptibility to political rather than purely constitutional considerations, which is one reason that some commentators insist on labelling it a quasi-federal system. It has certainly not been rigid, and it has responded actively to two major developments. One is the development of multipolar politics; the other is the liberalization of the economy from the 1990s.

The proliferation of political parties allowed the states to be more independent, controlled by regional leaders with their own agendas. In the post-1989 era, central parties have had to strike deals with these leaders to make up majorities, and the flow of central funds has followed the lines of alliance. It was usually the centre that suffered, especially when coalition partners at the geographical margins decided to make demands in foreign policy. Thus Tamil parties have frequently brought pressure to bear over relations with Sri Lanka. More recently, Mamata Banerjee in West Bengal was able effectively to veto the proposed agreement with Bangladesh over the waters of the Teesta river. Neither the AIADMK nor the TMC are currently in the NDA, so this pressure may be reduced for at least five years.

The other development, economic liberalization, brought about a profound change in the federal relationship in 2000, when Chandrababu Naidu, chief minister of Andhra Pradesh and a partner in the then ruling NDA, challenged the established system of regional allocation of revenues under the five-yearly Financial Commission, then in its eleventh avatar. The Commission's allocation had always been uneven, because states are not of uniform size and have different requirements; the original policy was to redistribute income from rich to poor states. But after the free market reforms of the 1990s the moral hazard in this system – the protection it offered to profligate states – caused the wealthier states to question whether the criteria for distribution should continue to be based on 'need'. The 2000 revolt led to the passing of the Fiscal Responsibility and Budget Management Act 2003, which sought to discipline states' spending with a view to the long-term reduction of deficits and debt. The system never worked very well, and was abandoned under the strain of the global recession that began in 2008.

Here we can clearly see the passing of power to the more powerful within the nation, and if this trend continues poorer states may begin to suffer. At that point they will either clean up their acts to become leaner, less dependent and more productive, or the nation may face new tensions on a regional basis. This might exacerbate internal migration, which is already causing friction in specific areas, such as the resentment in Maharashtra of immigrant workers from other states.

Attempts to make the federal system more formally institutional have never gone very far. In principle, the constitution allowed for the creation of an Inter-States Council, but it was only inaugurated in 1990 and has had a fitful existence since, largely for political reasons; if allegiances line up between states, or between states and the centre, then formal bodies are not necessary to get things done. If, however, political alignments are not in place, then no one has much incentive to resort to a formal body; deals can be made instead. Rather than the statutory Inter-States Council, heads of regional governments have met in either the National Development Council or more informally in ad-hoc bodies that include some or all of the states, and whose effectiveness is largely determined by political considerations. Currently an 'empowered committee' of state finance ministers is considering the final details of the proposed new goods and services tax. This has opened a variety of divisions between the states and the centre,[95] but agreement has now been reached, and the new provisions are expected to be in place by April 2016.

One definite improvement in the federal machine has been the recent reluctance of central governments to impose President's Rule on states, a device that was relatively common between 1967 and 1994. Civil disorder was the standard pretext, and a report by the state's governor was the only evidence required to validate suspension of a government. The Supreme Court's 1994 ruling in *Bommai vs. Union of India* made this more difficult, and the general fluidity of party politics also made coalition governments more reluctant to impose President's Rule tactically on their opponents in case of retaliation, and because reversals of alliances were not uncommon. Moderation was seen to work better.

Tensions between centre and provinces have been a constantly recurring factor in Indian political life since the 1960s, and the 2014 election has not returned us to the simple world of the 1950s, because the BJP is not an unchallenged party of local government. On the contrary, the main opposition comes from the local level and from local parties, not just the Congress. None of this makes it easy for a central government to use a national mandate directly at local level.

This situation is complicated by the fact that NDA-II does not at present have a majority in the Rajya Sabha, and so understandings with local parties in Opposition must be made to ensure the passage of legislation – at least until elections can remedy the government shortfall. It is true that a joint session of Parliament can be used to force through legislation, and in a full sitting the NDA could muster a small majority (currently 401 out of 795 seats) to press through legislation in the face of obstruction in the upper house. This, however, represents a nuclear option, and a smarter way of circumventing opposition is to co-opt it. Deals with local parties can be done. The cabinet reshuffle of November 2014 was partly motivated by precisely these considerations, of central management and local support-building,[96] with the inclusion of influential figures from a variety of allied parties and wider support groups such as Dalits and Nishads. Specific regional balances were also maintained. In appointments from Rajasthan, new ministers included both a Jat and a Rajput.

But for all the complications of regional cooperation, the centre in India has many methods of getting its own way. It can spend money in the provinces directly via centrally sponsored schemes, which now far outstrip federal grants, and it has a list of Union powers – 97 in the original constitution – that it can exercise. This was the intention of the founding generation, and it is less likely to be the federal structure that acts as a brake on government than constraints of national finance, or the obstructiveness and inertia of the bureaucracy, or vested interests of all kinds, personal, social and economic. Radical or rapid change has never been easy to pursue in India, ancient or modern.

All of this means that if the Modi government is determined to get its way, it must attend to the prevailing political situation and work with it. The NDA has secured its mandate, but it has not transcended politics.

Establishing strong government from the centre is always possible, because the main elements of the constitution were designed to facilitate it under due supervision. Those main elements – the Supreme Court, the Parliament, the Presidency, the Election Commission, the CAG – are in relatively good order, and the turf wars between the three major branches of government – legislative, executive and judiciary – are not currently destructive or paralyzing. But the delivery of effective government depends on the management of personnel, and the NDA will have to prove that it has skills as well as principles.

India's future lies, above all, in the hands of her political parties, which are the most changeable element in the national structure. Their record shows that they have not been consistent or principled enough, and that they tend to have internal lives marked either by exaggerated peace or barely contained savagery. There is a long-standing need for them to rise above personal leadership and family connections, to be more democratic in their internal procedures, and to be more transparent in their funding.

The Modi victory is already bringing changes to the party system, in a number of different areas. There was an extensive realignment of the political scene in Maharashtra where the four main parties, the BJP, the Shiv Sena, the Congress and the NCP all severed long-standing ties with their local partners before the 2014 Assembly elections. All the players were trying to find new space for themselves; the BJP felt strong and the NCP felt that the Congress was weak. These changes radically affected the outcome of the poll. The BJP emerged as the largest party, though somewhat short of an absolute majority, while the Congress was relegated to third place.

This indecisive result soon began to have dramatic effects. With the BJP in need of a governing partner, a battle of wills began between the NCP (with 41 seats) and the Shiv Sena (with 63), in which the Sena appeared to over-pitch its demands, and the NCP simply offered unconditional support from outside. Cynical observers suspected that some secret deal had been made, assuring NCP leaders of immunity from investigation over an irrigation scam. This was furiously denied, but the real damage was to the Sena, which found it had no further leverage on its erstwhile partner. The NCP was thus able to deny the Sena a share in governing the state, and the focus switched to national concerns, with the Sena threatening to leave the NDA. The Sena then took a further blow when Suresh Prabhu assured his promotion to cabinet rank by simply defecting to the BJP, leaving its one central minister, Anant Geete, in a precarious position. The one factor that held back the BJP leadership was the prospect of losing the Sena's support in the Rajya Sabha, but a combination of the shrewdness of Sharad Pawar, the firmness of the Modi–Shah leadership and the apparent ineptitude of Uddhav Thackeray combined to redefine both local and national outcomes. Eventually the Sena became a junior partner in the state government with a handful of portfolios, and thus preserved its status as a member of the ruling central coalition.

The details of the result were significant in several other ways. First, in decisively ending 15 years of Congress–NCP government in such a large state, it represented another major step towards the 'Congress-*mukt*' India that Modi had declared to be his goal. Talk of taking Bihar in 2015 and UP in 2017 sprang up.[97] Secondly, though the revived nationalist tenor of Indian politics had convinced the Shiv Sena's leadership that it might find space on the right away from its former junior partner, it did not. Though there may be a demand for neo-nationalist politics in India, it does not necessarily extend as far as the militant localism expressed by the Sena. Thirdly, the perceived collapse in Congress effectiveness has opened new opportunities for parties that wish to attract Muslim support; the Hyderabad-based Majlis-e-Ittehad-ul Muslimeen (MIM) collected two assembly seats. With a Lok Sabha containing the fewest Muslims for 50 years,[98] and only one Muslim minister among 151 in BJP ruled states,[99] this factor is not likely to go away any time soon.

Nationally there is now a great deal more space for left-of-centre parties, the nominally socialist element in the political picture, to recalibrate their stances and to move away from the kind of socialism that is a euphemism for caste solidarity. By now, India's caste-based parties are, loosely speaking, like trade unions in industrial countries, which started as organizations dedicated to promoting equity but ended up enforcing their own rights within very narrow confines to such an extent that they actually reinforced sectional inequalities; eventually they became outright special interest groups. One of the greatest exponents of caste politics, Ram Vilas Paswan, a man who has managed to get himself a job in every national cabinet since 1996, even flatly denies that caste-based politics is his game at all, which may indicate that it has rather lost its lustre. 'My party [the Lok Janshakti Party] has six Lok Sabha winners in this Parliament. This includes a Bhumihar, an upper caste, a Rajput, also upper caste…we have Dalits, Muslims, other castes in the party. So how can we be a caste-based party?'[100] But he has used caste throughout his career to seek and enhance support – which that list rather confirms – and he has been very good at it.

Caste parties are not about to disappear, but they may well be living on borrowed time. Caste has powerful constituent aspects, including kinship, religion and shared economic interests, but for its political aspects it relies heavily on the public sector, which will not grow under an NDA government, and will be increasingly dwarfed by the private sector. Caste used to divide people by what they did. Now it divides people by what they can get, and this is becoming an increasingly complicated – and competitive – puzzle for everyone involved. Caste remains a local matter, and the future may see the current array of parties that rely on it slowly morphing into regional parties more closely based on specific class interests, a process that social scientist D.L. Sheth has termed 'classisation'.[101] But if caste parties do not continue to distribute benefits to their supporters, they may lose out to broader units that make promises and deliver. Fragmentation may then reverse.

India's democracy also currently faces another familiar but rather more pointed challenge – how to cope with an ambitious and popular individual. Last time it was Indira Gandhi, who wrote the manual on how politicians can work through every part of the fabric of government to protect themselves and extend their control. The obvious question now is how far Narendra Modi threatens to travel the same path. So what can we discern about his outlook, methods, and intentions?

As leaders go he is not fond of the interview format, though he was prepared to make an exception for CNN's Fareed Zakaria in September 2014. This was a shrewd piece of media management, allowing Prime Minister Modi to address the world, and especially the US. The interview itself was generally anodyne, though he did make a very supportive remark about India's Muslim population, asserting that 'Indian Muslims will live for India. They will die for India.'[102] In general he prefers making speeches. He made over 400 speeches through the 2014 campaign, which set out a very positive vision of India as a land of opportunity for all. But what kind of opportunities does he think are open to him?

One obvious thing to say about him is that he appears to have embraced a very indigenous brand of politics, based not in the traditions of imported socialism or rights-based philosophy or even 'fascism', but drawing on distinctly Indian ideas. This should not come as a surprise considering that his schooling came from practical experience and his time in the RSS. His opponents may sneer at his lack of formal education, but his view of the close relation between society and the nation is entirely compatible with his background and personal development. Where he currently departs from the standard RSS agenda is that he has displayed no hint of divisiveness in his recent public utterances. The metaphor of nation as family holds with him, and the idea of an inclusive national community lies at the heart of the '*sabka saath, sabka vikas*' message. Neither is any of this incompatible with his economic outlook; it is all a positive aid to development.

And seen another way, neither is it incompatible with the older BJP–RSS view of India as an organic whole. He has expressed a wish that all Indians should be able to identify with the BJP as a diverse party, that '[p]eople from all strata of society should feel that we have a representative in this vase of flowers.'[103] Swapan Dasgupta, among the shrewdest of Modi watchers, has taken all this as an indication that 'the BJP leadership appears to be avoiding the ideological route'[104] in its efforts to consolidate its current dominant position.

Modi has publicly professed admiration for Gandhi and Sardar Patel, though rather pointedly not for Nehru, and he has quoted Vivekananda regularly.[105] Much of the Gandhian social agenda appears very congenial to him. His Independence Day speech at the Red Fort in 2014 touched on several Gandhian themes; of cleanliness, with the Swachh Bharat Abhiyan; and of the elimination of untouchability, an idea he has reinterpreted to mean the inclusion of those outside the ambit of modern financial institutions, via the Jan Dhan Yojana. The former chimes with the 'toilets before temples' line he has followed before,[106] and it dovetails with the drive to get more girls into schools. The latter is also entirely compatible with the idea of reducing 'transmission loss' in the delivery of benefits. This is hardly the stuff of divisive demagoguery.

The neo-Gandhian Hindutva-wallahs cannot conceive of or support the kind of development Modi is talking about, with its foreign investment, industrialization and hi-tech solutions. He appears to be developing a new kind of indigenous cultural–social project that promotes Indian values without being as exclusive or exclusionary. There is a powerful echo of Swami Vivekananda's practical Vedanta in much of what we see of Modi in action. Vivekananda believed that happiness lay in independence, misery in dependence.[107] This is very much Modi's philosophy in both domestic and foreign policy; it fits comfortably with both 'Digital India' and 'India First'. We may finally be seeing the re-emergence of a truly indigenous Indian take on modernity, lost in the disaster of 1857 and never since recovered.

While still saddled with various inherited programmes of state socialism, the Modi regime has undoubtedly moved to the right in general economic terms, but this shift is much less important for many of his supporters than the recovery of Hindu majority rule, which has opened up possibilities for those nationalists who were never satisfied with developments through the twentieth century. Many have sensed opportunities to advance the saffron cultural agenda – by rewriting school books, asking to install the Bhagavad Gita as a 'national scripture',[108] or claiming that astrology towers over science.[109]

The arrival of a 'proud' Hindu ruler in Delhi for the first time in 800 years[110] does indeed present the opportunity for taking majoritarian advantage, but members of the Sangh Parivar would do well to distinguish between promoting national cohesion and avenging ancient wrongs. The BJP's majority was built on votes for good governance and development, not on a belief in the alleged proficiency of ancient Hindus in nuclear science and advanced transplant surgery. Such ideas were ill-conceived and barely supported even as propaganda designed to challenge the British Raj when first purveyed by the likes of Har Bilas Sarda a hundred years ago.

Some in the BJP may be conscious that they only command a voter base of around 31 per cent, and this, coupled with the party's weakness in the Rajya Sabha, may explain the lurch towards overtly Hindu issues, especially after the localized success of this strategy in May 2014. The imminent assembly elections in Delhi may have motivated the offensive remarks, since withdrawn, by Niranjan Jyoti,[111] just as the slightly more distant polls in UP may help us understand why Laxmikant Bajpai, the BJP's chief in UP, has suddenly revived the claim that the Taj Mahal is an ancient Hindu temple.[112]

All the lessons the BJP has learned over the last 30 years would indicate that it is a forlorn quest to try to use governmental power to remake India on some supposedly divinely ordained model of yore. Nor does such a project open a path to sustained electoral success.

Nervous observers may continue to wonder when Modi will break out into traditional Savarkar-style Hindutva, but this may be missing a deeper point. Modi is drawing on a wider stream of Indian philosophy within which Savarkar, as a combative atheist, was a deviation, not the fulfilment. The tradition of service, carried down through Gokhale and Gandhi, is alive; Prime Minister Modi is the *pradhan sevak*. After something of an enforced absence, dharma is now centrally involved in Indian politics again. Dharma downplays social justice, or rather circumvents it, in that it views not just individuals but the whole of society as engaged in the work of right action, which goes beyond the simple fulfilment of *varna* obligations. Modi is promoting a vision of India in which people fend for themselves and improve their daily conditions of life. Modi-nomics reflect this. We can all make money for ourselves within inclusive growth. We can all work out our own paths away from the guiding hand of the state. Hence the slogan of 'minimum government, maximum governance', an idea which stands not so far away from the centre of Gandhian political philosophy.

Let none of this promote the idea that Modi is other-worldly or unduly saintly for a politician; he is neither. He is a driven, unsentimental, ambitious man, working within an established party structure; he is not a loose individual about to wreak havoc on the state. He certainly has big boots, and has treated his close colleagues with ruthlessness, kicking the old guard of Vajpayee, Advani and Joshi upstairs into the party's newly created Margdarshak Mandal. He has imposed his authority on every institution he needs to work through, upbraiding civil servants, ticking off cabinet colleagues, abolishing the Planning Commission, denying the position of Leader of the Opposition to the Congress, rejecting a Supreme Court judge, 'nudging' out UPA-appointed state governors,[113] sending A. Surya Prakash to run Prasar Bharati and even appointing his own man, Yellapragada Sudershan Rao, as chairman of the Indian Council of Historical Research.

Modi is a hands-on pragmatist, and he intends to supervise the system in as much detail as he can. Though somewhat similar in appearance, this can be distinguished from the behaviour and attitude of Indira Gandhi, who gradually backed away from any kind of policy agenda and eventually destroyed her own party in an effort to be free of rivals. Modi believes completely in the programme, and needs his party to remain in good health to see it through.

Where Indians have to be vigilant is in detecting if and when his activities move from the cut and thrust of politics into an assault on the constitution, though at present he does not have the Parliamentary muscle to do this. Nor does he need to, in order to achieve his aims as currently set out. He is, however, entitled to be as savage as he likes within his own party; no one is likely to show him much mercy there. But constitutional or legal infringements would be a different matter. We wait to see how far he feels he can bend the rules.

He may not do so, for there is a pattern here, related again to Vivekananda, but this time to the Swami's views on the ideal dharmic route to political success. Vivekananda set out a four-fold path of 'conciliation, bribery, sowing dissension and open war to win over an adversary'.[114] Here is the whole Modi approach. First the smooth words at Vadodara, then a little in the way of handouts, along with polarization in UP, and open war on all who resist him, including party rivals and the privileged Congress leadership. We can allow that autocratic management of government systems is entirely permissible. It facilitates delivery. We could then take a view about the decisiveness of his actions – that he is merely securing his space at the top.

There is also good reason to believe that his regime may not be as iconoclastic or severe as some liberal commentators have feared. Meghnad Desai believes that Modi, in his first Independence Day speech, has already signalled that he does not intend to overthrow the work of his predecessors. 'I offer my respects to all previous governments and prime ministers,' he declared on the ramparts, because all the previous governments, including state governments, 'have had a hand in developing India'.[115] According to Desai, these are the words of a man who has decided 'that you cannot disrespect previous governments, because you cannot disrespect the nation.'[116] As further proof of a commitment to continuity, Desai cites the first Modi budget, which was indeed more respectful of the previous government's policies – and figures – than most had expected. The rules of politics dictate that if he intended to make a truly radical break with the past, this was the time to do it, and he didn't.

Fareed Zakaria tends to agree. Noting the absence of early radical changes, he was driven to wonder, in the *Washington Post*, whether with Modi it may turn out to be 'not that he is too bold but rather that he is not bold enough'.[117] Many in India's business community are beginning to agree, with voices raised among senior members of the Confederation of Indian Industry (CII) that the pace of reforms is too slow.

Modi has talked the talk on women's rights, India's Muslims, a moratorium on communal violence, anti-nepotism and the work ethic in public service. But his critics insist that he has not said enough to distance himself and his government from those among his notional allies who have regularly made contentious and divisive comments about 'revenge', 'Hindu' areas of towns, building the Ram temple 'at any cost', 'love jihad', conversions, 'reconversions' and other traditional Hindutva pet issues. 'Will the real BJP please stand up?' they ask. Modi's sustained public silence is troubling, amid so much strident rhetoric from the fringes of the nationalist movement. The Indian press has noticed, and several high-profile cheerleaders for the Modi business project have called on him not to sacrifice his prosperity agenda for traditionalist goals. Other commentators see a clear split between Modi's headline national project of development and the logic of the BJP's local election drives in the regions, where identity politics has been seen to play out well for the party. Hence, we have two different messages and two different methods for two different audiences. Little in the way of restraint is acting on the local political project, whereas the national and international dimensions of the economic project require more selective rhetoric.

There is certainly some uncharted, dark territory beyond Modi's public position, but he has to tread a fine line here. To spend any significant amount of time in rebutting the crazier elements within the Hindu nationalist fraternity will do him no good; he will never be able to say enough to reassure those that believe him to be an extremist, and the more time he spends on rebuttal, the more he effectively derails his own project. Over FDI, GM crops, rural mechanization, ease of doing business and modernization in general, he seems to be siding with the number crunchers within the nationalist-right rather than the culture vultures. Above all, he has talked economics – the laws of money, not Manu.

So where, if anywhere, is the much vaunted Hindutva agenda that his opponents fear? We can take some reassurance from the fact that an intense love of social conformity is not compatible with development as Modi speaks of it, and he must know this. Business competitiveness is damaged by discriminatory practices, and foreign investors are wary of social troubles of all kinds. One of the very topmost priorities of the Modi *sarkar* has been to attract overseas investment, especially in manufacture.

Columnist, scholar and ex-BJP member Sudheendra Kulkarni recently asked: 'Is it not intriguing that the words "Hindutva" and "Hindu Rashtra", which the RSS believes are the non-negotiable markers of India's national identity, do not even appear in the constitution of the BJP?'[118] Perhaps there is further reassurance to be found in this observation.

It may not, in the end, be a matter of enforcing Hindutva at all. The Modi pitch to the nation was not about conformity in the Hindutva manner, it was about opportunity and self-improvement. This creed of self-reliance in a free market is not really the same sort of message as the quasi-religious cultural project that Hindutva types feel strongly about. Instead the danger to the Indian polity may not be that the Modi government is too strong or doctrinaire, but that it is lopsided and short of talent at the top. At the same time, as he has disposed of rivals from the party's past, Modi is not attracting other big figures towards the centre of Indian politics. Those who wish to build their own careers and power bases may well opt to stay in the provinces, where he himself found room to grow and create the momentum to storm Delhi on his own terms, unrivalled within his own party. Modi is the tallest poppy in the cabinet and is without equal. His most trusted ally is Arun Jaitley, whom he made finance and defence minister, but Jaitley has recently not been well. If he fails to recover his full capacities, it might be that the burden of leadership that Modi has to take on, the sheer mass of detail he would have to deal with, would be debilitating. Lord Curzon was nearly killed by that sort of burden, and that was many years ago when the volume of business was very much smaller.

Again, the November reshuffle addressed these issues, and the induction of Goa's chief minister, Manohar Parrikar as *raksha mantri*, killed two birds with one stone. It brought a confirmed Modi loyalist to Delhi, and allowed Jaitley to swap the burden of the defence portfolio for lighter and more familiar duties in charge of information and broadcasting.

But whatever Modi's intentions, who can stop him? The opposition would be expected to come from the Congress, so what are the prospects of the party holding the government to account? Have the wheels finally come off the Congress vehicle, the Mahayana that aspired to inclusivity and seemed to have perfected a locally relevant socialism? Demand for a party like the Congress will not diminish, especially if the rightward drift under Modi does not produce all that has been hoped for. But the Congress is currently much weakened. The centre-left agenda has been remorselessly stolen from it in small pieces, whereas the centre-right has remained open to monopolization by the BJP. National politics has come together under a centre-right umbrella, and until this changes, which it surely will in historical time, the BJP stands to do well.

The Congress's problem is that it has slowly become just one of many left-of-centre parties, with several disadvantages that have robbed it of character and purpose. It became a welfare party forced to tinker with its local support base, lacking true regional character or strong regional leaders. Eventually it was a national party without convincing national leaders either. Although the dynasty is the one thing that is holding the party together, it is also the one thing stopping it from changing, growing or reforming. From a great democracy, the Congress has reduced itself to a petty despotism, a fact disguised by ten years in power. But those ten years inflicted an enormous amount of political damage, internally and externally, that threatens to be irreparable. From where within the Congress will the demand for reform come? After the Antony Report it seemed unlikely that it would come from the top, though there are now signs that the party may be about to address its perceived image as 'anti-Hindu', and that the initiative may be coming from Rahul Gandhi himself. How this might play out in policy terms is not yet clear, but trying to outbid the BJP for the 'religious' vote will surely, in the long run, prove a fool's errand.

The Nehru–Gandhi dynasty managed in recent times to have its cake and eat it, content to hold power behind the throne for ten years. But it was then unable to come out. A fourth generation was perhaps too much to ask. Despite a small burst of defiance from Rahul Gandhi, including a trip to the well of the Lok Sabha to protest about communal violence, the fight may have temporarily gone out of the GOP, with too many senior members all watching each other rather than their opponents. It has already split in Tamil Nadu, with the departure of G.K. Vasan,[119] and other regional units may yet desert, as many have done before.

After 2014 we do not have two equally balanced national parties. Currently the right is mobilized, strongly led and clear on policy, whereas the left is not. We can expect it to rebuild and regroup, though not necessarily led by the Congress.

The original Congress concept of India has come into being, but the Congress itself has been left behind. The time may have come to rearrange the centre-left away from dynastic concerns and in full engagement with the public. Could a grand alliance of all the smaller parties come together in an anti-BJP popular front? This has been happening under the pressure of BJP success across UP and Bihar, but the prospect of such an alliance spanning the whole country seems unlikely, though fear of annihilation is prompting talk among leading players of a 'Janata Parivar-II'.[120] There are far too many egos, and far too many conflicting personal interests to faciltiate an effective, coordinated socialist revival. 'Third Fronts' of the kind seen after 1989 did not cohere very well either in or out of government, and if Modi can retain the political high ground – good economic numbers, a united party and the national organizing capability of the RSS – the disparate local left parties will struggle to offer an alternative national platform.

Looking further to the future, mixed messages about the sustainability of democracy in India can be found in some statistical trends, relating to levels of income and national age profile. No state that has exceeded an annual per capita income of around $7,000 has thus far relapsed into dictatorship. According to the World Bank, India currently has an average adjusted per capita income of $5,410,[121] which may afford a degree of immunity. But societies with an older average age are also safer from dictators. This may play against the much discussed 'demographic dividend' that Indians are about to collect, as India becomes 'the world's youngest country' with a median age of 29 by the year 2020.[122] Will that be old enough? Will the nation's impatient youth be put to the test?

On current performance India seems perfectly able to tackle the subject of self-criticism and reform. The post-independence history of India is full of it, though not all of these schemes worked well. The Mandal reservations played a very ambivalent role in both politics and the economy, as did Mrs Gandhi's nationalization of the banks. But the liberalization of 1991, the introduction of Panchayati raj two years later, and the Right to Information Act of 2005 have all been popular and successful. One lesson might be that reforms undertaken with clear party agendas have been much less helpful to the project of enhancing democracy.

Indian democracy has generally fallen somewhat short in delivering the material side of governance, and the country's problems with power and water are well documented. But the drive for reform remains strong, especially in areas of government activity that involve mass contact. The Aadhar universal identity card scheme, the UPA's star hi-tech project, was an attempt to use modern cyber capabilities to improve the distribution of benefits, enhancing their speed and accuracy and reducing fraud. It may yet deliver on all counts, especially if successfully married into the National Population Register, which the NDA prefers because it is based on proof of citizenship. And in creating literally millions of new bank accounts for those who had never previously had one, the Jan Dhan Yojana may bring a range of benefits to the poorest, as well as further promoting efficiency in the distribution of welfare payments and putting some of India's inert savings capacity to work.

These schemes are set to become integral parts of India's democracy because they control the points where it touches the masses most closely. If they can be permanently established and efficiently maintained, they should become binding tissue within the hard skeleton of the constitution. A government fully in touch with its people is a democratic ideal, and such inter-penetration of social and administrative systems is a hallmark of advanced Western democratic systems.

It may be harder, and less immediately rewarding, to address some other problems, such as chronic undercapacity in the judiciary, underprovision of basic healthcare and primary education or the widespread malnourishment of children. But there is a direct financial incentive to remedy some others, such as the environmental degradation that is estimated to be costing the country 5.7 per cent of GDP,[123] or India's scandalously small tax base, with only around 3 per cent of the population showing any taxable income. Crucially, all these shortcomings are widely known, and that itself may be half the battle. No one can hide them, and the system can probably brace itself to confront them. Compare the situation in Pakistan, and the contrast is telling. There is no central authority and no popular mass formation in Pakistan capable of tackling such difficulties. The missing ingredient is functioning democracy.

What can ordinary Indians do to help democracy stay strong? They can do what all citizens in all democratic states are well advised to do:

- Avoid over-expectation: democracy does not fix anything by itself.

- Don't over-value leadership: all leaders are fallible. Even if they are not corrupt and are gifted with vision – like Gandhi and Nehru – they still make mistakes, and can sometimes stay in power too long. Ambedkar warned against *bhakti*, and he was right.
- Be sparing with trust: Western experience shows beyond doubt that trust is abused time and again by those in power, be they politicians, bankers, or celebrities.

More constructively, India's people can:

- Cultivate serenity, the ability to make decisions outside the parameters of fear.
- Develop patience. The world will not change tomorrow, and if it did you might want it changed back if you were not fully consulted. Revolutionary change is a seductive notion, but one with enormously dangerous implications.
- Demand high standards. If the public does not demand high standards from their leaders, they are most unlikely to appear.

And here the door is slightly ajar. With the introduction of the None of the Above (NOTA) option in elections, India's voters now have a very direct method of expressing displeasure that avoids the time, trouble and danger of rioting, and is more effective than sulky apathy. Six million people, approximately 1 per cent of the electorate, took this option in 2014. If this figure mounts, the message will be clear, and in an ironic twist, the disgruntled may turn themselves into a new vote bank available to any political party willing to listen. Democracy can only be better served in this event.

Meanwhile, among all the options and lofty goals, poverty is set to remain the defining issue within Indian politics, the meridian that defines all measurements of progress.

Tackling poverty in Western countries has been a very complicated affair, and not always entirely popular among parties and voters on the right. But in India no one has ever been able to argue that poverty does not exist, or is simply a matter of indolence and moral turpitude, as many did (and do) in Europe and America.

In India, the problem for parties has been subtler. With poverty so ever-present and options limited, the question was not so much how to remove it but how to manoeuvre it into some kind of electoral asset; this has included redefining the ways it is measured. Western political parties routinely accuse each other of causing poverty, or perpetuating it. In India no one disputes its existence, and it has been all too easy to declare it to be a malign legacy of colonialism. As such, no one fears that bringing up the subject is likely to draw severe criticism onto themselves. Mrs Gandhi's famous '*Garibi Hatao*' slogan absolutely followed these rules.

Politicians in India found that simply announcing handouts of various kinds – especially subsidies and loans to the agrarian sector – was an effective way of securing popular support. The British Raj had a horror of this kind of open-ended generosity, fearing for its limited funds and dreading the prospect of having to feed an entire nation indefinitely. Modern Indian politicians have shown no such restraint. The culture of massive handouts dates from the mid-1970s, and has remained a fixture of Indian electoral politics ever since. The long-term effect of this relationship has been not to banish poverty but to lock politicians and poor people into a mutual dependency on welfare. The upside of this partnership is that India may have avoided a peasant revolution because of it.

India's democracy has always been closely intertwined with poverty because of the demographics of the country. All the while the nation avoided the temptation to gorge itself on credit. But this was never going to be a way to catch up in global terms. Electioneering strategy eventually led Modi to try another twist. But is he the deliverer?

It may well be that India will simply prove as unmanageable and as reluctantly amenable to Modi's schemes as she has done many times before to many others. India is a difficult country to govern, and the top echelons of the establishment are set in their ways and jealous of their knowledge. Reforming regimes from Dalhousie onwards have always found it difficult to bring about rapid constructive change. In the long run Modi may be exposed as nothing more than a clever slogan-maker with a remarkably focused public persona. Even if he is not, it may well be that even ten years of Modi sarkar will scarcely make a dent in the many ingrained systems of privilege and injustice within Indian society, whatever gloss may then be placed upon such a failure. Modi's coronation marked one sort of triumph for Indian democracy. Its next test may be in the manner of his removal.

Will India be stronger globally in ten years time? Almost certainly yes, for a multitude of very sound reasons. Economically, India is now a world player, representing an enormous market that cannot be ignored or taken out of global calculations by anyone. She is already a nation with a successful space programme, sending missions to the moon and to Mars, and is on the way to developing her own satellite-based positioning network, the Indian Regional Navigation Satellite System (IRNSS). This will remove dependence on existing systems controlled by other powers, thus enhancing national security, and opening up a potential avenue of foreign earnings.

But success and enhanced status will also bring new responsibilities, and will present a range of new dilemmas to consider. One of these is working out what it means, in the era of international climate change agreements, to be simultaneously a developing country, a global super-economy *and* a democracy. What is the will of the Indian people? Will the government lead or follow? And the incongruity of domestic poverty will appear in ever-sharper focus against a background of exalted diplomatic dealings. Where is the logic in aspiring to superpower status when up to half the Indian population practices open defecation, a rate 50 times that of China, and even five times that of Bangladesh?

India, though, might turn out to be a new kind of superpower.

Indians are often stronger on identity than opinion, which is what Jinnah feared. But they can also be stronger on spirituality than religion, which is what Gandhi hoped, and this offers a way in which India might develop a new kind of political consciousness. The threads are all there to be picked up – cultural confidence, ancient tolerance and economic potential. If India can solve the problems of citizenship in a plural society – by evolving sustainable attitudes to wealth and striking a balance between individualism and community identity – then the world might learn how to enrich its inhabitants while stabilizing its social structures.

Bluntly, this would mean less religion in Indian politics. Not less politics in Indian politics, or less God in the daily lives of Indians. But no large body of humanity has ever agreed sufficiently closely on matters of religion for it to be a reliable guide to wise and just policy, especially in large political units. Indeed, large political units have always loosened religious ties, and the largest, whether imperial or democratic, have never had a strong religious component.

The foundation of any state must be something upon which solid agreement can be found. Orderliness and prosperity are two such things, and both enhance daily life and render civilized behavior more sustainable. But religion can never serve as an adequate basis for agreement, especially if it becomes obsessed with preventing people from doing things or demonizing sections of society. Nor is nationalism always a stable basis upon which to form or sustain a state, and compensating for its inadequacies by narrowing its focus is no way forward either. States do not have to be built around a pre-existing nation. In Europe this was a convenience, but it was also largely a fiction. A state can have anyone in it, as long as they all agree to comply fully with the legislative and judicial system. A state can become a nation, and the US has spent a great deal of time trying to do this; the USSR largely failed in the same enterprise. The basic requirements for a state are agreed laws and agreed borders. Nothing more needs to be specified about the population – and indeed to do more can be actively unhelpful to peace and prosperity.

There is a solution to the problems of reconciling diversity and unity, as faced by India, and it lies in finding common purposes, even in the area of religion.

India has been uniquely fertile ground for religious ideas, and she now has a potential role to play in humanity's collective journey to sustainable political modernity by demonstrating that a successful democracy rests ultimately on a constructive quest for unity, as approached through the portal of individual choices. The debate about secularism can be redefined – and dissolved – in these terms. Spirituality has no political implications: it is a road out of politics. Spirituality is personal; religion is for communities. Religion by its nature is thus a road directly into politics. All religions are mass movements and inevitably develop political interests of their own. Spirituality allows for individuality in a way that religion does not. India has a long tradition in exactly this area, and has performed better under its influence than European states obsessed with religious conformity. The examples are clear.

The debate about minorities can be similarly dissolved by a small alteration in attitude. All states have minorities of some kind. There is no one fixed majority – it depends on how citizens perceive themselves in larger groups. And how well the state functions depends on whether the most stable majority chooses to be tyrannical and exclusive, or generous and inclusive; whether the majority is scared or secure.

Large social blocks in India have tended to be soft and shifting; political alignments have not been permanent, making it difficult for politicians to decide who to represent and how. Demagogues tend to assume that the alliances they create are somehow imbued with special inner strength and purpose. This has hardly ever been true anywhere over any long period, and India has seen all sorts of mass movements come and go. Flexibility, adaptability and evolution have all been present and have all been beneficial; moderation generally serves a nation better than extremism. India, the land of anti-incumbency, has managed to change her mind whenever the need arose. This is not a weakness.

Can the future bring better days? Will the *achhe din* moment come to look like a collective delusion?

There is a long and well-attested history of pessimism about democracy in India. In the 1930s Winston Churchill thought Indians would use it simply to exploit each other more effectively;[124] in the late 1950s Seymour Martin Lipset reiterated the classic case that India was too diverse, too illiterate, too poor and so forth.[125] Nor was it just foreigners in the distant past. Writing in the mid-1980s, Indian journalist Sasthi Brata described adult democratic franchise as 'essentially foreign to the Oriental temperament',[126] though he did then go on to take a more optimistic tone, even daring to hope that the 'novice' Rajiv Gandhi, recently installed, would be able to bring a speedy end to deference in India. All this shows the permanent perils of punditry, from which no writer is immune.

But there is another view, less judgmental and based on longer experience, which says that India's muddling through is much more like the Western 'mature' democracies than it seems. The background may be more colourful and apparently volatile, but the same processes are essentially at work. The democratic paradox, of stability within instability, is India through and through. The greatest strength of democracy is in its ability to absorb, contain and organize high degrees of chaos. Nowhere has it been required to do so more than in the brilliant chaos of India.

So, what of the great rope trick? Democracy has stretched itself to the limit in India but it has worked. It has allowed Indians to generate wealth and keep it. It has given them self-government, nurtured their identities, guaranteed their self-expression and showered them with a range of benefits both notional – new rights – and material – state handouts.

India got the theory, practice and purpose of democracy from a range of sources, including the French Revolution, British liberalism, Italian nationalism, the vision of Ambedkar and the best qualities of Nehru. There are many paths to democracy, and India eventually worked out her own.

In modern India liberty is secured, and equality is available, but the presiding spirit of democracy still comes from the fraternity preached by Gandhi. Above all, that spirit is what will keep the rope upright.

Bibliography

Alam, J., *Who Wants Democracy?*, New Delhi, Orient Black Swan, 2012

Chandra, B., *Indian National Movement: The Long Term Dynamics*, New Delhi, Har-Anand Publications, 2014

Charney, M. W., *A History of Modern Burma*, Cambridge University Press, 2009

Chibber, V., *Postcolonial Theory and the Specter of Capital*, London, Verso, 2013

Deb, S., *The Beautiful and the Damned: A Portrait of the New India*, London, Viking, 2011

Desai, M., *The Rediscovery of India*, London, Penguin, 2009

Desai, M., and Ahsan, A., *Divided By Democracy*, New Delhi, Roli Books, 2005

Drèze, J., and Sen, A., *An Uncertain Glory: India and Its Contradictions*, London, Penguin, 2014

Fukuyama, F., *The End of History and the Last Man*, London, Penguin, 1992

Gandhi, M. K., *Hind Swaraj, and Other Writings*, ed. A.J. Parel: Cambridge University Press, 2009

ed. Ganguly, S., *South Asia*, University of New York, 2006

Guha, R., *India After Gandhi*, London, Macmillan, 2007

Guha, R., *Makers of Modern India*, Cambridge, Mass.: Belknap Press of Harvard University Press, 2011

ed. Hasan, Z., *Parties and Party Politics in India*, New Delhi, Oxford University Press, 2002

Huntington, S. P., *The Clash of Civilizations*, London, Simon and Schuster, 1996

Jalal, A., *Democracy and Authoritarianism in South Asia*, Cambridge University Press, 1995

ed. Jayal, N. G., *Democracy in India*, New Delhi, Oxford University Press, 2001

Jha, P., *Battles of the New Republic: A Contemporary History of Nepal*, New Delhi, Aleph, 2014

Kamdar, M., *Planet India: The Turbulent Rise of the Largest Democracy*, London, Simon and Schuster, 2007

Keay, J., *History of India*, London, HarperCollins, 2000

Keay, J., *Midnight's Descendants*, London, Collins, 2014

Kohli, A., *Democracy and Discontent: India's Growing Crisis of Governability*, Cambridge University Press, 1990

Kothari, R., *Caste in Indian Politics*, New Delhi, Orient Black Swan, 2010
Kothari, R., *Politics in India*, New Delhi, Orient Black Swan, 2013
Krishna, S., *Postcolonial Insecurities*, University of Minnesota, 1999
Kumarasingha, H., *A Political Legacy of the British Empire*, London, I. B. Tauris, 2013
Luce, E., *In Spite of the Gods: The Strange Rise of Modern India*, New York, Doubleday, 2007
Menon, K.D., *Everyday Nationalism: Women of the Hindu Right in India*, New Delhi, Social Science Press, 2012
Nehru, J., *The Discovery of India*, London, Meridian, 1946
Raychaudhuri, T., *Perceptions, Emotions, Sensibilities: Essays on India's Colonial and Post-colonial Experiences*, New Delhi, Oxford University Press, 2005
Runciman, D., *The Confidence Trap*, Princeton University Press, 2013
ed. Shafqat, S., *New Perspectives on Pakistan*, Karachi, Oxford University Press, 2007
Sharma, V., *Hindutva*, New Delhi, Viking, 2003
van Schendel, W., *A History of Bangladesh*, Cambridge University Press, 2009
Varma, P. K., *Being Indian: Inside the Real India*, London, Heinemann, 2005
Wickramasinghe, N., *Sri Lanka in the Modern Age*, London, Hurst, 2006

Notes

1 http://timesofindia.indiatimes.com/india/Narendra-Modi-gives-mantra-to-take-on-China/articleshow/36265685.cms
2 http://www.rediff.com/news/report/ls-election-modi-reaches-out-to-all-parties-in-vadodara-victory-speech/20140516.htm
3 http://news.rediff.com/commentary/2014/may/16/live-narendra-modi-tweets-india-has-won-achhe-din-aanewale-hain/c6b047b00b7dcf24d9786ea5c7dbeaa3
4 quoted in Hobsbawn, E., *Age of Empire*, London, Weidenfeld and Nicholson, 1987, p. 148
5 Vaezi, A., *Shi'a Political Thought*, London, Islamic Centre of England, 2004, p. 178
6 Huntington, S. P., *The Clash of Civilizations*, London, Simon and Schuster, 1996, p. 41
7 ibid., p. 29
8 ibid., p. 29
9 ibid., Map 1.3, pp. 26-27
10 Runciman, D., *The Confidence Trap*, Princeton University Press, 2013, p. xiii
11 ibid., p. 294
12 ibid., p. xv.
13 http://www.bbc.co.uk/news/uk-24146572
14 http://www.nytimes.com/2013/10/14/world/asia/in-indias-politics-jail-time-is-a-badge-of-honor.html?pagewanted=all&_r=0
15 http://timesofindia.indiatimes.com/home/stoi/deep-focus/Its-criminal-how-Indians-vote/articleshow/29743590.cms
16 http://www.jaagore.com/power-of-49/i-know-what-you-did-last-election
17 http://www.thehindu.com/todays-paper/tp-opinion/by-the-ruling-class-for-the-ruling-class/article5939027.ece
18 http://timesofindia.indiatimes.com/india/SC-refuses-to-disqualify-ministers-facing-criminal-charges/articleshow/40984042.cms

19 http://www.thehindu.com/todays-paper/tp-opinion/in-2014-hindutva-versus-caste/article5832913.ece
20 http://timesofindia.indiatimes.com/news/Election-Results-2014-BJP-turncoat-is-surprise-winner/articleshow/35221572.cms
21 http://www.outlookindia.com/printarticle.aspx?269931
22 http://articles.economictimes.indiatimes.com/2010-08-21/news/27594515_1_crorepati-mps-bjp-mp-indian-mps
23 http://www.outlookindia.com/article/The-Princely-State-Of-India/269931
24 http://indiatoday.intoday.in/story/dynasty-politics-in-india-sons-of-politicians-enter-politics/1/292128.html
25 Kothari, R., *Caste In Indian Politics*, New Delhi, Orient Black Swan, 2010, p. xvii
26 Roberts, A, Salisbury: *Victorian Titan*, London, Orion, 2000, p. 279
27 http://blogs.timesofindia.indiatimes.com/cursor/muslim-population-myths/
28 http://timesofindia.indiatimes.com/india/Amit-Shah-in-Kerala-as-BJP-struggles-to-find-foothold-in-state/articleshow/41364530.cms
29 https://www.uni-bielefeld.de/tdrc/ag_comcad/downloads/workingpaper_103_negi_ganguly.pdf
30 Metcalf, T. R., *Ideologies of the Raj*: Cambridge University Press, 1995, p. 21
31 http://timesofindia.indiatimes.com/india/Ancient-caste-system-worked-well-ICHR-head-says/articleshow/38401312.cms
32 http://ccnmtl.columbia.edu/projects/mmt/ambedkar/web/section_4.html
33 Brass, P. R., *The Production of Hindu–Muslim Violence in Contemporary India*, New Delhi, Oxford University Press, 2003.
34 quoted: http://www.unafei.or.jp/english/pdf/RS_No56/No56_31VE_Raghavan.pdf
35 http://indianexpress.com/article/opinion/columns/the-abrupt-end-of-emergency/
36 http://www.outlookindia.com/printarticle.aspx?281456
37 http://www.hindustantimes.com/india-news/allaboutnarendramodi/modi-tears-into-chidambaram-says-hardwork-not-harvard-pays/article1-1182094.aspx
38 http://www.ibtimes.com/pakistani-army-offers-conditional-support-besieged-government-amid-intensifying-protests-1663748

39 http://timesofindia.indiatimes.com/world/pakistan/Pakistan-accounts-for-80-of-polio-cases-WHO/articleshow/44857068.cms

40 Katsiaficas, G. N., *Asia's Unknown Uprisings: 1947–2009*, Oakland CA, PM Press, p. 216

41 http://www.nytimes.com/2014/08/04/world/asia/nepal-enthralled-by-visit-of-indian-prime-minister-narendra-modi-who-hits-the-right-notes.html?_r=0

42 Personal e-correspondence, 11 September 2014

43 http://indianexpress.com/article/opinion/columns/facing-up-to-1971/99/#sthash.IlKicSsb.dpuf

44 http://www.thedailystar.net/maiming-limon-tib-for-exemplary-punishment-46152

45 http://www.janes.com/article/38843/bangladesh-increases-defence-budget-by-8-4

46 quoted in Rogers, B., *Burma: A Nation At The Crossroads*, London, Ebury, 2012, p. 2

47 http://www.rfa.org/english/news/myanmar/world-bank-01272014180632.html

48 http://www.worldpolicy.org/blog/2013/07/11/myanmar's-future-poised-real-democratic transition

49 http://www.bbc.co.uk/news/business-29592263

50 http://www.upi.com/Top_News/World-News/2014/10/17/Myanmar-jails-five-at-newspaper-for-public-alarm/5251413570854/?spt=sec&or=tn

51 http://content.time.com/time/magazine/article/0,9171,2146000,00.html

52 http://www.theguardian.com/world/2013/apr/18/buddhist-monk-spreads-hatred-burma

53 http://online.wsj.com/articles/elections-will-test-burmas-new-democracy-1407258010

54 ed. Cheran, R., *Pathways of Dissent: Tamil Nationalism in Sri Lanka*, New Delhi, Sage, 2009, p. xxix

55 http://curia.europa.eu/jcms/upload/docs/application/pdf/2014-10/cp140138en.pdf

56 http://www.firstpost.com/world/sri-lanka-rajapaksa-hits-opposition-taking-pro-tamil-stand-1764811.html

57 http://www.nation.lk/edition/news-features/item/34365-did-the-european-court-of-justice-slip-mahinda-a-trump-card?.html

58 https://www.colombotelegraph.com/index.php/five-ways-the-rajapaksas-hijacked-parliament-2/

59 http://www.dailymirror.lk/54727/india-to-provide-two-naval-ships-to-sl
60 http://timesofindia.indiatimes.com/india/Chinese-submarine-docking-in-Lanka-inimical-to-Indias-interests-Govt/articleshow/45025487.cms
61 http://indianexpress.com/article/india/india-others/5-indian-fishermen-sentenced-to-death-by-sri-lankan-court/
62 http://thediplomat.com/2014/10/sri-lanka-to-hold-early-presidential-elections/
63 http://www.nidahasa.com/news/news.php?go=fullnews&newsid=1356
64 http://www.sundayobserver.lk/2014/11/02/pol01.asp
65 See Drèze, J., and Sen, A., *An Uncertain Glory: India and Its Contradictions*, London, Penguin, 2014, passim
66 http://blogs.timesofindia.indiatimes.com/the-irreverent-lawyer/what-is-the-congress-partys-biggest-weakness/
67 http://www.firstpost.com/politics/undone-by-kerala-congress-politics-shashi-tharoor-sacked-as-spokesperson-1754607.html
68 http://en.wikipedia.org/wiki/The_Strange_Death_of_Liberal_England
69 http://www.thehindu.com/opinion/op-ed/the-story-of-dalit-vote-between-the-bjp-and-the-bsp/article6090744.ece
70 http://www.thehindu.com/opinion/lead/mayawatis-broken-dream/article6117048.ece?homepage=true
71 http://thediplomat.com/2010/08/25/will-india's-military-revolt/
72 http://www.outlookindia.com/article/Is-The-Coup-Finally-Upon-Us/290589
73 http://timesofindia.indiatimes.com/india/Alongside-gunfire-India-Pakistan-track-II-talks-continued-in-Dubai/articleshow/44941891.cms
74 See ed. Jayal, N.G., *Democracy in India*, New Delhi, Oxford University Press, 2001, p. 524
75 http://www.thehindu.com/todays-paper/tp-opinion/a-prime-ministerial-form-of-government/article6121384.ece
76 ed. Dressel, B., *The Judicialization of Politics in Asia*, Abingdon, Routledge, 2013, p. 57
77 http://articles.economictimes.indiatimes.com/2013-08-01/news/40917663_1_harit-pradesh-smaller-states-upa-government
78 http://www.satp.org/satporgtp/countries/india/maoist/data_sheets/arrsurrender.htm
79 http://www.tehelka.com/top-maoist-leader-ganapathi-admits-to-leadership-crisis-in-party/
80 http://timesofindia.indiatimes.com/india/Hardly-any-Indian-Muslim-indulges-in-terrorism-Pranab-Mukherjee-says/articleshow/44802414.cms

81 http://articles.economictimes.indiatimes.com/2014-07-22/news/51882082_1_nctc-chief-ministers-national-counter-terrorism-centre

82 http://indianexpress.com/article/india/uttar-pradesh/express-investigation-part-i-over-600-communal-incidents-in-up-since-ls-results-60-near-bypoll-seats/#sthash.qoMoKzi3.dpuf

83 http://www.thehindu.com/news/national/historians-protest-as-delhi-university-purges-ramayana-essay-from-syllabus/article2538301.ece

84 http://www.theguardian.com/world/2014/feb/13/indian-conservatives-penguin-hindus-book

85 http://www.udayindia.in/english/content_19january2013/cover-story.html

86 http://indiatoday.intoday.in/story/political-corruption-kiran-kumar-reddy-civil-services-probationer/1/305526.html

87 http://www.financialexpress.com/news/column-tackling-corruption-seriously/1236977/0

88 http://timesofindia.indiatimes.com/india/Redrawing-a-state-in-India-drives-land-prices-to-the-sky/articleshow/41414127.cms

89 http://timesofindia.indiatimes.com/india/Goa-CM-Parrikar-says-ready-to-quit-if-nepotism-allegations-proved/articleshow/19111431.cms

90 http://indianexpress.com/article/news-archive/web/will-release-proof-of-cong-jds-scams-bsy/

91 http://www.thehindu.com/opinion/lead/mandal-20-versus-the-new-hindutva/article6234697.ece?homepage=true

92 see ed. Jayal, N. G., *Democracy in India*, New Delhi, Oxford University Press, 2001, pp. 462-466

93 Sury, M.M., *Fiscal Federalism in India*, Delhi, Indian Tax Institute, 1998, pp. 80-81

94 Kothari, R., *Politics in India*, New Delhi, Orient Black Swan, 2013, p. 428

95 http://timesofindia.indiatimes.com/business/india-business/Centre-states-differences-persist-over-key-aspects-of-GST/articleshow/45111615.cms

96 http://articles.economictimes.indiatimes.com/2014-11-11/news/55990891_1_pm-narendra-modi-cabinet-expansion-state-elections

97 http://ibnlive.in.com/news/bihar-up-bengal-our-focus-states-says-rajiv-pratap-rudy/511990-37-64.html

98 http://www.thehindu.com/opinion/editorial/the-virtue-of-inclusiveness/article6575480.ece

99 http://www.thehindu.com/news/national/just-one-muslim-among-151-ministers-in-bjpruled-states/article6564908.ece

100 http://www.outlookindia.com/printarticle.aspx?291427

101 Kothari, R., op. cit., p. xlv; Sheth, D.L., *Secularisation of Caste and Making of New Middle Class* p. 2504: ttp://jan.ucc.nau.edu/~sj6/epwshethmclass1.htm

102 http://www.firstpost.com/india/full-text-pm-narendra-modis-world-exclusive-interview-with-cnns-zakaria-1723367.html

103 http://timesofindia.indiatimes.com/india/BJP-should-emerge-as-a-diverse-party-PM-Modi-says/articleshow/45005620.cms

104 http://www.hindustantimes.com/comment/analysis/outreach-based-on-governance/article1-1282597.aspx#sthash.un78UCBI.dpuf

105 http://www.swamivivekanandaquotes.org/2014/03/narendra-modi-swami-vivekananda.html

106 http://timesofindia.indiatimes.com/india/Build-toilets-first-and-temples-later-Narendra-Modi-says/articleshow/23422631.cms

107 Sharma, V., *Hindutva*, New Delhi, Viking, 2003, p. 122

108 http://www.thehindu.com/opinion/editorial/one-book-for-india/article6676859.ece?homepage=true

109 http://timesofindia.indiatimes.com/india/Now-BJP-says-science-a-pygmy-compared-to-astrology/articleshow/45364802.cms

110 http://zeenews.india.com/news/india/a-proud-hindu-in-power-in-delhi-after-800-years-ashok-singhal_1502548.html

111 http://timesofindia.indiatimes.com/india/Modis-minister-regrets-abusive-remark-but-opposition-wants-her-to-resign/articleshow/45345671.cms

112 http://timesofindia.indiatimes.com/india/Taj-Mahal-part-of-ancient-temple-claims-UP-BJP-chief/articleshow/45404592.cms

113 http://timesofindia.indiatimes.com/india/NDA-government-nudges-7-governors-to-quit-one-refuses/articleshow/36677778.cms

114 Sharma, op cit, p. 101: *Vivekananda's Complete Works*, Vol VIII, pp. 355-56

115 http://www.ndtv.com/article/india/pm-narendra-modi-s-independence-day-speech-at-red-fort-highlights-576248

116 Personal interview with author: London, 22 September 2014

117 http://www.washingtonpost.com/opinions/fareed-zakaria-is-indias-honeymoon-with-narendra-modi-coming-to-an-end/2014/09/18/65521878-3f74-11e4-b03f-de718edeb92f_story.html

118 http://www.outlookindia.com/article/The-First-Republic-Will-Stand/291861

119 http://indianexpress.com/article/india/politics/senior-leader-vasan-quits-congress-to-float-new-party-in-tn/

120 http://timesofindia.indiatimes.com/india/Janata-Parivar-II-Lalu-Nitish-MSY-Gowda-form-anti-BJP-front/articleshow/45064079.cms

121 http://data.worldbank.org/indicator/NY.GDP.PCAP.PP.CD

122 http://www.thehindu.com/news/national/india-is-set-to-become-the-youngest-country-by-2020/article4624347.ece

123 http://blogs.economictimes.indiatimes.com/YieldCurve/make-in-india-why-india-cant-afford-to-go-the-china-way-in-manufacturing/?utm_source=Popup&utm_medium=Old&utm_campaign=TOIHP

124 Hansard, Vol. 296, col. 456

125 1959 *American Political Science Review* 53(1) pp. 69-105: http://www.jstor.org/discover/10.2307/1951731?uid=3738032&uid=2&uid=4&sid=21104693686163

126 Brata, S., *India: The Perpetual Paradox*, Calcutta, Rupa, 1986, p. 321

Index